Scott Foresman

Scott Foresman

Reading
Seeing Is Believing

Seeing Is Believing

Focus on Family

A Wider View

Keys to Success

Timeless Stories

Other Times, Other Places

Express Yourself!

About the Cover Artist

As a child, Daniel Craig was crazy about dinosaurs, but in his Minneapolis home, his only pets are his cats, Isaac and Noah, and Winston, a dog. His pets often appear in his paintings.

Daniel Craig: cover

ISBN 0-328-03937-3

7 8 9 10 V057 10 09 08 07 06 05 04

Scott Foresman
Reading
Seeing Is Believing

Program Authors

Peter Afflerbach

James Beers

Camille Blachowicz

Candy Dawson Boyd

Wendy Cheyney

Deborah Diffily

Dolores Gaunty-Porter

Connie Juel

Donald Leu

Jeanne Paratore

Sam Sebesta

Karen Kring Wixson

PEARSON

Scott Foresman

Editorial Offices: Glenview, Illinois • Parsippany, New Jersey • New York, New York
Sales Offices: Parsippany, New Jersey • Duluth, Georgia • Glenview, Illinois
Coppell, Texas • Ontario, California • Mesa, Arizona

Unit 1 · Contents

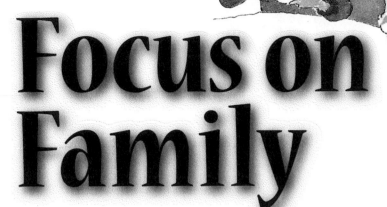

Focus on Family

Unit 2 · Contents

A Wider View

Unit 3 · Contents

Keys
to Success

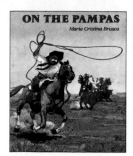

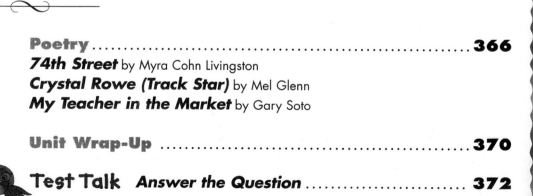

Unit 4 • Contents

Timeless Stories

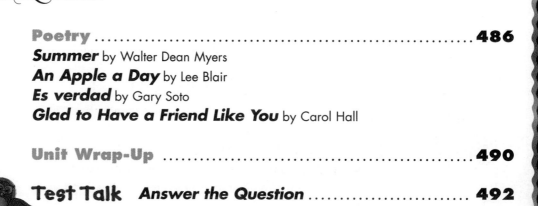

Unit 5 · Contents

Other Times, Other Places

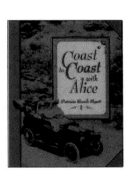

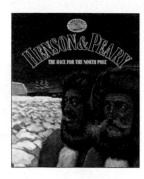

Unit 6 · Contents

14

Dear Reader,

I learned to read when I was a little less than two years old. At the time, I was living in Beijing, the capital city of China, and the first words I learned to read were Chinese characters. Many Chinese characters look like pictures of the things they stand for. The character for "mountain," for instance, looks like a mountain range with three peaks, and the character for "river" looks like a flowing stream. So it's easy for a child to get the idea that these squiggles on paper stand for words.

In spite of my early start in reading Chinese, my progress was slow, and it was some years before I could read even an easy book. Most Chinese characters are complicated ones made up of simple characters, and it's not always easy to guess what they mean. The character for "good" consists of the one for "woman" plus the one for "child." The character for "home" is a "pig" under a "roof." You have to memorize several thousands of these characters to be able to read.

Things are different in English. In English the word *mountain* doesn't look anything like a mountain. Can you think of an English word that looks like what it's supposed to represent? I can't. To read English you need to learn only the twenty-six letters of the alphabet, instead of thousands of different symbols. Since the letters stand for certain sounds, it's a matter of combining them to make a word.

Our family came to America when I was eight. Although I was way ahead of the other kids my age in math, I couldn't read or understand English. I still remember reading and sounding out my very first sentence. It was "Ben had a fine red sled." Maybe this doesn't seem like much to you, but to me it was the most exciting sentence. I'll remember it for the rest of my life.

Why did it make such an impression on me? Because I realized that the letter *e* had a particular sound, and that it had the same sound in three of the words: *Ben, red,* and *sled.* I also saw that the final letter *d* in *red* and *sled* produced the same sound. The power of these letters struck me as truly awesome. The alphabet must be one of the greatest inventions in the history of mankind!

Once I had mastered the use of the alphabet, I made pretty fast progress in reading. Although I had been reading Chinese books until our family moved to America, it wasn't too long before I found it easier to read in English. It also helped that we lived close to a public library, and I discovered that I could borrow all the books there for free! I didn't have to wait until my parents or one of my older sisters had finished a book before I could get my hands on it. I could just walk into the library, where the shelves had literally hundreds of books sitting there waiting for me. These days I can still read some Chinese. But for pleasure reading, I prefer English books now.

Reading has always been my greatest pleasure. There are times when my friends are busy, my husband is working in his office, and there isn't a good movie or a concert playing in town. I don't have to wait for a good program on television or radio. I don't have to sit back and meekly accept what someone else offers me. *I'm* the one who decides *what* to read and *when* to read it. It's the freedom to choose that I like best about reading.

Ben had a fine red sled.

Focus on Family

Who helps us find our talents, abilities, and dreams?

Setting

- **Setting** is the time and place in which a story occurs.

- Sometimes the setting is important to the plot of a story. At other times, setting is only background.

- Pictures sometimes show the setting of a story. At other times you have to imagine the setting. Details the author has written can help you see, hear, feel, and smell what it is like to be there.

Read the beginning of the short story "The Red Fox" by Donna Stringfellow, from *Spider* magazine.

Talk About It

1. Imagine you are going to illustrate the setting. Describe to a friend the scene you would sketch or paint.

2. What details in the story helped you decide what to draw?

The Red Fox

by Donna Stringfellow

It was cold in the forest. A bitter March wind rattled bare trees like skeletons and whipped up the dark clouds in an iron gray sky. The approaching snowstorm probably would not be the last one of the winter.

The red fox couldn't have chosen a worse time to bring a litter of kits into the world. Nestled in a small hollow beneath a hickory tree, curled against their mother's plush fur, the three young kits were warm and comfortable. But when the freezing storms came, the shallow nest would surely let in the snow. And it would be too easy for predators to find the

babies when their mother left them
to search for food. The fox knew she
would have to seek a new home,
and soon.

She nuzzled her kits, whose eyes were
not yet open. She licked them, and they
mewed about her like kittens. Then she
left them. Outside her den, cold air
stung her nose as she sniffed about for
danger. Then she padded off into the
gray, wintry forest.

She ducked beneath a wooden fence
and followed a path across a familiar
field, where during the summer she'd
chased rabbits. She was near a farm, a
place she'd always avoided because of
the fearful smell of humans. But now,
the warmth and protection of the barn
drew her close.

LOOK AHEAD

A Visit with Grandpa

In "A Visit with
Grandpa,"
Justin visits his
grandfather's
ranch. Read and get ready to
describe or sketch the setting.

Words to Know

biscuits   dough   prairie

raisins   rumpled   teasing

wrinkled

When you read, you may come across words that you don't know. Look for clues in the words or sentences near the unknown word to help you figure out the word's meaning.

Read this paragraph. Figure out the meaning of *wrinkled*.

A Day with Grandpa

Jake's freshly ironed clothes were getting dusty and rumpled from riding around the prairie, working with Grandpa. But Jake didn't mind that his clothes were so creased and wrinkled. He was having a great time, though he was working hard and getting hungry. When they stopped for lunch, Grandpa built a fire and made biscuits. At first, Jake was teasing Grandpa about putting raisins in the dough, but after tasting them, Jake decided they were the best biscuits ever. And this day with Grandpa was the best day ever too.

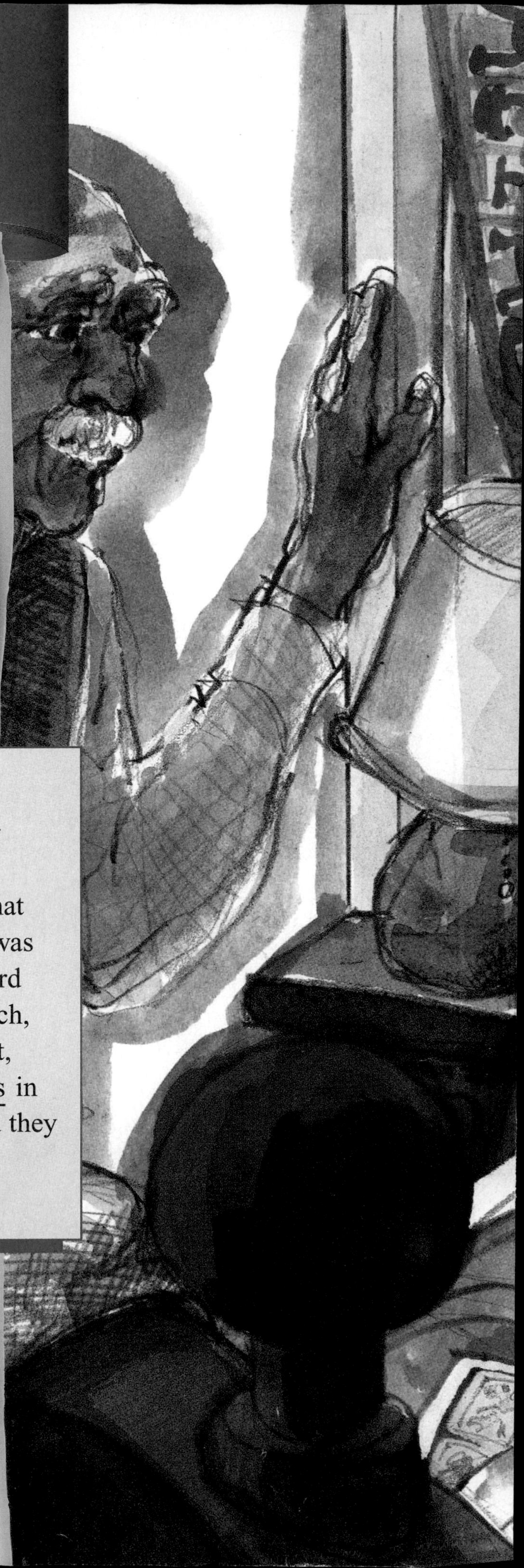

Write About It

What kind of work do you think Jake and Grandpa did out on the prairie? Write a story about their day. Use vocabulary words.

A Visit with Grandpa

from *Justin and the Best Biscuits in the World*

by Mildred Pitts Walter
illustrations by Catherine Stock

Justin has been having a hard time at home. He complains to his friend Anthony that his mother and sisters are always after him to make his bed, clean his room, or do dishes, all of which he considers "women's work." In frustration, Justin starts crying while Grandpa is visiting, so Grandpa invites him to come back with him to his ranch in Missouri for a week. They'll be able to attend the Western festival and see parades, games, and rodeos.

Justin and Grandpa have just arrived at Grandpa's house, where he lives alone and does all of his own housework. Grandpa shows Justin how a man makes a bed and then tucks him in for the night.

The smell of coffee and home-smoked ham woke Justin. His grandpa was already up and downstairs cooking breakfast. Justin jumped out of bed and quickly put on his clothes.

Grandpa had hot pancakes, apple jelly, and ham all ready for the table. Justin ate two stacks of pancakes with two helpings of everything else.

After breakfast, Grandpa cleared the table, preparing to wash the dishes. "Would you rather wash or dry?" he asked Justin.

"Neither," Justin replied, quickly thinking how little success he had with dishes.

Grandpa said nothing as he removed the dishes from the table. He took his time, carefully measuring liquid soap and letting hot water run in the sink. Then he washed each dish and rinsed it with care too. No water splashed or spilled. Soapsuds were not all over. How easy it looked, the way Grandpa did it.

After washing the dishes, Grandpa swept the floor and then went upstairs.

Justin stood around downstairs. He had a strange feeling of guilt and wished he had helped with the dishes. He heard Grandpa moving about, above in his room. Justin thought of going outside, down into the meadow, but he decided to see what was going on upstairs.

When he saw his grandpa busy making his own big bed, Justin went into his room. His unmade bed and his pajamas on the floor bothered him. But he decided that the room didn't look too bad. He picked up his pajamas and placed them on the bed and sat beside them. He waited.

Finally Grandpa came in and said, "Are you riding fence with me today?"

"Oh yes!"

"Fine. But why don't you make your bed? You'll probably feel pretty tired tonight. A well-made bed can be a warm welcome."

Justin moved slowly, reluctant to let Grandpa see him struggle with the bed. He started. What a surprise! Everything was tightly in place. He only had to smooth the covers. The bed was made. No lumps and bumps. Justin looked at Grandpa and grinned broadly. "That was easy!" he shouted.

"Don't you think you should unpack your clothes? They won't need ironing if you hang them up. You gotta look razor sharp for the festival." He gave Justin some clothes hangers.

"Are we *really* going to the festival every day?" Justin asked.

"You bet, starting with the judging early tomorrow and the dance tomorrow night." Grandpa winked at him.

Justin's excitement faded when he started unpacking his rumpled shirts. "They sure are wrinkled, Grandpa," he said.

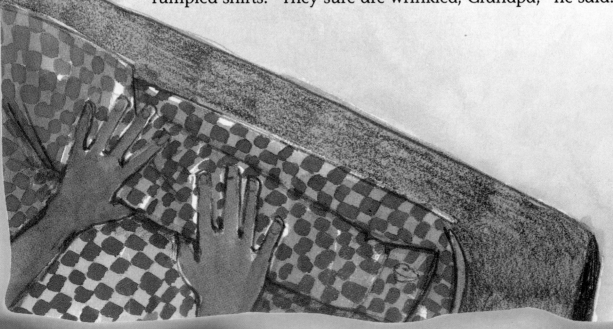

"Maybe that's because they weren't folded."

"I can't ever get them folded right," Justin cried.

"Well, let's see. Turn it so the buttons face down." Grandpa showed Justin how to bring the sleeves to the back, turning in the sides so that the sleeves were on top. Then he folded the tail of the shirt over the cuffs, and made a second fold up to the collar. "Now you try it."

Justin tried it. "Oh, I see. That was easy, Grandpa." Justin smiled, pleased with himself.

"Everything's easy when you know how."

Justin, happy with his new-found skill, hurriedly placed his clothes on the hangers. He hoped the wrinkles would disappear in time for the festival.

"Now you'll look sharp," Grandpa said.

Justin felt a surge of love for his grandpa. He would always remember how to make a bed snug as a bug and fold clothes neatly. He grabbed Grandpa's hand. They walked downstairs, still holding hands, to get ready to ride fence.

Riding fence meant inspecting the fence all around the ranch to see where it needed mending. Riding fence took a great deal of a rancher's time. Justin and Grandpa planned to spend most of the day out on the plains. Grandpa said he'd pack a lunch for them to eat on the far side of the ranch.

Justin was surprised when Grandpa packed only flour, raisins, shortening, and chunks of smoked pork. He also packed jugs of water and makings for coffee.

The horses stood in the meadow as if they knew a busy day awaited them. While Grandpa saddled Pal, he let Justin finish the saddling of Black Lightning. Justin tightened the cinches on Black, feeling the strong pull on his arm muscles. With their supplies in their saddlebags, they mounted Pal and Black, leaving Cropper behind to graze in the meadow.

The early sun shone fiery red on the hilltops while the foothills were cast in shades of purple. The dew still lingered heavily on the morning. They let their horses canter away past the house through the tall green grass. But on the outer edge of the ranch where the fence started, they walked the horses at a steady pace.

The fence had three rows of taut wire. "That's a pretty high fence," Justin said.

"We have to keep the cattle in. But deer sometimes leap that fence and eat hay with the cattle." When it got bitter cold and frosty, Grandpa rode around the ranch dropping bales of hay for the cattle. It took a lot of hay to feed the cattle during the winter months.

"I didn't think a cow could jump very high," Justin said.

"Aw, come on. Surely you know that a cow jumped over the moon." Grandpa had a serious look on his face.

"I guess that's a joke, eh?" Justin laughed.

Justin noticed that Grandpa had a map. When they came to a place in the fence that looked weak, Grandpa marked it on his map. Later, helpers who came to do the work would know exactly where to mend. That saved time.

Now the sun heated up the morning. The foothills were now varying shades of green. Shadows dotted the plains. Among the blackish green trees on the rolling hills, fog still lingered like lazy clouds. Insects buzzed. A small cloud of mosquitoes swarmed just behind their heads, and beautiful cardinals splashed their redness on the morning air. Justin felt a surge of happiness and hugged Black with his knees and heels.

Suddenly he saw a doe standing close to the fence. "Look, Grandpa!" he said. She seemed alarmed but did not run away. Doe eyes usually look peaceful and sad, Justin remembered. Hers widened with fear. Then Justin saw a fawn caught in the wire of the fence.

Quickly they got off their horses. They hitched them to a post and moved cautiously toward the fawn.

The mother rushed to the fence but stopped just short of the sharp wire. "Stay back and still," Grandpa said to Justin. "She doesn't know we will help her baby. She thinks we might hurt it. She wants to protect it."

The mother pranced restlessly. She pawed the ground, moving as close to the fence as she could. Near the post the fence had been broken. The wire curled there dangerously. The fawn's head, caught in the wire, bled close to an ear. Whenever it pulled its head the wire cut deeper.

Grandpa quickly untangled the fawn's head.
Blood flowed from the cut.

"Oh, Grandpa, it will die," Justin said sadly.

"No, no," Grandpa assured Justin. "Lucky we got here
when we did. It hasn't been caught long."

The fawn moved toward the doe. The mother, as if giving
her baby a signal, bounded off. The baby trotted behind.

As they mounted their horses, Justin suddenly felt weak in
the stomach. Remembering the blood, he trembled. Black, too,
seemed uneasy. He moved his nostrils nervously and strained
against the bit. He arched his neck and sidestepped quickly.
Justin pulled the reins. "Whoa, boy!"

"Let him run," Grandpa said.

Justin kicked Black's sides and off they raced across the plain.
They ran and ran, Justin pretending he was rounding up cattle.
Then Black turned and raced back toward Grandpa and Pal.

"Whoa, boy," Justin commanded. Justin felt better and
Black seemed calm, ready now to go on riding fence.

The sun beamed down and sweat rolled off Justin as he rode on with Grandpa, looking for broken wires in the fence. They were well away from the house, on the far side of the ranch. Flies buzzed around the horses and now gnats swarmed in clouds just above their heads. The prairie resounded with songs of the bluebirds, the bobwhite quails, and the mockingbirds mimicking them all. The cardinal's song, as lovely as any, included a whistle.

Justin thought of Anthony and how Anthony whistled for Pepper, his dog.

It was well past noon and Justin was hungry. Soon they came upon a small, well-built shed, securely locked. Nearby was a small stream. Grandpa reined in his horse. When he and Justin dismounted, they hitched the horses, and unsaddled them.

"We'll have our lunch here," Grandpa said. Justin was surprised when Grandpa took black iron pots, other cooking utensils, and a table from the shed. Justin helped him remove some iron rods that Grandpa carefully placed over a shallow pit. These would hold the pots. Now Justin understood why Grandpa had brought uncooked food. They were going to cook outside.

First they collected twigs and cow dung. Grandpa called it cow chips. "These," Grandpa said, holding up a dried brown pad, "make the best fuel. Gather them up."

There were plenty of chips left from the cattle that had fed there in winter. Soon they had a hot fire.

Justin watched as Grandpa carefully washed his hands and then began to cook their lunch.

"When I was a boy about your age, I used to go with my father on short runs with cattle. We'd bring them down from the high country onto the plains."

"Did you stay out all night?"

"Sometimes. And that was the time I liked most. The cook often made for supper what I am going to make for lunch."

Grandpa put raisins into a pot with a little water and placed them over the fire. Justin was surprised when Grandpa put flour in a separate pan. He used his fist to make a hole right in the middle of the flour. In that hole he placed some shortening. Then he added water. With his long delicate fingers he mixed the flour, water, and shortening until he had a nice round mound of dough.

Soon smooth circles of biscuits sat in an iron skillet with a lid on top. Grandpa put the skillet on the fire with some of the red-hot chips scattered over the lid.

Justin was amazed. How could only those ingredients make good bread? But he said nothing as Grandpa put the chunks of smoked pork in a skillet and started them cooking. Soon the smell was so delicious, Justin could hardly wait.

Finally Grandpa suggested that Justin take the horses to drink at the stream. "Keep your eyes open and don't step on any snakes."

33

Justin knew that diamondback rattlers sometimes lurked around. They were dangerous. He must be careful. He watered Black first.

While watering Pal, he heard rustling in the grass. His heart pounded. He heard the noise again. He wanted to run, but was too afraid. He looked around carefully. There were two black eyes staring at him. He tried to pull Pal away from the water, but Pal refused to stop drinking. Then Justin saw the animal. It had a long tail like a rat's. But it was as big as a cat. Then he saw something crawling on its back. They were little babies, hanging on as the animal ran.

A mama opossum and her babies, he thought, and was no longer afraid.

By the time the horses were watered, lunch was ready. *"M-mm-m,"* Justin said as he reached for a plate. The biscuits were golden brown, yet fluffy inside. And the sizzling pork was now crisp. Never had he eaten stewed raisins before.

"Grandpa, I didn't know you could cook like this," Justin said when he had tasted the food. "I didn't know men could cook so good."

"Why, Justin, some of the best cooks in the world are men."

Justin remembered the egg on the floor and his rice burning. The look he gave Grandpa revealed his doubts.

"It's true," Grandpa said. "All the cooks on the cattle trail were men. In hotels and restaurants they call them chefs."

"How did you make these biscuits?"

"That's a secret. One day I'll let you make some."

"Were you a cowboy, Grandpa?"

"I'm still a cowboy."

"No, you're not."

"Yes, I am. I work with cattle, so I'm a cowboy."

"You know what I mean. The kind who rides bulls, broncobusters. That kind of cowboy."

"No, I'm not that kind. But I know some."

"Are they famous?"

"No, but I did meet a real famous black cowboy once. When I was eight years old, my grandpa took me to meet his friend Bill Pickett. Bill Pickett was an old man then. He had a ranch in Oklahoma."

"Were there lots of black cowboys?"

"Yes. Lots of them. They were hard workers too. They busted broncos, branded calves, and drove cattle. My grandpa tamed wild mustangs."

"Bet they were famous."

"Oh, no. Some were. Bill Pickett created the sport of bulldogging. You'll see that at the rodeo. One cowboy named Williams taught Rough Rider Teddy Roosevelt how to break horses; and another one named Clay taught Will Rogers, the comedian, the art of roping." Grandpa offered Justin the last biscuit.

When they had finished their lunch they led the horses away from the shed to graze. As they watched the horses, Grandpa went on, "Now, there were some more very famous black cowboys. Jessie Stahl. They say he was the best rider of wild horses in the West."

"How could he be? Nobody ever heard about him. I didn't."

"Oh, there're lots of famous blacks you never hear or read about. You ever hear about Deadwood Dick?"

Justin laughed. "No."

"There's another one. His real name was Nat Love. He could outride, outshoot anyone. In Deadwood City in the Dakota Territory, he roped, tied, saddled, mounted, and rode a wild horse faster than anyone. Then in the shooting match, he hit the bull's-eye every time. The people named him Deadwood Dick right on the spot. Enough about cowboys, now. While the horses graze, let's clean up here and get back to our men's work."

Justin felt that Grandpa was still teasing him, the way he had in Justin's room when he had placed his hand on Justin's shoulder. There was still the sense of shame whenever the outburst about women's work and the tears were remembered.

As they cleaned the utensils and dishes, Justin asked, "Grandpa, you think housework is women's work?"

"Do you?" Grandpa asked quickly.

"I asked you first, Grandpa."

"I guess asking you that before I answer is unfair. No, I don't. Do you?"

"Well, it seems easier for them," Justin said as he splashed water all over, glad he was outside.

"Easier than for me?"

"Well, not for you, I guess, but for me, yeah."

"Could it be because you don't know how?"

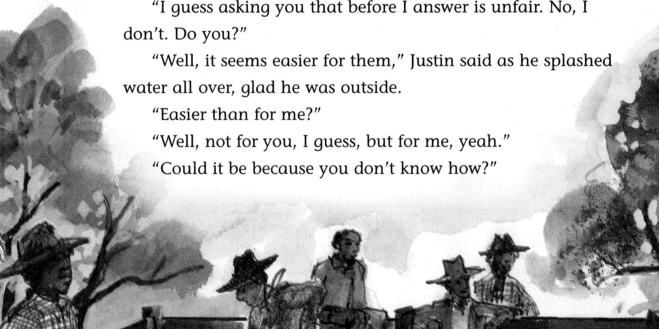

"You mean like making the bed and folding the clothes."

"Yes." Grandpa stopped and looked at Justin. "Making the bed is easy now, isn't it? All work is that way. It doesn't matter who does the work, man or woman, when it needs to be done. What matters is that we try to learn how to do it the best we can in the most enjoyable way."

"I don't think I'll ever like housework," Justin said, drying a big iron pot.

"It's like any other kind of work. The better you do it, the easier it becomes, and we seem not to mind doing things that are easy."

With the cooking rods and all the utensils put away, they locked the shed and went for their horses.

"Now, I'm going to let you do the cinches again. You'll like that."

There's that teasing again, Justin thought. "Yeah. That's a man's work," he said, and mounted Black.

"There are some good horsewomen. You'll see them at the rodeo." Grandpa mounted Pal. They went on their way, riding along silently, scanning the fence.

Finally Justin said, "I was just kidding, Grandpa." Then without planning to, he said, "I bet you don't like boys who cry like babies."

"Do I know any boys who cry like babies?"

"Aw, Grandpa, you saw me crying."

"Oh, I didn't think you were crying like a baby. In your room, you mean? We all cry sometime."

"You? Cry, Grandpa?"

"Sure."

They rode on, with Grandpa marking his map. Justin remained quiet, wondering what could make a man like Grandpa cry.

As if knowing Justin's thoughts, Grandpa said, "I remember crying when you were born."

"Why? Didn't you want me?"

"Oh, yes. You were the most beautiful baby. But, you see, your grandma, Beth, had just died. When I held you I was flooded with joy. Then I thought, *Grandma will never see this beautiful boy.* I cried."

The horses wading through the grass made the only sound in the silence. Then Grandpa said, "There's an old saying, son. 'The brave hide their fears, but share their tears.' Tears bathe the soul."

Justin looked at his grandpa. Their eyes caught. A warmth spread over Justin and he lowered his eyes. He wished he could tell his grandpa all he felt, how much he loved him.

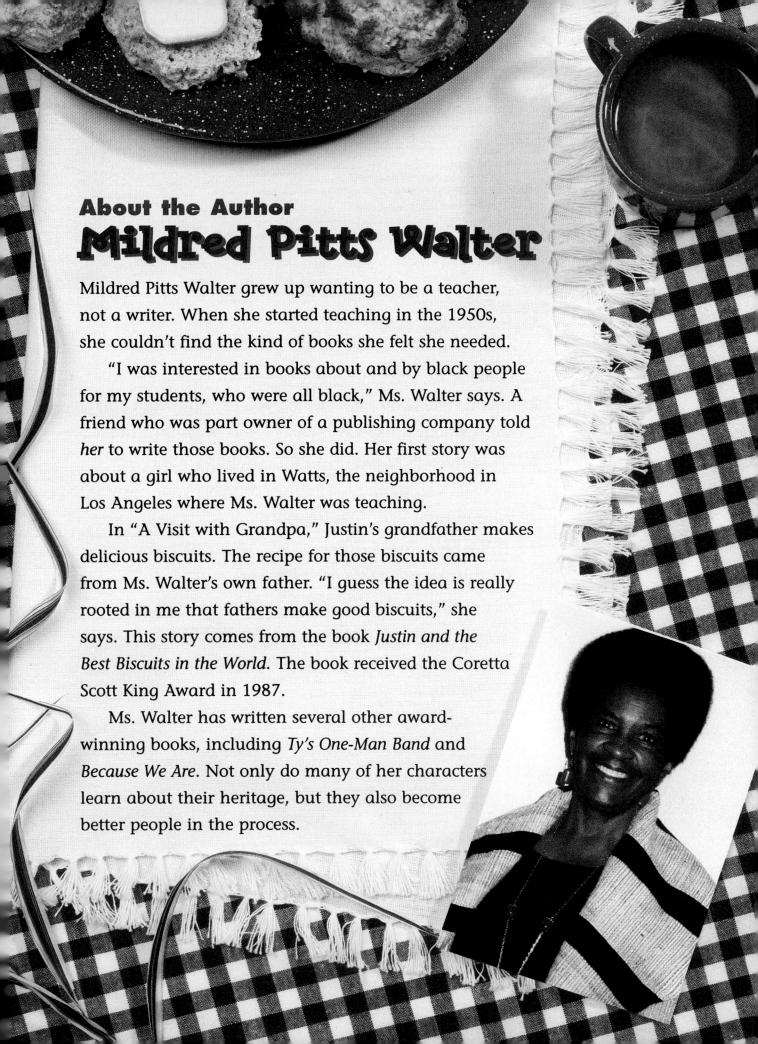

About the Author
Mildred Pitts Walter

Mildred Pitts Walter grew up wanting to be a teacher, not a writer. When she started teaching in the 1950s, she couldn't find the kind of books she felt she needed.

"I was interested in books about and by black people for my students, who were all black," Ms. Walter says. A friend who was part owner of a publishing company told *her* to write those books. So she did. Her first story was about a girl who lived in Watts, the neighborhood in Los Angeles where Ms. Walter was teaching.

In "A Visit with Grandpa," Justin's grandfather makes delicious biscuits. The recipe for those biscuits came from Ms. Walter's own father. "I guess the idea is really rooted in me that fathers make good biscuits," she says. This story comes from the book *Justin and the Best Biscuits in the World*. The book received the Coretta Scott King Award in 1987.

Ms. Walter has written several other award-winning books, including *Ty's One-Man Band* and *Because We Are*. Not only do many of her characters learn about their heritage, but they also become better people in the process.

Reader Response

Open for Discussion

When you remember this story, which scene do you think of first? Why?

Comprehension Check

1. If you were Grandpa, how would you tell and show what you think about work? Use story details to support your answer.

2. If you were Justin, how would you explain what you think about work? Give story details in your answer.

3. Grandpa tells Justin about famous black cowboys. Why do you think he does this? Support your answer with information from the story.

4. Think about the **setting.** What details help you know that the story takes place in the present? (Setting)

5. Details tell you about **setting.** Describe the place where Grandpa and Justin stop for lunch. What sights and sounds help you picture the setting? (Setting)

Test Prep
Look Back and Write

Look back at pages 30–31. Why does Justin's stomach feel weak? Use details from the story to support your answer.

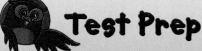

Test Prep

How to Read an Informational Article

1. Preview

- An informational article tells facts about something or someone.

- Look at the photographs. Read the title and the captions.

2. Read and Use Questions

- Think of questions to help you focus on important information. For example,

  Why do horses show their teeth?

  Write answers as you read.

3. Think and Connect

Think about "A Visit with Grandpa." Then read your answers from "Understanding Horses."

How could this article have helped Justin, from "A Visit with Grandpa," understand his horse's behavior better? Use details to support your answer.

Understanding Horses

by Peter R. Winkelaar

The horse, an animal with remarkably developed senses of hearing, smell, and sight, is always ready to gallop off in an instant. His ears can pick up the faintest of distant noises, and his eyes, positioned at the sides of his head, allow him to see a wide area around him. Because the horse cannot look directly backward, it is risky to pass close behind him unexpectedly. If he feels threatened, he will react quickly to defend himself.

A horse cannot move his eyes up and down as we can. To make out a distant object, he raises his head.

A horse that pulls the upper lip back, in a sort of smile, is smelling a very strong odor.

41

The horse's sense of smell, one of his most important senses, is comparable to that of a hunting dog's. When traveling over uneven ground, it's often best to allow the horse to pick his own way; he will instinctively find the best path. If your horse refuses to go where you want him to, it's most likely that he senses something wrong. Some riders, however, don't trust their horses' instincts and, because they don't understand these natural talents, they punish them. It is important to learn why horses act as they do, and your own horse's individual characteristics, for the best of relationships.

Horses take flight at any threat of danger, assuring their safety in nature.

THE HEAD

A horse can easily hold the head up, stretch it forward, let it hang, or make rocking motions side to side.

THE EARS

Horses can move their ears in all directions. In addition to their excellent hearing, they have a very good memory for sounds. The tone of a rider's voice is how the horse recognizes praise or punishment.

THE EYES

A horse's eyes can move from side to side, but not up or down.

THE NOSE

To horses, smell is the key to understanding the world around them. The sense is far more developed than in the human nose.

Left: In the herd, a colt quickly learns to play "Who is strongest?" The game allows him to measure himself physically against others without getting hurt.

Middle: When alert, a horse's ears are positioned forward.

Right: Horses sniff each other to recognize friends and learn about newcomers. It's possible that their sharp sense of smell allows them to recognize fear from a rider's perspiration. To understand horses, watch how they behave toward each other, such as when a colt joins a herd or as he grows up.

Outward display of the horse's mood

Horses express how they feel through their behavior. An animal whose neck is forcefully extended, with the head stretched upward, is in an aggressive mood, while one who lays back his ears, opens his eyes wide, swishes his tail, and steps around nervously feels threatened. Lifting the head with the ears pointed, the tail raised, and the nostrils flaring, wide open, is a sign of excitement in a horse. A horse that is agitated, in a sweat, with eyes bulging, is suffering and likely in pain. A satisfied horse will act calm and have a friendly, approachable look, with only a quiet movement of the tail.

Sequence

- **Sequence** means the order in which things happen. Sequence can also mean the steps we follow to do something.

- Clue words like *first, then, next,* and *finally* help you figure out the sequence of events. Dates and times of day also show sequence.

- Some events in a story may take place at the same time. Authors may use words like *meanwhile, while,* or *during* to show this.

- Sometimes events are told out of order. Verb tenses or clue words can show this.

Read "Will Sarah Return?" from *Sarah, Plain and Tall* by Patricia MacLachlan.

Write About It

1. Write a log listing the events of Anna and Caleb's day.

2. Which events occur at the same time? Which event occurred even before the events in this story?

WILL SARAH RETURN?

by Patricia MacLachlan

Anna and Caleb want Sarah to marry their father and be their new mother.

Caleb and I watched Sarah from the porch. Caleb took my hand, and the dogs lay down beside us. It was sunny, and I remembered another time when a wagon had taken Mama away. It had been a day just like this day. And Mama had never come back.

Seal jumped up to the porch, her feet making a small thump. Caleb leaned down and picked her up and walked inside. I took the broom and slowly swept the porch. Then I watered Sarah's plants. Caleb cleaned out the wood stove and carried the ashes to the barn, spilling them so that I had to sweep the porch again.

Outside, clouds moved into the sky and went away again. We took lunch to Papa, cheese and bread and lemonade. Caleb nudged me.

"Ask him. Ask Papa."

"What has Sarah gone to do?" I asked.

"I don't know," said Papa. He squinted at me. Then he sighed and put one hand on Caleb's head, one on mine. "Sarah is Sarah. She does things her way, you know."

"I know," said Caleb very softly.

Papa picked up his shovel and put on his hat.

"Ask if she's coming back," whispered Caleb.

"Of course she's coming back," I said. "Seal is here." But I would not ask the question. I was afraid to hear the answer.

We fed the sheep, and I set the table for dinner. Four plates.

LOOK AHEAD ➡

TRAIN TO SOMEWHERE

Notice how Marianne's expectations change throughout the sequence of events in *Train to Somewhere*.

Words to Know

adopt	atlas	misery
carriage	platform	couple

Sometimes you can figure out the meaning of a word by finding its antonym. Words with opposite meanings, such as *high* and *low*, are antonyms.

Read the following paragraph. Decide what *misery* means by thinking about its antonym *happiness*.

Diary Entry: May 25, 1880

My husband and I read about the <u>misery</u> of children without homes or families. We have so much happiness to share with a child of our own that we are going to be the first <u>couple</u> in our town in Iowa to <u>adopt</u> a little boy coming from the East. I checked the <u>atlas</u> to look at our route, and it will be a long journey—three days' travel by <u>carriage</u> to the train station. There, we'll wait on the <u>platform</u> for the train to arrive. We can hardly wait to meet our new son!

Write About It

What happens when the writer and her husband arrive at the train? Write their story. Use vocabulary words.

TRAIN TO SOMEWHERE

by Eve Bunting • illustrated by Ronald Himler

From the mid-1850s till the late 1920s, an estimated 100,000 homeless children were sent by train from New York City to small towns and farms in the Midwest. Charles Loring Brace of the Children's Aid Society hoped to place them with caring families.

Some of the children did well. Some did not. Some exchanged one kind of misery for another. Some found security and even love.

This is the story of fourteen orphan children, going West, dreaming of a better life. The orphan train itself is real; the route it takes and the place names are fictional. The town of Somewhere exists only on the map of the author's imagination.

"This is our train, Marianne," Miss Randolph says, and Nora clutches at my hand.

A conductor comes along the platform. "Are these the orphans, ma'am?" he asks.

Miss Randolph stands very straight. "Fourteen of them."

"We put on a special coach for you at the back," the conductor says.

The big boys carry the trunks and we take the rest of the bundles. Miss Randolph brings the emergency bag. This past week I watched her pack it with washcloths, medicine, and larkspur in case there are some stowaway fleas. None of us from St. Christopher's has any, of course. But those from the other homes and from the streets might.

"Going for a placing-out, are you?" the conductor asks Nora. "My, you look nice!"

"Thank you," Nora says. She's only five, but at St. Christopher's they teach us manners early.

"Good luck!" he says to me. "I hear there are still a lot of people in the New West wanting children to adopt."

"Yes, indeed," Miss Randolph says.

"We're not seeing as many going this year as last, though," the conductor adds. "1877 was a peak year for orphans."

We go aboard.

The train seats are hard. I let Nora sit by the window. We can see ourselves reflected in its dirty glass. She's wearing her new blue coat with the shiny buttons. Her hair twirls in bright ringlets under her bonnet. I can see my own long, thin face. I'm not pretty. I know Nora will be one of the first ones taken.

"Marianne?" She's got my hand again. "Will they believe we're sisters? We don't look a bit alike. I couldn't bear it if they split us up. Let's not go if. . . ."

"Shh!" I whisper.

But Miss Randolph has heard. "What's this?" she asks. "It won't work pretending to be sisters." Her voice softens. "Girls, listen. Most of the people will only want one child. Don't spoil it for each other."

It's all right, I tell myself. I slide my fingers into my pocket and touch the softness of the feather. *She'll be there. She'll want me.*

The train's moving. We're gliding fast and smooth past freight yards, past tenements with washing strung on lines, past warehouses. Then we're in the country and there are trees, trees with apples hanging on them. I knew this was the way apples grew but I'd never seen such a thing before.

Miss Randolph has me and another big girl, Jean, hold up a blanket to separate the boys from the girls. She opens one of the trunks and gives us our old clothes. We're to change.

"We don't want you looking messy at the first stop," she says.

She holds the blanket for Jean and me. We fold our new clothes and put them back into the trunks.

After a while we make sandwiches from the loaves and fillings Miss Randolph has brought and we have thick milk out of a can. When it gets dark we sleep, sitting up, leaning against one another.

The wheels mumble all night long.

Clickety-clack, clickety-clee,
I'm coming, Mama. Wait for me.

At Chicago we carry everything out and change trains. Then we're on our way again.

Days and nights have passed since we left New York. Now there's nothing to see outside but grass everywhere, rolling into the distance.

"The Great Plains," Miss Randolph tells us. She shows us in the atlas she's brought. Miss Randolph has made this trip with other orphans, other times. She says that now we should change back into our new clothes.

Not long after that we hear the call: "Porterville, Illinois!" This is our first stop. The town of Somewhere, Iowa, will be our last.

A crowd is waiting on the little platform.

"Cor blimey!" Zachary Cummings breathes when he sees so many people. Zachary came to New York on a boat from Liverpool, England, with his father, and then his father left him. Zachary has a funny way of saying things.

He's the first one out behind Miss Randolph.

There's a gentleman with a big box camera on legs. There are horses and wagons and dogs barking. I can see right away that my mother isn't here. She probably went farther west, farther than this.

A man leads us to the city hall with everyone following, like a parade.

"Smile and look pleasant," Miss Randolph whispers.

We sit on chairs on a stage and the people from the town look us over. They feel the boys' muscles through their coats. They say things like: "This here's a good one." And, "He'll be useful come harvest."

Zachary is taken right away along with two other big boys.

"Cheerio, mates," he calls to us.

Mavis Perkins is chosen by a little, scrawny woman. Mavis is tall and a bit heavy. She has a round face and the sweetest dimples.

"Dorothea!" the little woman calls out to another woman, just as scrawny. "Look at the one I got. She'll be a big help to me in the house. You should get one for your place."

"Mavis is a dear girl," Miss Randolph says as she signs the agreement papers. "Be good to her." She has her lips pressed tightly together. "There'll be an agent coming round to make sure the children are all right."

"So you think I won't treat her well, Missus? Is that what you're saying?" The woman glares at Miss Randolph. "Do you want me to give her back?"

Miss Randolph doesn't say anything. She hands over the papers, and the scrawny woman leads Mavis away.

A man and a woman stop in front of us.

My knees start trembling.

The woman has a soft fur muff. The man's carrying a cane with a gold head.

"Oh, Herbert. How sweet that little girl is!" The woman smiles at Nora. "Can we take her, Herbert? Can we?"

"This is my sister," Nora whispers, tugging at my hand. "Please, please, if you take me can you take her too?"

"Oh, dear!" The woman looks at Miss Randolph. "We couldn't possibly. We only want one little girl."

"Of course. And they're not sisters, just friends," Miss Randolph says quickly. "Now, stand up, Nora. You help her, Marianne."

I have to pry Nora's fingers from mine.

The woman bends down. "Do you know what's waiting for you in our carriage? A puppy, just for you."

"I don't want a puppy. I want Marianne," Nora cries.

Miss Randolph and the couple sign the agreement papers, and then they take her.

Nora's still crying and looking back.

I'm sniffling too.

But it's better if I'm not taken. I have to stay free for my mother. She told me she'd come for me. She kneeled in front of me on the steps of St. Christopher's the day she left me there. She was working in Gerrison's chicken factory at the time, and there was a white feather caught in her hair.

I lifted it off and held it against my cheek.

"I'm going West to make a new life for us," she said. "Then I'll come for you."

"When, Mama? When?" The feather stuck against the tears that ran down my face.

"Before Christmas," she said.

I've waited through so many Christmases.

But now I'm going West too.

Nine of us are left to get back on the train. Miss Randolph says we're to keep on our good clothes. We'll be getting off again soon.

At Kilburn we are walked to a hardware store to stand in line.

"I expect they took all the biggest boys in Porterville," one man says. "But still . . ."

Eddie Hartz, who is only seven, is taken. There's a boy who can stand on his hands and pretend to pull buttons out of people's ears. He makes the crowd laugh and he gets taken too.

As soon as the train has loaded on wood and fresh water, the rest of us get back aboard.

Miss Randolph wipes her eyes. "Anything's better than being on the streets of New York," she says. "A lot of you will do fine."

"We weren't on the streets," Susan Ayers says. Susan's only five, same as Nora, but she's sassy and not sweet. She was at St. Christopher's too.

"We couldn't keep all of you forever." Miss Randolph blows her nose on her white handkerchief. "We have to make room. There are other orphans in need."

Susan makes a face.

The next station is Glover. The crowd is smaller. My mother isn't here, either. Where is she? She must know I might be on this train. The story was in all the newspapers, Miss Randolph said. "Orphans from St. Christopher's among those riding the rails." "Children in need of homes." The papers listed every stop. I was sure my mother would be at one of them.

Wait, Mama, wait! I'm coming! Night after night at St. Christopher's I'd send my thoughts to her across the darkness and the distance. *You don't even have to come get me, Mama. I'm coming to you.* But where is she?

At Glover they line us up along the railway track.

Susan's pouting and whining. She says her new boots hurt her feet.

There's a nice-looking man and woman at the front of the crowd.

Susan stops pouting. She smiles and holds up her arms.

"Mama! Papa!" she begs.

The woman clutches at her heart. "James! She's calling out to us."

The man scoops Susan into his arms. "We'll take her," he says.

"Can I have a puppy?" Susan asks.

The man smiles. "I'll just bet you can, honey."

A boy who has his eyeglasses tied on with string is taken, too, and two other boys.

"There's not much left to pick from," a woman says in a bad-tempered way. "Next time we'll have to ride in as far as Porterville."

I have a terrible hurt inside of me. My mother didn't want me. It looks like nobody wants me. It's not that I'm hoping to be placed, because my mother could be at the very next stop. But what if she isn't?

The three of us who are left get back on the train with Miss Randolph. She gives us gingersnaps and milk from the can she got in Glover. The milk is sweet.

"We can't be down in the dumps, children," she says. "Let's sing." She begins, "Jesus loves me," but nobody joins in. She sings alone through three verses.

We're such a long way from Nora. I wonder if her puppy has a name. If somebody takes me, I'll ask if we can go visit her. "She's like my sister," I'll say.

"Memorial," the conductor calls. There are four people waiting at the station. None of them is my mother. I stumble out with the girl named Amy and the one named Dorothy. We sneak glances at one another. We're wondering which one of us looks best. They're not pretty, either. The taste of the sweet milk is still in my throat and it's making me sick.

One couple takes both Amy and Dorothy. "Two for the price of one," the man jokes, though of course there is no price.

"Marianne is very good with children," Miss Randolph tells the other couple. There's a sort of begging in her voice as she clutches the last agreement form, the one for me.

"My missus looks after our little one," the man grumps.

"We just came to look," the woman says. "But . . ." She takes an apple from her bag and gives it to me. "Have this, child."

"Thank you." I bend my head over the apple. It is blurry through my tears.

The train whistle's blowing.

Miss Randolph and I get on. There's only one stop left, I know. One.

Miss Randolph says I should eat my apple. She says she has a washcloth in case my hands get sticky. I say I don't want to eat anything just yet.

We look out the window, not talking, not singing. Miss Randolph has me take off my hat and she brushes my hair.

"There's a nice hotel farther down the line," she says. "If there's nobody at this next stop, why, we'll just go on. I'll be glad of the company. And on the journey back."

"Somewhere," the conductor calls. It's such a strange name. As if it thinks itself important. As if it's a place surrounded by nowhere.

I put my hat back on. My hands are shaking.

Outside there's a couple waiting by a wagon. The woman is small and round as a dumpling. She's wearing a heavy black dress and a man's droopy black hat. She is not my mother.

"Are you ready, Marianne?" Miss Randolph asks softly.

I pull myself back into the corner of the seat. "No," I whisper. "No."

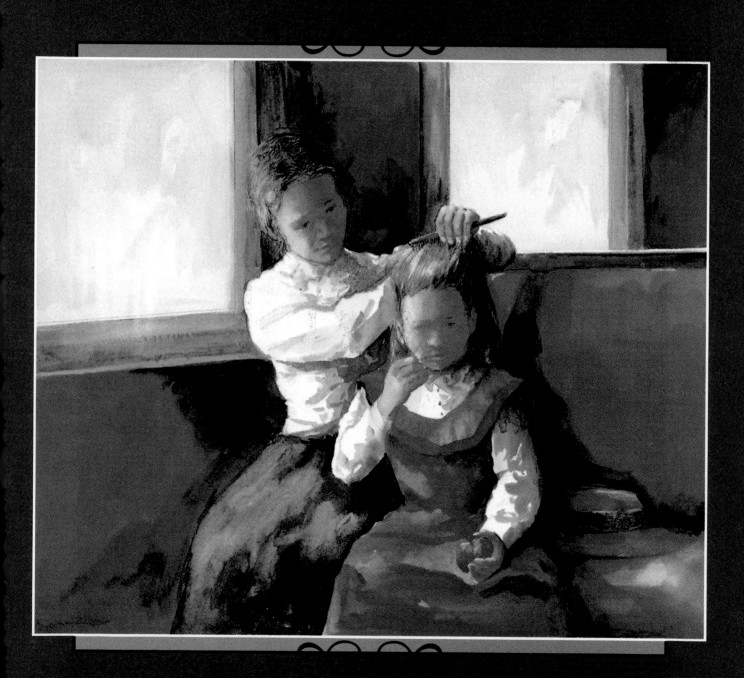

Miss Randolph holds my hand as we get down from the train.

The man is tall and stooped. He takes off his hat.

The woman doesn't take hers off.

I think they're both pretty old. The woman's holding a wooden toy locomotive.

"Are you . . . ?" the man asks Miss Randolph.

"Yes." Miss Randolph nudges me forward. "This is Marianne."

"Is she all . . ." The woman stops. I know she was going to say: "Is she all that's left?" But she doesn't. She looks at me closely and I see a change in her face. A softness. I'd thought my mother would look at me like that.

Somehow this woman understands about me, how it felt that nobody wanted me, even though I was waiting inside myself for my mother to come. Somehow she understands the hurt.

"I'm Tillie Book," she tells Miss Randolph. "This here's my husband, Roscoe." She holds the toy locomotive out to me. "We brought you this."

"I'm not what you wanted, am I?" I say. "You wanted a boy." The locomotive has red painted wheels and a blue smokestack.

"I won't lie to you. We did want a boy," Mrs. Book says.

"But we like girls fine," Mr. Book adds.

Mrs. Book squints at me. "I expect we're not what you wanted, either. Roscoe and I, we found each other late in life. I always thought I'd catch myself somebody a mite more handsome." She pats Mr. Book's hand and they smile at each other, and I can tell they like each other a lot. "Sometimes what you get turns out to be better than what you wanted in the first place," Mrs. Book says.

"Yes." There's a sort of crumbling inside of me. My mother's not in Somewhere. She's not waiting here or anywhere. "I . . ." I reach in my pocket and bring out the feather. It was white when

I took it from my mother's hair; now it's yellow. I smooth it with my fingers. "I brought you this."

"Why, thank you." Mrs. Book sticks the feather in the band of her droopy hat. It's funny the way it nestles there, as if it belongs, as if it has found its place at last.

Mr. Book takes the agreement papers, looks at them, then at me. "Will you come with us?"

"Yes," I whisper.

Miss Randolph leans forward and kisses my cheek.

"Are you ready now, Marianne?" she asks.

"I'm ready."

About the Author

EVE BUNTING

When Eve Bunting sits down to write a story, she doesn't have a problem coming up with ideas. In fact, her problem is just the opposite! "I couldn't possibly write about all the interesting thoughts that pop into my head," she says, because "there aren't that many hours in a day or that many days in a year!"

As a young girl growing up in Ireland, Ms. Bunting loved to listen to her father read poetry as the family sat by the fire in the evening. Those times with her father helped nurture her love for the sounds and rhythms that words make when they are put together in stories and poems.

Reader Response

Open for Discussion

What surprised or interested you most in this story?

Comprehension Check

1. Why do you think the author decided to have Marianne chosen last? Find examples to support your answer.

2. Miss Randolph is firm yet kind. Find examples of both her firmness and her kindness in the story.

3. What do you think it means when Marianne gives Tillie Book the feather? Use details from the story in your answer.

4. Think about **sequence**. What happens to Marianne's feelings between the beginning of her trip and the end? (Sequence)

5. The **sequence** of events is almost the same at each stop on the train's journey. Tell the events and number them in order. (Sequence)

Test Prep

Look Back and Write

Look back at page 54. Compare and contrast the reasons why Mavis and Nora are chosen to be adopted. Use details about each event to support your answer.

The American Railroad

by John Coiley

FEW NATIONS have had their history influenced so greatly by a new kind of transportation as the U.S. In Europe the new railroads were made to serve existing cities. But in the U.S., the railroads themselves created many large cities, in what had been a huge, empty continent. Progress was rapid. By 1869, people could cross the continent by rail. In the early 20th century, most North Americans lived within 25 miles of a railroad. Now, trains are used more in areas where the electric railroad has helped to cut down on traffic and pollution.

TOM THUMB

In 1830, *Tom Thumb*, a small experimental train, entered into a race with a horse-drawn train. The horse won.

"THE GOLDEN SPIKE"

On May 10, 1869, the U.S. was finally crossed by a railroad from east to west. The Union Pacific Railroad was connected to the Central Pacific Railroad.

BUILDING THE FUTURE

The opening up of the continent by the spread of the railroad was a great achievement. Railroads were important to the growth and wealth of many towns across the U.S.

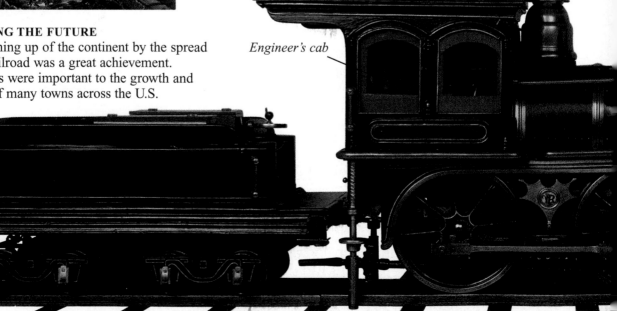

Engineer's cab

JOHN BULL

This was an early four-wheeled train, designed by Robert Stephenson. It was shipped in sections from England in 1831. The *John Bull* became one of the first trains to be fitted with a "cowcatcher."

DE WITT CLINTON

The first steam train in New York State was hauled by the locomotive *De Witt Clinton* on August 9, 1831. Passengers rode on top of the vehicles, as well as inside.

COWCATCHER

The absence of fences along many of the early tracks made it important to protect the front of a train. It could easily be derailed (knocked off the track) by large animals such as buffaloes. A cowcatcher pushed the animal aside.

IT'S A FIRST

The *Stourbridge Lion,* the first steam train with special wheels to run on rails in the U.S., was built in England in 1829.

A tall smokestack made the train more efficient—but there could be no low bridges on the line!

This model is based on an 1875 train that burned coal.

Steam whistle

Warning bell

Large headlight

Cowcatcher

ALL-AMERICAN TRAIN

This model of an 1875 train design is typically American, with outside cylinders, four driving wheels, and a four-wheeled truck in front. The large, ornate cab provides some protection for the engineer and fireman during severe weather.

Compare and Contrast

- To **compare** is to tell how two or more things are alike. To **contrast** is to tell how two or more things are different.

- Clue words such as *like* or *as* show comparisons. Clue words such as *but* or *unlike* show contrasts.

- Often authors don't use clue words. Readers must make comparisons for themselves.

Read "Anna's New School" from *From Anna* by Jean Little.

Talk About It

1. How is Anna's new classroom different from her old classroom? What clue words helped you to notice the differences?

2. How are Anna and Benjamin alike and different? What words are used to compare the two children?

Anna's New School

by Jean Little

She must not cry. She must *not!*

Then the desk itself caught her attention and distracted her. She had never seen one like it before. It had hinges on the sides and you could tip it up so that your book was close to you. She looked around wonderingly. The desk was not the only thing that was different. The pencil in the trough was bigger around than her thumb. The blackboards weren't black at all—they were green; and the chalk was fat too, and yellow instead of white.

Even the children were different. Most of them were older than Anna.

"We have Grades One to Seven in this room," Miss Williams had explained to Mama.

The desks were not set in straight rows nailed to the floor. They were pushed into separate groups. Miss Williams put Anna in one right beside her own desk near the front.

"You can sit next to Benjamin," she said. "Ben's been needing someone to keep him on his toes, haven't you, Ben?"

Anna had no idea how she was supposed to keep Benjamin on his toes. She looked sideways at his feet. They seemed perfectly ordinary.

Was it a joke, maybe?

Anna stared at the small boy with the black tufty hair and an impish face. He was a good head shorter than she was, though his glasses were as big as hers. Behind them, his eyes sparkled.

LOOK AHEAD

As you read "Yingtao's New Friend," compare and contrast Yingtao's family life with Matthew's and with your own.

Words to Know

instruments rehearsal triangle
orchestra measures

Many words have more than one meaning. To decide which meaning is being used, look for clues in the surrounding sentences or paragraph.

Read the note below. Decide whether *measures* means "bars of music" or "units of measure, such as inches."

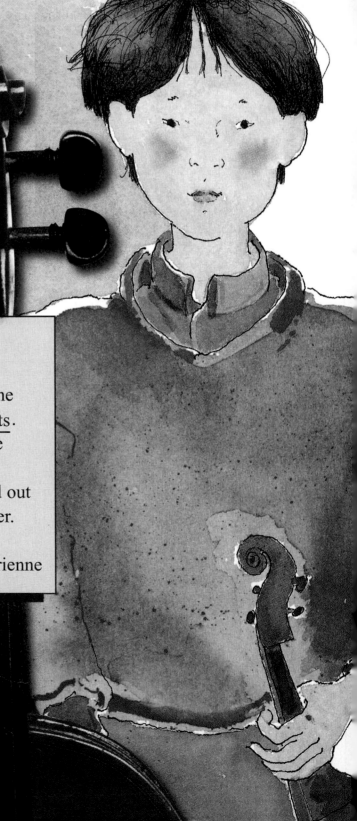

Right Place, Wrong Page!

Will,
Yesterday was my first day of <u>rehearsal</u> with the tri-city <u>orchestra</u>. There were many <u>instruments</u>. The director let me choose one, so I picked the <u>triangle</u>. I thought it would be easy, but I was always behind at least five <u>measures</u>! It turned out that two sheets of my music were stuck together. I hope things go better at the concert.

Adrienne

Talk About It

Imagine you went to the concert. Use vocabulary words to tell what you heard.

Yingtao's New Friend

from *Yang the Youngest and His Terrible Ear*

by Lensey Namioka • illustrated by Kees de Kiefte

The Yang family has just arrived in America from China. Yingtao is the youngest of the four children. By Chinese custom, he is called Yang the Youngest.

Everyone in the Yang family is musical—everyone, that is, but Yingtao. He wants very much to please his father by playing violin with his brother and sisters, but he simply can't hear how high or low a note really is. Add to this the new language and strange ways he encounters in his new school, and you will see that what Yingtao needs most right now is a friend.

We discovered that our school had an after-school orchestra, which met twice a week. My parents thought that Third Sister and I were very lucky, and they signed us up for the orchestra right away. They never even asked us whether we wanted to join.

Before Third Sister and I could play in the orchestra, the conductor gave us an audition; that is, he asked each of us to play a few bars of music alone.

He looked pleased when he heard Third Sister play the cello. He immediately put her near the front of the orchestra.

Then it was my turn to play the violin. He stopped me after only four measures and looked at me thoughtfully. "Would you like to try the triangle instead?"

Maybe I should have felt insulted, but in fact I was tempted to accept. You don't need a good ear to play the triangle, since all you do is just hit it with a stick. You only need to come in on time, and I was good at that. And besides, the triangle makes only a small tinkle, so you can't do much harm.

But I knew my parents would be upset. "I have my own violin," I told the conductor unhappily. "My parents will expect me to play it."

He sighed. "Very well. I know what parents are like." He put me in the very last row of the violin section—as far away from the audience as possible.

When I took my place, the boy sharing a music stand with me said, "Hi, looks like I'll be your stand partner."

It was Matthew, the boy who had gotten my pen back. I was very glad to see him.

Then the conductor raised his stick and the orchestra began to play.

When playing together with other people, my trick was to draw my bow back and forth, without quite touching the strings. This helped everybody. It helped me; it helped the other players; it helped the conductor; and most of all, it helped the audience.

After a few bars we stopped playing while the conductor tried to cheer up the trombone player, who was making bubbling sounds when he tried to blow.

Matthew turned to me. "You don't play very loudly, do you? I couldn't hear you at all."

"You're lucky," I told him.

He looked puzzled, but I had no time to explain because the conductor raised his stick again.

Matthew played with a dreamy look on his face. I couldn't tell if he was good or not, but he certainly seemed to be enjoying himself.

After the rehearsal the conductor asked Third Sister to stay behind and play a short piece for him. I waited for her outside so we could go home together.

Matthew came up to me while I was waiting. "I heard your sister tell the conductor that your father is a violin teacher."

"Yes, he is," I answered. Maybe this was a chance to get Father another student? "Do you want to take lessons?"

Matthew looked very uncomfortable. "I'd really like to, but my folks can't afford it."

"My father is cheap," I said eagerly, although I didn't actually know how much Father charged. But I felt sure he would love to have a new student, especially someone who really liked music.

When Third Sister came out, she was smiling. "The conductor wants me to play a solo for our first concert!"

I was very happy for her, and even Matthew looked glad. "Hey, that's great!" he said.

"This is my stand partner, Matthew," I said. "And this is my third sister—"

"Hi, my name is Mary," interrupted Third Sister.

I stared at her. I didn't even know she had an American name. She must have picked it without telling the rest of the family. Maybe she felt it would be easier for her new friends to remember.

I'd noticed that many Americans had trouble with Chinese names. When I told people my name was Yingtao, they always asked me to spell it. Even after I spelled it, they had trouble remembering it.

"I heard you play just now," Matthew said to Third Sister. "You're really good!"

Third Sister dimpled again. "I'm terrible. You're just saying that to be nice."

She didn't mean it, of course. That's the way my parents taught us to answer when someone praises us.

"Well, I guess I'd better run," said Matthew. But he didn't seem in a hurry to go.

Neither was Third Sister eager to have him go—not when he had just told her how much he admired her playing. "Would you like to come to our house and meet my elder brother and sister? They also play musical instruments."

Matthew grinned. "Sure, if it's okay with your folks."

"My parents would be glad to meet one of Fourth Brother's friends," she told him.

I liked the way she said that—as if Matthew was really my friend, as if I had lots of other friends.

My parents weren't home, but we found Second Sister in the kitchen, cutting tea bags. "This is my other sister," I told him. "She plays the viola."

Second Sister looked a little moody but not too moody to greet Matthew politely with "Hello."

I waited to see if she had chosen an American name too. But she just picked up her scissors again.

As we went up the stairs, Matthew looked at me. "What was your sister doing in the kitchen? It looked like she was cutting up tea bags."

"She was."

At the landing Matthew stopped and looked at me again. "What for?"

I was used to seeing Second Sister cutting tea bags, and it had never occurred to me that it might look funny. "When we make tea, we put some tea leaves in the bottom of the cup, and pour hot water over them," I said. "It's ready to drink when all the leaves are wet and sink to the bottom."

"But why do you need to cut the bags?"

"Well, my mother saw some tea for sale at the market one day, and she bought a big box. But it turned out to be all tea bags, not loose tea. So Second Sister cuts up a few bags every day and pours the loose tea into a jar."

It was perfectly obvious to me that tea would steep better when it's loose than when it's tightly packed into a tiny bag.

But I guess Matthew didn't think so. He was still shaking his head and looking puzzled.

I opened the door to the room I shared with Eldest Brother. He was inside, sitting on the floor and screwing knobs into the ends of orange crates. Beside him were a couple of boards and some bricks.

I introduced Matthew, who looked wide-eyed at the crates and boards. "What are you making?"

"I'm making a chest of drawers," said Eldest Brother. "The boards will sit over the piles of bricks to make a top, and the orange crates are the drawers. The knobs make it easier to pull them out."

Matthew peered into one of the crates, which already contained my shirts and underwear. "Why don't you put your clothes in a regular dresser?"

"We don't have enough money to buy much furniture," explained Eldest Brother.

"Gee, I'm sorry," Matthew said, turning red. "I didn't mean to sound rude or nosy." For some reason, he was very sensitive about money.

I had to show Matthew that we didn't mind. Chinese people aren't at all embarrassed to talk about money. When we meet someone, we often ask him how much money he makes.

"That's okay," I told Matthew. "I don't think you're rude or nosy at all."

"My mother was glad when she found all these orange crates she could have for free," Eldest Brother said.

As he continued to put the knobs in, I told him that Matthew loved music.

Eldest Brother looked pleased. "Are you in the school orchestra?"

"I play the violin," answered Matthew. "I'm Yingtao's stand partner."

Eldest Brother stopped smiling. "Did the conductor put you there after the audition?"

I knew why he asked that. He was trying to find out if Matthew was my stand partner because he played as badly as I did.

"I'm a beginner," said Matthew. "I only started playing the violin last fall. The school had an extra violin that nobody else was using, so I asked if I could borrow it."

"Do you take lessons?" asked Eldest Brother.

Again Matthew turned red. "My parents can't afford them," he mumbled. "My father is out of work right now."

I suddenly had an idea. "Maybe you can give him some free lessons," I said to Eldest Brother. "They don't have to be more than fifteen minutes, just long enough to show him what he's doing wrong."

Eldest Brother looked thoughtful. Finally he got up and went to his violin case. "Play something," he said, taking out the instrument and handing it to Matthew.

Matthew swallowed and wiped his hands on his pants. Then he took the violin carefully and looked at it with wide eyes. "Wow," he breathed. "This is beautiful!"

He closed his eyes for a minute and then began to play. From the expression on Eldest Brother's face, I knew that he liked the sound of what he was hearing.

When Matthew finished, Eldest Brother stood silent and then smiled. "It's certainly clear that you have not been playing very long. But you have a nice feel for the violin."

Matthew looked almost scared. "Then . . . then . . . "

Eldest Brother smiled more widely. "All right, I'll give you lessons. We can start after dinner tonight, if you want. Why don't you stay and eat with us?"

Matthew accepted and went to phone his parents for permission. When he came back he asked if he could go to the bathroom.

I was surprised. Did Americans always take a bath before dinner?

"Is it all right if you didn't take a bath just now?" I asked him. "Our tub has something in it."

It was Matthew's turn to look surprised. "I don't need a bath."

"Then why did you tell me you wanted one?" I demanded.

"I just want to go to the toilet," he explained. He began to laugh. "And you thought I actually asked to take a bath? Without someone making me?"

I laughed too. This was not like Jake and the others laughing at me for standing at attention when the teacher came in. We were laughing together because we were sharing a joke. I began to like Matthew very much.

When he came out of the bathroom, he looked shocked. "Was I seeing things, or were there really fish swimming in your bathtub?"

"That's just some carp my mother bought in Chinatown today. We're having them for dinner tonight."

"But they're alive!"

"Of course they're alive!" I snorted. "My mother would never buy dead fish. They're not fresh."

"I've never had live fish," Matthew said, as we went downstairs. "The fish I eat are nice and dead. They come in a can, or they're frozen sticks covered with bread crumbs."

When we came into the dining room, Matthew was muttering, ". . . cut-up tea bags, knobs on orange crates, fish in the bathtub . . ."

"Does your friend always talk to himself?" whispered Second Sister as I helped her set the table.

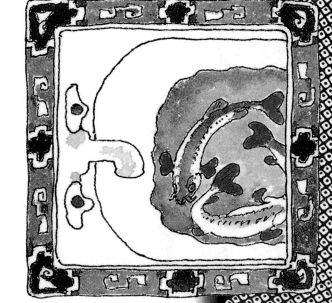

I just smiled. It was a good thing that Second Sister couldn't hear what he was saying.

Matthew was our first American dinner guest. Father nodded approval when Eldest Brother introduced him as my friend and said he had a very good ear.

When we eat dinner, we normally help ourselves to food from the platters in the middle of the table. But since Matthew was my guest, I acted as a host and served him with food.

After a while I noticed that he wasn't eating much. He spent most of the time staring at the chopsticks in my right hand.

"What's wrong?" I asked.

"I've never used chopsticks before," he admitted sheepishly.

"Why don't you give him a fork, Yingtao?" suggested Mother.

"No, please," Matthew said quickly. "I really want to learn how to use chopsticks."

So I taught him. I showed him how to grip one of the two sticks steady and jiggle the other stick to close down on a piece of meat.

He managed to eat most of the food I served him, but I noticed he didn't eat much of the fish. "I'm not used to eating someone I saw swimming just a little while ago," he whispered apologetically.

Matthew learned fast, and by the end of the meal he was using chopsticks pretty well. "Hey, this is good finger exercise!" he joked. "I bet it's going to help my violin playing."

"If that's true, then why doesn't Fourth Brother play a little better?" sniffed Second Sister. "He's been using chopsticks since he was two years old!"

Matthew gave me a sympathetic smile. I was used to remarks from the family about my violin playing, but it was still nice to have someone who was on my side.

From that day on Matthew was my best friend. I didn't have to stand by myself at recess anymore, and we helped each other a lot in school.

I was able to help Matthew with his math homework. Chinese schools are ahead of American schools in math, so everybody thought I was a math genius when I always finished my work long before anyone else. Matthew told me that most kids hated math, except those who were geniuses.

I'm certainly no genius, and Third Sister is much better at math than I am. But I was happy to have people think I was good at something, so I didn't say anything.

Matthew helped me with spelling. I had a lot of trouble because English just didn't sound the way it looked. So Matthew drilled me on tough words like *cough, enough,* and *dough.*

I was getting used to American schools. Not only did I stop jumping to attention when the teacher came into the room, I began to slouch in my seat like the other kids. Once I even interrupted to ask a question. In China, the only time we would interrupt the teacher would be if the building was on fire or one of the students was having a fit.

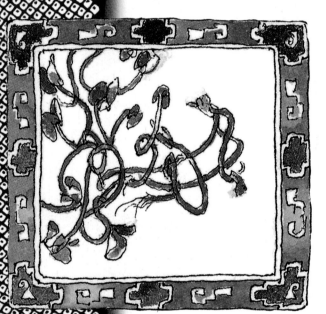

I began to eat lunch with Matthew and his friends. Third Sister looked relieved, because now she could sit and eat with her own friends.

Some of the boys made fun of my lunch, because I'd bring sandwiches with fillings like stir-fried bean sprouts. At first Matthew got angry when his friends laughed, but he soon saw that I didn't mind too much.

"Doesn't it bother you that those guys are always bugging you?" he asked afterward.

"No, it's okay," I said. "I'm used to it. I get a lot of it at home."

"You know, you're tough, Yingtao—a lot tougher than you look."

There was real admiration in his voice, and I suddenly felt twice as tall. There I was, Yang the scrawny, Yang the youngest, and my friend was telling me I was tough.

From the Author
Lensey Namioka

The question people most often ask me about *Yang the Youngest and His Terrible Ear* is whether the book is about myself. Since it's written in the first person, many readers jump to the conclusion that it's an autobiography.

Well, the answer to the question is no. Yang the Youngest is not Lensey Namioka. I differ from Yingtao Yang in several important ways: he's male, and I'm female. He's the youngest in his family, while I'm the third sister. Also, the Yang family are new immigrants to America, whereas I've lived in America for many years. Yingtao is very good at baseball, and I'm hopeless. The only times I was at bat, I struck out.

Yet in some ways I shared the experiences of Yingtao and the Yang family. Although it's been years since I came to this country, I'll never forget how scared I was when I started school here without being able to speak English.

Many readers also write to ask if I play a musical instrument and whether I have a terrible ear like Yingtao. The answer is yes to both these questions. I have a terrible ear, so I play the piano.

The good thing about playing the piano is that you can get somebody else to tune it for you. Of course you have to be able to count time, but I'm pretty good at that, like Yingtao.

I did play the violin for a short time—a very short time. My father, who was very musical, made the mistake of buying me a violin. Since everyone else in the family was musical, he took it for granted that I had a good ear too. No doubt he thought that a good ear should be in my genes. But my cat knew better. The first time I tried to play the violin, my cat streaked under the bed and refused to come out.

My father didn't give up, and he found a teacher to give me violin lessons. Once a week, this got me and my fiddle out of the house for an hour. But my practicing had to stop when my exercise book mysteriously disappeared. So I gave up the violin and took to the piano. Many years later, my eldest sister admitted that she stole my exercise book because she just couldn't stand the sound of my violin any more. (She has a very good ear, and eventually became a professor of music.)

Much of *Yang the Youngest and His Terrible Ear* is about a new immigrant family struggling to get used to the American way of life. Some of the episodes in the book do come from the experiences of my own family. No matter how hard we studied English, there were always idiomatic expressions that tripped us up and words that we mispronounced. Like Third Sister, I tried to keep a notebook with a list of new expressions I learned.

Describing the problems of adjusting to American life was only part of the reason why I wrote the book. The heart of the story is really about self-respect. I want to show that you're just as good as others even if you haven't learned yet how to behave in a world that's new to you.

Even closer to home is showing that you're just as good as others when you're different from the rest of your family. Yingtao may not have a good ear for music, but he turns out to be good at something else, namely baseball.

Still another reason for writing the book has to do with stereotyping. Some people think that all Asian boys are nerds who wear thick glasses, slave over their homework, and practice the violin for hours and hours. Some think that American boys care only about sports, and would rather die than be seen carrying a violin. But not all the people in any group are exactly the same. Therefore, I wanted to write about a Chinese boy, Yingtao, who prefers baseball to violin, while his Caucasian friend, Matthew, is the one who is musically gifted.

Oh, about the carp in the bathtub: many readers ask whether my mother really kept a carp swimming in our bathtub. Yes, she did. When we first came to America, we always bought live fish, because in China that was the only way we could count on its being fresh. So Mother kept it in the bathtub until it was ready to eat. Recently, I met someone who had arrived from China only a couple of months earlier. She told me that she was keeping a live carp in her tub at home.

Reader
Response

Open for Discussion

Is Matthew a good friend for Yingtao? Why or why not?

Comprehension Check

1. When Yingtao plays violin with others, he draws the bow back and forth without touching the strings. Why does he do this? Give details to support your answer.

2. Do you think Matthew behaves the right way at dinner with the Yangs? Explain with details from the story.

3. The author seems to understand both Chinese and American cultures very well. Having read "From the Author" on pages 90–92, you will understand why. Explain why the author understands both cultures. Use examples from the selection.

4. Yingtao and his sister both audition for the school orchestra. **Compare** and **contrast** the way the conductor reacts to the way each plays. (Compare and Contrast)

5. Make a chart to **compare** and **contrast** some of the Yang family's customs with some that Matthew's family may have. (Compare and Contrast)

Test Prep
Look Back and Write

Look back at pages 80–81. How does Matthew feel about discussing money? How does Yingtao feel about it? Use examples from the story to support your answer.

Making Music

by Barbara Taylor

In an orchestra the musicians make air vibrate to produce musical notes in three main ways—with strings, with pipes, or by hitting a surface. The size of the instruments affects the notes they make. Small instruments make high notes and large instruments make low notes.

In the picture, can you find examples of the different kinds of instruments? Look for stringed instruments (such as violin and cello), woodwind instruments (such as clarinet, flute, and bassoon), brass instruments (such as trumpet, trombone, and French horn), and percussion instruments (such as cymbals, drum, and triangle).

With Pipes

In woodwind and brass instruments, the note depends on the length of the pipe and the materials it is made from.

Trumpet

Violin

By Hitting Things

In percussion instruments sounds are produced by striking with the hand, with a special stick or hammer, or by hitting together the instruments themselves. Many of the instruments cannot produce definite notes, but some can be tuned.

With Strings

In a stringed instrument the note depends on the size and length of the string and how tightly it is stretched.

Drum

Author's Purpose

- An **author's purpose** is the reason or reasons an author has for writing.

- Authors usually don't tell their purposes, or reasons, for writing. You have to figure them out. Four purposes are to inform, to entertain, to express, and to persuade.

- Preview what you read to predict the author's purpose. Adjust how fast or how slowly you read depending on that purpose.

Read "Painting Mist and Fog" from a magazine article by author and illustrator Molly Bang.

Talk About It

1. What is Molly Bang's purpose for writing this article? Explain.

2. Should you read this article quickly or slowly? Why do you think this?

PAINTING
Mist and Fog
by Molly Bang

Sometimes warm air blows over a lake or the sea or very wet land, and as it blows, it pulls the water up into itself, and the water forms millions of tiny drops of mist or fog. Then everything around us looks soft and fuzzy. Things that are far away may disappear completely from our view.

Painting pictures of mist and fog is easy. You'll need a bamboo brush, India ink, and some absorbent paper, like Manila paper or white construction paper. For this lesson, you'll also need a small jar of ink and water mixed together to form a nice medium gray.

Dip your brush into the gray until it is completely wet. Then, starting at the upper left side of your paper, slowly paint all the way across the top in a straight line. Just underneath, paint another line so the two lines blend into one. Continue doing this until your whole paper is covered with gray. Make the gray as solid and regular as you can, but if there are some streaky patches, don't worry. Mist and fog have streaky patches too.

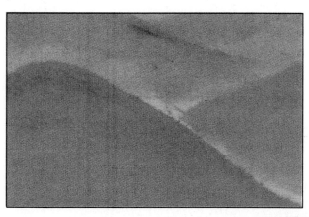

Author and artist Carmen Lomas Garza uses words and paintings to achieve her purpose. Preview *Family Pictures* to predict the author's purpose.

Vocabulary

Words to Know

memories	border	laundry
future	inspired	scene
involved	handkerchief	

To find the meaning of an unfamiliar word, look for its synonym. Words that have the same or a similar meaning are synonyms, such as *shout* and *yell*.

Read the following paragraph. Decide what *inspired* means by looking at its synonym *influenced*.

A Story from the Past

Lucinda tied back her long hair with a clean handkerchief from the laundry and went back to her notebook and pen. She had been inspired to write a scene in a story. The scene involved her own memories of moving across the border to the United States from Mexico with her parents when she was young. Her parents had influenced her through their hard work. Now she would work hard so that she could have a future as a writer.

Write About It

Why do you think Lucinda wants to write about this part of her childhood? Tell the rest of her story. Use vocabulary words.

The pictures in this book are all painted from my memories of growing up in Kingsville, Texas, near the border with Mexico. From the time I was a young girl I always dreamed of becoming an artist. I practiced drawing every day; I studied art in school; and I finally did become an artist. My family has inspired and encouraged me for all these years. This is my book of family pictures.

Los cuadros de este libro los pinté de los recuerdos de mi niñez en Kingsville, Texas, cerca de la frontera con México. Desde que era pequeña, siempre soñé con ser artista. Dibujaba cada día; estudié arte en la escuela; y por fin, me hice artista. Mi familia me ha inspirado y alentado todos estos años. Este es mi libro de cuadros de familia.

Family Pictures

Paintings and stories by Carmen Lomas Garza

Cuadros de familia

We were always going to my grandparents' house, so whatever they were involved in we would get involved in. In this picture my grandmother is hanging up the laundry. We told her that the oranges needed picking so she said, "Well, go ahead and pick some." Before she knew it, she had too many oranges to hold in her hands, so she made a basket out of her apron. That's my brother up in the tree, picking oranges. The rest of us are picking up the ones that he dropped on the ground.

Oranges
Naranjas

Siempre íbamos a la casa de mis abuelos, así que cualquier cosa que estuvieran haciendo ellos, nosotros la hacíamos también. En este cuadro, mi abuela está colgando la ropa a secar. Nosotros le dijimos que las naranjas estaban listas para cosecharse, y ella nos respondió: "Vayan pues, corten algunas." En un dos por tres, tenía demasiadas naranjas para sostenerlas en las manos, así que convirtió su delantal en canasta. Ése es mi hermano, en el árbol, recogiendo naranjas. Los demás estamos recogiendo las que él deja caer al suelo.

That's me hitting the piñata at my sixth birthday party. It was also my brother's fourth birthday. My mother made a big birthday party for us and invited all kinds of friends, cousins, and neighborhood kids.

You can't see the piñata when you're trying to hit it, because your eyes are covered with a handkerchief. My father is pulling the rope that makes the piñata go up and down. He will make sure that everybody has a chance to hit it at least once. Somebody will end up breaking it, and that's when all the candies will fall out and all the kids will run and try to grab them.

Birthday Party

Fiesta de cumpleaños

Ésa soy yo, pegándole a la piñata en la fiesta que me dieron cuando cumplí seis años. Era también el cumpleaños de mi hermano, que cumplía cuatro años. Mi madre nos dio una gran fiesta e invitó a muchos primos, vecinos y amigos.

No puedes ver la piñata cuando le estás dando con el palo, porque tienes los ojos cubiertos por un pañuelo. Mi padre está tirando de la cuerda que sube y baja la piñata. Él se encargará de que todos tengan por lo menos una oportunidad de pegarle a la piñata. Luego alguien acabará rompiéndola, y entonces todos los caramelos que tiene dentro caerán y todos los niños correrán a cogerlos.

In the early spring my grandfather would come
and get us and we'd all go out into the woods to
pick nopal cactus. My grandfather and my mother
are slicing off the fresh, tender leaves of the nopal
and putting them in boxes. My grandmother and
my brother Arturo are pulling leaves from the
mesquite tree to line the boxes. After we got home
my grandfather would shave off all the needles
from each leaf of cactus. Then my grandmother
would parboil the leaves in hot water. The next
morning she would cut them up and stir fry them
with chili powder and eggs for breakfast.

Picking Nopal Cactus

Cortando nopalitos

Al comienzo de la primavera, mi abuelo nos
venía a buscar y todos íbamos al bosque a cortar
nopalitos. Mi abuelo y mi madre están cortando
las pencas tiernas del nopal y metiéndolas en
cajas. Mi abuela y mi hermano Arturo están
recogiendo hojas de mesquite para forrar las cajas.
Al regresar a casa, mi abuelo le quitaba las
espinas a cada penca del cactus. Luego mi abuela
cocía las pencas en agua hirviente. A la mañana
siguiente, las cortaba y las freía con chile y
huevos para nuestro desayuno.

This picture is about the times my family went to Padre Island in the Gulf of Mexico to go swimming. Once when we got there, a fisherman had just caught a big hammerhead shark at the end of the pier. How he got the shark to the beach, I never found out. It was scary to see because it was big enough to swallow a little kid whole.

Hammerhead Shark
Tiburón martillo

Este cuadro trata de las veces en que mi familia iba a nadar a la Isla del Padre en el Golfo de México. Cuando llegamos una vez, un pescador acababa de atrapar un tiburón martillo al cabo del muelle. Cómo logró llevar al tiburón a la playa, nunca me enteré. Daba mucho miedo ver al tiburón, porque era tan grande que hubiera podido tragarse a un niño pequeño de un solo bocado.

This is a scene from my parents' kitchen.
Everybody is making tamales. My grandfather
is wearing blue overalls and a blue shirt. I'm right
next to him with my sister Margie. We're helping
to soak the dried leaves from the corn. My mother
is spreading the cornmeal dough on the leaves
and my aunt and uncle are spreading meat on
the dough. My grandmother is lining up the rolled
and folded tamales ready for cooking. In some
families just the women make tamales, but in
our family everybody helps.

Making Tamales

La tamalada

Ésta es una escena en la cocina de mis padres.
Todos están haciendo tamales. Mi abuelo lleva
puestos rancheros azules y camisa azul. Yo estoy
al lado de él, con mi hermana Margie. Estamos
ayudando a remojar las hojas secas del maíz.
Mi mamá está esparciendo la masa de maíz sobre
las hojas, y mis tíos están esparciendo la carne
sobre la masa. Mi abuelita está ordenando los
tamales que ya están enrollados, cubiertos y listos
para cocerse. En algunas familias sólo las mujeres
preparan tamales, pero en mi familia todos ayudan.

My sister and I used to go up on the roof on summer nights and just stay there and talk about the stars and the constellations. We also talked about the future. I knew since I was thirteen years old that I wanted to be an artist. And all those things that I dreamed of doing as an artist, I'm finally doing now. My mother was the one who inspired me to be an artist. She made up our beds to sleep in and have regular dreams, but she also laid out the bed for our dreams of the future.

Beds for Dreaming

Camas para soñar

Mi hermana y yo solíamos subirnos al techo en las noches de verano y nos quedábamos allí platicando sobre las estrellas y las constelaciones. También platicábamos del futuro. Yo sabía desde que tenía trece años que quería ser artista. Y todas las cosas que soñaba hacer como artista, por fin las estoy haciendo ahora. Mi madre fue la que me inspiró a ser artista. Ella nos tendía las camas para que durmiéramos y tuviéramos sueños normales, pero también preparó la cuna para nuestros sueños del futuro.

About the Author/Illustrator

Since she was young, Carmen Lomas Garza has always dreamed of becoming an artist. Ms. Garza's family encouraged her to follow her dream and study art in school.

Now that she is an artist, she has painted a book of memories. The art in *Family Pictures* shows her memories of what it was like to grow up in Kingsville, Texas, not far from the border with Mexico. The book *Family Pictures* was nominated for the Texas Bluebonnet Award in 1992.

Carmen Lomas Garza

Reader Response

Open for Discussion

If you could walk into one of these pictures and be part of it, which one would you choose? What would you look at, hear, and enjoy?

Comprehension Check

1. What activities does the author remember from her childhood? Use examples. What do these memories show about the author's family?

2. What people are important to the author? How did these people help her figure out who she is? Use examples from the selection.

3. Why do you think the author became an artist? Give evidence from the selection to support your answer.

4. An **author's purpose** can be to help the reader visualize a scene. Do you think this might have been one of Carmen Lomas Garza's purposes? Explain your answer. (Author's Purpose)

5. Think more about this **author's purpose**. What other reasons, besides visualizing a scene, may she have had for writing *Family Pictures?* Explain. (Author's Purpose)

 Test Prep

Look Back and Write

Look back at pages 100–101. How does the illustration help you understand what the author has written about this event in her life? Use details from the story to support your answer.

Family Photo

by Ralph Fletcher

One last picture
before we head off
in different directions.

One last group shot of
all of us, smirking,
with rabbit ears.

Three generations,
kids on shoulders,
a baby cousin on my lap.

And in the middle
Grandma and Grandpa
who started all this.

We're all ripples in a pond
spreading out
from a stone they threw.

New Baby

by Ralph Fletcher

Soon as the baby gets born
before she's two hours old
people start dividing her up

"She has Daddy's big ears"
"Got Grandma's double chin"
"She has my olive eyes"

like she's just a bunch
of borrowed parts
stitched together.

Well, I just got to hold her.
I touched her perfect head
and I'll tell you this:

My sister is whole.

Character

- **Characters** are the people or animals in a story or nonfictional article.

- You can learn about characters by what they think, do, and say.

- You can also learn about characters by paying attention to how other characters in the story treat them and what these other characters say about them.

Read "Ma on the Prairie" from *Black-Eyed Susan* by Jennifer Armstrong.

Talk About It

1. If Susie were to write to her relatives about her ma, what would she say?

2. Point out the parts of "Ma on the Prairie" that describe Ma.

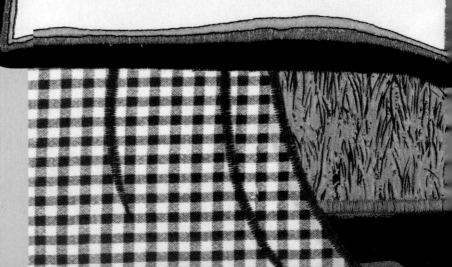

Ma on the Prairie

by Jennifer Armstrong

Susie has just noticed a stack of letters that Ma has written to relatives back in Ohio.

I never asked what she wrote to them about, as it didn't seem right to pry. But it gave me a left-out feeling to see how many letters she had written. I glanced at Ma, but she was miles away. It was awfully lonesome inside the house.

I had to clear my throat before I could talk. "Does that book have trees in it?"

Ma marked her place with one finger and looked up, and a smile slowly spread across her face. "Yes, it does. Lots of trees." She looked at me for a bit in a considering way, and then set the book down and held back the blankets. "Come on in here, Susie."

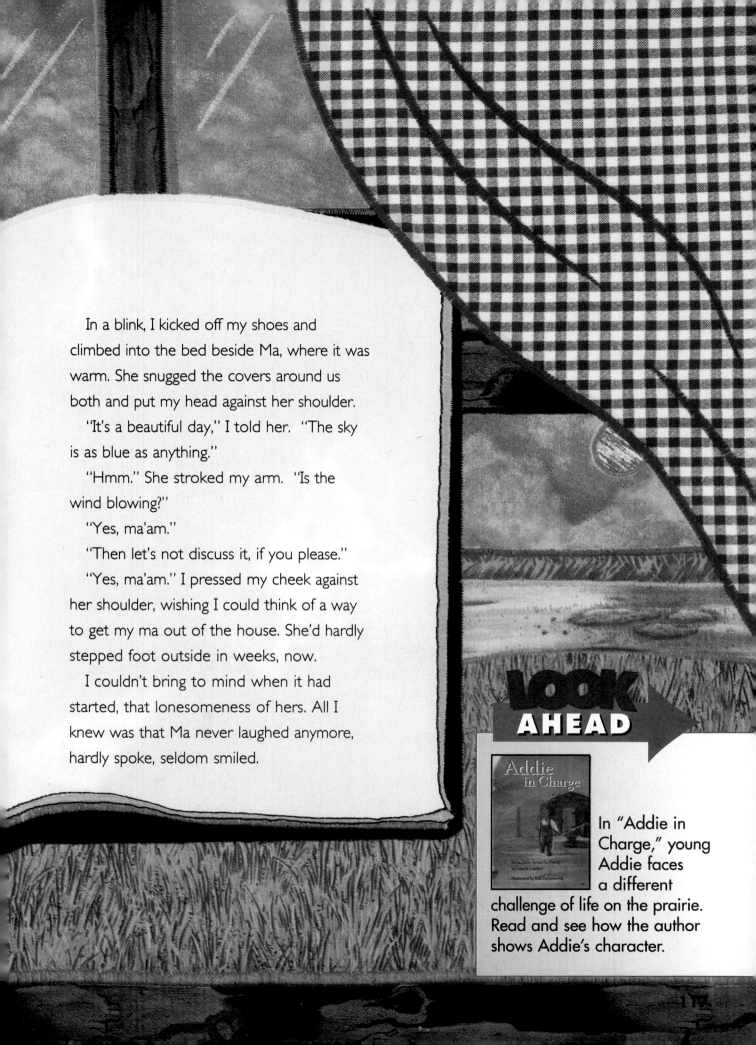

In a blink, I kicked off my shoes and climbed into the bed beside Ma, where it was warm. She snugged the covers around us both and put my head against her shoulder.

"It's a beautiful day," I told her. "The sky is as blue as anything."

"Hmm." She stroked my arm. "Is the wind blowing?"

"Yes, ma'am."

"Then let's not discuss it, if you please."

"Yes, ma'am." I pressed my cheek against her shoulder, wishing I could think of a way to get my ma out of the house. She'd hardly stepped foot outside in weeks, now.

I couldn't bring to mind when it had started, that lonesomeness of hers. All I knew was that Ma never laughed anymore, hardly spoke, seldom smiled.

LOOK AHEAD

In "Addie in Charge," young Addie faces a different challenge of life on the prairie. Read and see how the author shows Addie's character.

Words to Know

bellows smarted tufts
billows crouched

When you read, you may come across words you do not know. Look for clues in the words or sentences near the unknown word to help you figure out the word's meaning.

Read the paragraph below. Figure out the meaning of *bellows*.

Bravery Under Fire!

Billows of smoke filled the night sky as more tufts of grass went up in flames. Pedro could hear the loud, terrified bellows of animals running to escape the fire. Even though their eyes smarted from the smoke, Pedro and the other firefighters would not give up. They crouched down in a circle to decide what their next strategy should be. Their brave actions kept the forest from being completely destroyed.

Write About It

Pedro is receiving an award for his work. Write what should appear on his award certificate. Use vocabulary words.

Addie
in Charge

from *Addie Across the Prairie*

by Laurie Lawlor

illustrated by Bill Farnsworth

In the fall of 1883, nine-year-old Addie Mills and her family have come from Iowa to their 160-acre homestead in Dakota Territory. Addie hadn't wanted to leave Eleanor, her best friend in Iowa, and isn't sure she is strong enough to be a pioneer.

Before winter comes, the Mills family must build a sod house, called a soddy. Until their soddy is built, they are living with Mr. and Mrs. Fency.

Addie's parents and George, her eight-year-old brother, along with Mr. and Mrs. Fency, go to work on the soddy. For two days Addie is left in charge of the Fencys' farm and her two-year-old brother, Burt. With the company of Ruby Lillian, a doll, and Miss Primrose, a "person" Addie made by putting her sunbonnet over the bristles of a broom, Addie has survived the first day and night of being in charge.

When Addie had finished the milking and her other morning chores, she prepared a breakfast of gruel for herself and Burt. Carefully she dropped pinches of cornmeal into the boiling water. She felt pleased about how well she was doing on her own.

"Don't you think I'm doing just fine?" she asked Ruby Lillian, as she took her out from beneath the pillow and placed her on the table. Addie spooned gruel into two bowls.

"Mama! Mama!" Burt demanded.

"She'll be back, Burt. Pa's coming to get us soon as he can." Addie sighed. It still seemed like a long, long time to wait for her parents to return. But she had made it through the night. The worst was over.

She washed the breakfast dishes, swept, read Burt a story from Anna's book, and then took him outside to look for prairie dogs.

In the afternoon while Burt napped, Addie worked on her sampler again. Suddenly she heard low bellows from the cows. What was the matter with Bess and Missy? A gust of wind blew into the soddy, knocking the canvas flap against the wall. Addie looked outside. The sky seemed unusually dark for this time of the afternoon. Or had she lost track of time? Was it later than she thought?

The wind blew dust through the yard, and the cows continued making frightened noises. Addie hurried to the clothesline to make sure the laundry she had forgotten on the line since yesterday had not blown away. She gathered the bedding and Burt's clothes. Pulling the flapping sheets away from her face, she saw a queer sight in the southwestern sky. The far horizon was ablaze with orange and yellow, as if the sun were setting.

But Addie knew exactly where the sun set. She had watched the western horizon every day since they left Iowa. This glow wasn't from the sun.

She bundled the laundry together and tossed it inside the soddy, then scrambled up the ladder to the roof for a better look. As she climbed, the wind grew stronger. She crawled along the roof, shielding her eyes from flying dust and sharp pieces of brittle grass. A family of coyotes raced through Mr. Fency's plowed field, not even stopping to bother Anna's chickens, who frantically clucked near the lean-to. Addie wiped her eyes with her apron and discovered that her face was covered with black flecks. There were cinders flying in the air! The bright glow she saw was a prairie fire, and it was headed right for the Fency farm.

The palms of her hands broke into a cold sweat. She had to think of a way to save herself and Burt. She had to think of a way to save the farm. She scrambled off the roof and ran inside the soddy to wake her brother.

"Burt! Wake up!" she screamed. "We've got to get out of here!"

Burt's eyes flew open, and he began to whimper. He knew something was terribly wrong as he watched his sister gather Anna's books and stuff them back into the trunk. With all her strength she pushed the trunk across the room and opened the trap door to the root cellar. She shoved the trunk into the cellar with one terrific push. There was barely enough room for it. Neither she nor Burt would fit down there as well. She slammed the door.

"Where are we going to hide? What are we going to do?" she blurted and ran outside. The wind swept across the yard, picking up dried leaves and pieces of grass and sending them into the sky in little corkscrew formations. Addie remembered what Pa had said about a stiff wind behind a prairie fire. Would the Fencys' firebreak save them? The cows were bellowing in terror now. Addie decided to untie Bess and Missy and let them run from the fire. Their eyes rolled as they pulled against their ropes. "Run as fast as you can!" Addie shouted, hitting each cow on the rump. Should she and Burt try to run too? But how far could they get in bare feet?

Addie raced back into the soddy and put on her black, copper-toed boots. She quickly slipped Burt's shoes on him. Pulling him by the hand, she ran outside again. They were past the firebreak, running away from the fire as fast as Addie could go, when she realized she had left Ruby Lillian behind on the table. She picked Burt up and dashed back. The soddy's darkness and quiet made the fire seem farther away. She wanted to stay there, but she knew she couldn't. From the door she could see that the approaching flames were as tall as three houses stacked one atop the other. The wind was so strong the firebreak would never work. She knew there wasn't time to set a backfire, even if she knew how.

"A fire can't go where there's nothing to burn." Addie repeated Pa's words frantically, trying to think of a plan. She crouched and motioned to her brother. "Get on my back, Burt." The child sobbed tearfully but did as he was told.

She ran outside with Burt on her back and Ruby Lillian in her pocket. The wall of fire was closer; she could see tufts of grass exploding into flames. With each explosion the sky filled with more and more billows of black smoke. The roar was deafening, like a terrible, rolling summer thunderstorm.

"I promised to watch the farm and keep it safe," she told Burt, placing him on the ground near the well. "I can't let the Fencys' house burn." She lowered bucket after bucket into the water, soaking the soddy's walls as best she could. But even as she desperately tossed water, more pieces of burning grass landed on the roof. Saving the soddy seemed hopeless. Addie pulled the ladder away from the house and threw it on the ground just as it was about to catch fire, too. She would never be able to keep the house from burning all by herself.

Addie was exhausted, but she kept hauling bucket after bucket up the well as best she could. She could not think. Her arms kept working as if she had no control over them. As she pulled up one more bucket, she saw her reflection in the water, illuminated by the fire's glow. She and Burt had only a few minutes before the sea of flames would engulf them. Where could she find a place to hide from those awful, devouring explosions? "Where's there nothing to burn," Addie whispered. Suddenly she knew what to do. She dragged the ladder to the well, the way she had done to save her doll, Eleanor.* She pushed it down inside.

Burt was crying hysterically, crouched on the ground with his hands over his ears to stop the horrible noise.

* Eleanor is a doll Addie had made, which her brother George ruined by throwing in the well.

"Come on, Burt, we have to hurry. Climb on my back," Addie shouted.

"No, NO!" Burt sobbed.

"You have to!" Addie commanded. She knelt beside her brother. Reluctantly he grabbed around her shoulders, crying harder than ever.

Still kneeling on the ground, Addie used one foot to carefully feel for the ladder's highest rung. Slowly, she lowered herself, balancing Burt with great effort. Down into the well she went, step over step. Now they were below ground level. It was pitch black, and the water felt cold around Addie's knees as she reached the bottom rung. "Don't let go, Burt. Don't let go," she told her brother, who buried his face into the back of her neck so that her necklace dug deep into her skin.

The terrible roar of the fire grew louder. Addie wanted to cover both her ears, but she could not let go. She had to hold on tight to the ladder while standing as still as possible. Any minute the fire would be right over them. What would happen then? Would they melt? She remained motionless even as several stones and a handful of dirt came loose from the wall and tumbled into the water. Was the well going to cave in on them?

Now the noise was deafening. Pieces of burning grass hissed as they fell into the well water, just missing the children. Cinders smarted Addie's eyes. How long? How long until the fire came? Addie glanced up just as the flames roared over the mouth of the well.

Addie held her breath and closed her eyes. For one brief, horrible moment she was certain her hair would catch fire. The hot white light charged overhead with a howling ten times worse than the loudest locomotive Addie had ever heard. But as quickly as the flames appeared, they were gone.

A gust of wind blew more cinders and smoke into the well, and the children began coughing. Around the edge of the well, where Mr. Fency had laid sod bricks, Addie could see a few small flames sputter and go out as the last piece of dry grass was consumed.

"Burt? Are you all right?" she asked in a hoarse whisper.

"Mama! Mama!" his voice echoed in the well. He clung to Addie even more tightly.

Her legs shook in the cold water. A terrible pain shot up and down her back where her brother dug in with his knees. But still she did not move or change position. She felt as if she were frozen, clinging to the ladder for dear life. Nearly half an hour passed. There was no more roar to be heard, even in the distance, and the air seemed filled with an almost eerie silence.

Addie whispered again, "Burt, are you all right? I'm going to climb back up now. Don't touch the walls. Don't touch anything. Just hold on tight to me."

Addie climbed up one step. Then another. She stopped as some rocks tumbled past and splashed in the water. Burt whimpered and coughed. The top of the well seemed almost farther than Addie could manage. She was exhausted. Burt felt heavier by the minute, even though he weighed only a bit more than twenty-five pounds. If only Pa would come now and lift them both out. If only he would save them.

"Addie!" Burt cried, his voice echoing. "Out! Out!"

"Hush, Burt!" Addie hissed as a small section of the well wall crumbled and collapsed above them, sending dirt all over their faces and hair.

Pa wasn't going to save them. The only way they could get out was if she climbed out herself, with Burt on her back. Somehow she'd just have to trust that she could make it all nine feet up to the top. "Hold on, Burt. We're almost there," she said, her voice cracking. Only four more steps.

Suddenly Addie heard a familiar voice.

"Addie! Addie! Where are you?" someone called desperately.

It wasn't Pa. It was George!

"We're in the well!" Addie shouted. Another pile of dirt splashed into the water.

A face peered down at her. "Grab hold of my hand," George said, throwing his coat over the charred sod at the well's edge and lying on his stomach, his arms reaching down to them. "Careful now. Not too fast."

The ladder teetered as she reached the top-most rung. Addie made a desperate lunge for George's hands and solid ground. As her foot left the top rung, one side of the wall began to crumble. A section of stones and dirt broke loose and crashed into the water. Addie threw herself forward, grasped the well's edge with both hands, and scrambled to safe ground. Burt tumbled from her back, unharmed.

Addie hugged George as Burt jumped up and down with excitement. She couldn't believe how happy she was to see him. Her brother seemed just as happy to see her.

"You should take a look at yourself, Addie," George said, grinning. "Your face is black as a skunk's. Yours, too, Burt. Mother will hardly recognize you."

"Pa and Mother are all right? What about the others? You didn't get caught in the fire?" Addie asked anxiously.

"The fire passed to the south of us, heading straight east on the other side of the river. We were on our way back when we saw it coming. We headed to get you two as fast as we could travel. I rode ahead of the others to look for you. You sure scared me, Addie. When I got to the soddy, all I found was a burned scrap of your sunbonnet." George held out what was left of the bonnet Addie had used to decorate Miss Primrose. "I thought I'd never see you again."

"You won't get rid of me that easily, George Sidney," Addie said. She looked sheepishly at the toes of her dirty, wet boots. "I'm sorry about what I said to you before you left. I don't really hate you."

George blushed. "You aren't a crybaby, either. I just said that to be mean. You're about the bravest person I know. I don't believe I'd have been able to figure what to do if I'd gotten caught in a prairie fire."

"You really think I'm brave?" Addie asked, suddenly feeling wonderful in spite of her damp clothes and aching back. "But you know, George, I *was* afraid down there." She hesitated. "And I was afraid when the Indians came here too."

"Maybe you were scared, but you did something courageous anyway. I think that's what being brave's all about."

Addie was quiet for a moment. "Maybe the Indian necklace helped. Pa said it was special. I'll let you wear it sometime, if you want."

George looked pleased. "I'd like that, Addie. I'd like that a lot."

The children stepped over the smoldering black stubs that had once been Anna's garden. The fire had raced far enough to the east so that it was now a steady glow in the distance. The Fency soddy was charred black, but it was still standing. The prairie all around continued smoking. The ground was covered with blackened patches of brittle, burned grass, and the air was filled with the bitter, acrid smell of smoke. As they walked, the scorched ground crackled under their feet.

Addie looked in every direction and saw how horrible the firestorm had been. Straightening her shoulders, she felt a sudden pride. If she hadn't acted as quickly as she had, they would have been killed. Climbing into the well had been her own magnificent, new, wonderful idea. She had been very brave, just as George had said. She had saved her brother and herself. That was something, wasn't it? She had survived an Indian visit all alone too. Dakota didn't seem quite so frightening anymore. Maybe Eleanor was wrong. Maybe she *was* a sodbusting pioneer-type after all.

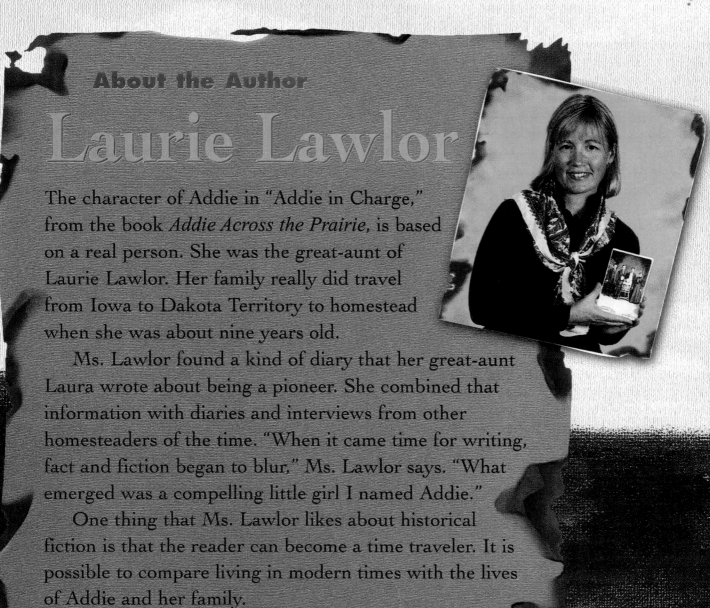

About the Author
Laurie Lawlor

The character of Addie in "Addie in Charge," from the book *Addie Across the Prairie*, is based on a real person. She was the great-aunt of Laurie Lawlor. Her family really did travel from Iowa to Dakota Territory to homestead when she was about nine years old.

Ms. Lawlor found a kind of diary that her great-aunt Laura wrote about being a pioneer. She combined that information with diaries and interviews from other homesteaders of the time. "When it came time for writing, fact and fiction began to blur," Ms. Lawlor says. "What emerged was a compelling little girl I named Addie."

One thing that Ms. Lawlor likes about historical fiction is that the reader can become a time traveler. It is possible to compare living in modern times with the lives of Addie and her family.

Reader Response

Open for Discussion

Suppose you are Addie. Someone asks, "What did you learn about courage that day you were in charge?" What would you say?

Comprehension Check

1. Before Addie sees the fire, what signs warn her that something is wrong? Give examples.

2. Addie tries to remember everything she has heard about prairie fires. How does this help her survive? Use story details to explain.

3. Imagine you are Addie. What sounds do you hear when you are down in the well? What do you feel? Use details from the story.

4. Think about Addie's **character**. What are her actions when she saves the Fency farm, Burt, and herself? What does this show about her character? (Character)

5. We learn about a **character** from how other characters treat and talk to him or her. How do Addie's parents treat her? How do Burt and George feel about Addie? Give examples. (Character)

Test Prep
Look Back and Write

Look back at pages 125–128. Describe the events in the story from when Addie and Burt first go into the well to when they climb out. Use details from the story to support your answer.

Search

How to Read an Internet Article

1. Preview

- Some informational articles on the Internet provide historical facts and compare them to something that is happening today.

- Read the title and the words in red type.

2. Read and Note Terms

- Terms are words or phrases about a specific subject, such as an event.

- As you read, make a list of the terms in red type. Add notes about what these terms mean.

3. Think and Connect

Think about "Addie in Charge." Then look over your notes for "Merle Builds a Sod House."

After reading this article, what do you know about how Addie would have lived? Use details to support your answer.

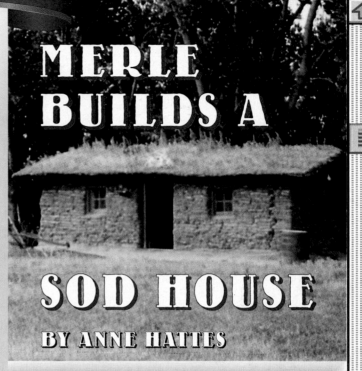

MERLE BUILDS A
SOD HOUSE
BY ANNE HATTES

Merle Block, a 20th-century descendant of Nebraska pioneer stock, built a sod house with his own hands. You'll find it in **Gothenburg, Nebraska**, along with a windmill, a giant sod-breaking plow, and a buffalo made from 4 1/2 miles of barbed wire. Last summer over 50,000 visitors came to see this unusual site, awarded a prize as Nebraska's most innovative tourist attraction using area resources.

According to Block, **prairie settlers** usually arrived with only two horses, a few hand tools, a plow, and a wagon. With the big cutting knife of the plow, they sliced the sod, laying it open to be chopped into building blocks for a house.

After building his **sod house**, Block thoroughly appreciates his

133

ancestors. Block's son came out from the city to help, but after three days he just sat in the shade and said, "Dad, you'll never finish it."

"It wasn't cutting the pieces," says Block, "but the continual picking up of the 100-pound sod rectangles that made the job such a struggle. The first one wasn't heavy, and the second wasn't heavy; the 13th and 14th and 1400th were. I lost 15 pounds in three weeks."

Block built his **"soddy"** nine years ago. He has photos showing that sod houses lasted for 70 years or longer. People still live in old sod houses in the **sandhill area** of Nebraska, according to Block, "but you wouldn't know it

from the outside, as they may have been covered with stucco. The only way you'll know is to see the three-foot-thick doorway and no air conditioner," he says. **Homesteaders**, with a little help, could put one up in a week. It took Block three weeks to build his.

Admitting he didn't have a team of horses or even the know-how to put on a harness, Block pulled his sod plow with a tractor. The plow cuts and lifts strips of sod 18 inches wide and 3 to 4 inches thick. The strips are chopped into 36-inch rectangles, each weighing about 100 pounds, he says.

The average size of a settler's house was about 12 by 14 feet. Sometimes they added rooms onto the end or side; a

The buffalo at Merle Block's Sod House Museum is made from barbed wire.

two-story sod house was a rarity. Block's, at 12 by 16 feet, is a little bigger than average. The sod is tied together, not with mortar, but with **buffalo grass** or bluestem. "I tried to use salt grass, which the cows won't eat anyway," comments Block, "but its root system won't hold the sod together."

Block estimates the total weight of his completed sod house to be about 70 tons. After allowing time for the sod to settle, he covered the inside walls with mud and whitewashed with a mixture of lime and water. He put on four or five coats of **whitewash** the first time and adds another coat every spring.

The lime in the whitewash keeps insects out. By keeping them out, mice and other rodents don't have much reason to come in, and farther up the food chain, snakes aren't as interested. Block says a letter from one of his ancestors talks about an old **bull snake** crawling across the cotton muslin on the ceiling. The snake was left alone up there because it kept the mice under control.

The muslin hanging from the ceiling kept dirt from falling through into the house. Every so often it would be taken down and washed. Stains in the muslin also showed where the sod roof was leaking. "And there's going to be a leak because it always rains for three days in Nebraska," says Block. "It rains for a day and then seeps through for two!"

Almost always the floor was of dirt. Wood floors were expensive, and there would have been the ever-present problem of snakes and other crawly things getting between the dirt and the wood. Lumber to hold up the sod roof and for door and window frames was hard to come by. Settlers either traveled great distances to find trees to cut down or had lumber carted in—an expensive proposition for most. If they were lucky enough to be near a **railroad** and could afford it, they could get window glass by rail. Others used oiled paper for windows.

With three-foot-thick walls, the sod house is well insulated. Visitors note that when the nearby barn is hot, it's 10 to 15 degrees cooler in the soddy. As transportation improved and settlers prospered, they built **frame houses.** Anticipating luxury, those who moved from soddies to frame houses found the new structures drafty, cold in the winter and hot in the summer, compared to the sod houses they'd recently spurned.

That "home on the range"—made of the range—was better than they'd realized.

Changing

by Mary Ann Hoberman

I know what I feel like;
I'd like to be *you*
And feel what *you* feel like
And do what *you* do.
I'd like to change places
For maybe a week
And look like your look-like
And speak as you speak
And think what you're thinking
And go where you go
And feel what you're feeling
And know what you know.
I wish we could do it;
What fun it would be
If I could try you out
And you could try me.

Enchantment

by Joanne Ryder

On warm summer nights
the porch becomes our living room
where Mama takes her reading
and Dad and I play games
in the patch of brightness
the lamp scatters on the floor.
From the darkness, others come—
small round bodies
clinging to the screens
which separate us
from the yard beyond.
Drawn to our light,
the June bugs watch our games
and listen to our talk till bedtime
when Mama darkens the porch
and breaks the spell
that holds them close to us.

My Grandma's Songs

by Francisco X. Alarcón

My grandma's songs
would follow
the beat of
the washing machine

turning
our kitchen
into a dance floor

consoling
the chairs placed
upside down

delighting
the family portraits
on the walls

putting to sleep
the sheets
on the clothesline

giving flavor
to the boiling pot
of beans

the songs
my grandma
used to sing

could make
the stars
come out

could turn
my grandma
into a young girl

going back
to the river
for water

and make her
laugh and cry
at the same time

AUGUST
COWBOY

by Joyce Carol Thomas

I woke up at dawn and rode
Grandpa's horse 'til noon
Think I'll ride 'til I see the moon

"I can see the tiredness in your bones
    I know all about boys, my son
        Don't you know I used to be one?"

Grandpa spreads a pallet
Stitched with Buffalo Soldiers
For a bed
"Oklahoma cowboys," he says,
    "With a dark man at the head

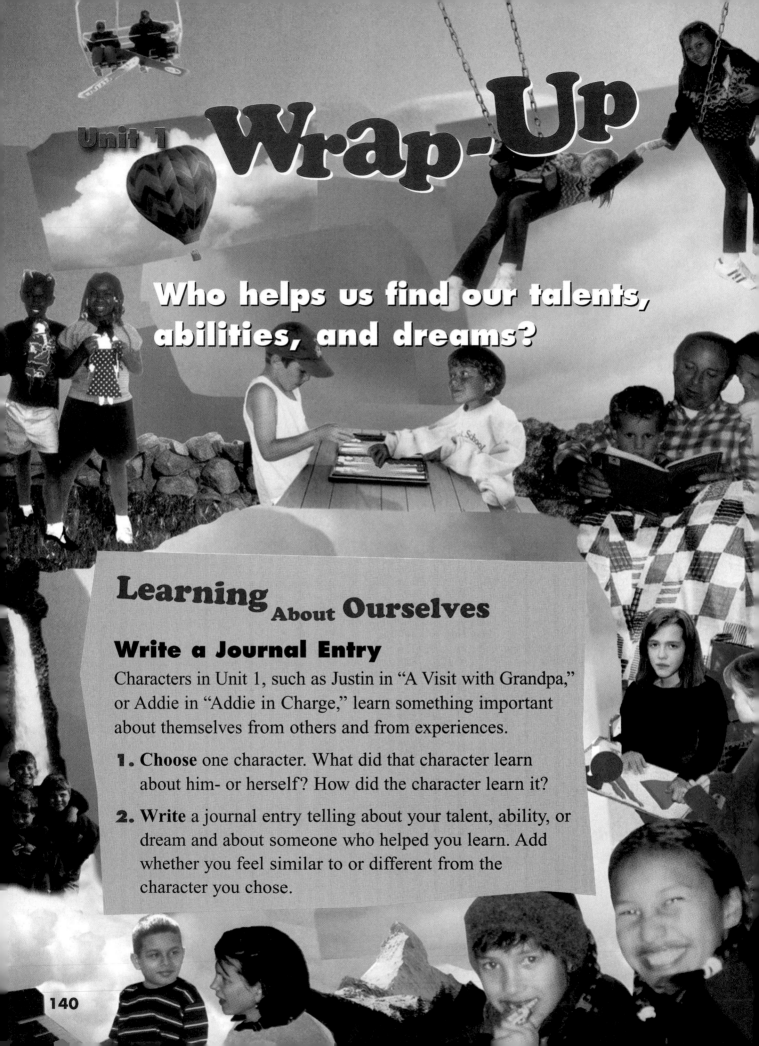

Wrap-Up

Who helps us find our talents, abilities, and dreams?

Learning About Ourselves

Write a Journal Entry

Characters in Unit 1, such as Justin in "A Visit with Grandpa," or Addie in "Addie in Charge," learn something important about themselves from others and from experiences.

1. **Choose** one character. What did that character learn about him- or herself? How did the character learn it?

2. **Write** a journal entry telling about your talent, ability, or dream and about someone who helped you learn. Add whether you feel similar to or different from the character you chose.

Family Treasures

Create a Photo Album

In *Family Pictures,* Carmen Lomas Garza illustrates family memories. Other characters in Unit 1 describe experiences too.

1. **Choose** a character from Unit 1. **Take notes** about the character's experiences.

2. **Create** a photo album for the character. Illustrate several of the character's experiences.

3. **Write** captions near each illustration.

Set Designer

Create a Movie Set

Details in a movie set, such as the inside of a kitchen, help the audience understand where and when the movie takes place. If a Unit 1 selection were to become a movie, what might the set look like?

1. **Look back** at one story in Unit 1. Jot down details about where most of the story takes place.

2. **Sketch** your set and write a short description. Include details from the story, such as the color of wallpaper.

3. **Display** your sketch and description.

Character Conversation

Compare Experiences

Marianne, in *Train to Somewhere,* and Yingtao, in "Yingtao's New Friend," have new experiences. Some are similar, and some are different.

1. With a partner, compare these characters' new experiences. **Write** your ideas in a Venn diagram.

2. **Discuss** which experiences you would like to share.

Yingtao / Both / Marianne

Test Talk

Understand the Question

Find Key Words in the Question

Before you can answer a test question, you have to understand it. A test about "Understanding Horses," pages 41–43, might have this question.

Test Question 1

How do a horse's eyes show its different moods? Use details from the article to support your answer.

Read the question slowly.
Ask yourself "Who or what is this question about?" The words that tell who or what the question is about are **key words**.

Look for other key words in the question.
- Often the first word of the question is a key word.

Turn the question into a statement.
Use the key words in a sentence that begins "I need to find out . . ."

See how one student makes sure she understands the question.

I've read the question. What is it about? Well, it's talking about a horse's eyes and its moods. **Horse's eyes** and **moods**—those must be key words.

Okay, I'm going to read the question again. There's the key word **how,** and there's the key word **different.** I need to find out how a horse uses its eyes to show its different moods.

Try it!

Now use what you learned to understand these test questions about "Understanding Horses," pages 41–43.

Test Question 2

What are two things a horse can learn by using its sense of smell? Use details from the article to support your answer.

Test Question 3

Why might a horse refuse to do what its rider tells it to do?

Ⓐ because it doesn't trust its rider

Ⓑ because the rider is not giving the right instructions

Ⓒ because it senses that something is wrong

Ⓓ because it doesn't understand the rider's instructions

A Wider View

What place do plants and animals have in the world around us?

Visualizing

- To **visualize** means to form a picture in your mind as you read.

- Look for details that tell how things look, smell, sound, taste, and feel.

- Think about what you already know about characters and places like those being described.

- If you cannot form a picture in your mind, reread or read more slowly to find details that will help you "see" the picture more clearly.

Read "Caught in the Kitchen" from *The Attic Mice* by Ethel Pochocki.

Talk About It

1. If you were an illustrator, what pictures would you draw to help readers visualize this scene?

2. What details in the story would help you know what to draw?

Caught in the Kitchen

by Ethel Pochocki

Before Omeletta could say "No!" Gertrude was on the rim, and the bowl, heavy under their weight, toppled. The cream splashed over the countertop, covering Gertrude and Omeletta, then dribbled down in several streams to the floor.

The mice screamed in panic and, momentarily blinded by the cream, ran madly in all directions. Gertrude stumbled and fell into the bowl of sugar and was followed by Omeletta, who jumped in after her mother. They opened their eyes, rubbed them dry, and screamed again when they saw each other.

"Omeletta?" squeaked Gertrude.

"Mother?" squeaked Omeletta in return.

"You look like a ghost!" said Gertrude.

"You too!" said Omeletta.

The steps came closer and then stopped at the sight of the spilled cream.

"What on earth—"

"Let's get out of here," whispered Gertrude, grabbing the heavy picnic basket.

The two sugar-coated mice made the journey from countertop to floor in no time.

While the mistress angrily wiped up cream from the counter, they ran along the woodwork of the kitchen, which was also white and so hid them somewhat. Once into the hallway, they dashed up the back stairs and attic stairs as fast as they could. They looked like two speeding blobs of cotton.

LOOK AHEAD

Visualize another small creature's new surroundings as you read *The Cricket in Times Square.*

Vocabulary

Words to Know

chirp	occasion	traffic
furiously	railroad	melody
venturing	subway	

Words with similar meanings are called **synonyms**. You can often figure out the meaning of an unknown word by finding a clue in the words around it. Sometimes this clue is a synonym.

Read the paragraph below. Notice how *song* helps you understand what *melody* means.

A Special Birthday

Samantha the cricket lived in the subway, where passenger trains travel under the street. She usually tried to avoid the traffic on the rails of the railroad, but today she was venturing out for an important occasion, her daughter's birthday. All the crickets would chirp a special melody, the song "Happy Birthday." As she furiously jumped over the track to get party supplies, Samantha smiled about her gift: her daughter would have a new home in the park!

Write About It

What will happen when Samantha gives her daughter the gift? Will they enjoy living in the park? Write the rest of the story. Use vocabulary words.

148

from
The Cricket
in Times Square

by George Selden   illustrated by Garth Williams

Normally Chester lives the quiet life of a country cricket. When he arrives without warning in New York City, he is nervous and uncomfortable in the strange new surroundings. Feeling alone and bewildered, he eventually makes his way to a subway station in Times Square. There, Mario Bellini, a boy whose parents own a newsstand in the subway station, finds Chester and makes a home for him in a matchbox lined with tissue.

One evening after the newsstand closes, Chester's chirping is overheard by Tucker, a mouse who also lives in the subway station. Tucker goes to investigate the noise.

Tucker Mouse had been watching the Bellinis and listening to what they said. Next to scrounging, eavesdropping on human beings was what he enjoyed most. That was one of the reasons he lived in the Times Square subway station. As soon as the family disappeared, he darted out across the floor and scooted up to the newsstand. At one side the boards had separated and there was a wide space he could jump through. He'd been in a few times before—just exploring. For a moment he stood under the three legged stool, letting his eyes get used to the darkness. Then he jumped up on it.

"Psst!" he whispered. "Hey you up there—are you awake?"

There was no answer.

"Psst! Psst! Hey!" Tucker whispered again, louder this time.

From the shelf above came scuffling, like little feet feeling their way to the edge. "Who is that going 'psst'?" said a voice.

"It's me," said Tucker. "Down here on the stool."

A black head, with two shiny black eyes, peered down at him. "Who are you?"

"A mouse," said Tucker, "Who are *you?*"

"I'm Chester Cricket," said the cricket. He had a high, musical voice. Everything he said seemed to be spoken to an unheard melody.

"My name's Tucker," said Tucker Mouse. "Can I come up?"

"I guess so," said Chester Cricket. "This isn't my house anyway."

Tucker jumped up beside the cricket and looked him all over. "A cricket," he said admiringly. "So you're a cricket. I never saw one before."

"I've seen mice before," the cricket said. "I knew quite a few back in Connecticut."

"Is that where you're from?" asked Tucker.

"Yes," said Chester. "I guess I'll never see it again," he added wistfully.

"How did you get to New York?" asked Tucker Mouse.

"It's a long story," sighed the cricket.

"Tell me," said Tucker, settling back on his haunches. He loved to hear stories. It was almost as much fun as eavesdropping—if the story was true.

"Well it must have been two—no, three days ago," Chester Cricket began. "I was sitting on top of my stump, just enjoying the weather and thinking how nice it was that summer had started. I live inside an old tree stump, next to a willow tree, and I often go up to the roof to look around. And I'd been practicing jumping that day too. On the other side of the stump from the willow tree there's a brook that runs past, and I'd been jumping back and forth across it to get my legs in condition for the summer. I do a lot of jumping, you know."

"Me too," said Tucker Mouse. "Especially around the rush hour."

"And I had just finished jumping when I smelled something," Chester went on, "liverwurst, which I love."

"You like liverwurst?" Tucker broke in. "Wait! Wait! Just wait!"

In one leap, he sprang down all the way from the shelf to the floor and dashed over to his drain pipe. Chester shook his head as he watched him go. He thought Tucker was a very excitable person—even for a mouse.

*I*nside the drain pipe, Tucker's nest was a jumble of papers, scraps of cloth, buttons, lost jewelry, small change, and everything else that can be picked up in a subway station. Tucker tossed things left and right in a wild search. Neatness was not one of the things he aimed at in life. At last he discovered what he was looking for: a big piece of liverwurst he had found earlier that evening. It was meant to be for breakfast tomorrow, but he decided that meeting his first cricket was a special occasion. Holding the liverwurst between his teeth, he whisked back to the newsstand.

"Look!" he said proudly, dropping the meat in front of Chester Cricket. "Liverwurst! You continue the story—we'll enjoy a snack too."

"That's very nice of you," said Chester. He was touched that a mouse he had known only a few minutes would share his food with him. "I had a little chocolate before, but besides that, nothing for three days."

"Eat! Eat!" said Tucker. He bit the liverwurst into two pieces and gave Chester the bigger one. "So you smelled the liverwurst—then what happened?"

"I hopped down from the stump and went off toward the smell," said Chester.

"Very logical," said Tucker Mouse, munching with his cheeks full. "Exactly what I would have done."

"It was coming from a picnic basket," said Chester. "A couple of tuffets away from my stump the meadow begins, and there was a whole bunch of people having a picnic. They had hard boiled eggs, and cold roast chicken, and roast beef, and a whole lot of other things besides the liverwurst sandwiches, which I smelled."

Tucker Mouse moaned with pleasure at the thought of all that food.

"They were having such a good time laughing and singing songs that they didn't notice me when I jumped into the picnic basket," continued Chester. "I was sure they wouldn't mind if I had just a taste."

"Naturally not," said Tucker Mouse sympathetically. "Why mind? Plenty for all. Who could blame you?"

"Now I have to admit," Chester went on, "I had more than a taste. As a matter of fact, I ate so much that I couldn't keep my eyes open—what with being tired from the jumping and everything. And I fell asleep right there in the picnic basket. The first thing I knew, somebody had put a bag on top of me that had the last of the roast beef sandwiches in it. I couldn't move!"

"Imagine!" Tucker exclaimed. "Trapped under roast beef sandwiches! Well, there are worse fates!"

"At first I wasn't too frightened," said Chester. "After all, I thought, they probably come from New Canaan or some other nearby town. They'll have to unpack the basket sooner or later. Little did I know!" He shook his head and sighed. "I could feel the basket being carried into a car and riding somewhere and then being lifted down. That must have been the railroad station. Then I went up again and there was a rattling and roaring sound, the way a train makes. By this time I was pretty scared. I knew every minute was taking me further away from my stump, but there wasn't anything I could do. I was getting awfully cramped too, under those roast beef sandwiches."

"Didn't you try to eat your way out?" asked Tucker.

"I didn't have any room," said Chester. "But every now and then the train would give a lurch and I managed to free myself a little. We traveled on and on, and then the train stopped. I didn't have any idea where we were, but as soon as the basket was carried off, I could tell from the noise it must be New York."

"You never were here before?" Tucker asked.

"Goodness no!" said Chester. "But I've heard about it. There was a swallow I used to know who told about flying over New York every spring and fall on her way to the North and back. But what would I be doing here?" He shifted uneasily from one set of legs to another. "I'm a country cricket."

"Don't worry," said Tucker Mouse. "I'll feed you liverwurst. You'll be all right. Go on with the story."

"It's almost over," said Chester. "The people got off one train and walked a ways and got on another—even noisier than the first."

"Must have been the subway," said Tucker.

"I guess so," Chester Cricket said. "You can imagine how scared I was. I didn't know *where* I was going! For all I knew they could have been heading for Texas, although I don't guess many people from Texas come all the way to Connecticut for a picnic."

"It could happen," said Tucker, nodding his head.

"**A**nyway I worked furiously to get loose. And finally I made it. When they got off the second train, I took a flying leap and landed in a pile of dirt over in the corner of this place where we are."

"Such an introduction to New York," said Tucker, "to land in a pile of dirt in the Times Square subway station. Tsk, tsk, tsk."

"And here I am," Chester concluded forlornly. "I've been lying over there for three days not knowing what to do. At last I got so nervous I began to chirp."

"That was the sound!" interrupted Tucker Mouse. "I heard it, but I didn't know what it was."

"Yes, that was me," said Chester. "Usually I don't chirp until later on in the summer—but my goodness, I had to do *something!*"

The cricket had been sitting next to the edge of the shelf. For some reason—perhaps it was a faint noise, like padded feet tiptoeing across the floor—he happened to look down. A shadowy form that had been crouching silently below in the darkness made a spring and landed right next to Tucker and Chester.

"Watch out!" Chester shouted, "A cat!" He dove headfirst into the matchbox.

Chester buried his head in the Kleenex. He didn't want to see his new friend, Tucker Mouse, get killed. Back in Connecticut he had sometimes watched the one-sided fights of cats and mice in the meadow, and unless the mice were near their holes, the fights always ended in the same way. But this cat had been upon them too quickly: Tucker couldn't have escaped.

There wasn't a sound. Chester lifted his head and very cautiously looked behind him. The cat—a huge tiger cat with gray-green and black stripes along his body—was sitting on his hind legs, switching his tail around his forepaws. And directly between those forepaws, in the very jaws of his enemy, sat Tucker Mouse. He was watching Chester curiously. The cricket began to make frantic signs that the mouse should look up and see what was looming over him.

Very casually Tucker raised his head. The cat looked straight down on him. "Oh him," said Tucker, chucking the cat under the chin with his right front paw, "he's my best friend. Come out from the matchbox."

Chester crept out, looking first at one, then the other.

"Chester, meet Harry Cat," said Tucker. "Harry, this is Chester. He's a cricket."

"I'm very pleased to make your acquaintance," said Harry Cat in a silky voice.

"Hello," said Chester. He was sort of ashamed because of all the fuss he'd made. "I wasn't scared for myself. But I thought cats and mice were enemies."

"In the country, maybe," said Tucker. "But in New York we gave up those old habits long ago. Harry is my oldest friend. He lives with me over in the drain pipe. So how was scrounging tonight, Harry?"

"Not so good," said Harry Cat. "I was over in the ash cans on the East Side, but those rich people don't throw out as much garbage as they should."

"Chester, make that noise again for Harry," said Tucker Mouse.

Chester lifted the black wings that were carefully folded across his back and with a quick, expert stroke drew the top one over the bottom. A "thrumm" echoed through the station.

"Lovely—very lovely," said the cat. "This cricket has talent."

"I thought it was singing," said Tucker. "But you do it like playing a violin, with one wing on the other?"

"Yes," said Chester. "These wings aren't much good for flying, but I prefer music anyhow." He made three rapid chirps.

Tucker Mouse and Harry Cat smiled at each other. "It makes me want to purr to hear it," said Harry.

"Some people say a cricket goes 'chee chee chee,' " explained Chester. "And others say, 'treet treet treet,' but we crickets don't think it sounds like either one of those."

"It sounds to me as if you were going 'crik crik crik,' " said Harry.

"Maybe that's why they call him a 'cricket,' " said Tucker.

They all laughed. Tucker had a squeaky laugh that sounded as if he were hiccuping. Chester was feeling much happier now. The future did not seem nearly as gloomy as it had over in the pile of dirt in the corner.

"Are you going to stay a while in New York?" asked Tucker.

"I guess I'll have to," said Chester. "I don't know how to get home."

"Well, we could always take you to Grand Central Station and put you on a train going back to Connecticut," said Tucker. "But why don't you give the city a try. Meet new people—see new things. Mario likes you very much."

"Yes, but his mother doesn't," said Chester. "She thinks I carry germs."

"Germs!" said Tucker scornfully. "She wouldn't know a germ if one gave her a black eye. Pay no attention."

"Too bad you couldn't have found more successful friends," said Harry Cat. "I fear for the future of this newsstand."

"It's true," echoed Tucker sadly. "They're going broke fast." He jumped up on a pile of magazines and read off the names in the half light that slanted through the cracks in the wooden cover *Art News—Musical America.* Who would read them but a few long-hairs?"

"I don't understand the way you talk," said Chester. Back in the meadow he had listened to bullfrogs, and woodchucks, and rabbits, even a few snakes, but he had never heard anyone speak like Tucker Mouse. "What is a long-hair?"

Tucker scratched his head and thought a moment. "A long-hair is an extra refined person," he said. "You take an Afghan Hound—that's a long-hair."

"Do Afghan Hounds read *Musical America?*" asked the cricket.

"They would if they could," said Tucker.

Chester shook his head. "I'm afraid I won't get along in New York," he said.

"Oh sure you will!" squeaked Tucker Mouse. "Harry, suppose we take Chester up and show him Times Square. Would you like that, Chester?"

"I guess so," said Chester, although he was really a little leery of venturing out into New York City.

The three of them jumped down to the floor. The crack in the side of the newsstand was just wide enough for Harry to get through. As they crossed the station floor, Tucker pointed out the local sights of interest, such as the Nedick's lunch counter—Tucker spent a lot of time around there—and the Loft's candy store. Then they came to the drain pipe. Chester had to make short little hops to keep from hitting his head as they went up. There seemed to be hundreds of twistings and turnings, and many other pipes that opened off the main route, but Tucker Mouse knew his way perfectly—even in the dark. At last Chester saw light above them. One more hop brought him out onto the sidewalk. And there he gasped, holding his breath and crouching against the cement.

They were standing at one corner of the Times building, which is at the south end of Times Square. Above the cricket, towers that seemed like mountains of light rose up into the night sky. Even this late the neon signs were still blazing. Reds, blues, greens, and yellows flashed down on him. And the air was full of the roar of traffic and the hum of human beings. It was as if Times Square were a kind of shell, with colors and noises breaking in great waves inside it. Chester's heart hurt him and he closed his eyes. The sight was too terrible and beautiful for a cricket who up to now had measured high things by the height of his willow tree and sounds by the burble of a running brook.

"How do you like it?" asked Tucker Mouse.

"Well—it's—it's quite something," Chester stuttered.

"You should see it New Year's Eve," said Harry Cat.

Gradually Chester's eyes got used to the lights. He looked up. And way far above them, above New York, and above the whole world, he made out a star that he knew was a star he used to look at back in Connecticut. When they had gone down to the station and Chester was in the matchbox again, he thought about that star. It made him feel better to think that there was one familiar thing, twinkling above him, amidst so much that was new and strange.

About the Author

George Selden

Like Chester Cricket in *The Cricket in Times Square*, George Selden was from Connecticut. Mr. Selden later moved to New York City. One night he was in the Times Square subway station, and he unexpectedly heard a cricket chirping. An idea came into his mind for a story about a cricket who landed in the city by accident and missed his home in the country. That was the beginning of *The Cricket in Times Square*. This book has won many awards, including a Newbery Honor Book Citation.

About the Illustrator

Garth Williams

When Garth Williams illustrated children's books, he tried to draw pictures the way the author imagined them while writing. "Illustrating books is not just making pictures of the houses, the people, and the articles mentioned by the author; the artist has to see everything with the same eyes," Mr. Williams said.

Besides *The Cricket in Times Square*, Mr. Williams illustrated many other famous books. These include *Stuart Little*, *Charlotte's Web*, and many books by Laura Ingalls Wilder.

Reader Response

Open for Discussion

After reading about Connecticut and New York City in the story, where would you rather live? Why?

Comprehension Check

1. How does Tucker Mouse make Chester feel at home? Give examples.

2. If you could have Chester, Tucker, or Harry for a pet, which would you choose? Why? Support your answer with details from the story.

3. After the tour of Times Square, when Chester is back in his matchbox, one thing makes him feel better. What is it? Why?

4. Chester tells Tucker how he got to New York. **Visualize** as you reread that part of the story. Describe what you see, hear, feel, smell, and taste. (Visualizing)

5. **Visualize** Chester's life in the country and in New York City. What are some of the differences? (Visualizing)

Test Prep
Look Back and Write

Look back at pages 152–154. What events caused Chester Cricket to become trapped in the picnic basket? Use details from the story to support your answer.

Test Prep
How to Read a Fable

1. Preview

- A fable is a story that is usually about animals. It teaches a lesson, or moral.

- Read the title and look at the illustrations.

2. Read and Take Notes

- Read the fable. As you read, take notes about events in the story to help you follow the action and understand the moral at the end.

> 1. City Mouse visits Country Mouse.

3. Think and Connect

Think about *The Cricket in Times Square.* Then look over your notes on "The Country Mouse and the City Mouse."

Do you think that Chester Cricket would agree with the moral of this fable? Give evidence to support your answer.

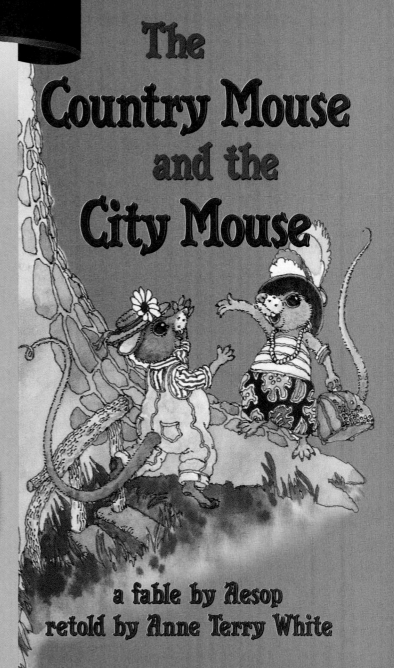

The Country Mouse and the City Mouse

a fable by Aesop
retold by Anne Terry White

"My dear, how are you?" said the Country Mouse. She kissed her cousin the City Mouse and made her welcome in her snug little hole.

"How good of you to travel all this way to visit me," she went on. "Well, you shall see how we country folk live. Not badly at all."

With that she began to carry food out of the house. The best of everything should be put on the table for her guest. They would eat outdoors in the fresh air under a tree and the birds would sing to them while they feasted.

It took a long time to carry out the moldy crust, the cheese parings, the bacon rind, and the dry peas and beans she had stored up. But all was ready at last. The dessert would be two stalks of fresh wheat which she had brought home from the field that very day. She laid them proudly on a mushroom, and very pretty they looked too.

The Country Mouse ate heartily, but the City Mouse only nibbled at the food. She was used to better things. After the dessert she said:

"My dear, how can you bear to live in this poky way? I call this starving. You don't know what happiness is. Come with me and let me show you my way of life. You will be done with loneliness. You will live in plenty and enjoy all the pleasures your heart desires."

The Country Mouse saw nothing wrong with her way of life, but she agreed to go with her cousin and they set off at once. It was night when they reached the city.

"This is my house," the City Mouse said and led the way up the stairs and into the dining room. It was brightly lighted. On the table were the remains of a fine feast, for there had been a party that night.

"Help yourself," the City Mouse invited her cousin.

The Country Mouse scampered over the snowy cloth and stared at the dishes. She could hardly believe it wasn't all a dream. She didn't know which to taste first—the pudding, the cheese, the cakes, the jellies, or the nuts. She sniffed at the grapes and pears. They didn't look real, but yes, they were. She was very thirsty, so first of all she took a sip out of a tall, sparkling glass.

"How silly I have been to waste my life in the country," she thought. "This is heaven!"

Then she started nibbling on a piece of cake. But she had taken no more than two bites when the doors flew open. In came the servants with their friends and a couple of roaring dogs. They were going to enjoy the leavings of the feast too.

The mice ran for their lives and hid in a corner. They lay trembling, hardly daring to breathe. Not till everybody had gone away did they dare to creep out.

"Well, my dear," said the Country Mouse, "if this is city life, good-by. I'll go back to the country. I would rather have my moldy crusts and dry peas in my own quiet hole than feast like this in fear of my life."

Crusts eaten in peace are better than cakes eaten in fear.

Cause and Effect

- A **cause** is why something happens. An **effect** is what happens.

- Sometimes there are clue words, such as *because, so, if, then,* or *since,* to help you figure out what happened and why. At other times there are no clue words.

Read "Super Cooper Scoopers," an article from *Kid City* magazine.

Write About It

1. Make a chart with the first column labeled *Cause* and the second labeled *Effect*. Write the three causes talked about in this article and the effect of each one.

2. Did you use any clue words to help you figure out what happened and why? If so, write them down.

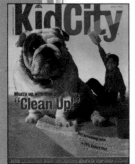

Super Cooper Scoopers

from *Kid City* magazine

Longfellow Creek in Seattle, Washington, was in trouble. The salmon that used to swim there stopped coming. Salmon are fish that love creeks. But Longfellow Creek was too dirty for them. So the students and teachers of Cooper Elementary School started a super cleanup!

"Our creek was one of only three left in Seattle that the salmon could live in," says Jackie Silverman, 10. "It was sad that they didn't have anywhere to lay their eggs."

Cleaning up water can be harder than cleaning up stuff on land. Garbage gets ripped apart in creeks and spreads everywhere. The kids had to use nets and shovels to get the trash out of the creek.

"It was our idea to do something for the fish," adds Chris Bowerman, 11. "It felt good to get our feet wet and help out."

Good news! The kids made the creek so clean, the salmon are swimming there again.

Jackie is even happier than the fish. "I think they're cute!" she says.

Glub!

LOOK AHEAD

A Big-City Dream

Now learn about the causes and effects of another cleanup project as you read "A Big-City Dream."

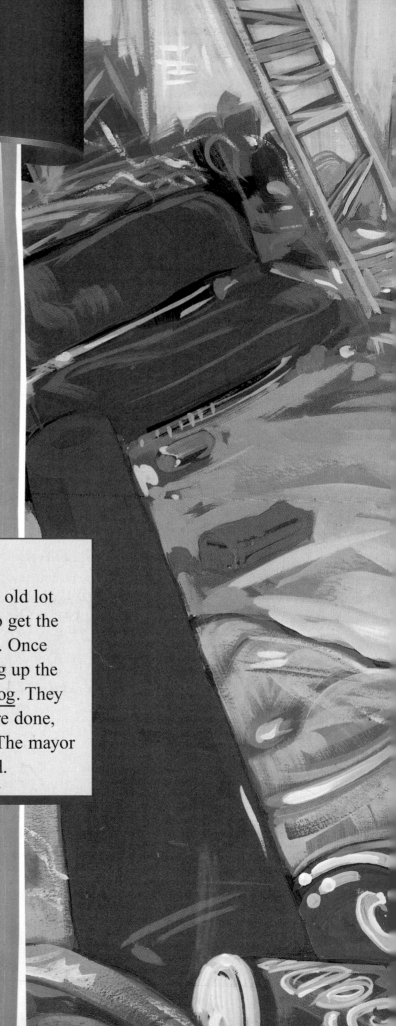

Vocabulary

Words to Know

impressed   celebrate   blisters
catalog   padlock

When you read, you may come across a word you don't know. To figure out the meaning of an unfamiliar word, look for clues in the surrounding sentences. A clue might be found in specific details or examples given near the unknown word.

Notice how *padlock* is used in the paragraph below. Find the specific details or examples in the paragraph. What do you think *padlock* means?

Teamwork!

Manuel and his friends wanted to turn the old lot on the corner into a park. First they had to get the key to open the large <u>padlock</u> on the gate. Once they opened the lock, they started cleaning up the lot. Then they ordered plants from a <u>catalog</u>. They had <u>blisters</u> on their hands when they were done, but they had something to <u>celebrate</u> too. The mayor was so <u>impressed</u> she gave them an award.

Talk About It

What could you do to make a neighborhood a better place to play? Talk about it with a friend. Use vocabulary words.

A Big-City Dream

from *The Big Idea* ~ by Ellen Schecter

Luz dreams of turning an empty lot in her neighborhood into a vegetable and flower garden. Officer Ramirez suggests she contact Ms. Kline of the Green Giants, a group that supports community projects. Ms. Kline says she can help only if Luz can guarantee workers to do the job. Will friends and family come through for her? Will Luz's best friend Rosie be willing to help even though she's moving away in July?

Saturday's bright and sunny. My eyes pop open way before my alarm rings. And I know right away why I'm so happy: It's the very first day of my garden. It's not a dream anymore!

I run to my window and do a little dance in a warm patch of sunshine. Then I jump into my clothes, grab one of Mami's sweet rolls, and run down to the corner to meet Ms. Kline. While I'm waiting, I look for the red tulip. There it is, blooming away in the middle of all the old newspapers and all the junk.

I pace up and down on the sidewalk outside the fence. I'm the first one there. In fact, I'm the only one there. And I'm still not sure who will show up.

I can't help wishing Rosie would come. I feel awful about our fight. But I'm not sure how to say sorry. That's because I'm still mad at her too. I know it's hard for her to think about moving away. But it's hard for me to lose her. Especially when she's still living right downstairs.

But I can't think about Rosie right now. Because I see a lady who might be Ms. Kline. She's parking an old, beat-up car near the corner. She gets out and starts to unload stuff—rakes and brooms, big plastic bags, lots of work gloves.

She's sort of round and plump. Wisps of gray hair poke out from under her big straw hat. She's wearing an old sweatshirt and jeans. Her sneakers are full of mud.

"Hi!" I say, and wave both hands.

"Luz? Luz Mendes?" she calls out to me.

"Hi, Ms. Kline. Want some help?"

"You bet." She's having trouble balancing all her stuff. The rakes fall with a clatter when she tries to pick up the brooms.

I run and grab the rakes with my left hand, then hold out my right hand to shake. I try to look as grown-up as I can.

"Glad to meet you, Luz." Ms. Kline smiles. Then she looks around to see who else is with me.

Nobody. Yet.

She stares down at me through her thick glasses, then looks up and down the block again. As if maybe she somehow missed seeing all the people in that big Dream Garden Group I'm supposed to have. She clears her throat.

"Uh—where is everybody?" Ms. Kline asks.

"They're not here. Yet. But don't worry," I tell her, trying not to look one bit worried myself. "The Dream Garden Group is on its way. And I'm very, *very* energetic. You'll see!" I pick up another rake to show how much I mean it.

Ms. Kline gives me one of those tiny grown-up smiles that's just pretend-friendly. It makes me feel nervous instead of good.

But then Papi turns the corner, and I start to feel better. I feel even better when Mrs. Chapman shows up right behind him.

The grown-ups shake hands and introduce themselves. Then Ms. Kline gives us all thick work gloves and puts on a pair herself. She takes a key out of her jeans' pocket and sticks it in the rusty padlock. Here's the big moment I've been waiting for! The gate screeches as we push it back. And we're inside!

The four of us get right to work. We start picking up cans and bottles, raking trash out of corners, and shoveling junk into bags.

But it's not like in the movies when you start a hard job and *presto!*—two seconds later it's all done.

No way. After what feels like a million hours, I'm still picking up cans and bottles. Papi is still raking trash out of corners. And Ms. Kline and Mrs. Chapman are still shoveling junk into bags.

Lots of people walk past. Most of them don't even notice what we're doing. And nobody offers to help.

Then, all of the sudden, I see Rosie and her mom turn the corner. My heart rises straight up in my chest.

Yay! I want to shout. You're coming after all!

I wipe my sweaty face on my sleeves. I get ready to run over and open the gate extra wide to let her in. But Rosie doesn't even look at me.

My heart falls down, hard, when she walks right past without even turning her head. She's wearing her favorite denim shirt and a new belt I've never seen.

Get real, I tell myself. Rosie's not coming to help. She's on her way to pick up that girl from down the block. Then they're going out to brunch and the movies.

I turn around fast so Rosie won't see me watching her. I start picking up cans and bottles and shoving them into my garbage bag. It gives me something to do besides worry about Rosie.

Then—total surprise! My brother, Lorenzo, shows up.

"*¡Hola, Luzita!* Need a hand?"

"I need about a hundred." I grin.

"Well, will you settle for two?" Lorenzo grins back, then puts on gloves and starts picking up stuff. With two of us working side by side, we seem to work more than twice as fast.

"You know, Luz, you got me thinking about Lito and his garden. When you were talking to Mami about *your* dream garden." Lorenzo speaks quietly, but I can hear every word. "I remember how cool it was when we played there. How bright the flowers were. How it almost felt like a magic place."

Lorenzo stops working for a second, and so do I. "You're right, Luz. We do need a garden around here. I'm glad we're doing this."

We go back to work without saying anything else. But the word "we" sings in my ears.

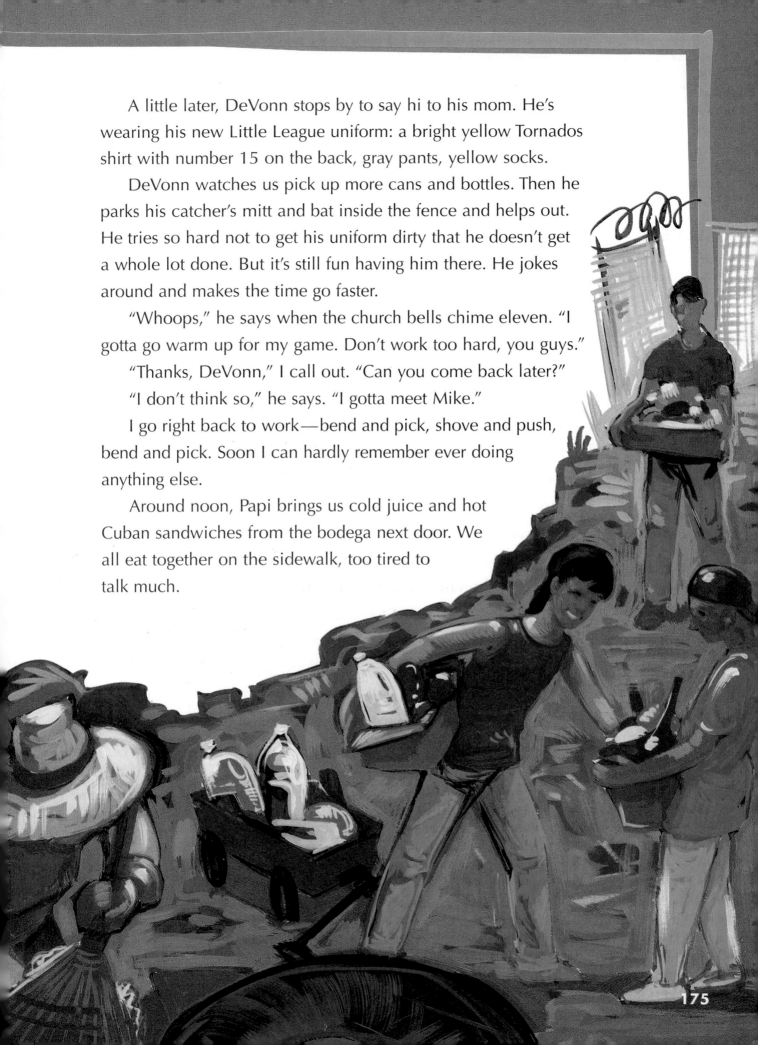

A little later, DeVonn stops by to say hi to his mom. He's wearing his new Little League uniform: a bright yellow Tornados shirt with number 15 on the back, gray pants, yellow socks.

DeVonn watches us pick up more cans and bottles. Then he parks his catcher's mitt and bat inside the fence and helps out. He tries so hard not to get his uniform dirty that he doesn't get a whole lot done. But it's still fun having him there. He jokes around and makes the time go faster.

"Whoops," he says when the church bells chime eleven. "I gotta go warm up for my game. Don't work too hard, you guys."

"Thanks, DeVonn," I call out. "Can you come back later?"

"I don't think so," he says. "I gotta meet Mike."

I go right back to work—bend and pick, shove and push, bend and pick. Soon I can hardly remember ever doing anything else.

Around noon, Papi brings us cold juice and hot Cuban sandwiches from the bodega next door. We all eat together on the sidewalk, too tired to talk much.

I count eighteen huge garbage bags piled up at the curb. I've got blisters on my hands, sunburn on my nose, and aches in strange muscles I never knew I had. But the lot still looks like a junk heap.

When it's time to get started again, my legs are so stiff I can hardly get up. But I don't want to act chicken, so I'm the first one back to work. The others follow me slowly.

Finally, around three o'clock, Ms. Kline puts down her rake.

"I've had it," she says.

"Me too," Mrs. Chapman groans, rubbing her shoulders.

I've never been so tired in my whole life. But I'm afraid to say one word of complaint. Otherwise, Ms. Kline will think I can't do this. And I'm trying so hard to convince her!

Now I count twenty-eight bags stuffed with garbage. Most of the small junk is gone. Papi and Ms. Kline drag the bedsprings and other big stuff out to the curb where the garbage truck can pick it up Monday morning.

I look around the lot. You can actually see the ground! And there's the red tulip, standing straight up in the middle. No old newspapers hide it now. It waves in the wind like a brave red flag that says, "You can do it! You can!" But we still have a long way to go.

"Well, Luz, you certainly are energetic." Ms. Kline stretches her back. "But you've still got to get more people to help." She frowns at me. But at least it's not one of those pretend smiles. She thinks for a minute, then digs in her pocket for the key. She dangles it in the air.

"I'm going to give this key to you and your papi, Luz. I'll be back next Saturday to see how much progress your group has made."

She sighs. "If you can't get this place cleaned up by then, the Green Giants just can't sponsor you. I'll have to take back the key and lock up this place for good."

I try to smile. "Don't worry, Ms. Kline, we'll do it. I'll get lots of people to help. You'll see."

I only hope I'm right.

That night I realize I only have six days to get the lot cleaned up *and* come up with the rest of the Dream Garden Group. Otherwise, Ms. Kline will take back the key and lock up the lot for good. I know I'll have to spend every spare minute either working on the garden or trying to convince other people to help me.

On Sunday, Mami forbids me to go anywhere near the garden. Instead, I have to get all dressed up and go to Mass. Then I have to help Mami for the rest of the day while about a dozen of my most boring relatives come for dinner.

On Monday, I rush home after school, change into my grungy clothes, grab my gloves and key, and go to work. Whenever somebody I know walks by, I invite them to come in, look around, maybe even give me a hand. But Mrs. Chapman and Papi are my only helpers. We fill two more bags with cans and bottles before it's time for supper and homework.

On Tuesday, Lorenzo, DeVonn, and Shrimp help for about an hour before it starts pouring. We get most of the old newspapers picked up and stuffed into bags.

On Wednesday, Lorenzo drags Mike over. "How's Luz's nightmare?" Mike teases. But Lorenzo convinces him to come in and help pick up the last of the bottles. For a grand total of twenty minutes. After he leaves, Lorenzo and I start raking chunks of glass out of the weeds near the fence. Papi stops by to help.

On Thursday, I see Kenya and Shuwanza, two first-grade girls from my school, playing hopscotch across the street. They're real curious when they see me open the gate. "Want to come in?" I yell. "We're making this into a garden. You can help if you want."

They come in and help me rake leaves. But after about half an hour they get tired and start giggling and go back to their game.

"Maybe we'll come back tomorrow," says Kenya. Maybe.

On Friday, Lorenzo and DeVonn help after school till suppertime. Melinda Park stops in to help after her violin lesson. We rake the last of the trash out of the corners. DeVonn says, "This place is starting to look much better, you guys." We all agree.

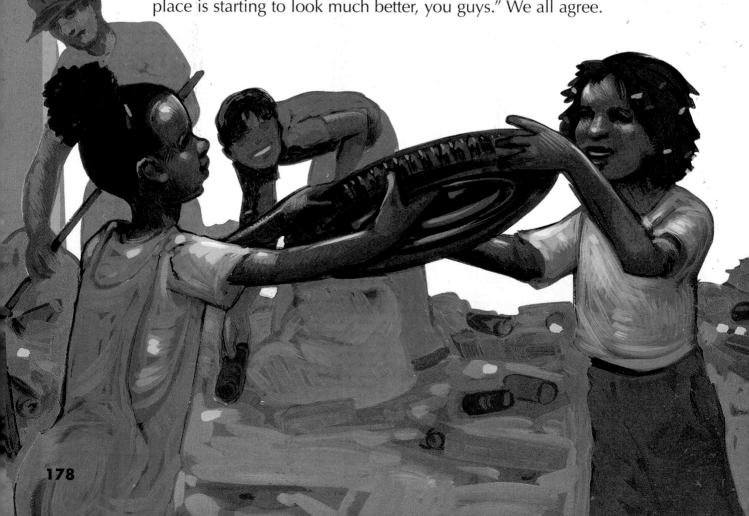

My papi was the only one I could count on to show up every single day—even if it was only for a few minutes after work. But as the week went by, I noticed more and more people stopping to watch instead of just walking past.

Some even offered free advice. "Don't forget, you'll need some nice, rich topsoil before you can grow anything in there," Mrs. Hodges told me.

"That lot is looking much nicer, Luz," Mrs. Pazzalini calls out as we're getting ready to leave late Friday afternoon.

"Want to help, Mrs. P.?" I call back.

"I can't now, dear. I'm running to the bookstore. Maybe some other time." But I can't tell if "some other time" will ever come.

I make sure to tell everybody who stops to show up tomorrow morning when the lady from the Green Giants will be here again. But—you guessed it—I still get mostly maybes.

One thing I do know: Rosie still won't help. Not even a little. She skates by a lot—sometimes by herself, sometimes with the girl down the block. She sees me, all right. But she doesn't come in. She hardly even says hi.

On Saturday morning, Lorenzo and I race over to the lot extra early to make sure things look really great for Ms. Kline.

Lorenzo beats me to the corner. Then he stops short, and I bump right into him.

"Oh, no!" he groans. "Look at that."

I can't believe what I see. During the night—after we locked up to go home for supper yesterday—somebody dropped a whole, huge load of garbage over the fence. Soda cans, rotten salad, yucky old coffee grounds, eggshells. And stacks and stacks of newspapers, which the wind blew all around during the night. Ripped pages are stuck in the fence and flying like dirty flags near the wall.

"Oh, no! What a mess." I sigh. Lorenzo just shakes his head. "C'mon," I say. "We better get busy."

We unlock the padlock and push open the gate. We grab two garbage bags and rake stuff in as fast as we can. We've got to get this cleaned up before Ms. Kline comes!

Just then, Mike, DeVonn, and Shrimp pass by on their way to baseball practice. "Hey, what happened?" Shrimp calls. "I thought we finished cleaning up this place already."

"We did," I call back. "But now we have to do it again. And we have to do it fast, before Ms. Kline shows up. If she sees this mess, she'll take back the key, lock up the lot, and good-by garden."

"Want some help?" DeVonn asks. Without waiting for an answer, he and Shrimp come in and get busy.

Mike yells to them, "Hey, what do you guys think you're doing? We've got practice in half an hour."

"So we'll help for half an hour," DeVonn says. "Keep your baseball shirt on, Mike. We'll get there in time to win the pennant." Mike turns his hat backward on his head. He stands there punching his mitt to break it in. Then he comes in too. We all keep stuffing the new trash into bags as fast as we can.

Mrs. Hodges passes by, walking her little white poodle with the pink hair bows. When she sees what happened, she ties her dog's leash to the fence. "Now you stay right there while Mama helps clean up," she says in fake baby talk. Then she picks up a rake and gets busy.

When Lorenzo sees I have plenty of help, he dashes to the gate. "I'm going for Papi, Luz. We'll be right back." I'm too busy to answer.

Mrs. Chapman and DeVonn's big sister, Keisha, pass by on their way home from the supermarket. Mrs. Chapman takes one look and clicks her tongue. "Look at that mess!" she says.

"Come on, Mom," DeVonn yells. "We need you!"

Mrs. Chapman taps Keisha on the shoulder. They both come in, set down their grocery bags, and get right to work.

Lorenzo and Papi come back with Pony. "We caught him on his way home from the night shift," Lorenzo explains quickly. He hands Pony a garbage bag and all three of them start picking up newspapers.

Soon, about a dozen people are busy stuffing the last of the new garbage into bags, tying them closed, and hauling them out of the lot.

And just in time! We're stacking the last of the bags by the curb when Ms. Kline's old rattletrap car turns the corner.

She gets out and slams the door. She's wearing exactly the same clothes as last week. She pushes that old straw hat back on her head and stands there grinning, hands on hips.

I meet her at the gate. "Good morning, Ms. K.," I say in my happiest voice.

"Good morning, Luz. Well, I must admit I'm pretty impressed. I see your Dream Garden Group isn't just a pipe dream after all."

Ms. Kline sounds like she can hardly believe it. No wonder. I can hardly believe it myself!

"You've got quite a work crew this week. And your garden looks just about ready for planting."

It's true. Almost every scrap of trash is gone. Most of the broken glass is raked out of the dirt. There's a bunch of big green weeds sticking up over by the wall, but that just makes it look more like a garden.

Ms. Kline looks around one more time, then looks me straight in the eye. This time her smile is one hundred percent real.

"Well, if you've got your one dollar rent, Luz, I guess you and your Dream Garden Group will be in business!"

I dig down into my jeans and pull out a carefully folded one-dollar bill. I smooth it out and hand it to Ms. Kline. We shake. Then I break into a yell and do a victory dance up and down the sidewalk.

Mrs. Chapman, DeVonn, and Keisha clap and cheer. "Bravo! *Bravissimo!*" Mrs. Hodges calls out in her fancy voice. Mike lets out an earsplitting whistle. Shrimp yells, "Hurray!"

Everybody crowds around, shaking my hands and clapping me on the back. And suddenly, everybody is full of ideas about what to plant, and where.

The only thing missing is Rosie.

The whole next week, I work on a map of our garden. I study the Green Giants catalog that shows all the stuff we can order. There are pages and pages of bright-colored flowers, all kinds of trees, and pictures of the most scrumptious vegetables you ever saw.

I bring the catalog down to our stoop after school and ask people in the Dream Garden Group to help decide what to get. I use chalk to sketch different ideas on the sidewalk. I figure lots of people will stop by and help. And that's just what happens. Before long, we pick out what we want, and I call in our order to Ms. Kline.

Then suddenly it's next Saturday. Delivery day. I run to open the gate at nine sharp. But this time, I'm not alone! Lots of people are there to help: Papi and Lorenzo, the Chapmans, the Pazzalinis, Melinda Park, Mrs. Hodges (and her dog), even Mike. Pony stops by on his way home from the night shift. There's a big buzz of talk, and lots of laughing. Everybody says good morning when Ms. Kline comes.

Best of all, Mami shows up! Right now she's standing outside the fence, as if she's not quite sure whether to come in or leave.

I feel like a big deal, standing by the gate when the delivery truck pulls up. It's much bigger than I expected. And it's right on time. A tall, husky man climbs out and checks some papers.

"I'm lookin' for Mrs. Luz Mendes," he calls out. "Is she here?"

Everybody laughs, and the man looks a little confused.

"Anybody know where Mrs. Luz Mendes is?" he says, scratching his head.

I feel myself turn bright red. Then I get up my courage and walk to the front of the crowd. But the man is looking right over my head. He doesn't even notice me. I make myself as tall as I can and tap him on the elbow.

"Hi," I say. "I'm *Ms.* Luz Mendes."

He looks down at me, totally surprised. I guess he never made a delivery to a kid before.

"Well, I guess you better sign here," he says. I use my very best script.

"Okay, Pete—you ready? Let's unload," he calls to his helper.

We all watch the back of the huge truck swing open. Inside, we can see giant bags full of soil and sand. There are piles of lumber, big cans of bright green paint, buckets, boxes of tools and supplies, packets of flower and vegetable seeds, and dozens of teeny tiny little plants called seedlings. There are even real live trees and bushes!

Papi and Mr. Pazzalini help the men unload the truck. Other people help carry everything into the garden. Everyone asks me where to put things. I look at my map and tell them, "Boards and paint over by the wall, please. Sand in the middle. Soil along the fence."

When I look up, I catch a glimpse of Mami. She's still watching me. I can see a little smile start to perk up her mouth. Then it reaches her eyes. It's like someone turned on a happy switch when that light starts shining in her eyes.

Then come the trees—eight of them! Two apple, two cherry, two sycamore, and two maple. Tags show their names and pictures of them. We'll have pink and white in the spring; green all summer; and red and gold in the fall. I get so excited telling the men where to put each tree that I forgot to watch Mami watching me.

Then I turn around—and there she is, right beside me. She reaches out and gives me a quick, hard hug. "Ah, Luzita, I am so proud of you! So proud! *¡Qué orgullosa me siento!* I wish Lito could see you and your garden!"

I feel at least six feet tall.

The empty truck pulls away with a roar. The delivery guys lean out the windows and wave. "Go, Luz!" they yell. "Lotsa luck!"

Now Papi gets busy measuring and sawing and hammering benches. Mr. Pazzalini, Shrimp, and Pony work on the vegetable garden. Mrs. Chapman and Ms. Kline help me measure the flower beds with stakes and string. Even Mami helps!

Lorenzo and DeVonn start digging up the hard, packed-down dirt. They mix in soft, dark topsoil to get the ground ready to plant. Mike horses around a little, but finally gives them a hand.

Then, when Papi says we should water our newly planted trees, I almost panic. I realize something I absolutely, totally forgot: water!

I think fast. Then I grab one of the buckets and run next door to the bodega. Ali shows me where his sink is and says we can use the water whenever we want. "Just don't water my customers," he kids me. I practically have to drag the heavy bucket back to the garden. From then on, people take turns helping get water.

We work all day, but the time flies past. And more and more people come to help out. Soon it seems like half the neighborhood is there, helping this garden happen.

Then, one more surprise. Mami and I are carrying another bucket of water when I hear a *beep-beep!* from the street. At first I pay no attention. Then it comes again—*beep-beep!* This time I turn and look.

I see a blue-and-white patrol car sitting at the curb. Officer Carter is at the wheel, looking impatient and arguing with somebody on her two-way radio.

But Officer Ramirez rolls down his window and waves. I run over. He's smiling from ear to ear.

"Well, well, well," he says, reaching out and shaking my hand. "Looks like you're a girl who really means what she says, huh?"

"I called the Green Giants, just like you said. It wasn't exactly easy—but here we are." I bow and say, "Ta-da! One super-special Dream Garden coming right up!"

Ramirez puts up his hand for a high five. I give him ten.

Then I get an idea.

"Listen, I've been thinking. We'll probably finish planting the garden next Saturday. Then we're having a big party Saturday night to celebrate. Want to come? You were my very first helper, you know."

Ramirez takes off his cap and bows his head, like to a grown-up lady. "*Muchas gracias, señorita.* I'd be delighted."

The two-way radio buzzes and crackles as Officer Carter signs off. For the first time, she turns to take a really good look at my garden. She stares at the hustle-bustle of all the people working. She watches Mrs. Chapman brush a coat of fresh white paint over the graffiti on the back wall.

"That looks nice, kid. Real nice. I bet your parents are pretty proud of you."

Mami is kneeling behind the fence, chucking stones out of the soil. She doesn't say anything, but I can see her smiling.

Now it seems like everybody in the whole world believes in my dream garden.

Even though Rosie does not help with the project, she lets Luz know that they will always be friends by bringing to the celebration party a big sign that reads:

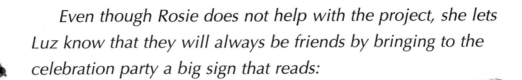

LUZ'S GARDEN: A DREAM COME TRUE

About the Author
Ellen Schecter

Do story ideas come from an author's mind? They do, but Ellen Schecter also gives her own mother and daughter part of the credit for the story in *The Big Idea*. In the dedication of the book, she thanks her mother, "who helped me dream of gardens," and her daughter, "who helped this one grow."

Ms. Schecter has worked in many different ways to help children learn. She has been a teacher, and she has written children's books. She also has done many projects for television. You may have seen episodes she wrote for *The Magic School Bus* or *Reading Rainbow*. Her work on television has won her many awards, including an Emmy.

Reader Response

Comprehension Check

1. Would you want to have Luz as a friend? Use story details to tell why or why not.

2. Luz's dream garden is created in stages. Write or tell three or four stages as though they were chapter titles in a book.

3. Even though Luz's dream comes true, there are some problems along the way. Using one of the problems, write or tell a different ending for the story.

4. We know that Luz is happy when the story opens on page 172. Why is she happy? (Cause) How do we know she's happy? (Effect)

5. Why does Luz get in touch with Ms. Kline of the Green Giants? (Cause) What happens as a result of the call? (Effect)

Test Prep
Look Back and Write

Look back at pages 179–181. What was the big problem Luz and her friends faced, and how did they solve it? Use details from this section of the story to support your answer.

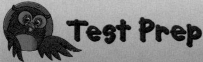 **Test Prep**

How to Read a Magazine Article

1. Preview

- Magazine articles often provide information about events that are taking place now, or other topics that have been in the news recently.

- Read the title. Look at the map and the photographs.

2. Read and Use Questions

- As you read the article, stop and ask yourself questions to focus on important information. For example,

  What is the river of grass?

- Write answers to your questions.

3. Think and Connect

Think about "A Big-City Dream." Then look over your answers for "River of Grass."

Do you think that Luz, from "A Big-City Dream," would like to help protect the "River of Grass"? Use evidence to support your answer.

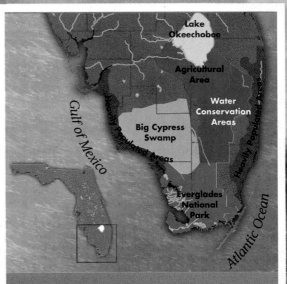

IN 1947, Congress set aside the southern part of the Everglades as a protected area, creating Everglades National Park. Soon after, Florida's nearby coastal population started to rise dramatically. Land north of the park was increasingly drained for agriculture, and water was diverted from Lake Okeechobee to irrigate the new farmland, greatly reducing the water that flows into the park. In addition, runoff from the fertilized fields pollutes the water that does get to the park. In recent years there has been much discussion about how to balance the needs of Florida's population with the desire to protect one of the world's natural wonders.

River of Grass

from Kids Discover magazine

It's a swamp! It's a marsh! It's the Everglades! Stretching across most of the southern end of the Florida peninsula is a unique wetlands system that includes marshes, sloughs (places with deep mud), freshwater swamps, coastal mangrove swamps, and pine woods. At the heart of this watery world is a 50-mile-wide, 100-mile-long "river of grass" that is on average about six inches deep. Beginning at Lake Okeechobee, the Everglades stretches south and southwest toward Florida Bay, providing shelter for a wide variety of wildlife. Come visit the land the Seminoles call Pa May-okee, "grassy waters."

ONE HUNDRED years ago, feathers on women's hats were all the rage. And egrets were hunted to near extinction for their plumes. Through protective laws—and a change in fashion—the egrets have made a comeback, only to find their Everglades home under new threat—from farming and development.

IS IT A CROCODILE or an alligator? Both are found in the Everglades, but it's easy to tell the difference—when their mouths are closed! Crocodiles have a distinctive fourth tooth on the lower jaw that sticks out when the mouth is closed. Alligators (above) make good mothers. After laying eggs, they stick around to make sure the babies can get out, sometimes cracking a shell in their mouth to help the baby emerge.

GALLERY OF 'GLADERS

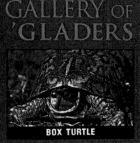

BOX TURTLE

EVERGLADES PANTHER

RATTLESNAKE

TREE SNAILS

PANTHER CROSSING NEXT 1 MI.

ORCHIDS

DRIVEN OUT OF Georgia and northern Florida by white settlers, the Seminoles learned to thrive in the harsh environment of the Everglades. When the U.S. government made its last attempt to remove these Native Americans from Florida in the Seminole War (1835–1842), most left and moved to Oklahoma. Today's Seminoles can no longer live off the land, but they still hunt and fish in the Everglades and farm on their reservations.

IN 1947, Marjory Stoneman Douglas brought the Everglades to the world's attention with her book *The Everglades: River of Grass*. Douglas was one of the century's leading conservationists. She never spent much time in the Everglades, which she once described as "too buggy, too wet." She added, "The Everglades and I have the kind of friendship that doesn't depend on constant physical contact."

LEFT: Aerial view of part of Everglades National Park.

Text Structure

- **Text structure** is the way a piece of writing is organized. The two main kinds of writing are fiction and nonfiction.

- Fiction tells stories of made-up people and events. The stories are often told in the order in which things happen.

- Nonfiction gives information, or it tells of real people and events.

- One way to organize nonfiction is to have main ideas followed by supporting details. Other ways are cause and effect, fact and opinion, and comparison and contrast.

Read "Your Best Friend" from *Me and My Pet Dog* by Christine Morley and Carole Orbell.

Talk About It

1. Is "Your Best Friend" fiction or nonfiction? How do you know?

2. How is the text of "Your Best Friend" organized? Explain.

Your Best Friend

by Christine Morley and Carole Orbell

Owning a dog can be fantastic fun. You can take it on long walks, feed and groom it, and in return it'll love you to bits! But to be a perfect dog owner, you need to know a few things about dogs.

Wild Wolves

Your dog has a fearsome relative— the wolf. Thousands of years ago, some wolves gave up their wild ways and settled with humans. All the different types, or breeds, of dog you see today are relatives of these tame wolves.

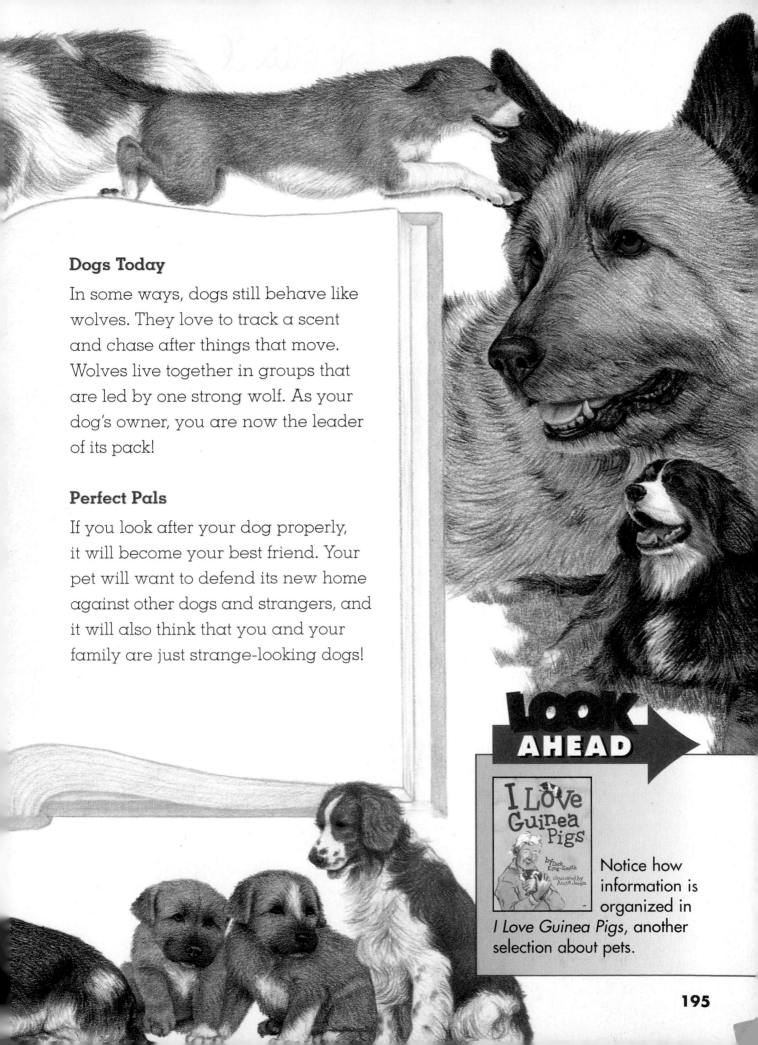

Dogs Today

In some ways, dogs still behave like wolves. They love to track a scent and chase after things that move. Wolves live together in groups that are led by one strong wolf. As your dog's owner, you are now the leader of its pack!

Perfect Pals

If you look after your dog properly, it will become your best friend. Your pet will want to defend its new home against other dogs and strangers, and it will also think that you and your family are just strange-looking dogs!

LOOK AHEAD

Notice how information is organized in *I Love Guinea Pigs*, another selection about pets.

Words to Know

sow	gnawing	boars
fond	varieties	

Words that are spelled the same but pronounced differently are called **homographs**—such as *sow,* rhyming with *go,* and *sow,* rhyming with *now.* To understand the correct meaning of a homograph, look for clues in the surrounding words and sentences.

Read the paragraph below, paying special attention to its meaning as a whole. Decide whether *sow* rhymes with *go* and means "to plant seeds," or rhymes with *now* and means "a female pig."

Guinea Pigs: Popular Pets

Do you want a gentle and curious pet? Try a guinea pig! There are several <u>varieties</u>, some with short hair and others that are silky. Guinea pigs like to eat grass and are also <u>fond</u> of <u>gnawing</u> on raw vegetables. A <u>sow</u>, or female, can have babies five or six times a year. The <u>boars</u>, or males, make good pets too. Guinea pigs aren't really pigs, but they are fun!

Write About It

Do you want a pet guinea pig? Write a note to your parents explaining why it's a good pet. Use vocabulary words.

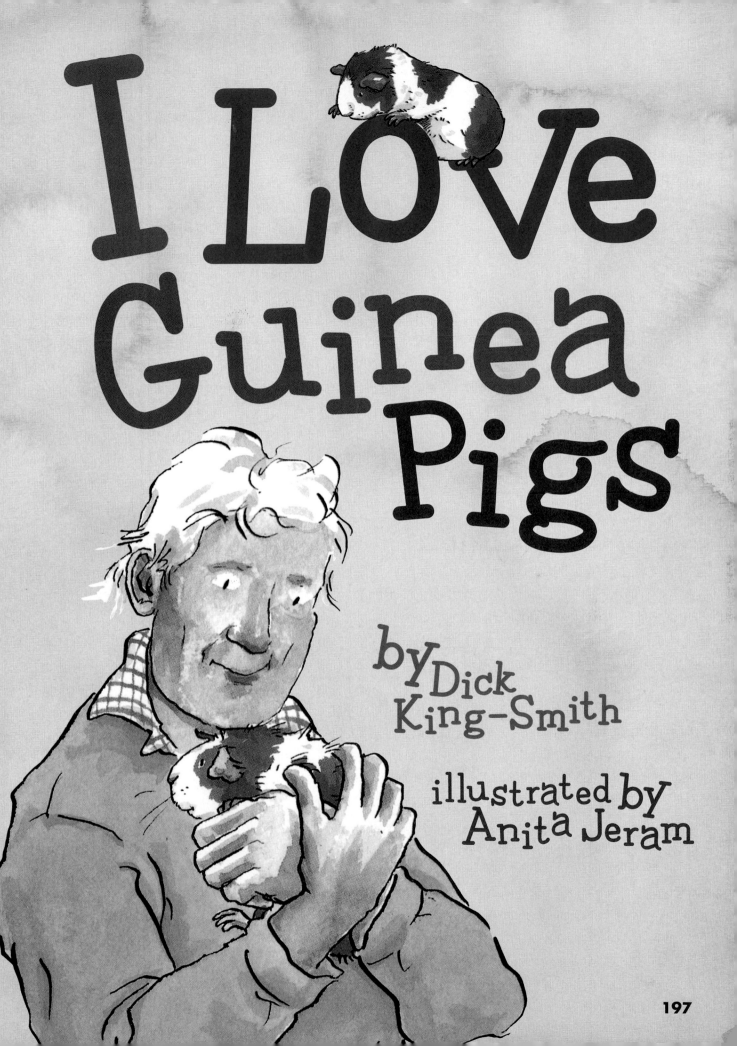

I Love Guinea Pigs

by Dick King-Smith

illustrated by Anita Jeram

There's a silly old saying that if you hold a guinea pig up by its tail, its eyes will drop out.

Well of course they wouldn't, even if you could—which you couldn't, because guinea pigs don't have tails. And they aren't pigs either. They're rodents—like mice and rats and squirrels.

What do guinea pigs have in common with pigs?

The males and females are known as boars and sows.

Rodents have special front teeth that are great for gnawing things. These teeth go on growing throughout the animal's life and are self-sharpening.

As for the other part of their name, guinea pigs were first brought to Europe about four hundred years ago by Spanish sailors, probably from a country in South America called Dutch Guiana. And the sailors called them "guiana pigs."

In fact, the guinea pig is a member of the cavy family, and its Latin name is *Cavia porcellus* (which means a piggy-looking cavy).

Anyway, whatever they're called, it's the way they look that I've always liked. They're so chunky and chubby and cuddly, with their blunt heads and sturdy bodies and short legs.

Sheltie

Abyssinians

They come in tons of different colors, and they can be smooth-coated or rough-coated or long-coated, not to mention the other varieties. I've had hundreds of guinea pigs over the last fifty years, but I've always liked the Abyssinians best.

crested

smooth

Peruvian

Guinea pigs are such sensible animals. They're awfully easy to keep, because they aren't fussy. They don't like the cold, of course, or the damp, any more than you would, and they're not happy living in a poky little place, any more than you would be. But as long as they have a comfortable, warm, dry place to live, guinea pigs are as happy as can be.

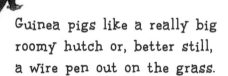

Guinea pigs like a really big roomy hutch or, better still, a wire pen out on the grass.

They're hardy animals and don't often get sick. Properly cared for, they can live a long time.

Most guinea pigs live for about five to eight years.

I once had a crested sow named Zen. She lived two years with me and then eight more with one of my daughters. People's hair grows whiter as they age, but Zen's grew darker.

Guinea pigs need plenty of food. They love eating, just like you do, and feeding them is half the fun of having them. Some people, of course, feed them nothing but hay and pellets from the pet store, and they're just fine. But how boring a diet like that must be, both for the piggy-looking cavy and its owner.

I always used to give my guinea pigs lots of other kinds of food as well: cabbage and cauliflower leaves, carrots, pieces of bread and apple peelings, and wild plants, like dandelions and clover. I gave them water, too, of course. Guinea pigs need clean drinking water every day. And their water bottle often needs washing, because they like blowing pieces of food back up the spout.

One especially nice thing about guinea pigs is that if you handle them regularly, and carry them around, stroke them, talk to them, and make a fuss over them, they become really fond of you.

The correct way to pick up a guinea pig is with one hand over its shoulders and the other supporting its bottom.

Another nice thing about guinea pigs is that they talk a lot. When they want food or water, they often give a sort of whistle, sometimes low, sometimes loud. Boars say *chutter* when they're squaring up for a fight. So do sows when their babies pester them too much.

Other things guinea pigs say are *putt, chut, tweet,* and *drr.*

But when one guinea pig says *purr* to another guinea pig, it's as plain as the nose on your face that it only means one thing: "I love you."

And that brings me to what's best of all about having guinea pigs—baby ones. Because their ancestors, the wild cavies of South America, lived out in the open with enemies all around them, their young ones had to be ready to run for it. So the guinea pig sow carries her unborn litter for a very long time, about seventy days, and they arrive in the world fully furred, with their eyes open and their mouths already filled with teeth. Newborn guinea pigs are such a comical sight. Their heads and feet look too big for their bodies.

Baby rabbits are born blind and naked and helpless, but not baby guinea pigs.

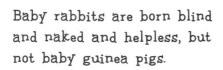

But almost immediately they show an interest in
those two favorite guinea pig pursuits—

eating

and conversation.

Of all the guinea pigs I've had, there were two that I will never forget. Both were Abyssinians, both were boars, and each in his time fathered dozens of lovely, big-headed, big-footed babies.

One was a bright golden color, and his name was King Arthur. The other was a blue roan named Beach Boy. Both are buried in my yard.

There's a solitary apple tree at the edge of my lawn, and I like to look at it and think that under it Beach Boy and King Arthur lie peacefully, one on one side of the tree, one on the other. I'm not sad about this—just happy to remember what a lot of pleasure I've had from all my guinea pigs.

About the Author
Dick King-Smith

Dick King-Smith was a farmer in England for twenty years before he started writing. When he was in his fifties, he got an idea for a children's story based on something that happened on his farm. That idea became his first book, *The Fox Busters*. Now Mr. King-Smith is always writing—to make up for all that lost time.

Many of his books have won awards in the United States and in England. One book that you may have heard of is *Babe: The Gallant Pig*. It was made into the movie *Babe*.

Reader Response

Open for Discussion

What do you think would be the best thing about having a guinea pig for a pet? What would be the worst thing?

Comprehension Check

1. How does the author feel about guinea pigs? Look back and find words he uses that are clues to his feelings.

2. Make a chart about guinea pigs. Look back at the selection and include details from it.

Things Guinea Pigs Like	Things Guinea Pigs Don't Like

3. If you had pet guinea pigs, could you leave them alone for a few days? Explain your answer with details from the selection.

4. **Text structure** is the way writing is organized. *I Love Guinea Pigs* is organized around facts about guinea pigs as well as the author's opinions of guinea pigs. Identify two facts and two opinions from this book. (Text Structure)

5. Look again at the **text structure** of this selection. Find one page that includes mostly facts and one page that is made up mostly of opinions. (Text Structure)

Test Prep
Look Back and Write

Look back at the whole selection. How do the illustrations and captions help you understand what the author wants you to learn? Use examples from the selection to support your answer.

Why doesn't a sleeping bird fall off its perch?

Z Z Z Z Z

by Dr. Ann Squire

Have you ever wondered why cats and dogs walk in circles before they go to sleep? If you have a pet, or you know someone who does, you might have some questions about what causes the animal to do certain things. Here are answers to some questions about pets.

If you have a parakeet, finch, or another type of bird as a pet, you may have wondered how it can sleep while sitting on its perch. Actually, the more deeply the bird sleeps, the *less* likely it is to fall. The grip of a bird's claws is controlled by a long tendon that runs around the back of the bird's leg. The more the tendon stretches, the tighter the claws grip. As the bird relaxes into deep sleep, it settles down onto the perch, bending its leg joints. As the leg joints bend, the tendon to the claws begins to stretch and the bird's hold on its perch gets tighter.

Do animals ever have pets?

There have been many stories about different kinds of animals being friends, but the first animal who actually had a pet was a "talking" gorilla named Koko. For many years Koko, a 230-pound female gorilla, has been learning to communicate with people by using American Sign Language (the same sign language used by the deaf). Her teacher is a scientist named Dr. Penny Patterson.

According to Dr. Patterson, Koko has always been interested in cats. She became excited whenever she saw a cat, either a real one glimpsed through the window or a photograph of a cat in a magazine. Finally, Dr. Patterson decided to surprise Koko with a cat of her own. Koko picked out her own pet, a tailless gray kitten she named "All Ball." Koko frequently used her sign language to tell her trainer how much she loved the kitten. Even though Koko was a giant compared to her tiny pet, she was always gentle and careful not to hurt her.

Why do dogs and cats turn around in circles before they lie down?

Like many other things that dogs and cats do, circling before lying down is a behavior that goes back to our pets' wild ancestors. When a wild dog or cat prepares to go to sleep, it looks around for a grassy spot. After choosing a place, the animal walks in circles to trample down the long grass, creating a soft, comfortable bed. Even though it's no longer necessary, this behavior is still shown by today's domestic pets.

Theme

- **Theme** is the underlying meaning of a story—a big idea that stands on its own outside the story.

- Sometimes an author states the theme directly. Sometimes readers have to figure out the theme on their own, using evidence from the text to support their big idea.

Read "Ant and Dove" from _Fables from Aesop_ retold by James Reeves.

Write About It

1. Write one sentence that you think states the theme of "Ant and Dove."

2. Explain what happens in the story that shows that theme, or big idea.

Ant AND Dove

an Aesop's fable retold by James Reeves

Ant was thirsty, and, going to a pool to drink, she fell in and was almost drowned. Now it happened that a dove was sitting on the branch of a tree overhanging the water. With her sharp eyes she saw the danger that Ant was in, and she dropped a leaf, which alighted on the pool. It fell just in front of Ant, who quickly climbed onto it and floated safely to the bank.

At that very moment a birdcatcher came along with his net, and he was just spreading it out to catch the dove. Ant saw what he was trying to do, and, noticing that the birdcatcher went barefoot, she bit him in the heel. It was not a very savage bite, but it was the worst that the ant could do; and it was enough to make the birdcatcher jump in the air with surprise. He lost hold of his net, so Dove was just able to escape with her life.

One good turn deserves another.

LOOK AHEAD

As you read "The Swimming Hole," think about the theme, or big idea, of the story.

Vocabulary

Words to Know

bristled	naughty	shallow
dugout	punish	rushes
jointed		

Words with opposite meanings are called **antonyms.** You can often figure out the meaning of an unknown word by finding a clue in the words around it. Sometimes this clue is an antonym.

Read the paragraph below. Notice how *deep* helps you understand what *shallow* means.

An Evening on the Prairie

Irene bristled when she heard a howl in the distance. She decided to keep busy. She waded through the shallow creek (it wasn't too deep to cross) and collected flowers and some rushes. The jointed rushes looked interesting against the smooth plants. Irene knew it was naughty to leave the dugout when her parents had told her to stay inside, but would they punish her when they saw the beautiful bouquet?

Talk About It

You are alone on the prairie. Tell a friend what you will do to keep busy. Use vocabulary words.

The Swimming Hole

by Laura Ingalls Wilder

illustrated by Garth Williams

from *On the Banks of Plum Creek*

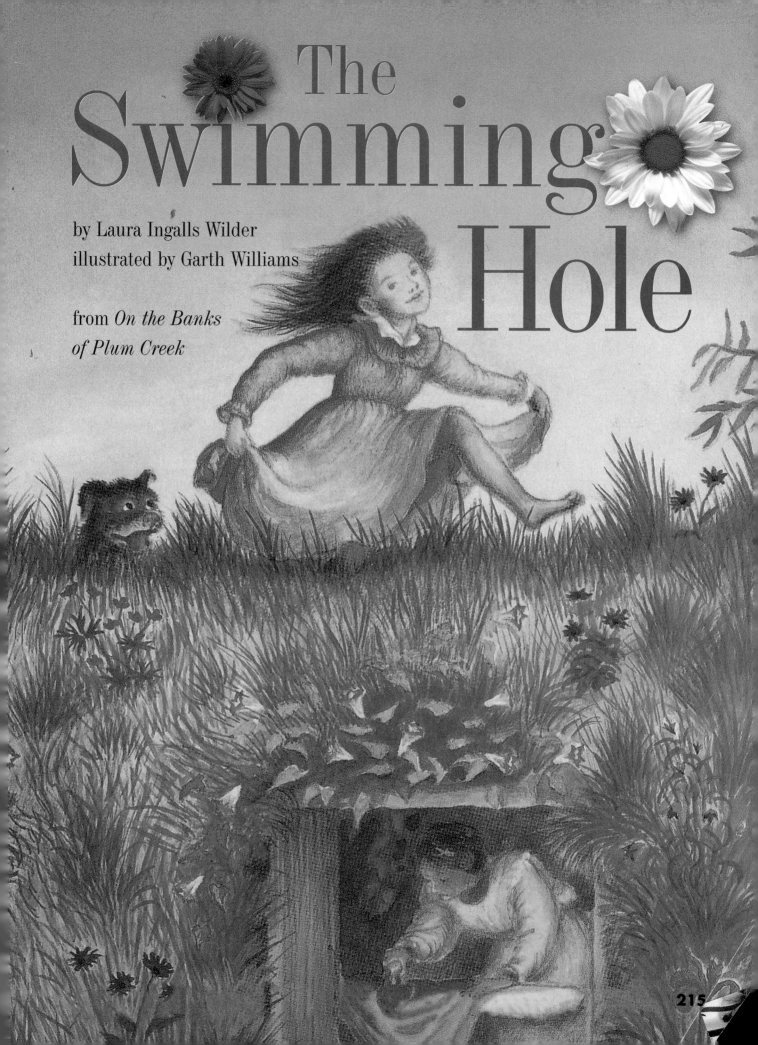

Every morning after Mary and Laura had done the dishes, made their bed and swept the floor, they could go out to play.

All around the door the morning glory flowers were fresh and new, springing with all their might out of the green leaves. All along Plum Creek the birds were talking. Sometimes a bird sang, but mostly they talked. "Tweet, tweet, oh twitter twee twit!" one said. Then another said, "Chee, Chee, Chee," and another laughed, "Ha ha ha, tiraloo!"

Laura and Mary went over the top of their house and down along the path where Pa led the oxen to water.

There along the creek, rushes were growing, and blue flags. Every morning the blue flags were new. They stood up dark blue and proud among the green rushes.

Each blue flag had three velvet petals that curved down like a lady's dress over hoops. From its waist three ruffled silky petals stood up and curved together. When Laura looked down inside them, she saw three narrow pale tongues, and each tongue had a strip of golden fur on it.

Sometimes a fat bumblebee, all black velvet and gold, was bumbling and butting there.

The flat creek bank was warm, soft mud. Little pale-yellow and pale-blue butterflies hovered there, and alighted and sipped. Bright dragonflies flew on blurry wings. The mud squeezed up between Laura's toes. Where she stepped, and where Mary stepped, and where the oxen had walked, there were tiny pools of water in their footprints.

Where they waded in the shallow water a footprint would not stay. First a swirl like smoke came up from it and wavered away in the clear water. Then the footprint slowly melted.

The toes smoothed out and the heel was only a small hollow.

There were tiny fishes in the water. They were so small that you could hardly see them. Only when they went swiftly sometimes a silvery belly flashed. When Laura and Mary stood still these little fishes swarmed around their feet and nibbled. It was a tickly feeling.

On top of the water the water bugs skated. They had tall legs, and each of their feet made a wee dent in the water. It was hard to see a water bug; he skated so fast that before you saw him he was somewhere else.

The rushes in the wind made a wild, lonely sound. They were not soft and flat like grass; they were hard and round and sleek and jointed. One day when Laura was wading in a deep place by the rushes, she took hold of a big one to pull herself up on the bank. It squeaked.

For a minute Laura could hardly breathe. Then she pulled another. It squeaked, and came in two.

The rushes were little hollow tubes, fitted together at the joints. The tubes squeaked when you pulled them apart. They squeaked when you pushed them together again.

Laura and Mary pulled them apart to hear them squeak. Then they put little ones together to make necklaces. They put big ones together to make long tubes. They blew through the tubes into the creek and made it bubble. They blew at the little fishes and scared them. Whenever they were thirsty, they could draw up long drinks of water through those tubes.

Ma laughed when Laura and Mary came to dinner and supper, all splashed and muddy, with green necklaces around their necks and the long green tubes in their hands. They brought her bouquets of the blue flags and she put them on the table to make it pretty.

"I declare," she said, "you two play in the creek so much, you'll be turning to water bugs!"

Pa and Ma did not care how much they played in the creek. Only they must never go upstream beyond the little willow valley. The creek came around a curve there. It came out of a hole full of deep, dark water. They must never go near enough to that hole, even to see it.

"Some day I'll take you there," Pa promised them. And one Sunday afternoon he told them that this was the day.

In the dugout Laura and Mary took off all their clothes and over their bare skins they put on old patched dresses. Ma tied on her sunbonnet, Pa took Carrie on his arm, and they all set out.

They went past the cattle path and the rushes, past the willow valley and the plum thickets. They went down a steep, grassy bank, and then across a level place where the grass was tall and coarse. They passed a high, almost straight-up wall of earth where no grass grew.

"What is that, Pa?" Laura asked; and Pa said, "That is a tableland, Laura."

He pushed on through the thick, tall grass, making a path for Ma and Mary and Laura. Suddenly they came out of the high grass and the creek was there.

It ran twinkling over white gravel into a wide pool, curved against a low bank where the grass was short. Tall

willows stood up on the other side of the pool. Flat on the water lay a shimmery picture of those willows, with every green leaf fluttering.

Ma sat on the grassy bank and kept Carrie with her, while Laura and Mary waded into the pool.

"Stay near the edge, girls!" Ma told them. "Don't go in where it's deep."

The water came up under their skirts and made them float. Then the calico got wet and stuck to their legs. Laura went in deeper and deeper. The water came up and up, almost to her waist. She squatted down, and it came to her chin.

Everything was watery, cool, and unsteady. Laura felt very light. Her feet were so light that they almost lifted off the creek bottom. She hopped, and splashed with her arms.

"Oo, Laura, don't!" Mary cried.

"Don't go in any farther, Laura," said Ma.

Laura kept on splashing. One big splash lifted both feet. Her feet came up, her arms did as they pleased, her head went under the water. She was scared. There was nothing to hold on to, nothing solid anywhere. Then she was standing up, streaming water all over. But her feet were solid.

Nobody had seen that. Mary was tucking up her skirts, Ma was playing with Carrie. Pa was out of sight among the willows. Laura walked as fast as she could in the water. She stepped down deeper and deeper. The water came up past her middle, up to her arms.

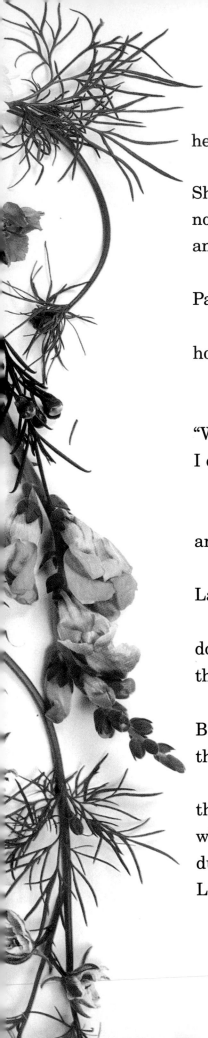

Suddenly, deep down in the water, something grabbed her foot.

The thing jerked, and down she went into the deep water. She couldn't breathe, she couldn't see. She grabbed and could not get hold of anything. Water filled her ears and her eyes and her mouth.

Then her head came out of the water close to Pa's head. Pa was holding her.

"Well, young lady," Pa said, "you went out too far, and how did you like it?"

Laura could not speak; she had to breathe.

"You heard Ma tell you to stay close to the bank," said Pa. "Why didn't you obey her? You deserved a ducking, and I ducked you. Next time you'll do as you're told."

"Y-yes, Pa!" Laura spluttered. "Oh, Pa, p-please do it again!"

Pa said, "Well, I'll—!" Then his great laughter rang among the willows.

"Why didn't you holler when I ducked you?" he asked Laura. "Weren't you scared?"

"I w-was—awful scared!" Laura gasped. "But p-please do it again!" Then she asked him, "How did you get down there, Pa?"

Pa told her he had swum under water from the willows. But they could not stay in the deep water; they must go near the bank and play with Mary.

All that afternoon Pa and Laura and Mary played in the water. They waded and they fought water fights, and whenever Laura or Mary went near the deep water, Pa ducked them. Mary was a good girl after one ducking, but Laura was ducked many times.

Then it was almost chore time and they had to go home. They went dripping along the path through the tall grass, and when they came to the tableland Laura wanted to climb it.

Pa climbed part way up, and Laura and Mary climbed, holding to his hands. The dry dirt slipped and slid. Tangled grass roots hung down from the bulging edge overhead. Then Pa lifted Laura up and set her on the tableland.

It really was like a table. That ground rose up high above the tall grasses, and it was round, and flat on top. The grass there was short and soft.

Pa and Laura and Mary stood up on top of that tableland, and looked over the grass tops and the pool to the prairie beyond. They looked all around at prairies stretching to the rim of the sky.

Then they had to slide down again to the lowland and go on home. That had been a wonderful afternoon.

"It's been lots of fun," Pa said. "But you girls remember what I tell you. Don't you ever go near that swimming hole unless I am with you."

All the next day Laura remembered. She remembered the cool, deep water in the shade of the tall willows. She remembered that she must not go near it.

Pa was away. Mary stayed with Ma in the dugout. Laura played all alone in the hot sunshine. The blue flags were withering among the dull rushes. She went past the willow valley and played in the prairie grasses among the black-eyed Susans and goldenrod. The sunshine was very hot and the wind was scorching.

Then Laura thought of the tableland. She wanted to climb it again. She wondered if she could climb it all by herself. Pa had not said that she could not go to the tableland.

She ran down the steep bank and went across the lowland, through the tall, coarse grasses. The tableland stood up straight and high. It was very hard to climb. The dry earth slid under Laura's feet, her dress was dirty where her knees dug in while she held on to the grasses and pulled herself up. Dust itched on her sweaty skin. But at last she got her stomach on the edge; she heaved and rolled and she was on top of the tableland.

She jumped up, and she could see the deep, shady pool under the willows. It was cool and wet, and her whole skin felt thirsty. But she remembered that she must not go there.

The tableland seemed big and empty and not interesting. It had been exciting when Pa was there, but now it was just flat land, and Laura thought she would go home and get a drink. She was very thirsty.

She slid down the side of the tableland and slowly started back along the way she had come. Down among the tall grasses the air was smothery and very hot. The dugout was far away and Laura was terribly thirsty.

She remembered with all her might that she must not go near that deep, shady swimming pool, and suddenly she turned around and hurried toward it. She thought she would only look at it. Just looking at it would make her feel better. Then she thought she might wade in the edge of it but she would not go into the deep water.

She came into the path that Pa had made, and she trotted faster.

Right in the middle of the path before her stood an animal.

Laura jumped back, and stood and stared at it. She had never seen such an animal. It was almost as long as Jack,* but its legs were very short. Long gray fur bristled all over it. It had a flat head and small ears. Its flat head slowly tilted up and it stared at Laura.

She stared back at its funny face. And while they stood still and staring, that animal widened and shortened and spread flat on the ground. It grew flatter and flatter, till it was a gray fur laid there. It was not like a whole animal at all. Only it had eyes staring up.

Slowly and carefully Laura stooped and reached and picked up a willow stick. She felt better then. She stayed bent over, looking at that flat gray fur.

It did not move and neither did Laura. She wondered what would happen if she poked it. It might change to some other shape. She poked it gently with the short stick.

A frightful snarl came out of it. Its eyes sparked mad, and fierce white teeth snapped almost on Laura's nose.

Laura ran with all her might. She could run fast. She did not stop running until she was in the dugout.

"Goodness, Laura!" Ma said. "You'll make yourself sick, tearing around so in this heat."

All that time, Mary had been sitting like a little lady, spelling out words in the book that Ma was teaching her to read. Mary was a good little girl.

Laura had been bad and she knew it. She had broken her promise to Pa. But no one had seen her. No one knew that she had started to go to the swimming hole. If she did not tell, no one would ever know. Only that strange animal knew, and it could not tell on her. But she felt worse and worse inside.

* Jack is the Ingalls family's dog.

That night she lay awake beside Mary. Pa and Ma sat in
the starlight outside the door and Pa was playing his fiddle.

"Go to sleep, Laura," Ma said, softly, and softly the fiddle
sang to her. Pa was a shadow against the sky and his bow
danced among the great stars.

Everything was beautiful and good, except Laura. She
had broken her promise to Pa. Breaking a promise was as
bad as telling a lie. Laura wished she had not done it. But
she had done it, and if Pa knew, he would punish her.

Pa went on playing softly in the starlight. His fiddle sang
to her sweetly and happily. He thought she was a good little
girl. At last Laura could bear it no longer.

She slid out of bed and her bare feet stole across the cool
earthen floor. In her nightgown and nightcap she stood
beside Pa. He drew the last notes from the strings with his
bow and she could feel him smiling down at her.

"What is it, little half pint?" he asked her. "You look like a little ghost, all white in the dark."

"Pa," Laura said, in a quivery small voice, "I—I—started to go to the swimming hole."

"You did!" Pa exclaimed. Then he asked, "Well, what stopped you?"

"I don't know," Laura whispered. "It had gray fur and it—it flattened out flat. It snarled."

"How big was it?" Pa asked.

Laura told him all about that strange animal.

Pa said, "It must have been a badger."

Then for a long time he did not say anything and Laura waited. Laura could not see his face in the dark, but she leaned against his knee and she could feel how strong and kind he was.

"Well," he said at last, "I hardly know what to do, Laura. You see, I trusted you. It is hard to know what to do with a person you can't trust. But do you know what people have to do to anyone they can't trust?"

"Wh—at?" Laura quavered.

"They have to watch him," said Pa. "So I guess you must be watched. Your Ma will have to do it because I must work at Nelson's. So tomorrow you stay where Ma can watch you. You are not to go out of her sight all day. If you are good all day, then we will let you try again to be a little girl we can trust.

"How about it, Caroline?" he asked Ma.

"Very well, Charles," Ma said out of the dark. "I will watch her tomorrow. But I am sure she will be good. Now back to bed, Laura, and go to sleep."

The next day was a dreadful day.

Ma was mending, and Laura had to stay in the dugout. She could not even fetch water from the spring, for that was

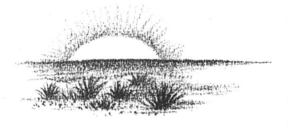

going out of Ma's sight. Mary fetched the water. Mary took Carrie to walk on the prairie. Laura had to stay in.

Jack laid his nose on his paws and waggled, he jumped out on the path and looked back at her, smiling with his ears, begging her to come out. He could not understand why she did not.

Laura helped Ma. She washed the dishes and made both beds and swept the floor and set the table. At dinner she sat bowed on her bench and ate what Ma set before her. Then she wiped the dishes. After that she ripped a sheet that was worn in the middle. Ma turned the strips of muslin and pinned them together, and Laura whipped the new seam, over and over with tiny stitches.

She thought that seam and that day would never end.

But at last Ma rolled up her mending and it was time to get supper.

"You have been a good girl, Laura," Ma said. "We will tell Pa so. And tomorrow morning you and I are going to look for that badger. I am sure he saved you from drowning, for if you had gone to that deep water you would have gone into it. Once you begin being naughty, it is easier to go on and on, and sooner or later something dreadful happens."

"Yes, Ma," Laura said. She knew that now.

The whole day was gone. Laura had not seen that sunrise, nor the shadows of clouds on the prairie. The morning glories were withered and that day's blue flags were dead. All day Laura had not seen the water running in the creek, the little fishes in it, and the water bugs skating over it. She was sure that being good could never be as hard as being watched.

Next day she went with Ma to look for the badger. In the path she showed Ma the place where he had flattened himself on the grass. Ma found the hole where he lived. It was a round hole under a clump of grass on the prairie bank. Laura called to him and she poked a stick into the hole.

If the badger was at home, he would not come out. Laura never saw that old gray badger again.

About the Author
Laura Ingalls Wilder

"I was born in the 'Little House in the Big Woods' of Wisconsin on February 7 in the year 1867," said Laura Ingalls Wilder. She was speaking about a house known to everyone who has read her famous book of that name. "I lived everything that happened in my books. It is a long story, filled with sunshine and shadow. . . ." Laura Ingalls Wilder spoke these words in a speech she gave in 1937.

When Mrs. Wilder's daughter, Rose, was young, she listened to her mother's stories about what life was like growing up on the prairie. When Rose grew up, she convinced her mother to write down the stories. She knew others would find them interesting too. Rose was right. Eight best-selling Little House books have been loved by generations of readers.

Other books in the series that you might enjoy reading are *By the Shores of Silver Lake* and *Little House on the Prairie*, which was made into a popular television show.

Reader Response

Open for Discussion

What did you see, hear, and feel as you read this story? Give examples.

Comprehension Check

1. Compare and contrast the characters of Laura and Mary. Use examples from the story.

2. Why do you think Pa ducks the girls when they get near deep water? Use story details in your answer.

3. What part does the badger play in the story? Use examples from the story to explain your answer.

4. The **theme** is the underlying meaning of a story. Which of the following best states a theme of this story? Explain. (Theme)

    a. Life in pioneer days was boring when you were not trusted.

    b. You earn freedom when you can be trusted.

    c. Some people can never be trusted.

5. Go back to "A Big-City Dream" and write or tell a **theme** for that story. (Theme)

Test Prep

Look Back and Write

Look back at pages 224–227. Compare how Laura feels *before* she tells her parents about breaking her promise to how she feels *after* she tells about it. Use details from this section of the story to explain your answer.

Badger Toes and Rabbit Feet

by Steve Parker

MAMMAL

Discover the fascinating world of mammals—
their natural history and secret lives

PARKER

Domestic cat

Front print

Fur on sole of foot

Hind print

WALKING THROUGH any wild place, we are aware of many animals. Birds fly above, insects buzz from one flower to another, and fish rise to snatch food from the water's surface. But where are all the mammals? Some make themselves scarce, fearing large creatures going past. Others are well hidden and asleep. Often, we only know the animals were there from the tracks and signs they left behind. These signs can be footprints and belly- or tail-drags in the ground, leftover bits of food with teeth marks, bits of hair caught on twigs and snagged on thorns, and castoffs such as antlers. The footprints shown here are actual size, and actual prints made by the walkers themselves. The prints were made by encouraging the animals (with food) to walk on a pad of nontoxic ink and then across the paper. Claw marks do not show up using this technique, but they will be found in trails in soft mud or snow.

Feet are covered with fur—no pads show

Print of fur would not show up in snow

Front print

Hind print

RUN, RABBIT, RUN
When sitting or hopping slowly, the rabbit's hind foot leaves a long imprint compared to the more circular front foot. But when running the difference is less easy to see because the animal tends to place only the tips of its hind feet on the ground.

Rabbit

Red fox

Badger

THE BADGER
The distinctive imprint of the badger has five toe pads in a curved line above the main pad, although the inner toe is small and may leave only a small mark. In its rolling walk, the badger's left and right limbs have a large gap between them.

Toe pads

Main foot pad

Front print

Hind print

LEAVING LITTLE IMPRESSION
Surprisingly, the heaviest land mammal, the elephant, often does not leave much of a mark with its feet. In soft ground there is a large, rounded print (left). But on looser, sandier soil the foot pads spread the weight so effectively that prints are shallow or not there at all.

Hedgehog

Four toe prints visible

Front print

Hind print

MISSING BIG TOES?
The five-toed hedgehog usually leaves a four-toed track, because its inner (first) toe is held farther from the ground. Like the badger, this animal walks with a straddle, with a gap of about two inches between right and left feet.

Front print

Fur between toes shows in print

Hind print

COMMON PRINTS: FOX OR DOG?
The red fox's prints can easily be mistaken for a dog's. The fox's claws are usually slightly longer and narrower than a dog's claws. Also, the fox's toe pads are relatively smaller than in a dog. As it trots, the fox puts each back paw in the print made by the front paw on that side of the body.

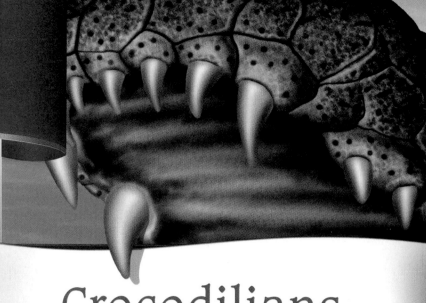

Context Clues

- When you are reading and you see an unfamiliar word, use **context clues**, or words around the unfamiliar word, to figure out its meaning.

- The context may give a definition or an explanation of the unfamiliar word. Often the definition or explanation comes just before or just after the word. For example, "Reptiles have an outer covering of thin, flat, hard plates called scales."

- Sometimes a synonym, a word with nearly the same meaning as another word, is used as a context clue.

Read "Crocodilians" from *Roaring Reptiles* by D. M. Souza.

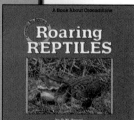

Write About It

1. Find the words *osteoderms*, *amphibious*, and *ectothermic* in the selection. Write a definition for each word without using a dictionary.

2. Write a synonym for the word *hides*.

Crocodilians

by D. M. Souza

Crocodilians, like other reptiles, have rows of scales that cover their bodies. Beneath thick pointed scales on their necks, backs, and tails are bony plates called osteoderms (AH-stee-oh-dermz). These plates make their skins, or hides, very strong and tough.

Crocodilians do not shed their skins the way other reptiles do. Each scale develops on its own. As the animal grows, new scales grow beneath the old ones and replace them. The scales and bony plates become larger as the reptile grows.

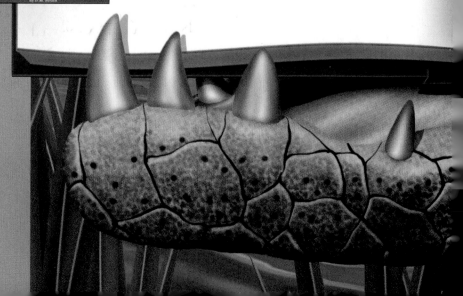

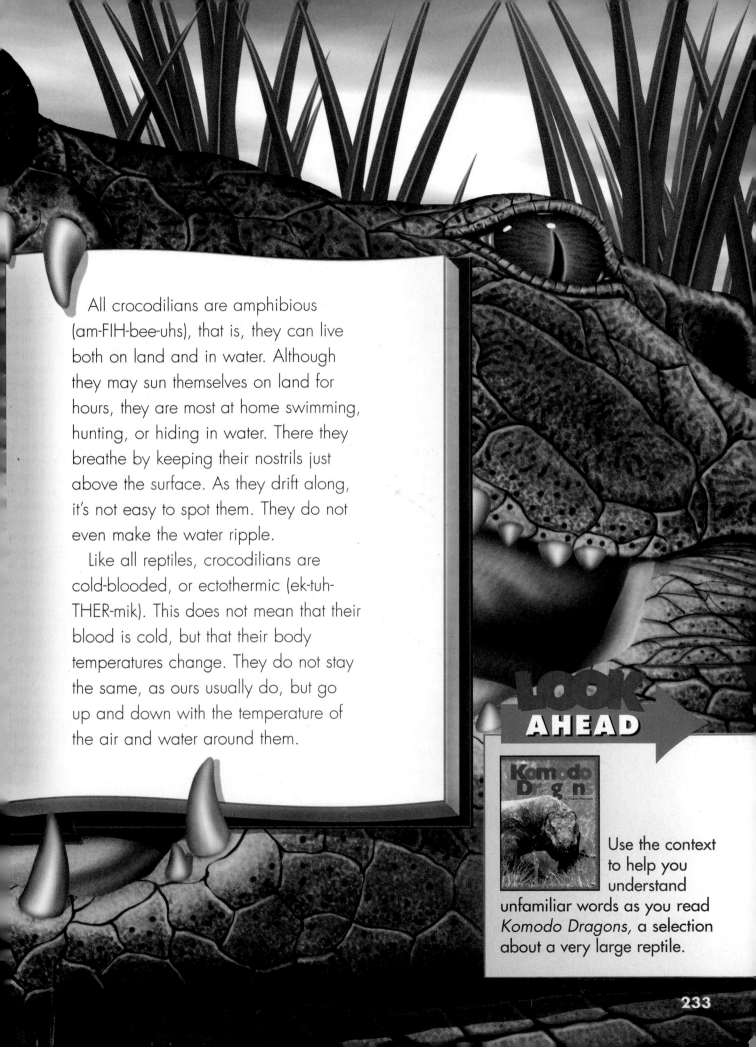

All crocodilians are amphibious (am-FIH-bee-uhs), that is, they can live both on land and in water. Although they may sun themselves on land for hours, they are most at home swimming, hunting, or hiding in water. There they breathe by keeping their nostrils just above the surface. As they drift along, it's not easy to spot them. They do not even make the water ripple.

Like all reptiles, crocodilians are cold-blooded, or ectothermic (ek-tuh-THER-mik). This does not mean that their blood is cold, but that their body temperatures change. They do not stay the same, as ours usually do, but go up and down with the temperature of the air and water around them.

LOOK AHEAD

Komodo Dragons

Use the context to help you understand unfamiliar words as you read *Komodo Dragons,* a selection about a very large reptile.

Words to Know

armor	lizards	roam
fierce	prey	reptiles
harshest		

When you read, you may come across a word that you do not know. To figure out its meaning, look for clues in the sentences around it.

Notice how *lizards* is used in the paragraph. Find a definition of *lizards*. What does *lizards* mean?

Komodo Dragons—Not for Pets!

Although both snakes and lizards are reptiles, cold-blooded animals with backbones and lungs, lizards have legs and movable eyelids. Komodo dragons are the largest lizards. They roam around Komodo Island, part of the country of Indonesia. Komodo dragons have the harshest skin—their armor feels rough. But you wouldn't want to touch it! They are fierce animals who can kill their prey (birds, insects, and other reptiles) by biting. Their mouths are full of deadly bacteria—Komodo dragons' bites can kill.

Write About It

Imagine you work at a zoo. Design a sign for the Komodo dragons' cage using as many vocabulary words as you can.

Komodo Dragons

by Thane Maynard

Dragons

Meet the Komodo Dragon!

Some people think that dragons are only make-believe animals—like the flying, fire-breathing dragons in books and movies. But if you travel to the far-off islands of a country called Indonesia, you can find real-life dragons! Komodo dragons.

Komodo dragons don't fly. They don't breathe fire, either. So why are they called "dragons"? Because they are the biggest lizards in the world. They look like little dragons.

or Lizards?

237

Where Do Komodo Dragons Live?

Komodo dragons are a type of lizard called a monitor. They come from the Komodo Island area of Indonesia, near the northwest shore of Australia. It is one of the harshest and hottest places in the world. Often, the temperature is over 100°F. Sometimes it even gets as hot as 110°F.

On the hottest days, dragons escape the heat by getting out of the sun. They rest in underground burrows. But in the morning, when they first wake up, they lie in the sun to warm up. They do that on cooler days too. That is because, like all lizards, they are reptiles. Reptiles are cold-blooded animals. They need outside heat (like sunlight) to warm them up.

Like most lizards, Komodo dragons are active during the day and sleep at night. Both males and females dig burrows. They sleep in their burrows at night and often rest in them during the hot day. They like to dig their dens in open hillsides or alongside streams.

One of the Hottest,

Harshest
places on Earth

Dragons

What Do Komodo Dragons Look Like?

Reptiles have scales instead of soft skin. Komodo dragons are covered with rough scales. These scales are bumpy and look like armor. The bumps help protect the lizards as they move around.

The dark color of adult dragons helps them soak up the heat of the sun.

Komodo dragons walk on bowed legs. Their tails swish back and forth to help them balance. They hold their heads high so that they can see and smell the slightest hint of a nearby animal.

Adult dragons can grow to be over ten feet long. They can weigh as much as 250 pounds! Males are usually bigger than females.

Komodo dragons are very strong. They also have claws that are two to three inches long. These claws help the dragons to dig holes and to grasp their prey.

can grow to over **10** feet long.

What Do Komodo Dragons Eat?

Komodo dragons hunt and eat other animals. Animals that eat other animals are called predators. Komodo dragons are fierce hunters. They eat anything they can catch, from rats to goats. They can catch and eat animals that are much bigger than they are. Sometimes they even eat water buffalo, which can weigh over one thousand pounds!

These giant lizards don't have very big teeth—but they have a lot of them! These teeth are very sharp, just perfect for biting chunks of meat. The edges of the teeth have ridges. The ridges are good for biting and holding on to their dinner.

Komodo dragons stick their tongues out all the time. They don't do it to tease each other. They do it for the same reason snakes do—to smell! They pick up smells as they wave their tongues through the air. That's why the tongue is forked, or shaped like a Y. That gives the tongue a wider surface to tell which direction a smell is coming from.

Usually Komodo dragons wait quietly for their dinner to come to them. If they need to, though, they can run as fast as eight miles per hour! They can't run that fast for very long, but it can help them catch their dinner.

Sometimes they eat

Water
Buffalo.

Eggs **Bigger** than a **Baseball**

How Are Baby Komodo Dragons Born?

Like most reptiles, Komodo dragons hatch from eggs. Dragon mothers lay their eggs on the ground. Then they dig a big hole and bury the eggs under the sand. This keeps the eggs nice and warm—about 81°F. It also protects them until they hatch. Hatching takes about eight months. Mother dragons usually lay between ten and twenty-seven eggs.

Dragon eggs have a soft, smooth shell. They are much bigger than chicken eggs. In fact, they are usually bigger than a baseball! That's a good thing, because baby dragons are about sixteen inches long when they hatch.

How Do Baby Komodo Dragons Grow Up?

Baby dragons take care of themselves right from the beginning. When they are young, they eat insects and small rodents. Soon, though, they move on to bigger animals. Komodo dragons grow up fast. In their first six months they grow to nearly three feet long—twice as big as when they hatch.

Baby Komodo dragons have many more spots than their parents do. That helps them hide from other hungry animals. They are also good climbers when they are young, and often live up in trees. That is probably to help them keep away from adult dragons. The adults will eat them if they get the chance!

Are Komodo Dragons in Danger?

Komodo dragons are rare animals. They live on only a few islands. As more and more people move into those areas, there is less and less room for the dragons.

For the dragons to survive, they need protected areas where they are free to roam and hunt, as they have for millions of years. Long live the dragons!

Thane Maynard

About the Author

Thane Maynard grew up in central Florida where he enjoyed catching scarlet king snakes and baby alligators. His interest in the world of nature led to a love for all types of animal wildlife. Mr. Maynard has shared this love with audiences through two television series, *Animals in Action* and *Secrets at the Zoo,* and a daily radio feature, *The 90-Second Naturalist,* on National Public Radio. He is the director of education at the Cincinnati Zoo and Botanical Garden.

In addition to *Komodo Dragons,* Mr. Maynard has written many other books about animals. These include *Animal Inventors, Endangered Animal Babies,* and *A Rhino Comes to America.* He dedicated his book *Saving Endangered Mammals* to all of tomorrow's conservationists with these words: "May you have the good sense to live as if the future matters."

Reader Response

Open for Discussion

What surprised you most about Komodo dragons?

Comprehension Check

1. Use details from the selection to describe Komodo dragons.

2. Compare baby and adult Komodo dragons. Explain how the babies and adults are different. Give examples from the selection.

3. Why are Komodo dragons in danger? What can people do to help them? Support your answers with details from the selection.

4. Some words have more than one meaning. Use **context clues** to figure out the meaning that makes sense in the sentence. What is a *monitor* in this selection? What are other meanings of the word *monitor?* (Context Clues)

5. Sometimes **context clues** give a definition or explanation for a difficult or unusual word. Find an example of a definition or explanation in this selection. (Context Clues)

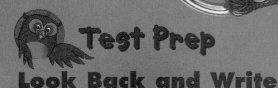 **Test Prep**

Look Back and Write

Look back at pages 238–240. What is a cold-blooded animal? Include details from the selection about how Komodo dragons act and look.

TWO UNCOMMON LIZARDS

from the Microsoft® Encarta® 96 Encyclopedia

Horned Lizard

Horned Lizard or **Horned Toad,** common name for a genus of short-tailed, short-legged lizards in the iguana family. They are called "horned" for the hornlike spines on the back of the head and sides of the body, and "toad" for their rounded, toadlike shape. Found mostly in dry regions of the western United States and Mexico, they are diurnal and can often be seen sitting motionless near ant mounds. Most species feed heavily on ants, but they will also eat other types of small insects and spiders. Their wide, flat bodies are about 8 cm to 13 cm (about 3 in. to 5 in.) long. For defense, many species, including the coast horned lizard, can spray an intruder from the corners of their eyes. The Texas horned lizard, once commonly sold as a pet, has disappeared from many parts of its former habitat and is protected in Texas.

Scientific classification: Horned lizards make up the genus *Phrynosoma* of the family Iguanidae. The coast horned lizard is classified as *Phrynosoma coronatum* and the Texas horned lizard as *Phrynosoma cornutum.*

The regal horned lizard is the largest of the American species.

Glass Lizard

Glass Lizard, common name for members of a genus of lizards named for the smooth, hard, highly polished, shinglelike scales that ring the legless body. They are frequently mistaken for snakes and are sometimes called glass snakes; however, unlike snakes, they have movable eyelids and external ear openings. Glass lizards are found in both Eurasia and the Americas, and six species are found in North America, from Virginia and southern Wisconsin to Texas and northeastern Mexico.

Color varies among the different species. Some are black with a green spot on each scale; others are tan or brown with longitudinal dark stripes. Glass lizards feed mainly on insects. They have a fragile tail that is two times or more the length of the body and that breaks off readily when handled. The tail serves as a defense mechanism against predators, which are often distracted by the broken, wriggling segment of tail. As in most lizards, the tail grows back after being broken, but the regenerated portion is usually shorter and of a different color than the original. A deep fold runs along each side of the glass lizard's body, which may reach a length of about 1 m (about 3.3 ft). The largest species is the scheltopusik, a European species that reaches a length of about 1.2 m (about 4 ft).

Scientific classification: Glass lizards make up the genus *Ophisaurus* of the family Anguidae. The scheltopusik is classified as *Ophisaurus apodus*.

The glass lizard is superficially similar to a snake.

Poetry

The Circle of Thanks

retold by Joseph Bruchac, from Micmac Native Americans

As I play my drum
I look around me
and I see the trees.
The trees are dancing
in a circle about me
and they are beautiful.

As I play my drum
I look around me
and I see the sun and moon.
The sun and moon are dancing
in a circle about me
and they are beautiful.

As I play my drum
I look around me
and I see the stars.
The stars are dancing
in a circle about me
and they are beautiful.

As I play my drum
I look around me
and I see my people.
All my people are dancing
in a circle about me
and my people, they are beautiful.

Food

by Victor M. Valle

One eats
the moon in a tortilla
Eat frijoles
and you eat the earth
Eat chile
and you eat sun and fire
Drink water
and you drink sky

Comida

por Victor M. Valle

Uno se come
la luna en la tortilla
Comes frijol
y comes tierra
Comes chile
y comes sol y fuego
Bebes agua
y bebes cielo

House Crickets

by Paul Fleischman

Voice One	Voice Two
We don't live in meadows	
crick-et	crick-et
or in groves	
	We're house crickets
	living beneath
	this gas stove
crick-et	crick-et
Others may worry	
crick-et	crick-et
about fall	
	We're scarcely aware
	of the seasons at all
crick-et	crick-et
Spring, to house crickets,	
crick-et	crick-et
means no more	
	than the time
	when fresh greens
	once again grace the floor
crick-et	crick-et
Summer's the season	
crick-et	crick-et
for pie crumbs:	
	peach, pear, boysenberry,

Voice One	Voice Two
	quince, apricot, plum
crick-et	crick-et
Pumpkin seeds tell us	
crick-et	crick-et
fall's arrived	
	while hot chocolate spills
	hint that it's
	winter outside.
No matter the month	No matter the month
we stay well fed and warm,	
	unconcerned about cold fronts
	and wind chill and storms.
For while others are ruled	For while others are ruled
by the sun in the heavens,	
	whose varying height brings
	the seasons' procession,
we live in a world	we live in a world
of fixed Fahrenheit	
crick-et	crick-et
	thanks to *our* sun:
our unchanging	
	reliable
steadfast and stable	
bright blue	bright blue
pilot light.	pilot light.

Unit 2 Wrap-Up

What place do plants and animals have in the world around us?

Read All About It!

Form Opinions from Facts

In many selections in Unit 2, plants and animals are cared for by humans. For example, *Komodo Dragons* gives information about caring for endangered animals.

1. **Look** in a local newspaper. Find an article about a plant or animal that people in your community are concerned about.

2. **Take notes** on the issue. Include all sides.

3. Which side will you take? **Write** a paragraph explaining your opinion.

WANTED: ONE BADGER

Create Posters

Did you see that badger escape? With a classmate, choose two animals from Unit 2 and create wanted posters for them.

1. **Look back** at the selections and choose two animals.

2. **Brainstorm** ideas for your posters. Include details, such as what they look like and what they eat.

3. **Create** your posters and show them to others.

It's in the Details

Research On-Location

When Thane Maynard, author of *Komodo Dragons,* says, "Baby Komodo dragons have many more spots than their parents do," he is using details that he observed.

1. **Look back** at the Unit 2 selections. Find ways that others observed details. Write three examples.

2. **Visit** a place or an animal that interests you.

3. **Take notes** about details, such as sounds and sights.

4. Use details to **write** about the place or animal.

Decisions, Decisions

Write a Letter

Characters in this unit make important choices. Luz, from "A Big-City Dream," starts a project without knowing if she can find help.

1. **Focus** on one character's decision or action and decide whether you agree or disagree with it.

2. **Write** a letter to the character explaining your opinion. If you agree, compliment the character. If you disagree, suggest what he or she might do differently.

Test Talk

Understand the Question

Find Key Words in the Text

Before you can answer a test question, you have to know where to look for the answer. Look at pages 184–185 in "A Big-City Dream." A test on that section of the story might have this question.

Test Question 1

How do Luz's family, friends, and neighbors help Luz create her garden? Use details from the story to support your answer.

Make sure that you understand the question.

Find the key words. Finish the statement "I need to find out . . ."

Decide where you will look for the answer.

- Some test questions tell you to look in one place in the text. The answer is *right there* in the text.

- Other test questions tell you to look for information in different parts of the selection. You have to *think and search*.

- Still other test questions tell you to combine what *you* know with what the *author* tells you. The answer comes from the *author and you*.

See how one student figures out where to look for the answer.

How do they help Luz . . . I think they want to know what people do to help her. Most of this section talks about that. So, this must be a question where I'll have to think and search for the answer.

Here's **helper** on page 184, but that's talking about the deliveryman's helper, not Luz's. Farther down I see, "Other people help carry everything into the garden." That is one thing people do to help.

Try it!

Now figure out where to look for the answer to these test questions about "A Big-City Dream," pages 184–185.

Test Question 2

Why is the first deliveryman surprised when he sees Luz? Use details from the story to support your answer.

Test Question 3

Why does Luz "feel at least six feet tall"?

Ⓐ because she is standing on a pile of dirt

Ⓑ because her mother is very proud of her

Ⓒ because she gets to tell people what to do

Ⓓ because she is working with younger children

Keys to Success

How do learning and working lead to success?

Making Judgments

- **Making judgments** means thinking about and deciding how to react toward people, situations, and ideas in stories and articles that you read.

- Use what you know and your experience as you make judgments.

- Ask yourself if the author is trying to influence you. Does the author support the ideas he or she presents in the text?

Read the tall tale "Welcome to McBroom's Farm" from *McBroom's Ear* **by Sid Fleischman.**

Talk About It

1. Is McBroom's farm like the farms that you know about? Explain.

2. How do you think the author wants you to react as you read about McBroom?

Welcome to McBroom's Farm

by Sid Fleischman

I guess you've heard how amazing rich our farm is. Anything will grow in it—quick. Seeds burst in the ground and crops shoot right up before your eyes. Why, just yesterday our oldest boy dropped a five-cent piece and before he could find it that nickel had grown to a quarter.

Early one morning a skinny, tangle-haired stranger came ambling along the road. My, he was tall! I do believe if his

hat fell off it would take a day or two
to reach the ground.

"Howdy, sir," he said. "I'm Slim-Face
John from here, there, and other places.
I'll paint your barn cheap."

That man was not only tall, skinny, and
tangle-haired, he was nearsighted. "We
don't own a barn," I said.

He squinted and laughed. "In that
case," he said, "I'll paint it free."

"Done," I smiled.

He painted that no-barn in less than
a second, with time left over.

LOOK AHEAD

As you read the legend *John Henry*, make a judgment about him. Could he and his sledgehammers win a contest against a machine?

Words to Know

boulder	horizon	tunnel
hollered	glimpse	rhythm
shivered		

Many words have more than one meaning. To decide which meaning of a word is being used, look for clues in the surrounding sentences or paragraph.

Read the paragraph below—paying special attention to its meaning as a whole.

Digging Out!

Fran <u>shivered</u> in the cold. The crew had started work on the <u>tunnel</u> at 4:00 A.M., and it was still dark. First they blasted a large <u>boulder</u> blocking the entrance. Then the boss <u>hollered</u> loudly enough for the workers to develop a <u>rhythm</u> as they shoveled small rocks out of the way. At last, Fran caught a <u>glimpse</u> of the sun peeking over the <u>horizon</u>. The work was hard, but at least it would warm up soon.

Write About It

Write a letter applying for a job as a road builder or construction worker. Use as many vocabulary words as you can.

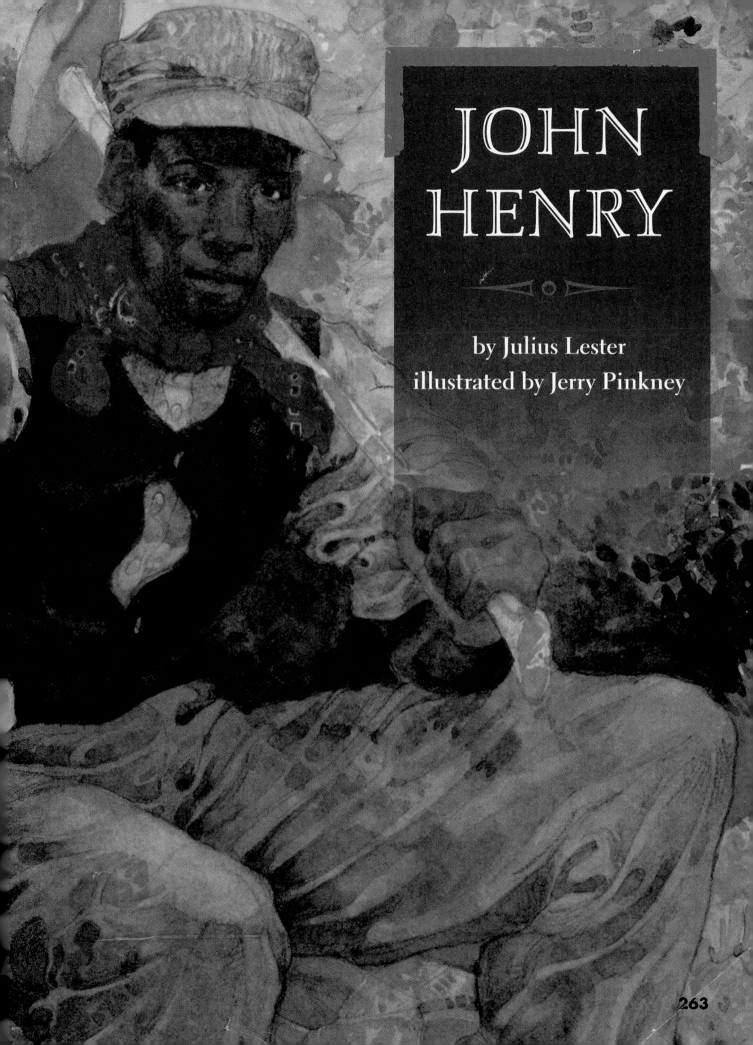

JOHN HENRY

by Julius Lester

illustrated by Jerry Pinkney

You have probably never heard of John Henry. Or maybe you heard about him but don't know the ins and outs of his comings and goings. Well, that's why I'm going to tell you about him.

When John Henry was born, birds came from everywhere to see him. The bears and panthers and moose and deer and rabbits and squirrels and even a unicorn came out of the woods to see him. And instead of the sun tending to his business and going to bed, it was peeping out from behind the moon's skirts trying to get a glimpse of the new baby.

Before long the mama and papa come out on the porch to show off their brand-new baby. The birds "oooooooohed" and the animals "aaaaaaahed" at how handsome the baby was.

Somewhere in the middle of one of the "oooooooohs," or maybe it was on the backside of one of the "aaaaaaaahs," that baby jumped out of his mama's arms and started growing.

He grew and he grew and he grew. He grew until his head and shoulders busted through the roof which was over the porch. John Henry thought that was the funniest thing in the world. He laughed so loud, the sun got scared. It scurried from behind the moon's skirts and went to bed, which is where it should've been all the while.

The next morning John Henry was up at sunrise. The sun wasn't. He was tired and had decided to sleep in. John Henry wasn't going to have none of that. He hollered up into the sky, "Get up from there! I got things to do and I need light to do 'em by."

The sun yawned, washed its face, flossed and brushed its teeth, and hurried up over the horizon.

That day John Henry helped his papa rebuild the porch he had busted through, added a wing onto the house with an indoor swimming pool and one of them jacutzis. After lunch he chopped down an acre of trees and split them into fireplace logs and still had time for a nap before supper.

The next day John Henry went to town. He met up with the meanest man in the state, Ferret-Faced Freddy, sitting on his big white horse. You know what he was doing? He was thinking of mean things to do. Ferret-Faced Freddy was so mean, he cried if he had a nice thought.

John Henry said, "Freddy, I'll make you a bet. Let's have a race. You on your horse. Me on my legs. If you and your horse win, you can work me as hard as you want for a whole year. If I win, you have to be nice for a year."

Ferret-Faced Freddy laughed an evil laugh. "It's a deal, John Henry." His voice sounded like bat wings on tombstones.

The next morning folks lined up all along the way the race would go. John Henry was ready. Ferret-Faced Freddy and his horse were ready.

BANG! The race was on.

My great-granddaddy's brother's cousin's sister-in-law's uncle's aunt was there that morning. She said everybody saw Ferret-Faced Freddy ride by on his big white horse and they were sho' 'nuf moving. Didn't nobody see John Henry. That's because he was so fast, the wind was out of breath trying to keep up with him. When Ferret-Faced Freddy crossed the finish line, John Henry was already on the other side, sitting in a rocking chair and drinking a soda mom.

After that Ferret-Faced Freddy was so nice, everybody called him Frederick the Friendly.

John Henry decided it was time for him to go on down the big road. He went home and told his mama and daddy good-by.

His daddy said, "You got to have something to make your way in the world with, Son. These belonged to your granddaddy." And he gave him two twenty-pound sledgehammers with four-foot handles made of whale bone.

A day or so later, John Henry saw a crew building a road. At least, that's what they were doing until they came on a boulder right smack-dab where the road was supposed to go. This was no ordinary boulder. It was as hard as anger and so big around, it took half a week for a tall man to walk from one side to the other.

John Henry offered to lend them a hand.

"That's all right. We'll put some dynamite to it."

John Henry smiled to himself. "Whatever you say."

The road crew planted dynamite all around the rock and set it off.

KERBOOM BLAMMITY-BLAMMITY BOOMBOOM BANGBOOMBANG!!!

That dynamite made so much racket, the Almighty looked over the parapets of Heaven and hollered, "It's getting too noisy down there." The dynamite kicked up so much dirt and dust, it got dark. The moon thought night had caught her napping and she hurried out so fast, she almost bumped into the sun who was still climbing the steep hill toward noontime.

When all the commotion from the dynamite was over, the road crew was amazed. The boulder was still there. In fact, the dynamite hadn't knocked even a chip off it.

The crew didn't know what to do. Then they heard a rumbling noise. They looked around. It was John Henry, laughing. He said, "If you gentlemen would give me a little room, I got some work to do."

"Don't see how you can do what dynamite couldn't," said the boss of the crew.

John Henry chuckled. "Just watch me." He swung one of his hammers round and round his head. It made such a wind that leaves blew off the trees and birds fell out of the sky.

RINGGGGGG!

The hammer hit the boulder. That boulder shivered like you do on a cold winter morning when it looks like the school bus is never going to come.

RINGGGGGG!

The boulder shivered like the morning when freedom came to the slaves.

John Henry picked up his other hammer. He swung one hammer in a circle over his head. As soon as it hit the rock—RINGGGG!—the hammer in his left hand started to make a circle and—RINGGGG! Soon the RINGGGG! of one hammer followed the RINGGGG! of the other one so closely, it sounded like they were falling at the same time.

RINGGGG!RINGGGG!
RINGGGG!RINGGGG!

Chips and dust were flying from the boulder so fast that John Henry vanished from sight. But you could still hear his hammers—RINGGGG!RINGGGG!

The air seemed to be dancing to the rhythm of his hammers. The boss of the road crew looked up. His mouth dropped open. He pointed into the sky.

There, in the air above the boulder, was a rainbow. John Henry was swinging the hammers so fast, he was making a rainbow around his shoulders. It was shining and shimmering in the dust and grit like hope that never dies. John Henry started singing:

I got a rainbow

RINGGGG!RINGGGG!

Tied round my shoulder

RINGGGG!RINGGGG!

It ain't gon' rain,

No, it ain't gon' rain.

RINGGGG!RINGGGG!

John Henry sang and he hammered and the air danced and the rainbow shimmered and the earth shook and rolled from the blows of the hammer. Finally it was quiet. Slowly the dust cleared.

Folks could not believe their eyes. The boulder was gone. In its place was the prettiest and straightest road they had ever seen. Not only had John Henry pulverized the boulder into pebbles, he had finished building the road.

In the distance where the new road connected to the main one, the road crew saw John Henry waving good-by, a hammer on each shoulder, the rainbow draped around him like love.

John Henry went on his way. He had heard that any man good with a hammer could find work building the Chesapeake and Ohio Railroad through West Virginia. That was where he had been going when he stopped to build the road.

The next day John Henry arrived at the railroad. However, work had stopped. The railroad tracks had to go through a mountain, and such a mountain. Next to it even John Henry felt small.

But a worker told John Henry about a new machine they were going to use to tunnel through the mountain. It was called a steam drill. "It can hammer faster and harder than ten men and it never has to stop and rest."

The next day the boss arrived with the steam drill. John Henry said to him, "Let's have a contest. Your steam drill against me and my hammers."

The man laughed. "I've heard you're the best there ever was, John Henry. But even you can't outhammer a machine."

"Let's find out," John Henry answered.

Boss shrugged. "Don't make me no never mind. You start on the other side of the mountain. I'll start the steam drill over here. Whoever gets to the middle first is the winner."

The next morning all was still. The birds weren't singing and the roosters weren't crowing. When the sun didn't hear the rooster, he wondered if something was wrong. So he rose a couple of minutes early to see.

What he saw was a mountain as big as hurt feelings. On one side was a big machine hooked up to hoses. It was belching smoke and steam. As the machine attacked the mountain, rocks and dirt and underbrush flew into the air. On the other side was John Henry. Next to the mountain he didn't look much bigger than a wish that wasn't going to come true.

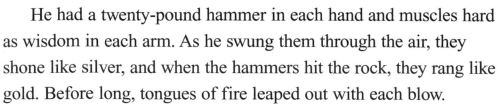

He had a twenty-pound hammer in each hand and muscles hard as wisdom in each arm. As he swung them through the air, they shone like silver, and when the hammers hit the rock, they rang like gold. Before long, tongues of fire leaped out with each blow.

On the other side the boss of the steam drill felt the mountain shudder. He got scared and hollered, "I believe this mountain is caving in!"

From the darkness inside the mountain came a deep voice: "It's just my hammers sucking wind. Just my hammers sucking wind." There wasn't enough room inside the tunnel for the rainbow, so it wrapped itself around the mountain on the side where John Henry was.

All through the night John Henry and the steam drill went at it. In the light from the tongues of fire shooting out of the tunnel from John Henry's hammer blows, folks could see the rainbow wrapped around the mountain like a shawl.

The sun came up extra early the next morning to see who was winning. Just as it did, John Henry broke through and met the steam drill. The boss of the steam drill was flabbergasted. John Henry had come a mile and a quarter. The steam drill had only come a quarter.

Folks were cheering and yelling, "John Henry! John Henry!"

John Henry walked out of the tunnel into the sunlight, raised his arms over his head, a hammer in each hand. The rainbow slid off the mountain and around his shoulders.

With a smile John Henry's eyes closed, and slowly he fell
to the ground. John Henry was dead. He had hammered so hard
and so fast and so long that his big heart had burst.

Everybody was silent for a minute. Then came the sound
of soft crying. Some said it came from the moon. Another one
said she saw the sun shed a tear.

Then something strange happened. Afterward folks swore
the rainbow whispered it. I don't know. But whether it was
a whisper or a thought, everyone had the same knowing at the
same moment: "Dying ain't important. Everybody does that.
What matters is how well you do your living."

First one person started clapping. Then another, and another.
Soon everybody was clapping.

The next morning the sun got everybody up early to say
good-by to John Henry. They put him on a flatbed railroad car,
and the train made its way slowly out of the mountains. All along

the way folks lined both sides of the track, and they were
cheering and shouting through their tears:

"John Henry! John Henry!"

John Henry's body was taken to Washington, D.C.

Some say he was buried on the White House lawn late one
night while the President and the Mrs. President was asleep.

I don't know about none of that. What I do know is this: If you
walk by the White House late at night, stand real still, and listen
real closely, folks say you just might hear a deep voice singing:

I got a rainbow
RINGGGG!RINGGGG!
Tied round my shoulder
RINGGGG!RINGGGG!
It ain't gon' rain,
No, it ain't gon' rain.
RINGGGG!RINGGGG!

About the Author
JULIUS LESTER

When Julius Lester was growing up in the 1940s and 1950s, he loved to read. Books provided an escape from the world around him. He has said that he is not sure exactly what led him to become a writer. As a teenager and young adult, he gradually became aware that writing was what he was "supposed to do with his life."

Mr. Lester began by writing several books for adults. Then, through the advice of an editor, he turned to writing children's books. It was important to him to help African American children become aware of their heritage. In his books for young people, he doesn't focus on the history of wars and politics, but rather on the lives and experiences of ordinary people. His books have won many awards, and some have been translated into other languages.

If you enjoyed reading *John Henry,* you may like these books by Julius Lester: *Black Folktales* and *The Knee-High Man and Other Tales*. Mr. Lester also has published retellings of the Uncle Remus stories.

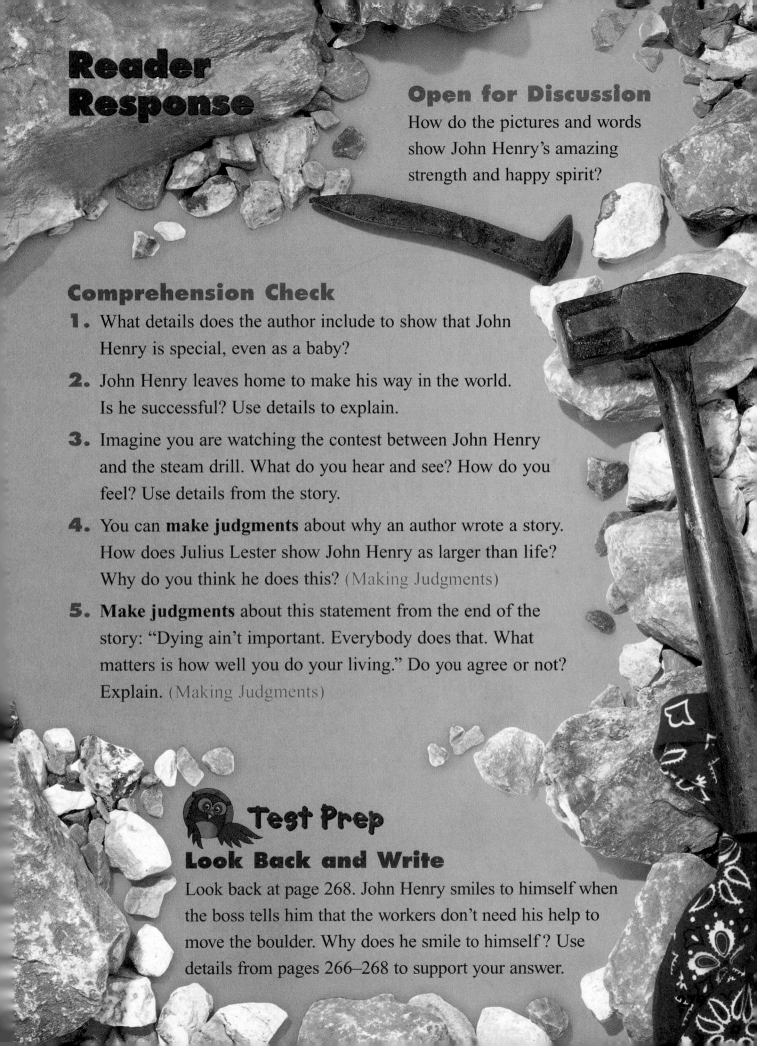

Reader Response

Open for Discussion

How do the pictures and words show John Henry's amazing strength and happy spirit?

Comprehension Check

1. What details does the author include to show that John Henry is special, even as a baby?

2. John Henry leaves home to make his way in the world. Is he successful? Use details to explain.

3. Imagine you are watching the contest between John Henry and the steam drill. What do you hear and see? How do you feel? Use details from the story.

4. You can **make judgments** about why an author wrote a story. How does Julius Lester show John Henry as larger than life? Why do you think he does this? (Making Judgments)

5. **Make judgments** about this statement from the end of the story: "Dying ain't important. Everybody does that. What matters is how well you do your living." Do you agree or not? Explain. (Making Judgments)

Test Prep

Look Back and Write

Look back at page 268. John Henry smiles to himself when the boss tells him that the workers don't need his help to move the boulder. Why does he smile to himself? Use details from pages 266–268 to support your answer.

Test Prep

How to Read a Poem

1. Preview

- Many poems have lines that rhyme. This poem was written as a song and set to music.

- A poem may also tell a story. Read the beginning of each verse (group of lines in a poem). What do these lines tell you about how much of John Henry's life will be described?

2. Read and Find Poem Parts

- A refrain is a line or lines which are repeated in a poem.

- As you read, look for repeated words and phrases that form refrains.

3. Think and Connect

Think about the story "John Henry." Then think about the poem "John Henry."

Which of these versions more clearly shows that people thought John Henry was a hero? Give examples to support your answer.

JOHN HENRY

*from **Doc Watson Sings Songs for Little Pickers***

When John Henry was just a little
    bitty baby
You could set him on the palm of your hand
John Henry's mama looked down on him
    and said,
"My Johnny gonna be a steel drivin'
    man, papa,
Johnny gonna be a steel drivin' man."

Then when John Henry was just a little
    old boy
And could sit on his papa's knee
Picked up a hammer, then he said to
    his papa,
"Hammer be the death of me;
    hammer be the death of me."

Now John Henry was a steel drivin' man
He drove steel all over this land
Said, "'Fore I let that old steel drill beat
    me down
Gonna die with my hammer in my hand;
    die with my hammer in my hand."

Well, John Henry's captain, he set out
    on a rock
Said "I think this tunnel's cavin' in."
John Henry smiled at his captain and
    he said,
"Hey, man, that's my hammer suckin' wind;
    That's my old hammer suckin' wind."

John Henry hammered in the Big
    Bend Tunnel
'Till his hammer caught on fire
The last word that poor John Henry said,
"Give me a cool drink of water 'fore I die;
Cool drink of water 'fore I die."

Well, they buried John Henry by the
    railroad track
Put him six feet under the sand
And every time a freight train would come
    a-rollin' by, they'd say,
"Yonder lies a steel drivin' man;
Yonder lies that steel drivin' man."

Drawing Conclusions

- Authors don't always tell you everything. Instead, they may give you a few details about what happens or about characters.

- You can use the details and what you know to **draw conclusions,** or figure out things about people or animals and what they do.

- A conclusion is a decision you reach that makes sense after you think about the details or facts that you have read.

Read "Winter of the Snowshoe Hare" by Gillian Richardson from *Cricket* magazine.

Talk About It

1. What would have happened to the hare if the dog hadn't obeyed the whistle? What makes you think so?

2. What conclusions can you draw about how fast the dog is? What details help you reach those conclusions?

3. What conclusions can you draw about the snowshoe hare?

WINTER OF THE SNOWSHOE HARE

by Gillian Richardson

Through the trees he raced, zigzagging this way and that. Faster, faster. The sound of pounding paws behind him grew ever louder, the harsh breathing nearer. His own huge feet barely touched the ground in his haste. He was almost flying!

Suddenly a shrill whistle split the air. The snowshoe hare sped on. But the dog slowed, reluctantly obeying the call of his master. He sniffed the trail once more, then turned and trotted back the way he'd come.

Cricket

Panic pushed the hare another half-mile through the woods before he became aware of the silence behind him. He darted into a dense patch of alders where he froze, his heart hammering inside his small chest. Gradually, the frightened creature grew calmer. His flattened ears lifted cautiously, and his nose twitched.

The frantic chase had begun near the pasture fence, a dangerous place for the hare to feed. The farm buildings were far too close, and the dog often hunted the hedgerows. But now the hare was deep in the safety of the mixed woods. He would survive another day.

LOOK AHEAD

Draw your own conclusions about Marven, his friends, and his family as you read about his experience working in a lumber camp in *Marven of the Great North Woods.*

Vocabulary

Words to Know

cord   flapjacks snowshoes
depot grizzly

Many words have more than one meaning.
To decide which meaning of a word
is being used, look for clues in the
surrounding sentences or paragraph.

Read the paragraph below—paying
special attention to its meaning as a
whole. Decide whether *cord* means "a
unit of measure" or "a string or rope."

From an Idaho Logging Camp, 1902

After a big breakfast of flapjacks and sausage,
I strapped on my snowshoes. I walked over the
powdery snow to the pile of freshly cut wood. All
of us in the logging camp were preparing the wood
to take it to the depot so the train could carry it back
east. I was a little afraid. Would I see a grizzly in the
woods on the way to the train station? As I loaded
cord after cord of wood into the big wagon, I wished
I could come home too. Hope to see you soon.

Talk About It

What would be the best thing about
working in a logging camp? the worst?
Talk about it with a friend. Use as many
vocabulary words as you can.

Marven
— of the —
Great North Woods

by Kathryn Lasky • illustrated by Kevin Hawkes

A Note from the Author

Marven at age ten

Marven Lasky was born in 1907 in Duluth, Minnesota. He was the first child born in America to Ida and Joseph Lasky, who had emigrated from Tsarist Russia to escape the persecution of Jews. The story of their escape in 1900 was told in my novel *The Night Journey*.

In 1918 an influenza epidemic swept through the United States. The disease was the worst in the cities, among large populations. Old people and young children were the most vulnerable. Ida and Joseph believed that they might save at least one of their children if they could arrange for that child to go far from the city. Marven was not chosen because he was loved most; Joseph and Ida loved all of their children. Girls in that era, however, were never permitted to travel far from home by themselves—and the last place a girl would ever be sent was to a logging camp. Marven, therefore, was sent by himself on a train to a logging camp in the great north woods of Minnesota.

Marven Lasky, my father, is now more than ninety years old. The last time he skied was at age eighty-three in Aspen, Colorado. He still has a good head for figures.

Marven in his late sixties

Ten-year-old Marven Lasky has left his parents and sisters and has traveled to the north woods to work there as a bookkeeper. Mr. Murray, who manages the lumber camp, shows Marven around the camp.

As they entered the camp, the longest shadows Marven had ever seen stretched across the snow, and he realized with a start that the shadows were the lumberjacks walking in the moonlight. He could smell hay and manure and saw the silhouettes of horses stomping in a snowy corral. From a nearby log building he heard the lively squeaks of a fiddle. It seemed for a moment as if the horses were keeping time to the music. Mr. Murray must have thought the same. "You want to watch the horses dance, or the jacks?" He laughed. "Come along, we'll take a look."

When they entered the building, the long shadows from the yard suddenly sprung to life. Marven stared. Immense men with long beards and wild hair were jumping around to the fiddler's tunes like a pack of frantic grizzly bears. They were the biggest and wildest men Marven had ever seen.

Marven could have watched the dancing all night, but Mr. Murray said, "Come on, Marven. We start early in the morning. I'll show you where you'll be living."

Mr. Murray took Marven to the small office where he would work and sleep. In Duluth, Marven had to share a bedroom with his two younger sisters and all of their dolls and toys, but this room was his—all his—and he liked it. A bed with a bearskin on it sat across from a woodstove; nearby, wood was stacked neatly. The big desk had cubbyholes for papers, envelopes, glue pots, and blotter strips. And on the desk there were blocks of paper and a big black ledger. There were pencils in a blue glass jar, as well as an inkwell. Marven hoped that somewhere there was a very good pen—a fountain pen.

"In addition to keeping the payroll," Mr. Murray said, "you have another job. The first bell in the morning is at four o'clock; second bell at four-fifteen. Third bell is at four-twenty. By four-twenty-five, if any jack is still in the sack, he's *en retard*, 'late.' So you, son, are the fourth bell. Starting tomorrow, you go into the bunkhouse and wake *les en retards*."

"How?"

"You tap them on the shoulder, give 'em a shake, scream in their ear if you have to."

Then Mr. Murray said good night, and Marven was alone again.

It seemed to Marven he had just crawled under the bearskin when he heard the first bell. The fire was out and the room was cold and dark. He lit the kerosene lamp and pulled on his double-thick long underwear, two pairs of socks, two pairs of knickers, and two sweaters. Then he put on his cut-down overcoat.

After the second bell, Marven heard the jacks heading toward the eating hall. It was nearly time for his first job.

He ran through the cold morning darkness to the bunkhouse, peeked in, and counted five huge lumps in the shadows. Five jacks in the sacks. Marven waited just inside the door.

At the third bell, Marven was relieved to see two jacks climb out of bed. He thought there must be a *broche*, a Hebrew blessing, for something like this. His father knew all sorts of *broches*— blessings for seeing the sunrise, blessings for the first blossom of spring. Was there a *broche* for a rising lumberjack? If he said a *broche*, maybe the other three would get up on their own.

One lump stirred, then another. They grunted, rolled, and climbed out from under the covers. Their huge shadows slid across the ceiling.

One jack was still in the sack. Marven took a deep breath, walked bravely over to the bed, reached out, and tapped the jack's shoulder. It was like poking a granite boulder. The jack's beard ran right into his long, shaggy hair; Marven couldn't even find an ear to shout into. He cupped his hands around his mouth and leaned forward.

"Up!"

The jack grunted and muttered something in French.

"Get up," Marven pleaded.

Another jack pulled on his boots, boomed, "*Lève-toi!* Jean Louis. *Lève-toi,*" and shuffled out the door.

"*Lève-toi!* Jean Louis. *Lève-toi,*" Marven repeated.

Jean Louis opened one eye. It glittered like a blue star beneath his thick black eyebrow. He squinted, as if trying to make out the shape in front of him, then blinked and sat up.

"*Bonjour,*" Marvin whispered.

"*Qui es tu? Quel est ton nom?*"

"I don't speak French—just *bonjour, derrière,* and *lève-toi.*"

"That's all? No more?" The man opened his eyes wide now. "So what is your name?"

"Marven."

"Ah . . . Marven," Jean Louis repeated, as if tasting the sound of his name.

"Will you get up?" Marven asked anxiously.

Jean Louis growled and fixed him in the hard blue squint of one eye.

"Please." Marven stood straight and tried not to tremble.

Jean Louis grunted and swung his feet from beneath the covers. They were as big as skillets, and one of his huge toenails was bruised black and blue. Marven tried not to stare.

Marven and Jean Louis were the last to arrive at the breakfast table. The only sounds were those of chewing and the clink of forks and knives against the plates. At each place were three stacks of flapjacks, one big steak, eight strips of bacon, and a bowl of oatmeal. In the middle of the table were bowls of potatoes and beans with molasses, platters with pies and cakes, and blue jugs filled with tea, coffee, and milk.

Marven stared at the food in dismay. *It's not kosher,* he thought. In Marven's house it was against ancient Jewish law to eat dairy products and meat together. And never, ever, did a Jew eat bacon. Marven came to a quick decision. One day he would eat the flapjacks and oatmeal with milk. The next day he would eat the steak and the oatmeal without milk. And never the bacon.

After breakfast, as they did every morning, the jacks went to the toolhouse to get their saws and axes. Then, wearing snowshoes and pulling huge sleds piled with equipment, they made their way into the great woods, where they would work all day.

Marven went directly to his office after breakfast. Mr. Murray was already there, setting out Marven's work. A fresh pot of ink was thawing in a bowl of hot water on the woodstove. There were two boxes on the desk filled with scraps of paper.

"Cord chits," Mr. Murray said. "The jacks are paid according to the number of cords they cut in a pay period—two weeks.

You figure it out. I'm no good as a bookkeeper and have enough other things to do around here. Each chit should have the jack's name—or, if he can't write, his symbol."

"His symbol?" Marven asked weakly.

"Yes. Jean Louis's is a thumbprint. Here's one!" He held up a small piece of paper with a thumbprint on it the size of a baby's fist. Marven blinked.

It was all very confusing. Sometimes two names were on one chit. These were called doublees; there were even some triplees. This meant more calculations. And sometimes chits were in the wrong pay-period box.

Marven sat staring at the scraps. "There is no system!" he muttered. Where to begin? His mother always made a list when she had many things to do. So first Marven listed the jacks' names alphabetically and noted the proper symbol for those who could not write. Then he listed the dates of a single pay period, coded each chit with the dates, and, with a ruler, made a chart. By the end of the morning, Marven had a system and knew the name or symbol for each man. There were many chits with the huge thumbprint of Jean Louis.

Every day Marven worked until midday, when he went into the cookhouse and ate baked beans and two kinds of pie with Mr. Murray and the cook. After lunch he returned to his office and worked until the jacks returned from the forest for supper.

By Friday of the second week, Marven had learned his job so well that he finished early. He had not been on his skis since he had arrived at camp. Every day the routine was simply meals and work, and Marven kept to his office and away from the lumberjacks as much as he could. But today he wanted to explore, so he put on his skis and followed the sled paths into the woods.

He glided forward, his skis making soft whisking sounds in the snow. This certainly was different from city skiing in Duluth, where he would dodge the ragman's cart or the milkman's wagon, where the sky was notched with chimney pots belching smoke, where the snow turned sooty as soon as it fell.

Here in the great north woods all was still and white. Beads of ice glistened on bare branches like jewels. The frosted needles of pine and spruce pricked the eggshell sky, and a ghostly moon began to climb over the treetops.

Marven came upon a frozen lake covered with snow, which lay in a circle of tall trees like a bowl of sugar. He skimmed out across it on his skis, his cheeks stinging in the cold air, and stopped in the middle to listen to the quietness.

And then Marven heard a deep, low growl. At the edge of the lake a shower of snow fell from a pine. A grizzly bear? Marven gripped his ski poles. A grizzly awake in the winter! What would he do if a bear came after him? Where could he hide? Could he out-ski a grizzly?

Marven began to tremble, but he knew that he must remain still, very still. Maybe, Marven thought desperately, the grizzly would think he was a small tree growing in the middle of the lake. He tried very hard to look like a tree. But concentrating on being a tree was difficult because Marven kept thinking of the bundle on the train platform—his mother, his father, his two big sisters, his two little sisters. He belonged in Duluth with them, not in the middle of the great north woods with a grizzly. The hot tears streaming down his cheeks turned cold, then froze.

When another tree showered snow, Marven, startled, shot out across the lake. As he reached the shore, a huge shadow slid from behind the trees. The breath froze in Marven's throat.

In the thick purple shadows, he saw a blue twinkle.

"Aaah! Marven!" Jean Louis held a glistening ax in one hand. He looked taller than ever. "I mark the tree for cutting next season." He stepped closer to the trunk and swung the ax hard. Snow showered at Marven's feet.

"Ah, *mon petit,* you cry!" Jean Louis took off his glove and rubbed his huge thumb down Marven's cheek. "You miss your mama? Your papa?" Marven nodded silently.

"Jean Louis," he whispered. The huge lumberjack bent closer. "I thought you were a grizzly bear!"

"You what!" Jean Louis gasped. "You think I was a grizzly!" And Jean Louis began to laugh, and as he roared, more snow fell from the tree, for his laugh was as powerful as his ax.

As they made their way back to the sled paths, Marven heard a French song drifting through the woods. The other jacks came down the path, their saws and axes slung across their shoulders, and Marven and Jean Louis joined them. Evening shadows fell through the trees, and as Marven skied alongside the huge men, he hummed the tune they were singing.

One day followed the next. Every morning, in that time when the night had worn thin but the day had not yet dawned, Marven shouted, "Up! *Lève-toi! Lève-toi!*" to Jean Louis. Together they would go to the dining hall, where one day Marven would eat steak and oatmeal without milk; the next day he would eat oatmeal with milk and flapjacks but no steak. Jean Louis always ate the bacon and anything else Marven left.

And every afternoon after that, Marven would finish his work well before sunset and ski into the woods. Although the worry that his family might catch the terrible sickness nagged at him constantly, when he was in the woods his fears grew dim in the silence and shadows of the winter forest. And every day he would fall in beside Jean Louis as the jacks returned to camp, and he would hum the French songs that Jean Louis told him were about a beautiful woman in the far, far north, or a lonely bear in its den, or a lovely maiden named Go With Clouds.

At night, after supper was done, Marven learned the lumberjacks' songs and how to play their games—the ones he could manage, like ax throwing. A jack would heave an ax from thirty paces at the tail end of a log; for Marven they moved the mark up to ten feet. The jacks challenged each other to barrel lifting and bucksaw contests, but Marven was too small for those.

He was not, however, too small to dance. Sometimes he danced on the floor, and sometimes Jean Louis lifted him and Marven did a little two-step right there in his stocking feet on the shoulders of the big lumberjack.

In April, four months after Marven had arrived at the camp, the snow began to melt. Mr. Murray said to Marven, "I promised your parents I'd send you back while there was still enough snow for you to ski on. Every day it grows warmer. You better go before you have to swim out of here. I'll send your parents a letter to say you're coming home. But I don't know what I'll do for a bookkeeper."

So it was planned that Marven would leave on the last day of the month. When the day came, he went to the bunkhouse to find Jean Louis.

"Ah, Marven." Jean Louis tasted Marven's name as he had the first time he had ever said it, as if it were the most delicious French pastry in the world. "I have something for you, *mon petit.*" He got up and opened the chest at the end of his bed.

"You are a woodsman now," he said, and handed Marven a brand-new ax. The head was sharp and glinting; the handle glistened like dark honey.

"*Merci,* Jean Louis. *Merci beaucoup,*" Marven whispered.

Jean Louis went with Marven all the way to the train station. When the snow ran out on the banks of a muddy creek near the depot, he turned to Marven, grinned widely, and said, "Up, up. *Léve-toi*, Marven." The giant of a man swung the small boy onto his shoulders, skis and all, and carried him across to the opposite bank.

As the train pulled away, Marven waved at Jean Louis through the window, which had become foggy with his breath. "*Au revoir*," he murmured. "*Au revoir*, Jean Louis."

Marven sat alone on the train and thought of his family. Who would be waiting for him at the station? He felt the edge of his new ax. It was so sharp, so bright. But it was good only for cutting wood. What could it do against the terrible flu that had sent him away?

With each mile the land slid out from under its snowy cover. When the train finally pulled into the station in Duluth, Marven pressed his face against the window, the glass fogging as he searched the crowd on the platform.

When Marven stepped down from the train he was still searching. Everyone looked pale and winter worn, and not a single face was familiar. Then suddenly he was being smothered with kisses and hugs. His little sisters were grabbing him around his waist, his big sisters were kissing his ears, and then all of them tumbled into Mama's and Papa's arms, and they were one big hugging bundle.

"You're not dead!" Marven said. His sisters, Mama, Papa, Aunt Ghisa, and Uncle Moishe crowded around him in a tight circle. He turned slowly to look at each face.

"Nobody's dead," Marven repeated softly.

"The sickness is over," said Mama. "And you are finally home!"

About the Author
Kathryn Lasky

Kathryn Lasky did her writing in secret when she was a child. She was constantly thinking up stories and sometimes writing them on paper. She never told anybody about them, though, until much later.

One warm summer night when Ms. Lasky was about thirteen years old, she was riding in the back seat of her family's convertible. While she was watching the clouds, she made a comment that it "looked like a sheepback sky." She remembers her mother turning and saying, "Kathy, you should be a writer." Her mother's belief in her started Ms. Lasky thinking that maybe she *could* be a writer. She started writing books, and her books have won many awards.

Like *Marven of the Great North Woods,* many of Ms. Lasky's stories are based on real events. She is not concerned with her readers learning a lot of facts or getting a message from her writing. She says, "What I do hope is that they come away with a sense of joy—indeed celebration—about something they have sensed of the world in which they live."

Open for Discussion

Imagine yourself as Marven. What do you remember best from living in the logging camp?

Comprehension Check

1. Describe the lumber camp. What details does the author use to help you experience it?

2. Marven took on responsibilities in return for being able to live at the lumber camp. Explain how he contributed to the work of the camp. Use details.

3. Marven and Jean Louis became friends. Give examples from the story that show their special friendship.

4. **Draw conclusions** about Marven's family. How did they feel about sending him away? How did they feel when he returned home? (Drawing Conclusions)

5. Now **draw conclusions** about Marven. What kind of person was he? What details support this conclusion? (Drawing Conclusions)

Test Prep
Look Back and Write

Look back at pages 290–291. Why do you think the author chose to include French words in this story? Use examples from the story to support your answer.

Test Prep

How to Read a Math Textbook

1. Preview

- This math lesson helps you learn how to do specific tasks. It provides directions and practice activities.

- Read the headings and the information in the first box.

2. Read and Find Important Information

- As you read, take notes about important information that is needed to teach someone how to count money.

- Notice other interesting information.

3. Think and Connect

Think about "Marven and the Great North Woods." Then look over your notes on "Counting Money."

If Marven had to train someone to do his job as a bookkeeper, could he use this lesson to help teach the person? Use details to support your answer.

You Will Learn
how to count and compare money

Vocabulary
decimal point a symbol (.) that separates dollar and cent amounts

Did You Know?
The average life of a $1 bill is 18 months, and that of a $10 bill is 3 years.

Learn

Philomena Okigbo sells clothing, arts, and crafts from Africa.

Suppose you have some bills and coins. Do you have enough money to buy this cowrie necklace?

Example

You can count dollar and coin amounts to compare money.

$8.75

Step I

Count the dollars.
You count: 5, 6, 7, 8 dollars.

Philomena Okigbo came from Nigeria, in western Africa. Now she works in Ithaca, New York.

Step 2

Count the coin amounts.

You count: 25, 50, 75 . . .   85, 90, 91, 92 cents.

You have: $8.92.
You need: $8.75.

Compare $8.92 and $8.75. Find the first place the digits are different.

90 cents > 70 cents. So, $8.92 > $8.75.

You have enough money to buy the necklace.

Talk About It

How is comparing money different from comparing whole numbers?

Check

Count the money. Write each amount with dollar sign and decimal point.

1. 3 dollars, 2 quarters, 3 pennies

2. one $20.00 bill, 2 $10.00 bills, 4 dimes, 1 nickel

Compare. Write >, <, or =.

3. $25.94 ● $25.49   **4.** $94.06 ● $94.01   **5.** $0.38 ● $1.37   **6.** $42.40 ● $4.24

7. Reasoning How could you make $37.95 with the fewest bills and coins?

Practice

Problem Solving and Applications

8. What is the greatest number of five-dollar bills you would need to buy the medium wall art?

9. Suppose you have 1 twenty-dollar bill, 1 ten-dollar bill, 2 five-dollar bills, 10 quarters, and 7 dimes. What is the largest wall art you could buy? Write the amount you have.

Wall Art from Africa	
Small	$40.00
Medium	$45.00
Large	$50.00

Generalizing

- A **generalization** is a broad statement or rule that applies to many examples.

- Often clue words, such as *all, most, many, some, sometimes, usually, seldom, few,* or *generally,* signal generalizations.

- When you read, you are sometimes given ideas about several things or people. You can generalize, or make a statement about all or most of them together.

- A **valid generalization** is supported by facts and your own knowledge. A **faulty generalization** is not.

Read "Salmon for All" from *Salmon Summer* by Bruce McMillan.

Write About It

1. Copy the sentence from the last paragraph that makes a generalization. Underline the clue word.

2. Is the generalization valid or faulty? Explain.

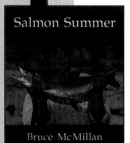

Salmon Summer

Bruce McMillan

Salmon for All

by Bruce McMillan

Alex cleans salmon alongside his father as seagulls watch from afar. He uses the same knife his grandmother's uncle used to skin bears. He cuts filets from one of the fish for dinner. With the others, he cuts off the head, pulls out the guts, and leaves the skin and tails on. They're for the smokehouse. But as the cleaned fish hang outside, uninvited visitors fly in to steal a meal.

Magpies sneak in for a bite when nobody's watching. They're not the only hungry birds. Alex leaves salmon scraps to wash away with the tide and be eaten by scavengers. The gulls swoop down for a fish feast. As always, they eat their favorite part of the salmon first—the eyes.

At dusk another animal arrives to take home more of Alex's scraps. A fox slinks by to pick up a meal. She takes

it back to her pups in their den near Alex's cabin.

Farther up the bay, at Dog Salmon Creek, a Kodiak bear grabs a king salmon to feed her two cubs. Later, when Alex goes by, the bears are gone. But he knows they were here. He follows claw tracks in the sand and discovers the remains of their meal.

There's an abundance of salmon for all. There's salmon for the eagles to catch. There's more salmon for Alex to catch and give to the people in town who are too old to fish.

LOOK AHEAD

In *On the Pampas*, María Cristina Brusca tells about a childhood summer that she spent at her grandparents' ranch on the pampas of Argentina. What generalizations can you make about life on a ranch?

Vocabulary

Words to Know

brand	corral	manes
bridles	herd	reins
calves	initials	

Words that are pronounced the same but spelled differently, such as *reins* and *rains*, are called **homophones.** Homophones also have different meanings. To understand the difference between homophones, look for clues in the surrounding words and sentences.

Read the paragraph below paying special attention to its meaning as a whole. Why is *reins* used, and not *rains?*

Adventure at the Ranch

I entered the horses' <u>corral</u> and chose Champ— he had one of the most beautiful <u>manes</u> of hair on his neck. I took one of the <u>bridles</u> and put it over Champ's head. I hopped on his back and grabbed the <u>reins</u>. Then I rode through a <u>herd</u> of cattle to rope young <u>calves</u> so I could help <u>brand</u> them with their owners' <u>initials</u>.

Write About It

You're visiting a ranch. Use vocabulary words in a postcard that you're sending home.

ON THE PAMPAS

by María Cristina Brusca

These pages will help you read and understand the meanings of Spanish words in the story *On the Pampas*.

GAUCHO CLOTHES

Gaucho *(GOU-choh)*
A cowboy on the southern plains, or pampas, of South America.

Boleadoras *(boh-lay-ah-DOOR-ahs)*
Gauchos used to catch ñandús and other animals with boleadoras, which they threw in such a way that the animals' legs were tangled up in them.

Bombacha *(bome-BAH-cha)*
Loose gaucho pants.

Rastra *(RAH-stra)*
A gaucho belt made from a wide strip of leather decorated with silver coins, usually from different countries. Some gauchos have their initials on the buckle.

Estancia *(eh-STAHN-see-ah)*
A South American cattle ranch.

Las Pampas *(las POM-pas)*
The pampas are the very flat, almost treeless grasslands that stretch for hundreds of miles through central Argentina and Uruguay. Ranch animals live on the pampas year round, even during the mild winter months, eating grass.

Asado (ah-SAH-doh)
Meat, usually beef, roasted outdoors over a fire.

La Carlota's Brand (la car-LOH-ta)
The brand represented two crossed fencing swords, but we called it "the scissors."

Hornero (or-NAIR-oh)
The hornero is a kind of oven bird. Its nest looks something like an oven and is built out of clay, usually on top of a post or pole.

Recado (ray-KAH-doh)
The gaucho saddle, made of many layers of leather and wool, with a sheepskin on the top.

Ñandú (nyon-DOO)
The ñandú, or South American ostrich, is the largest bird in the Americas. It grows to be five feet tall and to weigh about fifty pounds. Although it cannot fly, it can run very fast. The male ñandú guards the nest, hatches the eggs, and takes care of the chicks.

Mate (MAH-tay)
Mate is a bitter, greenish tea. It is sipped through a silver straw called a bombilla (bome-BEE-yah) from a hollow gourd that is passed around.

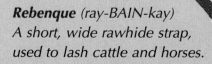

Rebenque (ray-BAIN-kay)
A short, wide rawhide strap, used to lash cattle and horses.

Yegua Madrina (YAY-goo-ah mah-DREE-na)
The yegua madrina, or leading mare of a herd of horses, keeps the herd together. She generally has a bell around her neck.

I grew up in Argentina, in South America. I lived with my family in the big city of Buenos Aires, but we spent our summers in the country, at my grandparents' *estancia*. One summer my parents and brother stayed in the city, so I went without them.

My grandmother met me at the station in Buenos Aires, and we had breakfast as we rode through miles and miles of the flattest land in the world—the *pampas*. All around us, as far as we could see, were fences, windmills, and millions of cattle grazing.

Our station, San Enrique, was at the end of the line, where the train tracks stopped. My grandfather was there to meet us in his pickup truck and take us the five miles to the estancia.

The ranch was called La Carlota, and the gates were made of iron bars from a fort that had been on that very spot a hundred years before. As we drove up to the gates, we were greeted by a

cloud of dust and a thundering of hooves—it was my cousin Susanita, on her horse.

Susanita lived at the estancia all year round. She knew everything about horses, cows, and all the other animals that live on the pampas. Even though she was three years younger than me, she had her own horse, La Baya. Susanita was so tiny, she had to shinny up La Baya's leg to get on her back. But she rode so well that the *gauchos* called her La Gauchita—"The Little Gaucho."

I didn't have a horse of my own, but old Salguero, the ranch foreman, brought me Pampita, a sweet-tempered mare, to ride. She wasn't very fast, but she certainly was my friend.

Susanita and I did everything together that summer. She was the one who showed me how to take care of the horses. We would brush their coats, trim their hooves, and braid their manes and tails.

Susanita was always ready for an adventure, no matter how scary. She used to swim in the creek holding on to La Baya's mane. At first I was afraid to follow her, but when she finally convinced me, it was a lot of fun.

I wanted to learn all the things a gaucho has to know. I wanted to ride out on the pampas every day, as Salguero did, and to wear a belt like his, with silver coins from all over the world and a buckle with my initials on it. Salguero said I'd have to begin at the beginning, and he spent hours showing Susanita and me how to use the lasso.

It was going to take a while for me to become a gaucho. The first time I lassoed a calf, it dragged me halfway across the

corral. But Salguero told me that even he had been dragged plenty of times, so I kept trying, until I got pretty good at it.

Whenever the gauchos were working with the cattle, Susanita was there, and before long I was too. Sometimes the herd had to be rounded up and moved from one pasture to another. I loved galloping behind hundreds of cattle, yelling to make them run. I never got to yell like that in the city!

One day we separated the calves from the cows, to vaccinate them and brand them with "the scissors," La Carlota's mark. That was more difficult—and more exciting too. I tried to do what Salguero told me to, but sometimes I got lost in the middle of that sea of cattle.

At noon, everybody would sit down around one big table and eat together. I was always hungry. Grandma, Susanita's mother, and María the cook had been working hard all morning too. They would make soup, salad, and lamb stew or pot roast, or my favorite, *carbonada,* a thick stew made of corn and peaches.

After lunch the grown-ups took a *siesta,* but not us. We liked to stay outdoors. Some afternoons, when it was too hot to do anything else, we rode out to a eucalyptus grove that was nice and cool, and stayed there until it got dark, reading comic books or cowboy stories.

Other times we would gallop for two hours to the general store and buy ourselves an orange soda. Then, while we drank it, we'd look at all the saddles and bridles we planned to have

when we were grown up and rich. Sometimes the storekeeper would take down a wonderful gaucho belt like Salguero's, and we would admire the silver coins and wonder where each one came from.

One day we rode far away from the house, to a field where Susanita thought we might find *ñandú* eggs. They are so huge, you can bake a whole cake with just one of them. After riding around all afternoon, we found a nest, well hidden in the tall grass, with about twenty pale-yellow eggs as big as coconuts.

Salguero had warned us to watch out for the ñandú, and he was right! The father ñandú, who protects the nest, saw us taking an egg. He was furious and chased us out of the field.

The next day we used the ñandú egg to bake a birthday cake for my grandmother. We snuck into the kitchen while she was taking her siesta, so it would be a surprise. The cake had three layers, and in between them we put whipped cream and peaches from the trees on the ranch.

We had a wonderful party for my grandmother's birthday. The gauchos started the fire for the *asado* early in the evening, and soon the smell of the slowly cooking meat filled the air.

There was music, and dancing too. We stayed up almost all night, and I learned to dance the *zamba*, taking little steps and hops, and twirling my handkerchief.

Most evenings were much quieter. There was just the hum of the generator that made electricity for the house. We liked to go out to the *mate* house, where the gauchos spent their evenings.

We listened to them tell ghost stories and tall tales while they sat around the fire, passing the gourd and sipping mate through the silver straw. We didn't like the hot, bitter tea, but we loved being frightened by their spooky stories.

The summer was drawing to a close, and soon I would be returning to Buenos Aires. The night before I was to leave, Salguero showed me how to find the Southern Cross. The generator had been turned off, and there was only the soft sound of the peepers. We could see the horses sleeping far off in the field.

The next morning, my last at the estancia, Susanita and I got up before dawn. Pampita and the other horses were still out in the field. Salguero handed me his own horse's reins. He told me he thought I was ready to bring in the horses by myself. I wasn't sure I could do it, but Susanita encouraged me to try.

I remembered what I'd seen Salguero do. I tried to get the leading mare, with her bell, to go toward the corral, and the others would follow her. It wasn't easy. The foals were frisky and kept running away. But I stayed behind them until finally the little herd was all together, trotting in front of me.

I was so busy trying to keep the foals from running off that I didn't notice the whole household waiting in the corral with Salguero. Everyone cheered as I rode in, and before I knew it, my grandfather was helping me off the horse. "You've become quite a gaucho this summer," he said. My grandmother held out a wonderful gaucho belt like Salguero's, with silver coins from around the world—and my initials on the buckle!

"And," she added, "there's something else every gaucho needs. Next summer, when you come back, you'll have your

very own horse waiting for you!" She pointed to the leading mare's foal, the friskiest and most beautiful of them all.

Before I could say a word, the foal pranced over to me, tossing his head. I would have the whole winter to decide what to name him, and to look forward to my next summer on the pampas.

About the Author/Illustrator
MARÍA CRISTINA BRUSCA

On the Pampas is a true story about María Cristina Brusca's childhood in Argentina. The summers spent at her grandparents' ranch meant so much to her that she dedicated the story to her grandparents and to her cousin, Susanita.

When she was older, Ms. Brusca moved to New York. Later she wrote and illustrated another book about her childhood, titled *My Mama's Little Ranch on the Pampas*. With her friend, Tona Wilson, Ms. Brusca has written two books of South American folk tales.

Reader Response

Open for Discussion

Pretend you have been asked to spend next summer at an *estancia* on the pampas. What will you plan to do there?

Comprehension Check

1. What kinds of work does a gaucho do? Give examples.

2. How did the author and Susanita spend their time after the work was done? Give details.

3. Did the author write *On the Pampas* to inform, to entertain, or to persuade? Explain your answer with examples from the selection.

4. Sometimes clue words show that an author is making a **generalization.** Read the following sentences from the story. Which one is a generalization? How do you know? (Generalizing)

   a. I grew up in Argentina, in South America.
   b. Most evenings were much quieter.
   c. The foals were frisky and kept running away.

5. Now make a **generalization.** Tell why this selection belongs in a unit called "Keys to Success." (Generalizing)

Test Prep
Look Back and Write

Look back at pages 311–313. The narrator and her cousin, Susanita, share adventures at the *estancia*. How are the two girls alike? How are they different? Use details from the story to support your answer.

A Closer Look at Argentina

by Michael Burgan

South America

The People

More than 35 million people live in
Argentina. Its citizens are called
Argentines. Nine out of ten Argentines
live in cities or large towns. The biggest
city is Buenos Aires, the country's capital.
More than 12 million people live in or
near this modern city.

The Regions

The people of Argentina live and work in
three major regions. In the north is the
Gran Chaco, a mixture of grassy plains
and pine forests. The fertile, flat lands of
the Pampa make up the central region of
Argentina. Most Argentines make the
Pampa their home. The largest and
southernmost region of Argentina is
Patagonia. It is a dry and windy plateau,
with rocky cliffs and canyons.

Farming and Ranching in Argentina

The most important part of the Argentine economy is farming. Farmers grow wheat, corn, and other grains on the rich soil of the Pampas.

They export (sell to other countries) most of these crops. Argentina is one of the world's leaders in growing wheat. The country also has vast fruit orchards and vineyards.

Some of Argentina's plentiful grain is used to feed cattle and sheep raised on large ranches. The ranchers own more than fifty million cattle. The beef from these cattle is another major export. Many Argentine factories make food products that are sold around the world.

Cattle in the U.S.

If you think of the western part of the U.S. when you hear the word *cattle*, you're right to think so. But thousands of people all over the U.S. earn their income by raising cattle for beef and dairy products. In fact, raising cattle for beef is the main source of farm income in the U.S. This graph shows some states in the U.S. where cattle are raised for beef.

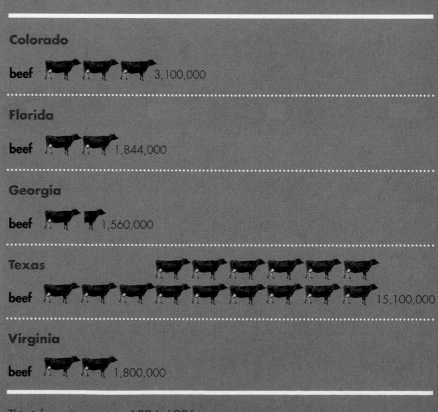

Colorado

beef 3,100,000

Florida

beef 1,844,000

Georgia

beef 1,560,000

Texas

beef 15,100,000

Virginia

beef 1,800,000

This information covers 1994–1996.

323

Predicting

- To **predict** means to tell what you think might happen next in a story or article based on what has already happened. Your prediction is what you say will happen next.

- When you make predictions, you also use your personal knowledge about a topic to help you.

- Predicting is a process of checking and changing your predictions as you read, based on new information.

Read "Summer Surfers" from *Seal Surfer* by Michael Foreman.

Talk About It

1. What information in the title helped you predict where the story would take place and who the main characters might be?

2. What details did you use to predict what would happen to Ben? What personal knowledge did you use to help you make your prediction?

Summer Surfers

by Michael Foreman

The next day the tide was perfect and the young seal was back. Again Ben and the seal surfed side by side.

Ben could not take his eyes off the seal as she flashed through the water. As he concentrated on watching her, the wave he was riding suddenly broke and plunged him headfirst off his board. He somersaulted through the surf and struck a rock. The water, thick with sand, filled his nose and mouth. His body was pulled deeper and deeper. He was sinking into darkness.

> **Predict what will happen to Ben.**

Then he felt a different sensation. His body was forced upward. Sunlight shone through the water onto Ben's face as the seal pushed his body up. With a final heave she flipped Ben onto his board. He held on, and the next wave carried him to shore. His friends crowded around to make sure he was all right. Once he caught his breath, Ben felt fine.

The next afternoon, and for the rest of the long, hot summer, Ben surfed with the seal.

LOOK AHEAD

Next you'll read *The Storm*, about a boy named Jonathan. Predict what might happen to him when a tornado touches down on his family's farm.

Words to Know

accident	nuzzled	tornado
coaxed	soothing	wail

Words with opposite meanings are called **antonyms.** You can often figure out the meaning of an unknown word by finding a clue in the words around it. Sometimes this clue is an antonym.

Read the paragraph below. Notice how *exciting* helps you understand what *soothing* means.

In the Path of the Twister

The <u>wail</u> of the wind was a signal Justin knew— a <u>tornado</u> might be on its way. Justin remembered that some of the animals were in the fields. He wanted to avoid an <u>accident</u> where they might be hurt in the storm, so he decided to bring them in for protection. First, Justin <u>coaxed</u> the horses into the barn. Then, instead of an exciting song, he sang them a <u>soothing</u> one to calm them. As the tornado passed south of the farm, Justin's favorite horse <u>nuzzled</u> him with his nose to say "Thank you."

Talk About It

Imagine you are Justin. Tell a friend what happened. Use as many vocabulary words as you can.

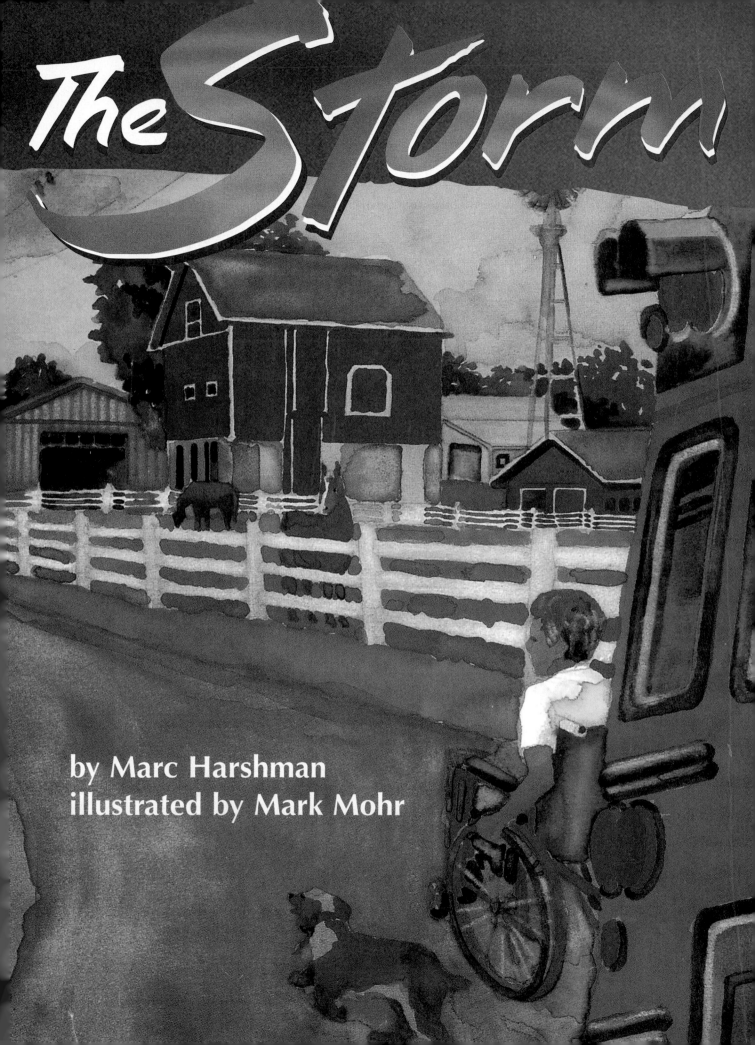

The Storm

by Marc Harshman
illustrated by Mark Mohr

School had gone just fine until then. Just an everyday class. And just like the beginning of every tornado season, the teacher began going over the usual information about the safety drill and then the storms themselves. After she explained the map of school exits, she showed a few slides of real tornadoes. Next she described what to do if caught outside in one.

It was then Roger had piped up.

"It must be real scary for Jonathan!"

"Jonathan stuck in his wheelchair is what he means," Jonathan muttered to himself.

This was what he hated. Just this. Being singled out. Different. And of all things, a storm. There were things he was scared of, but storms weren't one of them. He loved storms. He loved those evenings when he and Dad would watch a thunderstorm, and its spidering lightning, boom and flash the darkness into daylight.

What he was scared of was much more common and everyday. Cars. Traffic. The squealing of tires on pavement. He could still see, as if in a freeze-frame, the red truck the second before it blindsided him as he crossed US 40 under the flashing red light. And he was scared of moments like these, around others, when he realized everyone was thinking about him, or not really him, but his "condition"—his legs, his inability to use them, his wheelchair. He hated these moments when he felt everyone looking at him. He dreaded this as much as the flashbacks because this happened more often.

The rest of the class went on about funnel clouds and the conditions that caused them, how their ground speeds could reach sixty, and the winds inside them over two hundred miles per hour. Jonathan knew all this and he daydreamed while the class went over what he had heard before. He even yawned.

Jonathan didn't know it but people were yawning everywhere that day. And George Richardson's bunions were hurting him "something awful." Meg Thomas complained there wasn't a "breath of wind" to dry her washing. Cattle had lain down at midday at Whitesel's. "Storm's comin'." "Gonna rain." "Bad weather."

"What I really hate is this heat!" Jonathan complained to no one in particular as he wheeled himself away from the bus and down the long drive to the house. "Everything sticks to me in this chair." He was happy, though, to see his mom on the porch, knowing that she now understood about not meeting him at the bus.

"Jonathan, this car's giving me fits again. Dale said he'd take a look at it if I brought it in right away. I should be back in plenty of time, but supper is made if I'm not. Just put it in the oven. Your dad's still at Reynold's working on that roof. I've got the cows in the barn and the chickens fed. Storm's comin', Martha told me, and she's never wrong. Oh, and if I run late, could you get the horses?"

"Sure, Mom," he smiled. "Don't worry, I'll take care of them."

Ducking into the car, she yelled, "Thanks!" and drove off.

Ever since the accident, Jonathan had done everything he could, and his therapists as well, to make the rest of his body as strong as possible. Mom and Dad had helped a lot, too—making changes in the house, adding ramps outside, putting rope handles on the barn doors low enough to reach. They had even adjusted the horse

halters so it was easier for him to snap on a lead rope. It all helped.

Since he was already out, he decided to go ahead and whistle the horses into the lot. It wasn't easy but a short while later he was rolling himself back out of the root cellar toward the horse trough, carrots laid carefully across his lap.

As usual, Buster was first. Buster was his, the one he had hand-fed since a colt. Buster nickered and then nuzzled at his hand so hard he nearly spilled the carrots. "You want sugar, I know, but it's staying in my pockets for now."

Back in the barn he turned on Dad's milking radio:

"A line of thunderstorms approaching east-central Indiana could have severe hail and lightning and a tornado watch has been issued for Wayne, Randolph, Jay, and Delaware counties."

He'd heard this before. A "watch" meant there was a chance, nothing more—it seemed there were dozens every spring. Only the warnings got his attention. This did mean, though, that there was a good chance of a storm and Jonathan liked any kind of storm.

He put his hands to the rubber rims and pushed himself out the west doors. There were ripples in the grass and the skies had clouded. It was peaceful. Since his accident he felt more alert somehow. He liked watching those ripples in the grass, the tumbling of the clouds overhead, the way the fluffy tops of the sycamores by the creek bent and tossed in the rising wind.

But. That rising wind. He wasn't sure he liked the low wail that began moving through the farmyard, nor the green-yellow tint of the sky. They were signs the old-timers said meant "twister."

"Better get busy and see to closing things up," he told himself. "Who knows?"

The radio was still running the same advisory: "wind . . . hail . . . tornado watch . . ."

He called to the horses, reached up from his chair and undid the latch, backing away as the gate swung open. Buster nuzzled his ear as he wheeled along beside them into the barn. Once inside he gave them each a scoop of oats. Usually he liked to linger here, thinking and talking, but as he felt the barn creak and moan under the wind, he turned himself back out to take another look.

He could hear now a continuous rumble of thunder and to the southwest the sky had turned a deep, deep blue. Here and there it was fractured by lightning. For a moment the wind stopped. The cackling of the hens, the snorting of the hogs, the chittering of the birds—all went silent. Then a sharp whistling rose up from somewhere. There was a worried nicker from Henry.

Jonathan looked again at the sky. And there he saw it, saw the strange, black thumb press itself down out of the bulging mass of clouds and stretch into a narrow tongue just licking over the surface of the ground.

Tornado!

It was so incredible that for a moment he simply stared. From the rise of the farmyard he watched the snakelike funnel slowly twist across the distant fields and broaden into a larger blackness. Before his eyes it became a black wall headed straight for the farm. Fear replaced amazement. He hurried back across the lot. The wind was shrieking now. But before he could get to the house, he heard horses.

Looking back, there were Buster and Henry tearing madly around the inner lot. How could they have gotten out? He didn't know. And not just Buster, but Henry, pride and joy of his father. Jonathan couldn't think if he had time or not, if it was safe or not.

He raced toward them, his arms aching with the effort. His hands burned against the friction of the rubber wheels. He didn't think he could push any harder, but the horses had to be saved. He had to save them for Dad.

First he had to get Buster calmed. If he could get him calmed, Henry would follow. He held out his sugar cubes. After circling and snorting around him, Buster came, and with Jonathan's hand on his neck, allowed himself to be calmed enough so that Jonathan could snap on a lead rope. He then did the same with Henry. On their leads they followed him back.

Inside, one stall was shattered from where Henry must have panicked and kicked. It must have been easy for Buster to force his latch and so race to join Henry.

To keep them safe from panic now Jonathan would have to stay, too, inside the barn and not below ground in the safety of the cellar. He'd glanced back as he got inside and the wall of the tornado seemed to be standing just outside the lot. It was a thing of sound now as much as of color, so loud that even though the horses' mouths were working, he could not hear them. Their frantic fidgeting took all his strength as he tried to control them by touch, by voice, by will.

He finally coaxed them into an old stall. It wouldn't be any stronger than the shattered one, but he knew nothing would be strong enough now, except him, his soothing them, his hands on them, the scent of sugar on his palms. This would be all that would keep them from bolting again.

The barn shook. Like a freight train the twister kept coming. The screaming wail of it was inside as well as outside, was inside him. And though he was drenched in sweat, he was freezing with goose bumps too. Each second he expected to be his last.

Shading his eyes from the swirling chaff, he tried to squint through the slats of the siding to see. But it was darker than night,

the electric gone now. There was just himself and the animals and the pounding of the storm, so deep, so strong, it felt as if the earth itself was shaking. The dried chaff and straw choked him and he gave up trying to keep his eyes open.

Cra-aaack! Whuumph! Suddenly hay swooshed down all over them. Keeping hold of both leads in one hand, Jonathan tried to move his chair out from under the beam that seemed to hang just over them. Finally he got to where he could see it resting on the crossbars above the stall. It could have killed them.

To work their way out he had to pull the hay loose from his wheelchair and then tug on the leads, tug and coax. It was then that he realized the thumping had stopped, and the wind had lessened and been joined by the pleasanter sound of rain. "We're saved," he shouted to Buster and Henry. "We're saved!"

All along the south side of the barn was a mess of hay and straw, small boards, and other litter. The rain had settled to an easy shower and the sounds from the cattle sounded normal enough so he tied Buster and Henry to a post and wheeled himself outside.

What he saw took his breath away. The house had grown leaves, buried in the branches of the giant oak that had stood beside it. The barn's entire north side had collapsed. The haywagon, milking cans, feed buckets, Mom's bicycle, bird feeder, fences, clothesline had all changed places, gotten mixed up, twisted.

But it was when he looked beyond the house that his blood froze. Everything there was gone. Their hay barn, corncribs, hayrake, outbuildings, orchard, and— "ohh," Jonathan sucked in his breath, even the woods, the two-acre wood—it looked as if someone had gone through it with a scythe. He shook his head in disbelief. It was like something off the evening news.

Incredibly the only thing left was a neatly stacked, four-foot pile of corn with hardly a splinter of wood to show that there had been a crib around it. A few chickens were already gathering

around to claim their unlikely feast. He didn't notice that the rooster was not in his usual place at the head of his flock. The more he looked, the stranger it all seemed.

There was a feed bucket sitting on the slope of the house roof, perfectly, as if someone had set it there on purpose. Up in the elm that had remained standing, he could see one of the wheels from the haywagon, but no sign of the wagon itself. And sticking straight out from the front door of the house was a white slat from the picket fence driven straight in.

Finally, he turned back to the barn to check more carefully the other animals. Though he'd gone right past it, he hadn't seen the rooster lying on the ground like a dirty, crumpled rag. But when he picked it up and held the wet, limp body in his hands, he began to cry. He cried hard, and it wasn't like the crying we do when we're sad for someone we love. The rooster wasn't a pet. If anything, he was a bad-tempered, noisy, dumb bird. What mattered was that it was dead.

Jonathan knew then, at that moment, just how small he had been underneath the terrific power of the storm.

He laid the rooster down finally and started to see what he could do to really make sure the other animals were okay. Now that he had time to think more slowly, he also began to worry. Who could tell what else this storm had done? Mom and Dad— were they all right?

He heard them before he saw them—the honking of the horn and the rattling of Dad's truck through the soybeans. It was absolutely crazy. But everything this day had been crazy.

"Thank heavens you're all right," his mom said, climbing out and running to him and hugging him.

His dad was dead quiet for a long moment as he looked slowly around, but then he said, "Have a little bit of a storm here, Son?" and put his hand on Jonathan's shoulder. As Jonathan told them his story, he could see it all again, the blackness, the roaring of the wind, the funnel cloud, the cries of the animals, how he had to bring the horses in and stay, the battering of the barn itself. They listened. They didn't scold or baby him. He felt better than he had for a long time. He knew he had done a thing he could feel good about.

He wouldn't care so much now when people looked at him. He knew they would. They would still see his "condition," but when they knew this story they might begin to see a lot more. They might just see him. Jonathan.

Marc Harshman

About the Author

Marc Harshman loves language. Not only has he written seven picture books, but he is also a professional storyteller and a poet. One of his favorite activities is talking with young people about stories and writing. "I enjoy seeing them discover that writers are real people who use the same language that they do."

Mr. Harshman grew up in Indiana, where *The Storm* takes place. He has lived his adult life in West Virginia. Many of his tales reflect the influence of both of these regions.

Mark Mohr

About the Illustrator

Although *The Storm* is the first book that Mark Mohr has illustrated, he has always enjoyed drawing. When asked what one thing he would share with students about being an artist, he said it is that art gives him a way to express himself.

Mr. Mohr lost his younger brother, Nick, in a car accident just before he was asked to illustrate *The Storm*. He dedicated the book to Nick because he could not think of a better way to honor his brother's memory.

Reader Response

Open for Discussion

This is an exciting story because of the drama of the storm. Do you think the story also has a message? Explain.

Comprehension Check

1. Compare Jonathan's reactions with his classmates' reactions during the lesson about tornadoes. Give examples.

2. Is Jonathan brave or foolish to go out into the storm when he could be safe in the cellar? Support your answer with story details.

3. Describe the storm and its effects. Use examples.

4. How do the title and illustration on page 327 and the beginning of the story on page 328 help you make a **prediction** about what will happen? (Predicting)

5. Make a **prediction** about Jonathan. How will he be different in the future because of his experience in the storm? (Predicting)

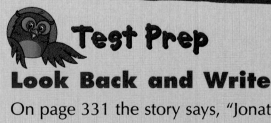

Test Prep
Look Back and Write

On page 331 the story says, "Jonathan liked any kind of storm." Look back at the whole story. As the storm comes, do you think he changes his mind? Use examples from the story to support your answer.

Tornado Tales

from *Weather Explained* by Derek Elsom

The power of a tornado can produce some strange effects. Stalks of straw have been driven into a telegraph pole, planks of wood shot through a barn door, and a playing card embedded on its edge more than an inch into a wooden door. Bark has been stripped from trees and feathers plucked from chickens. The amount of feathers lost by chickens was once suggested as a way of estimating the strength of a tornado's winds.

Trains have been lifted, turned around, and dropped onto the track facing the other way. Heavy refrigerators have been carried hundreds of yards while lighter objects have been carried for tens of miles.

Freak Falls

A tornado passing over a pond or river can suck up the contents like a huge vacuum cleaner. Hundreds of small frogs, toads, tadpoles, fish, and weeds may be carried along for many miles until the tornado weakens and

A waterspout can suck up objects from the sea or beach and carry them long distances before dropping them inland.

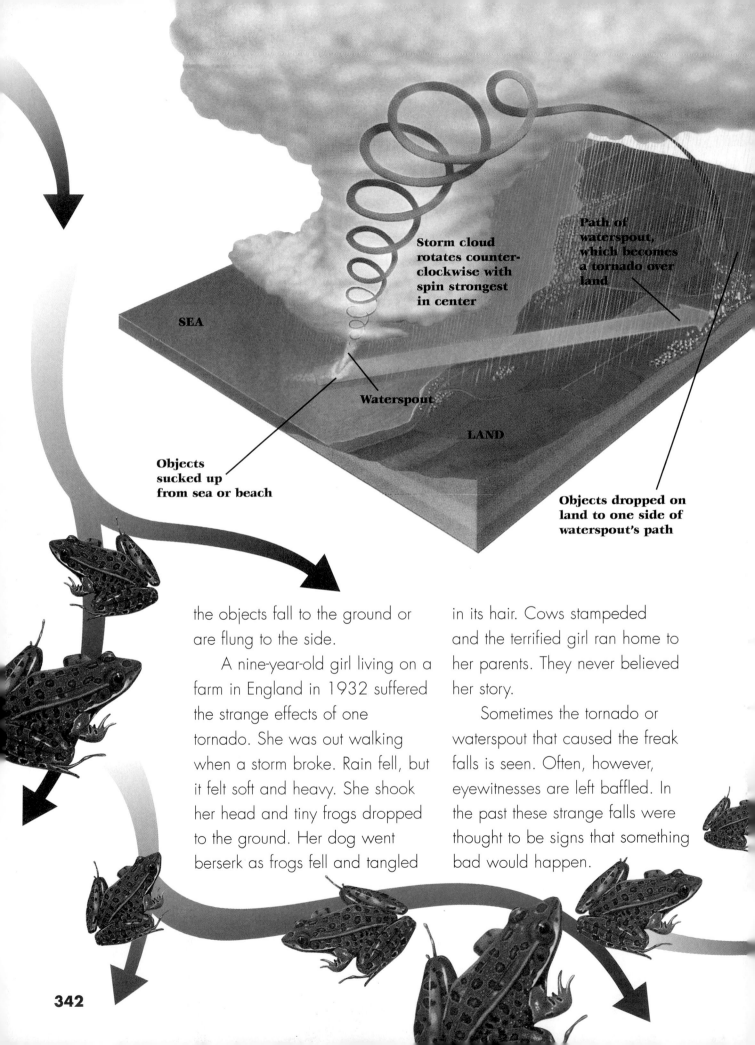

Storm cloud rotates counter-clockwise with spin strongest in center

Path of waterspout, which becomes a tornado over land

SEA

Waterspout

LAND

Objects sucked up from sea or beach

Objects dropped on land to one side of waterspout's path

the objects fall to the ground or are flung to the side.

A nine-year-old girl living on a farm in England in 1932 suffered the strange effects of one tornado. She was out walking when a storm broke. Rain fell, but it felt soft and heavy. She shook her head and tiny frogs dropped to the ground. Her dog went berserk as frogs fell and tangled

in its hair. Cows stampeded and the terrified girl ran home to her parents. They never believed her story.

Sometimes the tornado or waterspout that caused the freak falls is seen. Often, however, eyewitnesses are left baffled. In the past these strange falls were thought to be signs that something bad would happen.

In the Path of a Tornado

Being caught in a tornado can be very scary but most people survive, especially if they take shelter.

In 1995, a baby boy was plucked from his cot and carried away from his destroyed home in Des Arc, Arkansas, by a tornado. He was found safe in a ditch half a mile away, muddy and with just a few scratches and bruises. In 1992, a young girl escaped unhurt after being carried almost two miles by a tornado near Shanghai, China. She was set down in a treetop.

Trying to flee from a tornado in a car is not a good idea. A tornado is too fast and the direction it travels in is too unpredictable for drivers to know where to go to avoid it. This was made clear when a tornado with 200 mph winds struck Wichita Falls, Texas, in 1979. As it approached the city, some people jumped into their cars and tried to flee the tornado by driving away from it. However, twenty-six out of the forty-three people killed and thirty out of the fifty-nine people with serious injuries were in cars. Most of the victims' homes were left undamaged by the tornado's powerful winds.

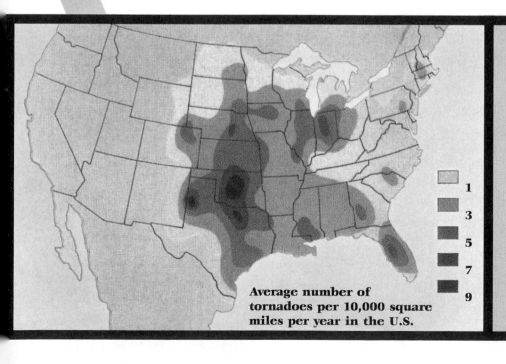

Average number of
tornadoes per 10,000 square
miles per year in the U.S.

| 1 |
| 3 |
| 5 |
| 7 |
| 9 |

Tornadoes occur so often in the Midwest that it is known as Tornado Alley. Typically there are 1,000 tornadoes in the United States each year. Tornadoes occur in other parts of the world, including the United Kingdom, which has 15–30 small tornadoes each year. In 1989, the world's worst tornado disaster killed 1,300 people in Bangladesh.

Drawing Conclusions

- As you read, look at the details and make decisions about the characters and what happens in the story or article.

- When you make decisions about the characters or events, you are **drawing conclusions.**

- Drawing conclusions is sometimes called making inferences.

Read "Another Death on the Ranch" from *The Original Adventures of Hank the Cowdog* **by John R. Erickson.**

Talk About It

1. Do you think that Hank the Cowdog is a good detective? What details lead to the conclusion you draw?

2. Based on these few paragraphs, would you conclude that *The Original Adventures of Hank the Cowdog* is a serious or a humorous book? Why?

Another Death on the Ranch

by John R. Erickson

In town I had been just another happy-go-lucky dog without a care in the world. But back on the ranch, I felt that same crushing sense of responsibility that's known to people in high places, such as presidents, prime ministers, emperors, and such. Being Head of Ranch Security is a great honor but also a dreadful burden.

I remembered the chickenhouse murder. I still didn't have any suspects, or I had too many suspects, maybe that was it. Everyone was a suspect, well, everyone but the milk cow, and I had pretty muchly scratched her off the list. And the porcupine, since they only eat trees.

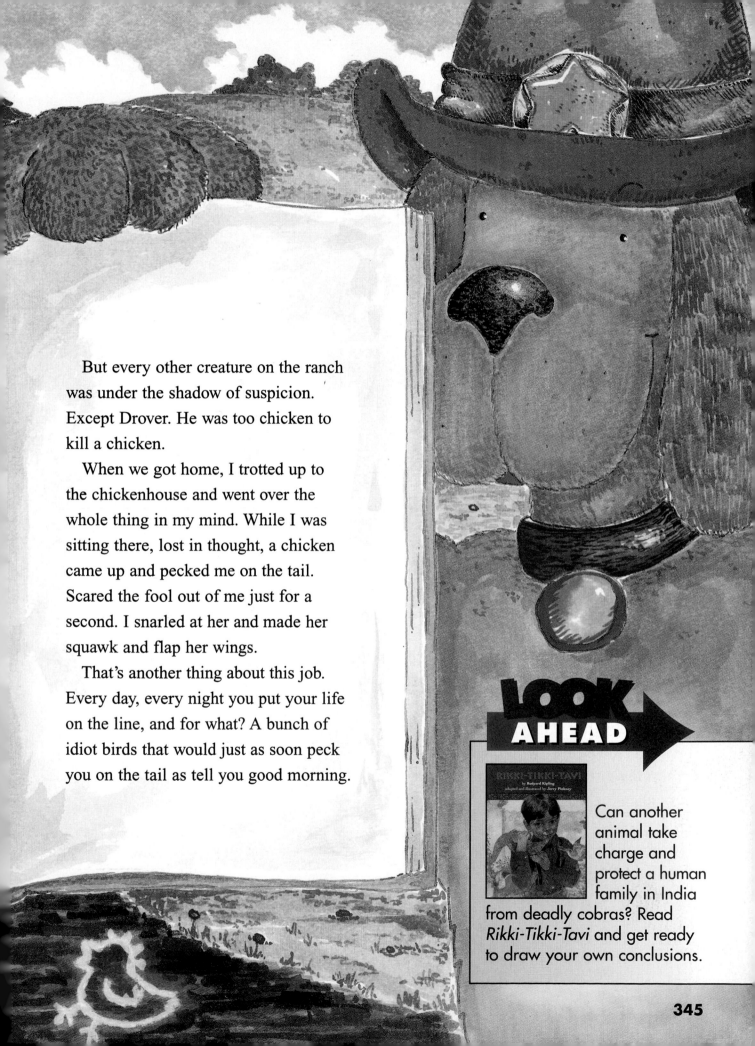

But every other creature on the ranch was under the shadow of suspicion. Except Drover. He was too chicken to kill a chicken.

When we got home, I trotted up to the chickenhouse and went over the whole thing in my mind. While I was sitting there, lost in thought, a chicken came up and pecked me on the tail. Scared the fool out of me just for a second. I snarled at her and made her squawk and flap her wings.

That's another thing about this job. Every day, every night you put your life on the line, and for what? A bunch of idiot birds that would just as soon peck you on the tail as tell you good morning.

LOOK AHEAD

RIKKI-TIKKI-TAVI
by Rudyard Kipling
adapted and illustrated by Jerry Pinkney

Can another animal take charge and protect a human family in India from deadly cobras? Read *Rikki-Tikki-Tavi* and get ready to draw your own conclusions.

Words to Know

cobra	plunged	lame
coiled	triumph	

When you read, you may come across a word you do not know. To figure out the meaning of the unfamiliar word, look for clues in the sentences or paragraph around it. A clue might be found in specific details or examples given near the unknown word.

Notice how *triumph* is used below. Find the specific details or examples near the word. What do you think *triumph* means?

Brave Dog!

Topper protected his family from the cobra, a poisonous snake coiled in a tight circle near the house. Topper thought it was asleep. He went to inspect, and the cobra lashed out and plunged its fangs into Topper's leg. The strike would have made any other dog lame instantly, but Topper fought until he defeated the cobra. Winning the battle was a triumph. Now the family was safe, and they could get medical help for Topper.

Write About It

Write a newspaper story about Topper. Use some vocabulary words.

RIKKI-TIKKI-TAVI

by **Rudyard Kipling**
adapted and illustrated by **Jerry Pinkney**

Rikki-tikki-tavi is a young mongoose who is washed by a summer flood into the garden of an English family living in India. Mongooses are the natural enemies of snakes, and the family is happy to have Rikki-tikki as a protector for their young son, Teddy. As Rikki-tikki explores his new home, he meets Darzee and his wife, a family of tailorbirds in the garden. They warn him of Nag and Nagaina, husband and wife cobras, who also live in the garden. Rikki-tikki, with the help of Teddy's father, kills Karait, a small brown snake whose bite is as dangerous as a cobra's. By saving Teddy from Karait, Rikki-tikki gains the gratitude of the family and becomes their honored guest.

Teddy carried him to bed and insisted that Rikki-tikki sleep under his chin. But as soon as Teddy was asleep, he went for his nightly walk around the house, and in the dark he ran up against Chuchundra, the muskrat, creeping near the wall. Chuchundra is a scared little beast. He whimpers and cheeps all night, trying to make up his mind to run into the middle of the room, but he never gets there.

"Don't kill me," said Chuchundra. "Rikki-tikki, don't kill me."

"Do you think a snake killer kills muskrats?" asked Rikki-tikki scornfully.

"Those who kill snakes get killed by snakes," said Chuchundra. "And how am I to be sure Nag won't mistake me for you some dark night?"

"There's no danger," said Rikki-tikki. "Nag is in the garden, and you don't go there."

"My cousin, the rat, told me—," said Chuchundra, and then he stopped.

"Told you what?"

"Hush! Nag is everywhere, Rikki-tikki. Can't you *hear?*"

Rikki-tikki listened. The house was as still as still, but he could just catch a soft *scratch-scratch* sound—a noise as quiet as the footsteps of a fly on a windowpane—the dry scratch of a snake's scales on brick.

"That's Nag or Nagaina," he said, "and whoever it is, is crawling into the bathroom drain. Thank you, Chuchundra."

He crept to Teddy's bathroom, but there was nothing there, and then to Teddy's parents' bathroom. At the bottom of the plaster wall there was a brick pulled out to make a drain for the bathwater, and as Rikki-tikki listened, he heard Nag and Nagaina whispering together in the moonlight.

"When the house is emptied of people," said Nagaina, "*he* will go away, and then the garden will be ours again. Go in quietly, and remember that the big man who killed Karait is the first one to bite. Then come out, and we will hunt for Rikki-tikki."

"But are you sure we must kill the people?" asked Nag.

"Yes. When there were no people in the house, did we have a mongoose in the garden? As long as the house is empty, we are king and queen of the garden. Remember that as soon as our eggs hatch, our children will need room and quiet."

"I had not thought of that," said Nag. "I will go, but there's no need to hunt for Rikki-tikki. I will kill the man and woman, and the child if I can. Then the house will be empty, and Rikki-tikki will leave."

Rikki-tikki tingled all over with rage at this, and then Nag's head came through the drain, and his five feet of cold body followed it. Angry as he was, Rikki-tikki was very frightened when he saw the size of the cobra. Nag raised his head and looked into the bathroom, and Rikki could see his eyes glitter in the dark.

"When Karait was killed, the man had a stick," said the snake, "but when he comes to bathe in the morning, he won't have it. I'll wait here till he comes. Nagaina—do you hear me?—I'll wait here till daytime."

There was no answer, so Rikki-tikki knew Nagaina had gone away. Nag coiled himself down, coil by coil, around the bottom of the water jar that was used to fill the bath. Rikki-tikki stayed as still as death. After an hour he began to move, muscle by muscle, toward the jar. Nag was asleep, and Rikki-tikki looked at him, wondering how to attack. "If I don't break his back at the first jump," thought Rikki, "he can still fight. And if he fights—Oh, Rikki!"

"It must be the head," he decided finally. "And I must not let go."

Then he jumped. As he bit, Rikki braced his back against the water jar to hold down the snake's head. Then he was battered back and forth as a toy is shaken by a dog—back and forth, up and down, and around in circles—but he held on as the snake's body whipped across the floor and banged against the side of the bathtub. He closed his jaws tighter and tighter, for he was sure he would be banged to death, and, for the honor of his family, he wanted to be found with his teeth locked. He was dizzy, aching, and felt shaken to pieces when something went off like a thunderclap just behind him, and red fire singed his fur. Teddy's father had been wakened by the noise and had fired a shotgun into Nag.

Rikki-tikki held on with his eyes shut, for now he was sure he was dead, but the man picked him up and said, "It's the mongoose again. The little guy has saved *our* lives now."

When morning came, Rikki-tikki was very stiff but well pleased with himself. "Now I have Nagaina to deal with, and she will be worse than five Nags. And there's no knowing when the eggs will hatch. I must go see Darzee," he said.

Without waiting for breakfast, Rikki-tikki ran to the thornbush where Darzee was singing a song of triumph at the top of his voice. The news of Nag's death was all over the garden, because his body had been put on the garbage heap.

"Oh, you stupid tuft of feathers!" said Rikki-tikki. "Is this the time to sing?"

"Nag is dead, dead, dead!" sang Darzee. "The valiant Rikki-tikki caught him by the head and held tight. The big man brought the bang stick, and Nag broke in two pieces! He will never eat my babies again."

"You're safe enough in your nest there," said Rikki-tikki, "but it's war for me down here. Stop singing a minute, Darzee."

"For the great Rikki-tikki's sake, I will stop," said Darzee. "What is it, O killer of the terrible Nag?"

"Where is Nagaina?"

"On the garbage heap by the stables, mourning for Nag, great Rikki-tikki of the white teeth."

"Never mind my white teeth! Do you know where she keeps her eggs?"

"In the melon bed, on the end nearest the wall, where the sun strikes nearly all day. Rikki-tikki, you're not going to eat her eggs?"

"Not eat exactly, no. Darzee, can you fly off to the stables and pretend your wing is broken, and let Nagaina chase you back to this bush? I must get to the melon bed, and if I went there now, she'd see me."

Darzee knew that Nagaina's children were born in eggs like his own, so he didn't think it was fair to kill them. But his wife was a sensible bird, and she knew that a cobra's eggs meant young cobras later on. So she flew from the nest and left Darzee to keep the babies warm. She flew in front of Nagaina and cried out, "My wing is broken! The boy in the house threw a stone at me and broke it."

"Before night, the boy in the house will lie very still. Now what's the use of running away? I'm sure to catch you."

Nagaina lifted up her head and hissed, "You've picked a bad place to be lame in." And she moved toward the bird, slipping along over the dust.

"The boy broke it with a stone!" cried Darzee's wife.

"Well! It may please you to know that when you're dead, I will deal with him. Before night, the boy in the house will lie very still. Now what's the use of running away? I'm sure to catch you."

But Darzee's wife fluttered on, never leaving the ground, and Nagaina slithered faster.

Rikki-tikki heard them going up the path, and he raced for the end of the melon patch near the wall. There, very cleverly hidden, he found twenty-five small eggs.

"I was just in time," he thought, for he could see the baby cobras curled up inside the skin, and he knew that the minute they were hatched, they could each kill a man or a mongoose. He bit off the tops of the eggs as fast as he could, crushing the deadly young snakes. At last there were only three eggs left. Then he heard Darzee's wife screaming.

"Rikki-tikki! I led Nagaina toward the house, and she has gone onto the porch and—oh, come quickly!—she means killing!"

Rikki-tikki smashed two eggs and, with the third egg in his mouth, scuttled to the porch as fast as he could. Teddy and his mother and father were there at breakfast, but they were not eating anything. They were stone still, and their faces were pale. Nagaina was coiled up within easy striking distance of Teddy's bare leg, and she was swaying back and forth, singing a song of triumph.

"Son of the man who killed Nag," she hissed, "stay still. Keep very still, all three of you. If you move, I strike, and if you do not move, I strike. Oh, foolish people who killed my Nag!"

Teddy's eyes were fixed on his father, but all his father could do was whisper, "Sit still, Teddy. Don't move. Keep still."

Then Rikki-tikki came up and cried, "Turn around, Nagaina! Turn and fight!"

"All in good time," said she, without moving her eyes. "I'll deal with *you* later. Look at your friends, Rikki-tikki. They dare not move, and if you come a step nearer, I strike."

"Look at your eggs in the melon patch," said Rikki-tikki. "Go and look, Nagaina." The snake turned half around and saw the egg. "Give it to me!" she said.

Rikki-tikki held the egg. "What price for a snake's egg? For a young cobra? For the last—the very last—of the brood? The ants are eating all the others, down by the melon patch."

Nagaina spun around, forgetting everything for the sake of the one egg, and Rikki-tikki saw Teddy's father grab Teddy by the shoulder and drag him across the table with the teacups, out of reach of Nagaina.

"Yes, you'll never come back, because you'll be dead. Fight, snake!"

"Tricked! Tricked! Tricked! *Rikk-tck-tck!*" called Rikki-tikki. "The boy is safe, and it was I—I—I that caught Nag last night in the bathroom. He threw me back and forth, but he could not shake me off. He was dead before the man killed him. I did it. *Rikki-tikki-tck-tck!* Come, Nagaina. Come and fight me."

Nagaina saw she had lost her chance of killing Teddy, and the egg lay between Rikki-tikki's paws. "Give me the egg, Rikki-tikki, and I will go away and never come back," she said.

"Yes, you'll never come back, because you'll be dead. Fight, snake! The man has gone for his gun. Fight!"

Rikki-tikki was bounding all around Nagaina, keeping just out of her reach. Nagaina gathered herself together and struck out at him. Rikki-tikki jumped up and back. Again and again and again she struck, and each time her head hit with a whack on the matting of the porch. Then Rikki-tikki danced in a circle to get behind her, and Nagaina spun around to face him.

Rikki-tikki had forgotten the egg. It lay on the porch. Nagaina came nearer and nearer to it, till at last, while Rikki-tikki was taking a breath, she caught it in her mouth, turned to the steps, and flew down the path, with Rikki-tikki behind her.

Rikki-tikki knew he must catch her or all the trouble would begin again. She headed straight for the long grass by the thornbush, and as he was running, Rikki-tikki heard Darzee still singing his song of triumph. But Darzee's wife was smarter. She flew off her nest as Nagaina came along and flapped her wings at Nagaina's head. Nagaina only lowered her head and went on. But the instant's delay let Rikki-tikki catch up to her, and as she plunged into the hole where she and Nag used to live, his little white teeth were clenched on her tail.

Rikki-tikki went down with her, and very few mongooses—however wise and old they may be—care to follow a cobra into its hole. It was dark in the hole, and Rikki-tikki never knew when it might widen and give Nagaina room to turn and strike at him.

When the grass by the mouth of the hole stopped waving, Darzee said, "It is all over with Rikki-tikki! We must sing his death song, for Nagaina will surely kill him underground." So he sang a very mournful song that he had just made up, and right at the saddest part, the grass quivered again, and Rikki-tikki dragged himself out of the hole, leg by leg, licking his whiskers. Rikki-tikki shook some of the dust out of his fur and sneezed. "It's all over," he said. "The snake will never come out again." And the red ants that live between the grass stems heard him and began to troop down the hole to see if he had spoken the truth.

When Rikki got to the house, Teddy and Teddy's mother and Teddy's father came out and almost cried over him. And that night he ate everything that was given to him until he could eat no more. He went to bed on Teddy's shoulder, where Teddy's mother saw him when she looked in late at night.

"He saved our lives," she said to her husband. "Just think, he saved all our lives."

Rikki-tikki woke with a jump, for all mongooses are light sleepers. "Oh, it's you," said he. "What are you awake for? All the cobras are dead, and if they weren't, I'm here."

Rikki-tikki had a right to be proud of himself. And he kept the garden as a mongoose should keep it, with tooth and jump and spring and bite, till never a cobra dared show its head inside the walls.

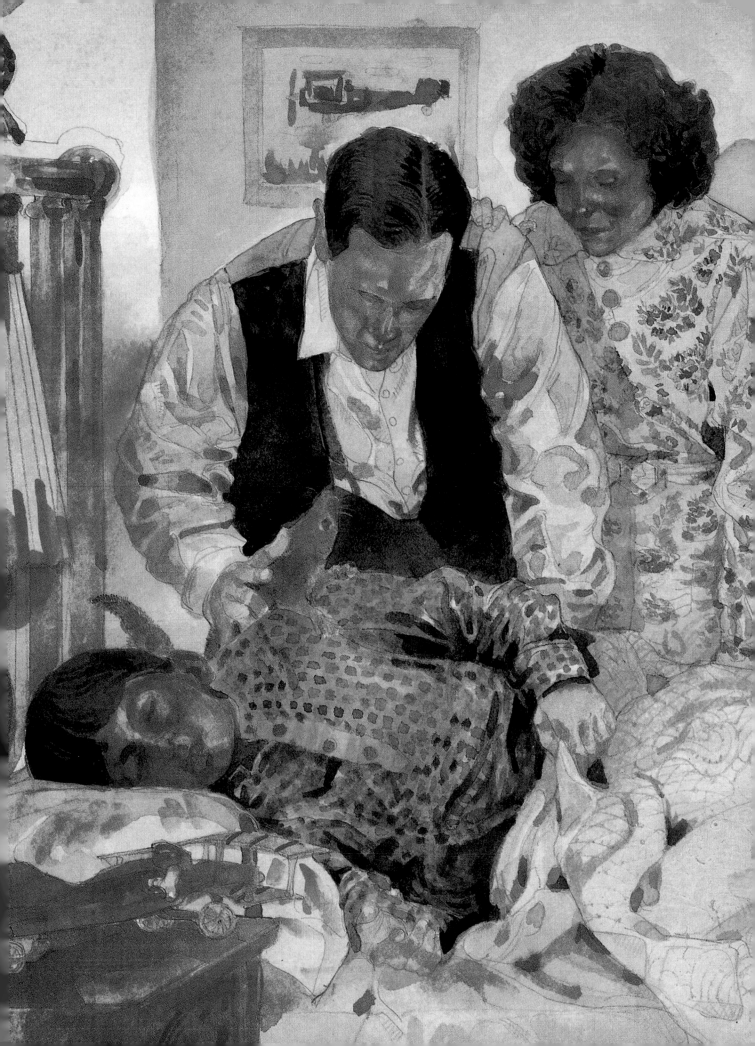

About the Author
RUDYARD KIPLING

Rudyard Kipling wrote *Rikki-tikki-tavi* more than a hundred years ago. The story takes place in India, where Mr. Kipling was born. Besides writing books and poems, he also invented stories to tell to his children. Although many of these stories were not written down, Mr. Kipling published a book, called *Just So Stories*, in honor of his daughter Josephine. She wanted stories told the same way each time, or "just so."

About the Illustrator
JERRY PINKNEY

Before Jerry Pinkney begins to draw, he does research to get a feeling for the people and places in the story. Next, he has models dress like the human characters and act out the events. After he studies the photos of the models, he is ready to begin his illustrations.

Mr. Pinkney says he appreciates "the opportunity to use my imagination, to draw and paint, and to travel through the voices of the characters in my stories, and above all else, to touch children." In *Rikki-tikki-tavi*, he reaches his audience by creating art and adapting the story for today's readers.

Reader Response

Open for Discussion

This classic story celebrates the great deeds of a mongoose. What are these deeds, and how do the words and illustrations celebrate them?

Comprehension Check

1. What is Rikki-tikki's job? How well does he do this job? Give examples from the story.

2. Why is Rikki-tikki an enemy of Nag and Nagaina? How does he get along with the other creatures? Give examples.

3. Characters in a story are shown by the way they act and by their words. How do Rikki-tikki's actions and words show his character? Use examples.

4. **Draw conclusions** about Nag and Nagaina. Why do they want to kill the people in the house? (Drawing Conclusions)

5. Now **draw conclusions** about Rikki-tikki. Why is he so loyal to the family? Why does he follow Nagaina into the hole? (Drawing Conclusions)

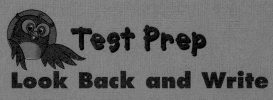

Test Prep
Look Back and Write

Look back at pages 356–357. Why does Rikki-tikki hold up the last cobra egg and show it to Nagaina? Use details from the story to explain your answer.

The Deadly Cobra

by Alexandra Parsons

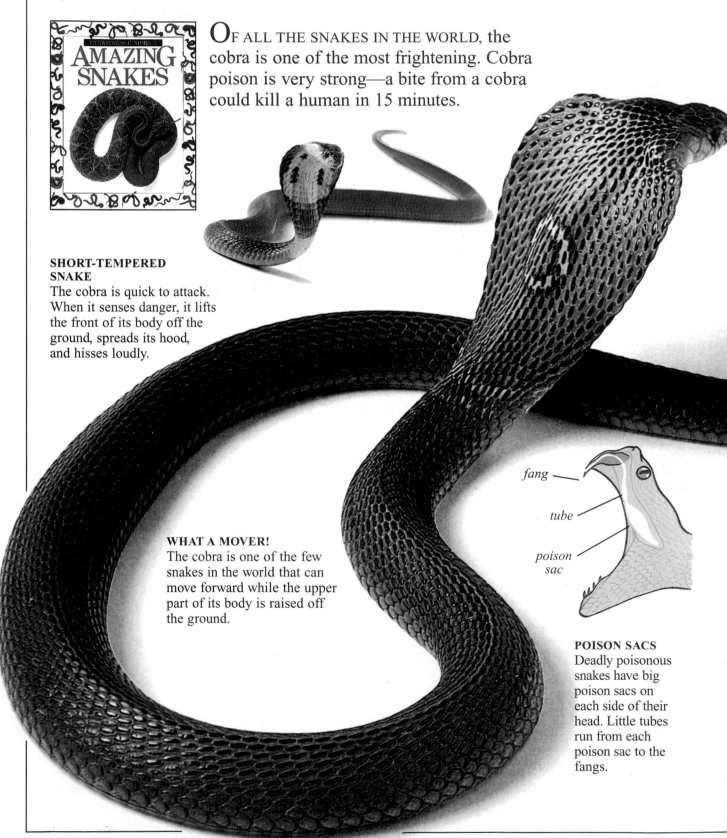

OF ALL THE SNAKES IN THE WORLD, the cobra is one of the most frightening. Cobra poison is very strong—a bite from a cobra could kill a human in 15 minutes.

SHORT-TEMPERED SNAKE
The cobra is quick to attack. When it senses danger, it lifts the front of its body off the ground, spreads its hood, and hisses loudly.

WHAT A MOVER!
The cobra is one of the few snakes in the world that can move forward while the upper part of its body is raised off the ground.

fang

tube

poison sac

POISON SACS
Deadly poisonous snakes have big poison sacs on each side of their head. Little tubes run from each poison sac to the fangs.

MEDUSA

In Greek mythology, Medusa's father gave her powers to transform herself into a beautiful woman. In return, she became mortal. In one story, Athena was jealous of Medusa's beauty and turned her hair into snakes.

CLEOPATRA

Long ago there was a beautiful queen of Egypt named Cleopatra. One myth says that she died because one of the royal cobras bit her.

DANGEROUS BABIES

Cobras can bite and kill as soon as they are born. Just one tablespoon of their poison—even dried—could kill 165 people or over 160,000 mice.

HOW CHARMING!

Snake charmers can make snakes dance to their music. At least that's what it looks like. In fact, the snake can't even hear the music and is just copying the swaying movements of the charmer and the flute.

DON'T SPIT!

"Spitting" cobras, found in Africa, don't really spit. When they feel threatened, they spray jets of poison into their attacker's eyes.

74th Street

by Myra Cohn Livingston

Hey, this little kid gets roller skates.
She puts them on.
She stands up and almost
flops over backwards.
She sticks out a foot like
she's going somewhere and
falls down and
smacks her hand. She
grabs hold of a step to get up and
sticks out the other foot and
slides about six inches and
falls and
skins her knee.

And then, you know what?

She brushes off the dirt and the
blood and puts some
spit on it and then
sticks out the other foot

again.

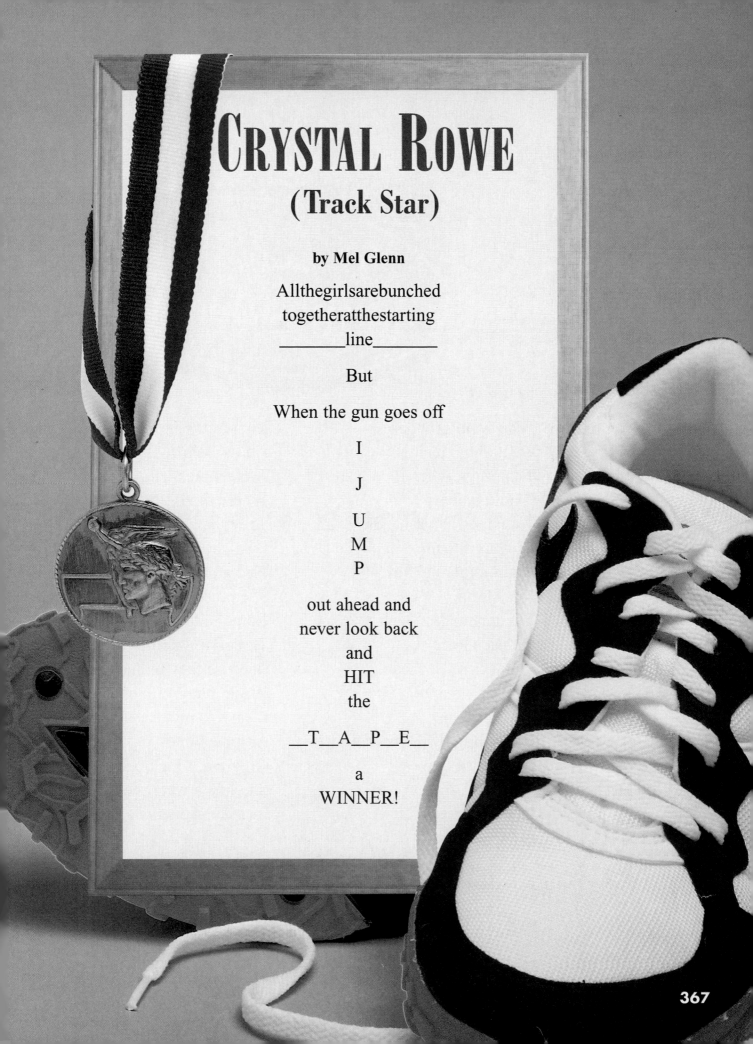

CRYSTAL ROWE
(Track Star)

by Mel Glenn

Allthegirlsarebunched
togetheratthestarting
_____line_____

But

When the gun goes off

I

J

U

M

P

out ahead and
never look back
and
HIT
the

__T__A__P__E__

a
WINNER!

My Teacher in the Market

by Gary Soto

Who would suppose
On a Saturday
That my teacher
Would balance
Tomatoes in her hands
And sniff them
Right under my nose.
I'm María,
The girl with a Band-Aid
On each knee,
Pink scars the shape
Of check marks
On homework.
I'm hiding by the bags
Of potatoes,
Tiptoeing and curious.
I've never seen

My teacher in jeans
And a T-shirt,
And tennies with a hole
Where the little
Toe rubs. She
Bags the tomatoes
And a pinch of chiles.
She presses a thumb
Gently into ripe avocados,
Three for a dollar
Because they're black,
Black, but pretty black.
I wave to my teacher
And then duck,
Giggling. I look up.
She lifts a watermelon
Into her arms,

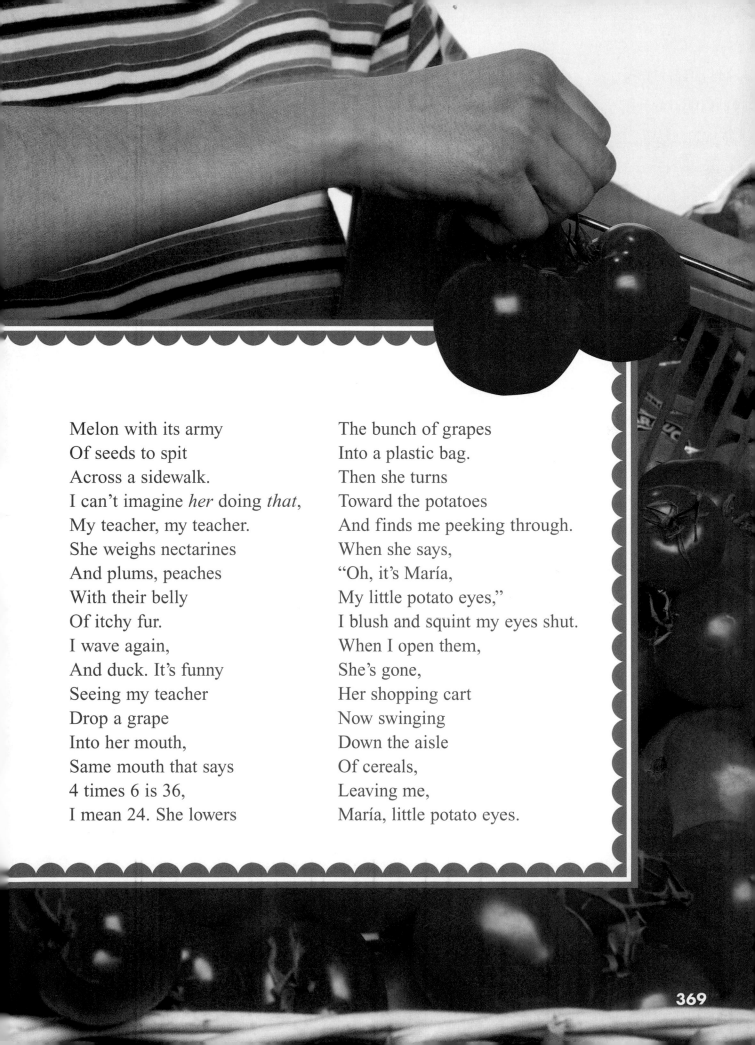

Melon with its army
Of seeds to spit
Across a sidewalk.
I can't imagine *her* doing *that*,
My teacher, my teacher.
She weighs nectarines
And plums, peaches
With their belly
Of itchy fur.
I wave again,
And duck. It's funny
Seeing my teacher
Drop a grape
Into her mouth,
Same mouth that says
4 times 6 is 36,
I mean 24. She lowers

The bunch of grapes
Into a plastic bag.
Then she turns
Toward the potatoes
And finds me peeking through.
When she says,
"Oh, it's María,
My little potato eyes,"
I blush and squint my eyes shut.
When I open them,
She's gone,
Her shopping cart
Now swinging
Down the aisle
Of cereals,
Leaving me,
María, little potato eyes.

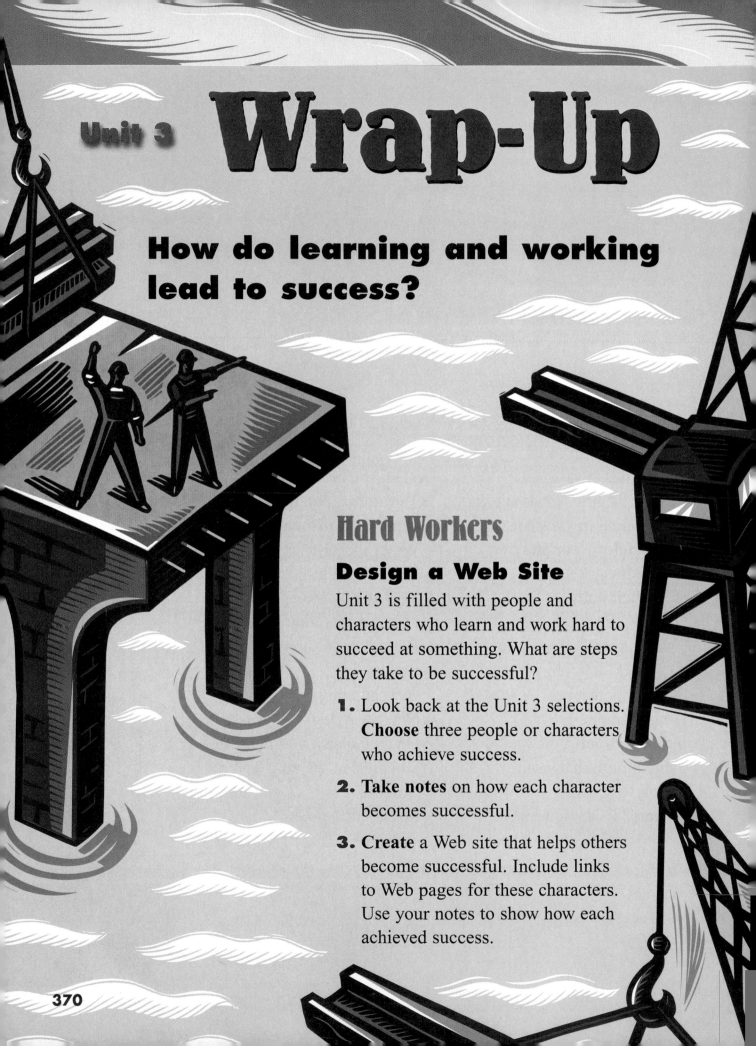

Unit 3 Wrap-Up

How do learning and working lead to success?

Hard Workers

Design a Web Site

Unit 3 is filled with people and characters who learn and work hard to succeed at something. What are steps they take to be successful?

1. Look back at the Unit 3 selections. **Choose** three people or characters who achieve success.

2. **Take notes** on how each character becomes successful.

3. **Create** a Web site that helps others become successful. Include links to Web pages for these characters. Use your notes to show how each achieved success.

Wish You Were Here!

Write a Postcard

Selections in this unit take place in the woods of Minnesota, in Argentina, and in other places.

1. **Imagine** you are a part of one selection.

2. **Look back** over the selection. Notice details that describe the setting.

3. **Illustrate** one side of an index card with a scene from the selection. On the other side, **write** a postcard to a friend. Describe the setting.

Whose Turn Is It?

Design a Board Game

Many characters and people in Unit 3 have exciting adventures before their stories end. What might it be like if their adventures were turned into a board game?

1. With two classmates, **choose** a selection. Find adventures and obstacles. Find happy and sad events.

2. **Design** a game board. Use your findings to make "moves" on the board.

3. **Create** game markers and play!

Glad to Meet You

Dramatize a Conversation

Imagine that all the characters in this unit meet for the first time at a party. Which characters might become friends?

1. **Look back** over the selections. Jot down a few notes about each character's personality and experiences.

2. With a classmate, **choose** two characters that might become friends.

3. **Pretend** that each of you is one of the characters. Have a conversation and plan to do something together that will interest both of you.

Test Talk

Answer the Question

Make the Right Choice

Before you can answer a multiple-choice test question, you have to decide on the best answer. A test about "Tornado Tales," pages 341–343, might have this question.

Test Question 1

According to the diagram on page 342, what causes objects to move from water to land?

Ⓐ Hurricanes cause waves to wash the objects onto land.

Ⓑ Hundreds of objects are carried for miles.

Ⓒ The tornado drops them into the water.

Ⓓ A waterspout sucks up objects and later drops them on land.

Understand the question.

Find the key words. Finish the statement "I need to find out . . ."

Narrow the answer choices.

Read each answer choice carefully. Rule out any choice that you know is wrong.

Look back at the text.

- Is the answer *right there* in one place, or do you have to *think and search*? Does the answer depend on the *author and you*?

Choose the best answer.

Mark your answer choice. Check it by comparing it with the text.

See how one student makes the right choice.

Okay, I need to find out how objects get from water to land. I don't need to know how far objects are carried or how they get in the water, so it's not **B** or **C**. That leaves **A** or **D**. I'm not sure, so I'll go back and look at the diagram.

The diagram shows a waterspout and a storm cloud. The first caption says, "Objects sucked up from sea or beach" and the last caption says, "Objects dropped on land to one side of the waterspout's path." So the right answer must be **D**.

Try it!

Now decide on the best answer to these test questions about "Tornado Tales," pages 341–343.

Test Question 2

Based on the information in this article, a tornado

Ⓐ can carry people and animals long distances without hurting them.

Ⓑ has a part called an "eye" which is quiet and still.

Ⓒ cannot hurt you if you are riding in a car.

Ⓓ only strikes the midwestern part of the United States.

Test Question 3

Why did the author write "Tornado Tales"?

Ⓕ to warn readers not to live in the Midwest

Ⓖ to inform readers about the effects of tornadoes

Ⓗ to tell readers how animals react to bad weather

Ⓘ to teach readers about the history of tornadoes

Timeless Stories

How do stories from the past help us live in the present?

Paraphrasing

- **Paraphrasing** is explaining something in your own words. A paraphrase should keep the writer's meaning.

- A paraphrase should include all of the author's ideas, but it should be easier to read than the original.

- Practice paraphrasing. It can help you understand what you read.

Read "Blue Jay Takes the Heat" from _When Birds Could Talk and Bats Could Sing_ told by Virginia Hamilton.

Write About It

1. Paraphrase the last sentence of the folk tale. Use your own words, but keep the author's meaning.

2. Paraphrase either the first or the fourth paragraph. Remember to use your own words and avoid copying from the story.

Blue Jay
Takes the Heat

told by Virginia Hamilton

There was no fire in all the world to warm Alcee Lingo except that owned by mean old Firekeeper—didn't have any last name. And he didn't like Alcee Lingo on account of Alcee hanging around trying to warm his hands and then running away real fast when Firekeeper tried to catch him. Firekeeper wouldn't like any other child when it came into this world, either. Just awful, he was.

It got so cold that even Bruh Blue Jay felt sorry for Alcee Lingo. "That child doesn't have feathers to warm him," he said one day to Sis Blue Jay.

So Bruh Blue Jay flew off.

He had to be swift if he was to take some fire and then get away. So he did it. But that quick-eyed Firekeeper saw him. He ran after Bruh Blue Jay in a flaming rage. And scared Bruh Blue Jay half to death. Bruh Blue Jay opened his mouth to warn all the birds that Firekeeper was burning mad, and—whoops!—he dropped the chunk of fire he'd taken.

"What business you have to take my fire?" Firekeeper yelled up at him.

Scared to death, Bruh Blue Jay hollered down, "It was only for Alcee Lingo. I'll pay, I'll pay, yes, I will! I'll pay you!" And until right yet, Bruh Blue Jay can be seen every day and most always taking stick pieces and fine little wood chips, nice and clean, over to Sis Squatty, old Firekeeper's wife.

LOOK AHEAD

Read about the adventures of an unusual chicken in *Half-Chicken*, another folk tale. Check your understanding of the story by paraphrasing sentences or paragraphs as you go along.

Vocabulary

Words to Know

farewells	tangled	flung
suggested	uniforms	vain

Words with similar meanings are called **synonyms.** You can often figure out the meaning of an unknown word by finding a clue in the words around it. Sometimes this clue is a synonym.

Read the paragraph below. Notice how *good-bys* helps you understand *farewells*.

A Fresh Start

Ingrid said her <u>farewells</u> to friends. After the good-bys, she was worried about the new school. What if her tongue felt <u>tangled</u> when she talked and she sounded silly? What if everyone had to wear ugly <u>uniforms</u>? What if all the girls there were <u>vain</u>, too stuck up to be her friend? Ingrid's mom <u>suggested</u> that she should just be herself. As they pulled up to the school, everyone looked friendly! Ingrid hopped out of the car and <u>flung</u> her hand back in a wave to her mom. She was off to a fresh start!

Write About It

Write a diary entry about a move to a new neighborhood or school. Use as many vocabulary words as you can.

Half-Chicken

by **Alma Flor Ada**

illustrated by **Kim Howard**

Have you ever seen a weather vane? Do you know why there is a little rooster on one end, spinning around to let us know which way the wind is blowing?

Well, I'll tell you. It's an old, old story that my grandmother once told me. And before that, her grandmother told it to her. It goes like this. . . .

A long, long time ago, on a Mexican ranch, a mother hen was sitting on her eggs. One by one, the baby chicks began to hatch, leaving their empty shells behind. One, two, three, four . . . twelve chicks had hatched. But the last egg still had not cracked open.

The hen did not know what to do. The chicks were running here and there, and she could not chase after them because she was still sitting on the last egg.

Finally there was a tiny sound. The baby chick was pecking at its egg from the inside. The hen quickly helped it break open the shell, and at last the thirteenth chick came out into the world.

Yet this was no ordinary chick. He had only one wing, only one leg, only one eye, and only half as many feathers as the other chicks.

It was not long before everyone at the ranch knew that a very special chick had been born.

The ducks told the turkeys. The turkeys told the pigeons. The pigeons told the swallows. And the swallows flew over the fields, spreading the news to the cows grazing peacefully with their calves, the fierce bulls, and the swift horses.

Soon the hen was surrounded by animals who wanted to see the strange chick.

One of the ducks said, "But he only has one wing!"

And one of the turkeys added, "Why, he's only a . . . half chicken!"

From then on, everyone called him Half-Chicken. And
Half-Chicken, finding himself at the center of all this attention,
became very vain.

One day he overheard the swallows, who traveled a great deal,
talking about him: "Not even at the court of the viceroy in Mexico
City is there anyone so unique."

Then Half-Chicken decided that it was time for him to leave
the ranch. Early one morning he said his farewells, announcing:
"Good-by, good-by! I'm off to Mexico City to see the court of
the viceroy!"

And *hip hop hip hop,* off he went, hippety-hopping along on
his only foot.

Half-Chicken had not walked very far when he found a stream
whose waters were blocked by some branches.

"Good morning, Half-Chicken. Would you please move the branches that are blocking my way?" asked the stream.

Half-Chicken moved the branches aside. But when the stream suggested that he stay awhile and take a swim, he answered: "I have no time to lose. I'm off to Mexico City to see the court of the viceroy!"

And *hip hop hip hop,* off he went, hippety-hopping along on his only foot.

A little while later, Half-Chicken found a small fire burning between some rocks. The fire was almost out.

"Good morning, Half-Chicken. Please, fan me a little with your wing, for I am about to go out," asked the fire.

Half-Chicken fanned the fire with his wing, and it blazed up again. But when the fire suggested that he stay awhile and warm up, he answered: "I have no time to lose. I'm off to Mexico City to see the court of the viceroy!"

And *hip hop hip hop,* off he went, hippety-hopping along on his only foot.

After he had walked a little farther, Half-Chicken found the wind tangled in some bushes.

"Good morning, Half-Chicken. Would you please untangle me, so that I can go on my way?" asked the wind.

Half-Chicken untangled the branches. But when the wind suggested that he stay and play, and offered to help him fly here and there like a dry leaf, he answered: "I have no time to lose. I'm off to Mexico City to see the court of the viceroy!"

And *hip hop hip hop,* off he went, hippety-hopping along on his only foot. At last he reached Mexico City.

Half-Chicken crossed the enormous Great Plaza. He passed the stalls laden with meat, fish, vegetables, fruit, cheese, and honey. He passed the Parián, the market where all kinds of beautiful goods were sold. Finally, he reached the gate of the viceroy's palace.

"Good afternoon," said Half-Chicken to the guards in fancy uniforms who stood in front of the palace. "I've come to see the viceroy."

One of the guards began to laugh. The other one said, "You'd better go in around the back and through the kitchen."

So Half-Chicken went, *hip hop hip hop*, around the palace and to the kitchen door.

The cook who saw him said, "What luck! This chicken is just what I need to make a soup for the vicereine." And he threw Half-Chicken into a kettle of water that was sitting on the fire.

When Half-Chicken felt how hot the water was, he said, "Oh, fire, help me! Please, don't burn me!"

The fire answered, "You helped me when I needed help. Now it's my turn to help you. Ask the water to jump on me and put me out."

Then Half-Chicken asked the water, "Oh, water, help me! Please jump on the fire and put him out, so he won't burn me."

And the water answered, "You helped me when I needed help. Now it's my turn to help you." And he jumped on the fire and put him out.

When the cook returned, he saw that the water had spilled
and the fire was out.

"This chicken has been more trouble than he's worth!"
exclaimed the cook. "Besides, one of the ladies-in-waiting just
told me that the vicereine doesn't want any soup. She wants to
eat nothing but salad."

And he picked Half-Chicken up by his only leg and flung
him out the window.

When Half-Chicken was tumbling through the air, he called
out: "Oh, wind, help me, please!"

And the wind answered, "You helped me when I needed help.
Now it's my turn to help you."

And the wind blew fiercely. He lifted Half-Chicken higher
and higher, until the little rooster landed on one of the towers
of the palace.

"From there you can see everything you want, Half-Chicken, with no danger of ending up in the cooking pot."

And from that day on, weathercocks have stood on their only leg, seeing everything that happens below, and pointing whichever way their friend the wind blows.

Alma Flor Ada

Alma Flor Ada once wrote about what it was like for her growing up. "My grandmother and one of my uncles were great storytellers. And every night, at bedtime, my father told me stories he invented to explain to me all that he knew about the history of the world. With all of these storytellers around me, it is not a surprise that I like to tell stories."

When she was still in school, she knew what she wanted to do in the future. "I made a firm commitment while in the fourth grade to devote my life to producing schoolbooks that would be fun—and since then I am having a lot of fun doing just that!"

Ms. Flor Ada was born in Cuba and came to the United States to do post-graduate work and teach. She speaks and writes both in Spanish and in English. It is important to her that children and adults know more than one language. Many of her stories are written in two languages. Her daughter, Rosalma Zubizarreta, helps her by translating between English and Spanish. *Half-Chicken* was translated by Ms. Zubizarreta.

About the Illustrator

Kim Howard

When Kim Howard was a child, she lived in Panama, a country in Central America. She has traveled in Mexico, where *Half-Chicken* takes place, and other parts of Latin America. She now lives in Idaho.

Reader Response

Open for Discussion

This is an old story the author heard from her grandmother. Why do you think the story has been told over and over again?

Comprehension Check

1. Why does Half-Chicken go off to the court of the viceroy in Mexico City? Use story details in your answer.

2. Who does Half-Chicken meet on the way to see the viceroy? How do the favors Half-Chicken does bring him good fortune? Find story details to support your answer.

3. How do you know that this story is a fantasy? Use examples to explain.

4. Reread the first paragraph on page 382. **Paraphrase,** or explain in your own words, the meaning of this paragraph. (Paraphrasing)

5. Now reread the last paragraph in the story on page 389. **Paraphrase** this paragraph. How does paraphrasing help you understand the purpose of the story? (Paraphrasing)

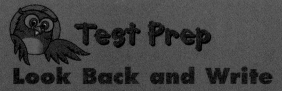

Test Prep
Look Back and Write

Look back at pages 381–382. What do the swallows mean when they say Half-Chicken is unique? Use context clues to answer.

Chicken Farming

by Ned Halley

THE CHICKENS PECK QUIETLY in the farmyard under the watchful eye of the rooster. Occasionally, as he has done since dawn, he throws back his head and crows: "Cock-a-doodle-do!" This is what many people think of when they picture poultry farming. Some flocks still do live in this way, now known as "free-range" farming. But most eggs and chickens in stores today come from "factory" farms. These farms have more than 100,000 birds at a time. Today's hens are hybrids, specially raised to produce more and better eggs and meat. Their eggs—they produce one or more every day—are collected automatically.

SAFE HOUSE
The coop has hinged shutters that can be closed at night for warmth and to keep foxes out.

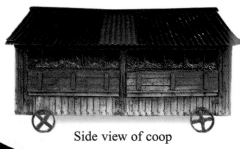

Side view of coop

Small door in roof or wall lets birds in and out while main door is closed.

HOME ON THE RANGE
Free-range chickens need a chicken coop, or house, in which to lay and sit on their eggs. Here they can be shut in at night, safe from predators such as foxes.

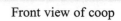

Front view of coop

BREEDER'S TREASURE
Traditional breeds are not kept by big farmers, but they have survived thanks to the efforts of some poultry breeders in many countries. Old breeds are still used to preserve characteristics that today's commercial breeds have lost.

The fleshy growth on top of the fowl's head is called the comb.

ROYAL CONNECTION
The Brahma, an Asian breed, became fashionable when a breeder brought a flock to England from an Indian town. He presented Queen Victoria with nine birds.

TALL BREED
Brought to Europe 200 years ago, Malay birds from southern Asia are up to 32 in. tall.

The part below the head is known as the wattle.

Buff Sussex chick

Silver Gray Dorking chick

BEFORE FACTORY FARMING
Until the modern farming era of the last 50 years, chickens were mostly reared on a small scale in farmyards. They gave fresh eggs—though far fewer than today's chickens do.

HANDSOME BIRDS
The Orpington breeds of duck and chicken were created in Orpington, England, in the 19th century.

Buff Orpington chicken

Compare and Contrast

- To **compare** is to tell how two or more things are alike. To **contrast** is to tell how two or more things are different.

- Clue words such as *like* or *as* show comparisons. Clue words such as *but, instead,* and *unlike* show contrasts. Other clue words are words of comparison, such as *smaller* and *more slender.*

- Often authors don't use clue words. Readers must make comparisons for themselves.

Read the beginning of the book *Wolves* by Gail Gibbons.

Talk About It

1. How are the gray wolf and the red wolf different? What clue words help you notice the differences?

2. What things about wolves did Gail Gibbons choose to compare and contrast?

Wolves

by Gail Gibbons

It is a snowy moonlit night in the northern woods. An animal shakes the snow from its thick fur, throws its head back, and joins its companions in a long howl. The animal is a wolf.

There are two different types of wolves. One is the gray wolf, or timber wolf. A gray wolf can have black, white, brown, or gray fur depending on where it lives. Thirty-two different kinds of gray wolves have been identified. Some of them don't exist anymore.

The other type of wolf is the red wolf. Red wolves aren't really red. Instead, they are a combination of black, gray, and reddish brown. They are smaller and more slender than gray wolves. Only one of the three original different kinds of red wolves exists today. Very few of them live in the wild.

The first ancestors of wolves lived more than fifty million years ago. Over time, these creatures developed into wolves.

Wolves are members of the dog family called Canidae. All dogs are related to wolves.

A few hundred years ago, wolves lived all around the world. People hunted them and also took over much of their territory. There were fewer wolves and they moved away. Today most wolves are found in the northern parts of the world.

Gray wolves

LOOK AHEAD

Wolves in fairy tales always seem to be the "bad guys." Compare and contrast the wolf in the play *Blame It on the Wolf* with the fairy tale wolves that you know about.

Words to Know

character **courtroom** **guilty**
evidence **rescued**

When you read, you may come across a word you do not know. To figure out the meaning of the unfamiliar word, look for clues in the words and sentences around it.

Notice how *evidence* is used in the paragraph below. Find an example in the sentence after *evidence*. What do you think *evidence* means?

Live News Report

We are here at the trial of Goldilocks, the famous story character. The courtroom is packed with people who want to watch the trial. Let's listen in: "Goldilocks is guilty of stealing the bears' breakfast. This empty bowl is evidence. It proves she ate all the porridge."

"But, Your Honor, I rescued Mama Bear! If it weren't for me, she would have had more dishes to wash!" Stay tuned for the rest of the story.

Talk About It

What will happen next? Act it out with friends. Use as many vocabulary words as you can.

Blame It on The Wolf

an original play by Douglas Love

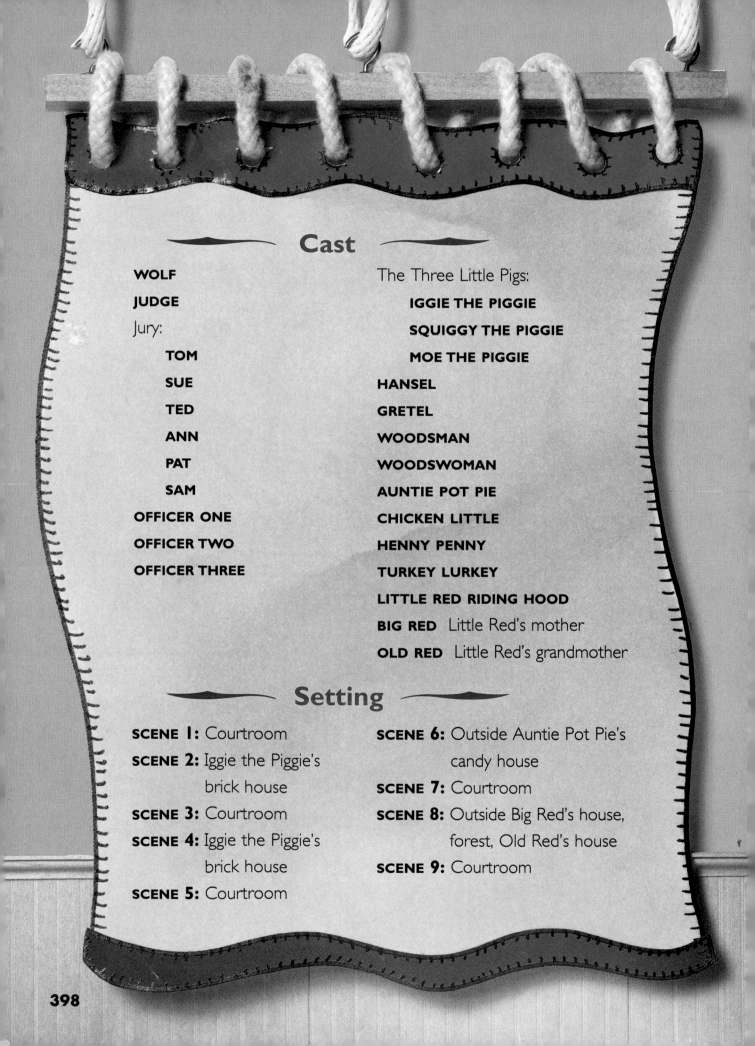

Cast

WOLF

JUDGE

Jury:

    TOM

    SUE

    TED

    ANN

    PAT

    SAM

OFFICER ONE

OFFICER TWO

OFFICER THREE

The Three Little Pigs:

    IGGIE THE PIGGIE

    SQUIGGY THE PIGGIE

    MOE THE PIGGIE

HANSEL

GRETEL

WOODSMAN

WOODSWOMAN

AUNTIE POT PIE

CHICKEN LITTLE

HENNY PENNY

TURKEY LURKEY

LITTLE RED RIDING HOOD

BIG RED Little Red's mother

OLD RED Little Red's grandmother

Setting

SCENE 1: Courtroom

SCENE 2: Iggie the Piggie's brick house

SCENE 3: Courtroom

SCENE 4: Iggie the Piggie's brick house

SCENE 5: Courtroom

SCENE 6: Outside Auntie Pot Pie's candy house

SCENE 7: Courtroom

SCENE 8: Outside Big Red's house, forest, Old Red's house

SCENE 9: Courtroom

Scene 1

The JURY *is seated on the stage. The* JUDGE *walks in and steps up to his podium.* WOLF *is downstage center.*

JUDGE: Jury, have you reached a verdict?

(Each jury member stands as he or she speaks.)

TOM: Yes—

SUE: Your . . .

TED: Honor.

ANN: We . . .

PAT: find . . .

SAM: the . . .

TOM: wolf . . .

WOLF: Stop! Wait! Freeze!

(All the actors onstage, except WOLF, *magically freeze, and* WOLF *talks directly to the audience.)*

WOLF: I didn't do it! I'm not guilty. You gotta believe me. Why do they always blame the wolf? They never bother to listen to my side of the story—until now! I'm going to tell you my side of the story. You can step into my shoes. You can look through my eyes. You'll decide if I'm guilty. They say that I ate Little Red Riding Hood's grandma, Old Red. I'll present my case, and you can decide. I know you'll be fair. It all started in this courtroom a few days ago when they asked one of the Three Little Pigs to tell the court all about the first time they met me.

(The actors move in slow motion to show the change in time, taking their places in the courtroom for the action a few days earlier when the trial began. IGGIE THE PIGGIE *is on the stand.)*

JUDGE: Please state your full name for the jury.

IGGIE: Iggie the Piggie.

JUDGE: Your witness, Mr. Wolf.

WOLF: Iggie, how long have you known the defendant?

IGGIE: Who's the defendant?

WOLF: Me! The wolf!

IGGIE: Oh. Two weeks, I guess.

WOLF: You guess? Do you always guess when you answer questions in a court of law?

IGGIE: I don't know.

WOLF: You don't know?

IGGIE: I've never been in a court of law before.

WOLF: Me neither; aren't you nervous?

IGGIE: Yes, I am. (*Pointing to the* JURY.) Who are they?

WOLF: They're the jury. They decide if I did it or not.

JUDGE (*getting impatient*): Can we get on with it?

WOLF: I'm sorry, Your Honor. (*To* IGGIE.) Please tell the court about the first day we met.

IGGIE: My two brothers were over at my brick house.

WOLF: For the record, Your Honor, Iggie the Piggie refers to his brothers, Squiggy and Moe.

JUDGE (*surprised at the corny names*): Iggie, Squiggy, and Moe?

IGGIE: Well, Your Honor, my parents already had an Iggie and a Squiggy, and they thought they should have one Moe.

Blackout.

Scene 2

Inside IGGIE's *brick house.* IGGIE, SQUIGGY, *and* MOE *are huddling in the corner, trembling with fright.* WOLF *is at the side of the stage, looking mean.*

WOLF *(in a mean voice):* Little pigs! Little pigs! Let me come in!

IGGIE: Not by the hair of my chinney chin chin!

SQUIGGY: You tell 'im, Iggie!

IGGIE: Thanks, Squiggy!

WOLF: Then I'll huff and I'll puff and I'll blow your house into another galaxy!
    (He tries huffing and puffing and cannot blow down the brick house.) Let me
    in, little pigs, or I'll make you my supper!

MOE: What did he say?

SQUIGGY: He says he'll make us his supper!

IGGIE: He'll make us his supper? Don't worry, brothers. My brick house
    is strong enough to protect us from the evil wolf!

*(WOLF tries to blow down the house and he cannot. The piggies
dance in celebration.)*

Lights fade.

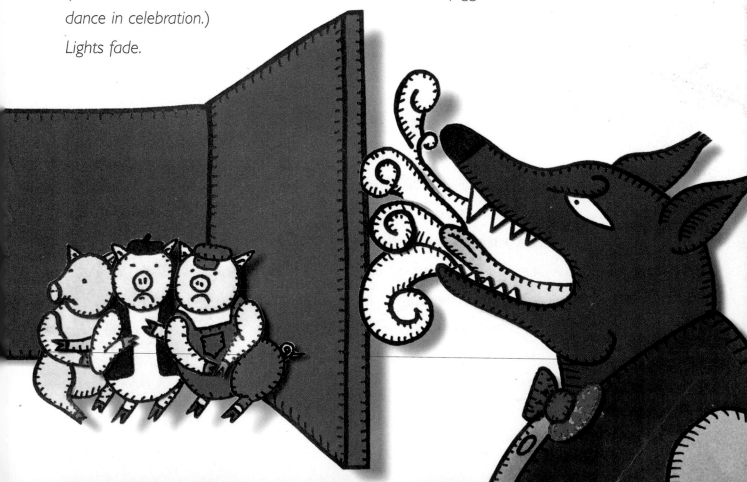

Scene 3

Back in the courtroom, at the trial.

JUDGE: Thank you, Iggie the Piggie. Do you have anything else to ask, Mr. Wolf?

WOLF: Yes, Your Honor, I would like to call Squiggy and Moe to the stand.

JUDGE: Squiggy and Moe, please take the stand.

(SQUIGGY *and* MOE *take the stand with* IGGIE. *All three sit in the same chair.*)

WOLF: What do you think I said outside your brick house? On the day in question?

IGGIE: I thought you said, "I'll huff and I'll puff and blow you into another galaxy!"

SQUIGGY: I thought he said, "My hands are rough. Can I borrow some moisturizing lotion?"

MOE: I thought he said, "I'll have a BLT on whole wheat—hold the mayo!"

WOLF: So you admit that you really aren't sure what I said. *(To* JURY.*)* I intend to prove that sometimes we don't hear everything clearly. Some people don't pay attention. . . .

JUDGE *(trying to get* WOLF*'s attention)*: Mr. Wolf . . .

WOLF *(continuing without hearing the* JUDGE*)*: Some people only hear what they want to hear. . . .

JUDGE *(again trying to interrupt* WOLF*)*: Mr. Wolf . . .

WOLF *(again he does not hear)*: And some people have wax . . .

JUDGE *(finally interrupting)*: Mr. Wolf, please make your point.

WOLF: Judge, with your permission, I would like to explain what really happened that day I met the three pigs.

JUDGE: All right, Mr. Wolf. But make it snappy!

Blackout.

Back at the brick house. The pigs are sitting around playing Monopoly®.

MOE (*moving his game piece around the board*): 1 . . . 2 . . . 3 . . .
Go directly to jail? Darn!

IGGIE (*taking the dice from* MOE): My turn!

(*They continue playing as* WOLF *enters the stage outside of their house.*)

WOLF (*talking to himself*): I always get a flat tire out in the middle of
nowhere! Now all I've got to do is find a phone! (*He notices the
brick house.*) Maybe the people who live in this brick house will
let me call the motor club from their phone!

(WOLF *begins to knock on the door of the pigs' house.*)

WOLF: Hello, hello!

IGGIE (*to his brothers*): Who's that?

SQUIGGY: Well, it can't be the Chinese food. That already came.

MOE: Maybe it's the three bears, Harry, Mary, and Epstein.

SQUIGGY: Those are the three little kittens. The three bears are
named Fritzie, Mitzie, and Hasenfrasen.

IGGIE: No, no. They're the three blind mice! The three bears are named Enrico, Pico, and Kinnicinnic.

(The three of them begin to argue, all talking at once. WOLF *knocks again to stop their arguing.)*

MOE: I'll look out the window and SEE who it is. *(He looks.)* Hey, it's the big bad wolf!

IGGIE: *(clinging to his brother):* A big bad wolf—I'm scared!

SQUIGGY: Just relax, brothers—he cannot hurt us in this strong brick house.

WOLF *(still talking to himself):* What does this welcome mat say? "The house of the three little pigs." *(knocking and calling through the door)* Little pigs . . . little pigs! Let me in! I've got a flat on the interstate, and I need to call a tow truck!

IGGIE: Not by the hair of my chinney chin chin!

SQUIGGY: You tell 'im, Iggie!

IGGIE: Thanks, Squiggy!

WOLF: Please! I'm so out of breath from walking all the way from my car. I'm huffing and puffing, and I need to blow my nose.

(They don't let him in.)

SQUIGGY: What did he say?

WOLF: Please help me, little pigs. I'm so hungry—I haven't had any supper!

MOE: What did he say?

SQUIGGY: He says he'll make us his supper!

IGGIE: He'll make us his supper? Don't worry, brothers. My brick house is strong enough to protect us from the evil wolf!

WOLF *(still knocking)*: Please help!

Lights fade.

Scene 5

The courtroom.

JUDGE: Members of the jury, please understand that the Piggies have appeared as character witnesses. It is your job to decide who was telling the truth. We will now hear from two more character witnesses. *(To* OFFICER ONE.*)* Officer One? Please call Hansel and Gretel to the stand.

OFFICER ONE *(turning to* OFFICER TWO*)*: Officer Two? Please call Hansel and Gretel to the stand.

OFFICER TWO *(turning to* OFFICER THREE*)*: Officer Three? Please call Hansel and Gretel to the stand.

OFFICER THREE: Officer Ffff . . . *(seeing that there is nobody else to delegate)* Hansel and Gretel, please take the stand!

(HANSEL *and* GRETEL *take the stand.*)

WOLF: Your Honor, I plan to reveal to the court that I could not possibly have eaten Old Red because I was saving the lives of these two children. *(To the children.)* Please state your names for the court.

HANSEL: Hansel.

GRETEL: Gretel.

WOLF: Where did we first meet?

GRETEL: At Auntie Pot Pie's house.

WOLF: And how did you happen to arrive there?

HANSEL: My sister and I lost our way in the woods . . .

405

GRETEL: It wasn't my fault. I told him to leave a trail.

HANSEL: I keep telling you. I did leave a trail!

GRETEL: You don't leave a trail of bread crumbs in a forest full of hungry little animals!

Blackout.

Lights shift to the HANSEL *and* GRETEL *setting.*

Scene 6

Flashback to the woods outside AUNTIE POT PIE'*s candy house.* WOODSMAN *and* WOODSWOMAN *enter with a lantern looking for their children.*

WOODSMAN: Hansel! Gretel!

WOODSWOMAN: Gretel! Hansel!

WOODSMAN: Children! Where are you?

WOODSWOMAN: They're nowhere to be found! What shall we do? Oh, it's my fault! If only I hadn't been so greedy about the firewood! I never should have sent them alone into the forest. What shall become of them?

WOODSMAN: Now, now. We shall find them. I know every inch of these woods. I will not give up until I've found our dear children. Their legs are short. They could not have gone far. . . .

GRETEL

HANSEL

WOODSWOMAN *(frightened):* Oh, my poor children. What shall become of them?

WOODSMAN: Do not fret! We will find them! *(They exit.)*

CHICKEN LITTLE *(enters in a fright.):*

It's falling! It's falling!

Tomorrow you'll be crawling

Under piles of clouds and sky.

It's frightful! Appalling!

There isn't any stalling.

How I wish these wings could fly!

I'd fly away above the sky

On Venus I would live.

The moon would be my neighbor

And there'd be no one to give the word . . .

It's falling! It's falling!

I tell ya that I'm bawling.

This news of doom I will be

spreading near and far.

I am getting very tired. How I wish I had a car!

It's falling! It's falling!

Tomorrow you'll be crawling

Under piles of clouds and sky.

(CHICKEN LITTLE *exits.*)

(HANSEL *and* GRETEL *enter, looking lost.*)

GRETEL: Where are we, Brother? I thought we left a trail!

HANSEL: We did leave one, Sister. Only I fear that I had no stones to drop behind us to mark our way.

GRETEL: What did you drop, Brother?

HANSEL: Bread crumbs from my peanut butter and pickle sandwich.

GRETEL *(very angry):* BREAD CRUMBS! The birds and animals of the forest must have eaten them all up!

HANSEL: What are we to do?

GRETEL: We must try to find our way on our own.

(They come upon a house made of gingerbread and candy.)

HANSEL: Look at that candy house.

GRETEL: It looks good enough to eat!

HANSEL: It is making me very hungry.

GRETEL: Let's take a small bite . . . no one will know!

AUNTIE POT PIE *(from inside the house):* Who is nibbling on my house?

HANSEL: What was that?

AUNTIE POT PIE *(entering):* Who is nibbling? Nibbling, nibbling on my house?

GRETEL: I am sorry, old woman. We are lost and haven't eaten a thing all day.

HANSEL: We are very hungry. May we eat your door post?

(CHICKEN LITTLE *enters with* TURKEY LURKEY *and* HENNY PENNY. HANSEL, GRETEL, *and* AUNTIE POT PIE *look at the three birds as if they have wandered into the wrong story.)*

ALL THREE BIRDS: It's falling! It's falling!

Tomorrow you'll be crawling

Under piles of clouds and sky.

HENNY PENNY: It's frightful! Appalling! There isn't any stalling.

TURKEY LURKEY: How I wish these wings could fly! *(Flap, flap.)*

I'd fly away above the sky

On Venus I would live.

CHICKEN LITTLE: The moon would be my neighbor

And there'd be no one to give the word . . .

ALL THREE BIRDS: It's falling! It's falling!

I tell ya that I'm bawling.

This news of doom I will be

spreading near and far.

I am getting very tired. How I wish I had a car!

It's falling! It's falling!

Tomorrow you'll be crawling

Under piles of clouds and sky.

(The three of them exit.)

AUNTIE POT PIE: Come inside and I'll give you some sweets, children.

Blackout.

Scene 7

The courtroom. HANSEL *and* GRETEL *are finishing their story.*

HANSEL: Then she put us in a cage until the wolf came by and rescued us.

WOODSMAN *(standing in his place on stage, crying tears of joy):* Thank you, Mr. Wolf, for saving my children!

JUDGE: Order in the court! Mr. Wolf, do you have any further questions for these witnesses?

WOLF: Just a few, Your Honor. Hansel, Gretel—how would you describe me?

GRETEL: Well . . . you're about 4 foot 9 and furry. . . .

WOLF: No, I mean as a person. . . .

HANSEL: You were very kind to us!

WOLF: I rest my case!

(HANSEL *and* GRETEL *leave the witness stand.*)

JUDGE: Officer One, please call Little Red Riding Hood to the stand.

OFFICER ONE (*turning to* OFFICER TWO): Officer Two, please call Little Red to the stand.

OFFICER TWO (*turning to* OFFICER THREE): Officer Three, please call Little Red to the stand.

OFFICER THREE: Officer Ffff . . . *(Turning to see there is not another officer.)* . . . um . . . Little Red Riding Hood, please take the stand.

(LITTLE RED *skips up to the witness stand and sits down.*)

LITTLE RED: The wolf ate my grandma! He came to her door and ate her up! I always visit on Thursdays! Last Thursday she was gone! He must have eaten her up. I say X-ray his stomach and look for her bifocals!

WOLF: I never even met your grandmother. I am going to explain what really happened that day.

End of scene.

Scene 8

BIG RED, LITTLE RED's *mother, is sending her off to bring a basket of goodies to* LITTLE RED's *grandmother,* OLD RED.

BIG RED: Now remember, Daughter, go to Grandma's with this basket of goodies and do not stray from the path. Do not talk to strangers. Do not pick the flowers. Do not speak out of turn. Do not pass go. Do not run in the halls. Do not chew gum in school. And don't count your chickens!

(CHICKEN LITTLE *enters with* TURKEY LURKEY *and* HENNY PENNY.)

CHICKEN LITTLE: Did somebody mention chickens?

TURKEY LURKEY: Or turkeys?

HENNY PENNY: Or hennys?

ALL THREE BIRDS: It's falling! It's falling!

Tomorrow you'll be crawling

Under piles of clouds and sky.

HENNY: It's frightful! Appalling!

There isn't any stalling . . .

TURKEY: How I wish these wings could fly!

I'd fly away above the sky

On Venus I would live . . .

CHICKEN: The moon would be my neighbor

And there'd be no one to give the word . . .

ALL THREE BIRDS: It's falling! It's falling!

I tell ya that I'm bawling.

This news of doom I will be

spreading near and far.

I am getting very tired. How I wish I had a car!

It's falling! It's falling!

Tomorrow you'll be crawling

Under piles of clouds and sky.

411

(The three of them exit.)

*(*LITTLE RED *walks around the stage, then stops at* OLD RED*'s house. She knocks on the door.* AUNTIE POT PIE *is inside, disguised as a wolf.)*

AUNTIE POT PIE *(evilly):* With this disguise Little Red will think that I am the wolf and I ate her grandmother. This way I can get back at that nasty wolf who helped those delicious little children, Hansel and Gretel, go! And I can also get back at Little Red Riding Hood's grandmother, my sweet twin sister! Yuck!

*(*AUNTIE POT PIE *opens the door.* LITTLE RED *thinks that she is talking to her grandma.)*

LITTLE RED: Here is a basket of goodies for the best grandma in the world!

AUNTIE POT PIE: I am not your grandma! I am the big bad wolf!

LITTLE RED *(not paying attention):* Grandma! What big eyes you have!

AUNTIE POT PIE: These are wolf eyes! Why don't you open yours and take a look?

LITTLE RED: Grandma! What big ears you have!

AUNTIE POT PIE: I'm not your granny! Open up your ears so I can tell you I'm the big bad wolf!

LITTLE RED *(not paying attention):* Grandma! What big wolflike teeth you have!

AUNTIE POT PIE: You better believe it, baby! What do you have to say about that?

LITTLE RED: So how've you been, Grandma?

*(*AUNTIE POT PIE *roars with anger.)*

LITTLE RED: Sore throat still?

*(*AUNTIE POT PIE *roars again.)*

LITTLE RED: Eek!

(A big chase follows that involves many cast members. We end up in the courtroom with the jury about to announce the verdict.)

Scene 9

The courtroom. The JUDGE *and* JURY *are seated.* WOLF *is downstage center.*

WOLF *(to audience):* See? I couldn't have eaten Old Red! All the
evidence is in. All of the witnesses have testified. I guess I have
to find out what the jury decides sooner or later. *(To audience.)*
Have you made up your mind? You don't think I did it, do you?
(Pointing to the jury.) Let's see what they think.

(The JUDGE *and the* JURY *unfreeze and the* JURY *is about to give its verdict.)*

JUDGE: Jury, have you reached a verdict?

TOM: Yes—

SUE: Your . . .

TED: Honor.

ANN: We . . .

PAT: find . . .

SAM: the . . .

TOM: wolf . . .

SUE: guilty

TED: as

ANN: charged.

PAT: Guilty.

SAM: Guilty.

TOM: Guilty.

SUE: Guilty.

TED: Guilty.

ANN: Guilty

PAT: as

SAM: charged!

413

(Suddenly from stage left OLD RED *enters.)*

OLD RED *(singing to herself):* Oh, I wanna go back to my little grass shack in Ka Wala Ka Koo Hawaii! La La La La La La La La La La.

*(*LITTLE RED *is surprised.)*

LITTLE RED: Grandma!

AUNTIE POT PIE *(seeing that she will soon be found out):* Uh-oh!

WOLF: See! I told you I didn't eat her!

OLD RED: I'm back! *(To* AUNTIE POT PIE.*)* Thank you, dear sister, for sending me on that lovely vacation. You know, I don't think I'll ever be able to get over how surprised I was when you offered me the trip. I always thought you didn't like me. I know better now, sweet sister!

AUNTIE POT PIE: Don't sweet sister me. . . . You always come in at the wrong time!

JUDGE: Jury—I think that we all owe Mr. Wolf an apology. We can only hope that he will accept it.

WOLF: Oh, I accept. It is not easy to see both sides of a story. But you'll never see the other side if you don't look!

AUNTIE POT PIE: This is all so sweet and mushy, I think I'm going to be sick! You all celebrate—I'm going home.

LITTLE RED: Wait! Stay and celebrate with us! Grandma is going to teach us all to hula!

*(*AUNTIE POT PIE *stays on stage, looking defeated.)*

WOLF: What's a hula?

LITTLE RED: It's a dance!

OLD RED: I picked it up in Hawaii. You're going to love it!

(Suddenly a loud boom is heard and clouds fall to the stage.)

ALL THREE BIRDS *(entering)*:

It's falling! It's falling!

We told you it was falling!

But you did not hear, did you?

We told you—We warned you.

We did not want to scorn you.

But, the foot's on the other shoe.

It is always good to listen to

Another point of view.

Hear all sides of the story and

You'll have a better clue.

We're happy, there's justice.

You'll really have to trust us.

We want you all to go out yelling up to every rafter,

The wolves and pigs, the Reds and Grets,

Live happily ever after!

Curtain.

Douglas Love

About the Author

Douglas Love started acting when he was just a child. "From the very first moment I stepped foot inside a theater," he says, "I came to realize that it was the most magical place in the world. My life would never be the same." Mr. Love acted in more than fifty plays as a child.

Because he wants other children to be able to enjoy the excitement that playacting can create, Mr. Love writes plays for children. For those who have never put on a play before, he explains how to do it. He also introduces his readers to new ideas. By writing *Blame It on the Wolf* from Wolf's point of view, he helps the readers see the story from a different angle.

Besides writing, Mr. Love runs theater workshops and is active in the Broadway Children's Theater. About children's theater he remarks, "In the world of children performing plays, there are no small parts—just some small actors."

Reader Response

Open for Discussion

Suppose your class is putting on a performance of this play. Which character would you want to be? Why?

Comprehension Check

1. Which of the characters from this play are familiar to you? How are they different from what you remember? Use examples to explain your answer.

2. "Some people don't pay attention. . . . Some people only hear what they want to hear." Do you think Wolf has a good reason for saying that? Does he have a good case? Use story details to explain why.

3. Remember that a theme is a big idea in a story. What theme do you discover as you read this play? Use examples.

4. **Contrast** Auntie Pot Pie and Wolf. How are the two characters different? (Compare and Contrast)

5. **Compare** this play to the story *Half-Chicken*. How are the two alike? (Compare and Contrast)

Test Prep

Look Back and Write

Look back pages 414–415. Old Red suddenly appears in the courtroom. How does this affect the jury's verdict? Use details from the play to explain why her appearance has this effect.

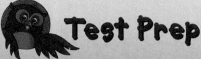

Test Prep

How to Read an Informational Article

1. Preview

- An author researches a topic and chooses important facts before writing an informational article.

- Read the title and the headings. What will you be reading about?

2. Read and Take Notes

- Write the title. Then jot notes when you read information that answers the question.

What Is the Supreme Court?

- place where final judgments are
  made about U.S. laws

3. Think and Connect

Think about *Blame It on the Wolf.* Then look over your notes on "What Is the Supreme Court?"

If animals could really go to court, would Mr. Wolf's case have to be settled in the Supreme Court? Use evidence from the selections to support your answer.

*F*rom the top row, left to right are Supreme Court Justices Ruth Bader Ginsburg, David Souter, Clarence Thomas, Stephen Breyer, (bottom left) Antonin Scalia, John Paul Stevens, William Rehnquist, Sandra Day O'Connor, Anthony Kennedy.

WHAT IS THE SUPREME COURT?

by Barbara Aria

Why Is the Supreme Court So Powerful?

The Supreme Court is where final judgments are made about the laws of the United States and about people's rights under the law. When the Supreme Court makes a decision, or ruling, that ruling applies to everyone, not just to the people involved in the case. Why is the Supreme Court so powerful? Because it has the final say—after the lower courts, Congress, and even the President—about what is legal.

The Supreme Court is a part of the United States government. Its home is in Washington, D.C., in a building so grand that it has been nicknamed "the Marble Palace." Here the nine judges, or justices, of the Supreme Court meet to decide many of the questions facing the people of this country. During its history, the Supreme Court has made decisions on questions of slavery, free speech, women's rights, children's rights, racial discrimination, and many others. These decisions have become a part of the law under which we live, affecting the day-to-day lives of millions of Americans.

The United States Supreme Court is the highest court of law in the land. Even the President has to obey its rulings. Like an ordinary law court, the Supreme Court settles arguments between people or between an individual and the government. And, like any other law court, it can only settle an argument that is presented in the form of a criminal or civil case. In a criminal case, someone is accused of breaking the law. In a civil case, two people or groups of people go to court to settle a dispute; perhaps they both claim ownership of a certain piece of land.

Different from Other Courts

The Supreme Court's special job is to make sure that the Constitution of the United States is upheld by the branches of the government. If the Court finds that a state law or an act of Congress goes against the Constitution, then that law or act can no longer stand. Even a presidential act can be found unlawful by the Supreme Court.

The Court does not have the power to make people obey its rulings. It has to rely on the government and citizens to carry them out. Nevertheless, most people feel that if we believe in living by the Constitution, then as President John F. Kennedy once said, "It's important that we support the Supreme Court decisions, even when we may not agree with them."

Text Structure

- **Text structure** is the way a piece of writing is organized.

- One way to organize writing is to put events in chronological, or time, order.

- Biographies and autobiographies, which tell about real people's lives, are often organized in chronological order.

- Important dates in a person's life and the age of a person at the time of an event can help you follow the order of a biography or autobiography.

Read "Cal Ripken, Jr." by Elizabeth Schleichert from *National Geographic World* magazine.

Write About It

1. Make a time line showing key events in the life of Cal Ripken, Jr.

2. List clue words that help you follow Cal's life story.

Cal Ripken, Jr.

by Elizabeth Schleichert

"All Cal ever wanted to be was a ballplayer," says Vi Ripken. She's referring to her son, Cal Ripken, Jr., a record-breaking player for the Baltimore Orioles.

Born August 24, 1960, Cal grew up in Aberdeen, Maryland, not far from the Orioles stadium in Baltimore. Cal often talked about baseball at home. His father, Cal Ripken, Sr., was a catcher for a minor league team and later a major league coach.

As young as age four, Cal took advantage of his father's job. He ran near the practice field, sometimes asking players to roll the ball to him. At age nine he was allowed to chase fly balls during batting practice. All the time, Cal studied how the pros played, asking his dad lots of questions and practicing. He was also developing a competitive spirit.

Cal worked hard to compete. As a freshman, he was determined to be on his high school baseball team, even though he was small. But he didn't qualify for the team because he couldn't run a mile in less than seven minutes. He convinced the coach to let him try again. The second time, Cal made it. Once he was on the team, he continued to work hard. By his senior year, he was pitching the ball an amazing eighty-six miles an hour.

AHEAD

Lou Gehrig
~ The Luckiest Man ~

Learn about Lou Gehrig, another great baseball player, as you read *Lou Gehrig: The Luckiest Man*. Then determine the text structure of the selection.

Words to Know

convinced	gradually
courageous	immigrants
engineer	

When you read, you may come across a word you do not know. To figure out the meaning of the unfamiliar word, look for clues in the sentences around the word. You might find a definition of the word in the paragraph.

Notice how *immigrants* is used in the paragraph below. Find its definition in the sentence. What does *immigrant* mean?

Lou Gehrig
1903 – 1941

Book Report: Lou Gehrig

Lou Gehrig's parents were courageous immigrants, brave people who came to the U.S. from another country. Lou was born in New York. The Gehrigs wanted their son to become an accountant or engineer, but Lou was convinced he wanted to be a baseball player. His parents gradually accepted his decision. They were probably proud of his choice—Lou Gehrig became one of the best baseball players of all time!

Write About It

Write a short report about a sports figure you admire. Use vocabulary words.

Lou Gehrig
~ The Luckiest Man ~

by David A. Adler
illustrated by Terry Widener

1903 was a year of great beginnings. Henry Ford sold his first automobile and the Wright Brothers made the first successful flight in an airplane. In baseball, the first World Series was played. The team later known as the Yankees moved from Baltimore to New York. And on June 19, 1903, Henry Louis Gehrig was born. He would become one of the greatest players in baseball history.

Lou Gehrig was born in the Yorkville section of New York City. It was an area populated with poor immigrants like his parents, Heinrich and Christina Gehrig, who had come to the United States from Germany.

Christina Gehrig had great hopes for her son Lou. She dreamed that he would attend college and become an accountant or an engineer. She insisted that he study hard. Through eight years of grade school, Lou didn't miss a single day.

Lou's mother thought games and sports were a waste of time. But Lou loved sports. He got up early to play the games he loved—baseball, soccer, and football. He played until it was time to go to school. In high school Lou was a star on his school's baseball team.

After high school Lou Gehrig went to Columbia University. He was on the baseball team there, too, and on April 26, 1923, a scout for the New York Yankees watched him play. Lou hit two long home runs in that game. Soon after that he was signed to play for the Yankees.

The Yankees offered Lou a $1,500 bonus to sign plus a good salary. His family needed the money. Lou quit college and joined the Yankees. Lou's mother was furious. She was convinced that he was ruining his life.

On June 1, 1925, the Yankee manager sent Lou to bat for the shortstop. The next day Lou played in place of first baseman Wally Pipp. Those were the first two games in what would become an amazing record: For the next fourteen years Lou Gehrig played in 2,130 consecutive Yankee games. The boy who never missed a day of grade school became a man who never missed a game.

Lou Gehrig played despite stomachaches, fevers, a sore arm, back pains, and broken fingers. Lou's constant play earned him the nickname Iron Horse. All he would say about his amazing record was, "That's the way I am."

Lou was shy and modest, but people who watched him knew just how good he was. In 1927 Lou's teammate Babe Ruth hit sixty home runs, the most hit up to that time in one season. But it was Lou Gehrig who was selected that year by the baseball writers as the American League's Most Valuable Player. He was selected again as the league's MVP in 1936.

Then, during the 1938 baseball season—and for no apparent reason—Lou Gehrig stopped hitting. One newspaper reported that Lou was swinging as hard as he could, but when he hit the ball it didn't go anywhere.

Lou exercised. He took extra batting practice. He even tried changing the way he stood and held his bat. He worked hard during the winter of 1938 and watched his diet.

But the following spring Lou's playing was worse. Time after time he swung at the ball and missed. He had trouble fielding. And he even had problems off the field. In the clubhouse he fell down while he was getting dressed.

Some people said Yankee manager Joe McCarthy should take Lou out of the lineup. But McCarthy refused. He had great respect for Lou and said, "Gehrig plays as long as he wants to play." But Lou wasn't selfish. On May 2, 1939, he told Joe McCarthy, "I'm benching myself . . . for the good of the team."

When reporters asked why he took himself out, Lou didn't say he felt weak or how hard it was for him to run. Lou made no excuses. He just said that he couldn't hit and he couldn't field.

On June 13, 1939, Lou went to the Mayo Clinic in Rochester, Minnesota, to be examined by specialists. On June 19, his thirty-sixth birthday, they told Lou's wife, Eleanor, what was wrong. He was suffering from amyotrophic lateral sclerosis, a deadly disease that affects the central nervous system.

Lou stayed with the team, but he didn't play. He was losing weight. His hair was turning gray. He didn't have to be told he was dying. He knew it. "I don't have long to go," he told a teammate.

Lou loved going to the games, being in the clubhouse, and sitting with his teammates. Before each game Lou brought the Yankee lineup card to the umpire at home plate. A teammate or coach walked with him, to make sure he didn't fall. Whenever Lou came onto the field the fans stood up and cheered for brave Lou Gehrig.

But Yankee fans and the team wanted to do more. They wanted Lou to know how deeply they felt about him. So they made July 4, 1939, Lou Gehrig Appreciation Day at Yankee Stadium.

Many of the players from the 1927 Yankees—perhaps the best baseball team ever—came to honor their former teammate. There was a marching band and gifts. Many people spoke too. Fiorello La Guardia, the mayor of New York City, told Lou, "You are the greatest prototype of good sportsmanship and citizenship."

When the time came for Lou to thank everyone, he was too moved to speak. But the fans wanted to hear him and chanted, "We want Gehrig! We want Gehrig!"

Dressed in his Yankee uniform, Lou Gehrig walked slowly to the array of microphones. He wiped his eyes, and with his baseball cap in his hands, his head down, he slowly spoke.

"Fans," he said, "for the past two weeks you have been reading about a bad break I got. Yet today I consider myself the luckiest man on the face of the earth."

It was a courageous speech. Lou didn't complain about his terrible illness. Instead he spoke of his many blessings and of the future. "Sure, I'm lucky," he said when he spoke of his years in baseball. "Sure, I'm lucky," he said again when he spoke of his fans and family.

Lou spoke about how good people had been to him. He praised his teammates. He thanked his parents and his wife, whom he called a tower of strength.

The more than sixty thousand fans in Yankee Stadium stood to honor Lou Gehrig. His last words to them—and to the many thousands more sitting by their radios and listening—were, "So I close in saying that I might have had a bad break, but I have an awful lot to live for. Thank you."

Lou stepped back from the microphones and wiped his eyes. The stadium crowd let out a tremendous roar, and Babe Ruth did what many people must have wanted to do that day. He threw his arms around Lou Gehrig and gave him a great warm hug.

The band played the song "I Love You Truly," and the fans chanted, "We love you, Lou."

When Lou Gehrig left the stadium later that afternoon, he told a teammate, "I'm going to remember this day for a long time."

In December 1939 Lou Gehrig was voted into the Baseball Hall of Fame. And the Yankees retired his uniform. No one else on the team would ever wear the number four. It was the first time a major-league baseball team did that to honor one of its players.

Mayor Fiorello La Guardia thought Lou's courage might inspire some of the city's troubled youths to be courageous too. He offered Lou a job working with former prisoners as a member of the New York City Parole Commission. Lou had many opportunities to earn more money, but he believed this job would enable him to do something for the city that had given him so much.

Within little more than a year, Lou had to leave his job. He was too weak to keep working. He stayed at home, unable to do the simplest task.

Lou had many visitors. He didn't speak to them of his illness or of dying. When he saw one friend visibly upset by the way he looked, Lou told him not to worry. "I'll gradually get better," he said. In cards to his friends Lou wrote, "We have much to be thankful for."

By the middle of May 1941, Lou hardly left his bed. Then on Monday, June 2, 1941, just after ten o'clock at night, Lou Gehrig died. He was thirty-seven years old.

On June 4 the Yankee game was canceled because of rain. Some people thought it was fitting that the Yankees did not play; this was the day of Lou Gehrig's funeral.

At the funeral the minister announced that there would be no speeches. "We need none," he said, "because you all knew him." That seemed fitting, too, for modest Lou Gehrig.

About the Author

David Adler was an artist and a math teacher in New York City before he started writing books. He has written over one hundred books on such topics as Roman numerals, redwood trees, and the Holocaust. Mr. Adler writes both fiction and nonfiction books, and he likes it that way. He says about writing, "I am able to vary my work even in a single day, from doing research on a nonfiction book to writing fiction to creating a silly riddle or poem."

Mr. Adler is also a devoted New York Yankees fan who spends a lot of time at Yankee Stadium during the baseball season.

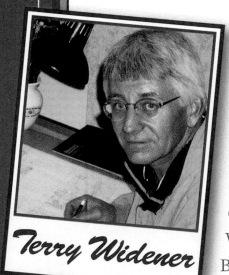

About the Illustrator

Terry Widener is an award-winning artist. He loves creating art. He also happens to be a baseball fan. His two loves came together in the book *Lou Gehrig: The Luckiest Man.* This is Mr. Widener's first book as an illustrator. Because of his knowledge of baseball, he was able to show how this famous baseball star looked and moved. Mr. Widener lives in Texas with his wife and children.

Reader Response

Open for Discussion

If you had heard Lou Gehrig's speech in Yankee Stadium, how would you have felt?

Comprehension Check

1. What made Lou Gehrig an amazing baseball player? Use details from the selection to explain your answer.

2. The author expresses a viewpoint when he writes, "It was a courageous speech." Do you agree with this view? Use examples to explain.

3. Do you think Lou Gehrig was a hero? Use examples to explain.

4. **Text structure** is the way a piece of writing is organized. The two main kinds of writing are fiction and nonfiction. How do you know that this is a piece of nonfiction? (Text Structure)

5. Chronological order is one of the ways to organize **text structure** in nonfiction. Tell the order of important events in Lou Gehrig's life. (Text Structure)

Test Prep

Look Back and Write

Look back at pages 424–425. Why was it important for the author to include information about Lou Gehrig's parents? Use details from the selection to support your answer.

The Baseball Hall of Fame

by Terry Janson Dunnahoo
and Herma Silverstein

A popular exhibit at the Baseball Hall of Fame is the No-Hitter Display.

How would you like to come face-to-face with Babe Ruth and Ted Williams? Or peek into Lou Gehrig's locker? Or see the nicks in the bat Willie Mays used when he hit four home runs in one game? You can. They're all on display in the Baseball Hall of Fame in Cooperstown, New York.

During the first year the Hall of Fame was open, 25,332 people paid 25 cents each to tour the Hall. Since then, millions of visitors have passed through its doors. So many souvenirs have been donated by baseball clubs, players, and fans that the Hall of Fame has become baseball's storage attic.

HANK AARON

Hank Aaron was one of the greatest home-run hitters of all time.

Almost every bat, ball, and glove that ever set a record is there. So are the shoes "Shoeless" Joe Jackson wore during the crooked 1919 Chicago White Sox World Series; the cap and ball Texas Rangers pitcher Nolan Ryan used when he pitched his record-breaking seventh no-hitter in 1991; and Babe Ruth's locker, complete with his bowling ball and shaving mug. Looking at his locker, you have the feeling that Babe will run in any minute to suit up and go hit another home run.

Enter the National Baseball Hall of Fame and Museum—its full name—and be transported into a baseball fantasyland. Straight ahead you'll spot life-size wooden statues of Babe Ruth and Ted Williams. They look so real you can see whisker stubs sprouting from Babe's face as he stares back at you.

In the Cooperstown Room you'll see the evolution of baseball, including a photo of the first Hall of Famers and the $5 Abner Doubleday Baseball that Stephen Clark bought from Abner Graves's family.

Highest Slugging Average
Based on at least 2,000 total bases.

Avg.	Player
.730	Mark McGwire
.729	Frank Thomas
.690	Albert Belle
.690	Babe Ruth
.670	Hank Greenberg
.646	Ken Griffey Jr.
.634	Ted Williams
.632	Lou Gehrig
.632	Juan Gonzalez
.609	Jimmie Foxx
.585	Joe DiMaggio
.577	Rogers Hornsby
.559	Stan Musial

Note: Slugging average is total bases divided by at-bats.

The Baseball Hall of Fame connects the past and the present with an Evolution of Equipment exhibit of bats, gloves, baseballs, and catcher's gear.

In the Sports Gallery, zero in on the stats of your favorite Hall of Famer. On the computer you can punch up Roy Campanella's lifetime batting average or find out how many bases Lou Brock stole or how many Gold Gloves Johnny Bench won.

Climb to the second floor and see the old-time baseball uniforms. Check out the baggy, knee-length pants, flannel shirts, and straw caps worn by some of the first organized baseball teams.

On the third floor are dugout benches, grandstand seats, turnstiles, and cornerstones from Ebbets Field, Forbes Field, Crosley Field, and the Polo Grounds. None of these parks exist any longer—they all are history.

Smell the memories of leather, dust, and sweat while you stroll by lockers that once belonged to Joe DiMaggio, Stan Musial, and Hank Aaron, who broke Babe Ruth's 714 home run record. The lockers stand side by side, like an all-star baseball team for all time.

Summarizing

- A **summary** is a short statement, no more than a few sentences, that tells the main idea of a selection.

- A story summary tells the goals of the characters, how they try to reach them, and whether they reach them.

- A summary of an article should tell the main idea, leaving out unnecessary details.

Read "Korean Foods" from *North and South Korea* by Gene and Clare Gurney.

Talk About It

1. Which of these statements is the better summary of this article? Explain your choice.

   a. Korean foods are not fattening.

   b. Basic foods in the Korean diet include *kimch'i,* rice, vegetables, and fish.

2. A summary is not a paraphrase. How would a paraphrase of "Korean Foods" be different from a summary?

Korean Foods

by Gene and Clare Gurney

Kimch'i is the Korean national dish. Like many Korean foods, it is highly seasoned. A combination of vegetables and strong spices, *kimch'i* is served with most meals.

   Rice is the principal food in the Korean diet. A Korean thinks he has eaten well if his meal has included rice. When other grains such as barley, wheat, or millet are eaten, they are mixed with rice if possible. Poor people who cannot afford rice every day try to have rice on New Year's Day and on their birthdays.

   Good Korean cooks prepare rice very carefully. They wash it several times and cook it in an iron pot in just the right amount of water. When the rice is removed from the cooking pot, water is added to the burned rice remaining on the bottom. The resulting mixture, called *sungyong* or rice tea, is served after the meal.

During the summer, Koreans eat a variety of fresh fruits and vegetables. Persimmons, peaches, pears, melons, apples, and berries are plentiful. Among the vegetables, potatoes, cabbage, *daikon,* turnips, hot peppers, leeks, and beans are especially popular. Both fruits and vegetables are pickled for winter use.

Fish is eaten throughout Korea. It may be fresh, salted, or dried. Fresh fish is sometimes served raw. Meat is expensive and not widely eaten. Eggs are considered a delicacy.

LOOK AHEAD

Read "The Disguise," the story of a young Korean girl born in 1896. Summarize the goals that Imduk's mother sets for her.

Words to Know

dangerous	chanting	cautious
suspected	squatted	recite
principal	disguise	

Words with opposite meanings are **antonyms.** You might be able to figure out the meaning of an unknown word by finding a clue word in the words around it. Sometimes the clue is an antonym.

Read the letter below. Notice how *careless* helps you understand what *cautious* means.

Letter to Mother from School

I am trying to be cautious here—if I'm careless, the others will find out I'm a girl wearing a boy's disguise. The first day was dangerous—I was almost found out! We were chanting a song when the principal came in. I thought he suspected the truth when he heard my voice, but he said nothing. I change my voice when I recite answers too. Yesterday we got to play my favorite game— baseball. As I squatted down behind home plate to catch, I started to feel better about being here.

Talk About It

In some places in the world, girls are not allowed to go to school. Do you think that's fair? Explain. Use as many vocabulary words as you can.

The Disguise

from *The Girl-Son*

by Anne E. Neuberger • illustrated by Cheryl Kirk Noll

In the year 1896, in a small village in Korea, a baby girl was born. She was named Imduk. At that time, girls in Korea were considered inferior to boys and never had a chance to go to school. But when Imduk's brother and father died of cholera, her mother made the decision that Imduk must get educated in order to earn the life that her father could no longer give her.

Early the next morning, I awoke as my mother began moving about the house. Opening one eye, I saw the bleak light of a winter morning.

"Imduk," Mother called, "I have asked a man to come and teach you the alphabet. Get up and dress quickly. He will be here soon."

Shivering, I pulled on my clothes, glancing at Mother wonderingly. Learn the alphabet? I knew no girls who could read!

I heard a soft knock and Mother hurried to the door. She opened it to let in a blast of frosty air and an old man.

He was frail, with a wispy beard the color of new-fallen snow. On his head he wore a tall, narrow stovepipe hat, which he removed upon entering. His long hair was braided and drawn into a knot at the top of his head, held tightly by a horsehair net. This topknot meant he was an educated man. I knew this, for my father, also a scholar, had worn his hair this way. How dignified this man looked in his white scholar's robe!

I wondered where his *podari* was. My father had had one, a small cloth bundle that held the soft, pointed Chinese brush, ink stone, and ink cake. With these my father had spent hours practicing his brush strokes that made up the thousands of characters of the Chinese alphabet.

But this man brought no *podari*, nor any roll of rice paper. Instead, he held a small pad of paper.

I studied his face, a map of wrinkles, and his hands, purpled with veins. He saw me staring.

Though he said nothing, his eyes twinkled at me. I relaxed a bit. Without a word, he sat down on the floor, cross-legged.

The silence among us was broken by a rasping sound. Mother was scraping the end of my blunt pencil with a knife. When it was sharp, she handed it to me, gesturing for me to sit on the floor next to the teacher. Awkwardly, I sat. My first lesson had begun.

Each day for two weeks, my teacher and I bent over the pad of paper, as I labored with my yellow pencil. Mother wove cloth, ever watchful in the background. She did not know if I could actually learn; most people did not think a girl could be taught to read and write. Mother would not waste her money on a teacher if they were right.

But I learned. Fast and well.

At the end of two weeks, my kindly teacher proclaimed me capable of reading and writing Han'gŭl, the Korean alphabet, and quietly took his leave.

"Oh, child!" Mother exclaimed, even giving a little jump for joy. "You can learn just like a boy! You must go to school!"

Holding the little pad now filled with letters, I watched my mother uneasily. It was rare that she showed so much excitement. Rarer still that she should talk so foolishly. Go to school? School was for boys!

Mother did not say how. For a week she was unusually quiet. She seemed deep in thought as she wove and cooked. I asked no questions.

One day Mother was squatting near her cooking pot, pouring rice into it. I liked the soft sh-sh sound the hard rice made as it was poured.

"Imduk, do you remember the tale of the Chinese girl who wanted to be a soldier?" she asked.

"Oh, yes, Mother! Tell it to me again, please?"

"She was young and beautiful but she did not want to live as a girl did. She longed to lead an exciting life. So she quietly left her village, dressed as a soldier, and went to war. Everyone assumed she was a man."

I nodded. I loved this story. Closing my eyes, I was no longer six years old but the woman warrior.

Mother stirred at the fire a bit. "She fought bravely and her fellow soldiers depended on her. Because she was such a good leader, she eventually became a general in the army.

She met another general who was a good man. She fell in love with him. After some time, she decided to risk everything and tell him that she was really a woman. He loved her too and later they married."

Opening my eyes, I saw Mother's face and knew she was not finished with her thoughts yet. I waited.

Suddenly she stood up and looked around at the small house. With determination, she said, "I have made a decision. We are going to move to the village of Dukdong, where a relative of mine runs a school for boys. I have thought of a way for you to get an education."

Mother's work-worn hands smoothed the fabric of her black skirt as it lay on the floor. Quickly she began cutting it.

We were in our new home, a single room, in the village of Dukdong. We had planned to live with Mother's brother, but they had quarreled.

He said Mother's idea to educate me was ridiculous. A girl couldn't learn! Where did she get such wild ideas from? No one in their family had such crazy notions!

Stubbornly, Mother clung to her plans and decided to make her own home. This decision took tremendous courage. I knew of no other woman who lived without at least one male relative in her home. By doing this, she was breaking yet another rule of our culture.

"Soon you will have some nice new pants, Imduk. I have made you a pink jacket, just like all the boys wear," Mother explained. Threading a needle with black thread, she began expertly sewing the skirt into pants. Her hands moved methodically. Never did she move unnecessarily.

"A pink jacket?" I asked softly, a little horrified. Pink was for boys.

"Yes. I've made all the arrangements with my relative, Kim Sung-No. He is the principal and has agreed that you may enter his school if I disguise you as a boy."

Disguised as a boy and go to school! I wondered what lay ahead for me. Thoughts of the warrior woman in Mother's story came back to me and I imagined her planning her change from girl to soldier.

I went to bed that night as a girl, but when I awoke, I began my life as a boy.

My red hair ribbons were laid aside. They were for girls. Boys also had long hair, but they braided a black ribbon into it. Mother carefully fixed my hair to look just like a boy's.

This made me think of my little brother, who had died when my father had died. I wondered if Mother also thought of him. I looked into her face. She was peering at my hair, determined that it be exactly right. No, all her thoughts were on me right now.

Next I put on the new pants she had finished late the night before, and the pink jacket.

Now Mother held me at arm's length, her sharp eyes examining me.

"Good," she said with satisfaction. "Now you look just like a boy."

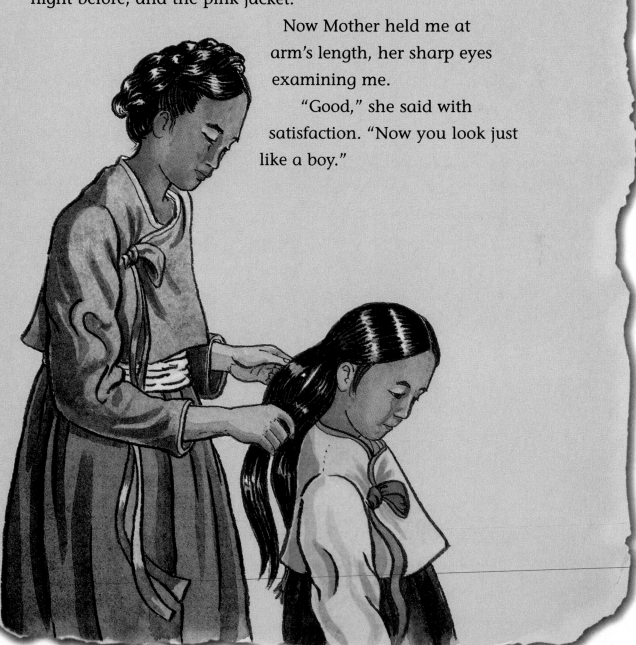

I wiggled a bit, feeling strange in these clothes. Did I really look like a boy?

Mother said solemnly, "You will no longer be called Imduk. You are beginning a new life. For this new life I name you Induk. It means 'benevolence.'"

"Benevolence?"

"Yes. One who does kindnesses. Now that you are Induk, you are my girl-son."

For a moment she paused, and there was silence between us. Then she said briskly, "Now come, Induk. We must leave for the school."

Together we walked through the village, mother and girl-son. She walked proudly and I knew she felt I was just as important as anyone else's boy. I was just as important as her cousin's three sons. I also knew that was a radical idea.

We reached the school quickly, too soon for my comfort. Mother squatted to look intently into my face. I studied her black eyes, understanding the seriousness of her plan.

"You are a boy now," Mother said in a low tone. "Remember your name. If you have been a good boy at school, I will give you all the chicken gizzards you want when you come home."

This was a favorite treat of mine, but first I had to face the school all by myself. Mother could not come with me. She would go back home. Home, where all the girls were.

Gathering all my seven-year-old courage, I entered the school doorway and looked around. The classroom was part of the teacher's home. The floor was made of mud and stone, then covered with oiled paper. As in most Korean homes, because pipes running under the floor were heated by the kitchen stove, the floor was warm.

On this floor sat fifteen boys. Some were little, a bit younger than me. The oldest were around ten years old. Each sat cross-legged and held a Chinese book in his hands, reading aloud. Their voices had a singsong sound. As they read, they swayed to and fro.

The teacher saw me. The principal had assured Mother he would not tell anyone I was a girl, but as the teacher came toward me, I wondered if he could tell I was only pretending to be a boy.

"Come in," he invited. "You may sit at the end of the row."

So I entered this world of boys and men.

Holding my head high as Mother would have, I walked past the seated boys.

Though the chanting of lessons did not stop, I knew every eye was upon me. I felt my face burning with embarrassment, and a feeling of fear began welling up inside of me. Did they guess my secret? Did I really look like a boy?

The end of the row seemed at the end of the world. Finally I reached it. I took my place, sitting cross-legged as the others did. Again I glanced at the teacher. Did he realize I was a girl? He was walking toward me. My heart pounded so loudly, I wondered if the boy sitting next to me could hear it.

But the teacher simply handed me a book called "One Thousand Characters."

I was now to learn the very complicated language of China. Highly educated Koreans still used Chinese, a tradition from long ago.

The teacher said in a kind voice, "You must learn the first eight characters. Tomorrow you will recite them aloud and write them without looking at the book."

Opening my book, I looked carefully at the unfamiliar letters. They were not the Han'gŭl letters my teacher in Monyangtul had taught me.

"If I learned those, I can learn these," I told myself.

And I learned sixteen of them.

It was a good day.

At the end of the school day, I gave a sigh of relief. No one had noticed all day that I was really a girl! But as we tumbled out of the classroom, I suddenly realized that pretending to be a boy in the quiet classroom was one thing. Being a boy outside was quite another.

The boys began running and shouting playfully. I paused. I had never been allowed to play with boys before.

"Come on, Induk! Race you home!" a boy named Kim Hyun Duk called.

Well, I told myself, I could run! And I chased after him.

When I reached home, Mother greeted me with interest.

"School was good, Mother!" I said. "I am learning the Chinese language. And, Mother—I think I will like being a boy!"

"Here," Mother replied. "I made the chicken gizzards for you."

I knew Mother was proud of me. I imagine she was also very relieved. I had managed to play the part of a boy and had liked it too!

As I relished the chicken gizzards, I realized that Mother had prepared them before I had come home from school. She had expected that I would succeed today. She had believed in me. The chicken tasted even better.

Each day was a little easier. I worked hard, but I enjoyed learning. I felt more comfortable being a boy as each afternoon ended.

Then one morning, the teacher announced it would soon be time for a review. Twice a month, every student recited what he had learned in the past two weeks.

"The student who has learned the most and the one who recites the loudest receives a prize," the teacher reminded us.

I listened, wondering what the prize was. On the way home, however, the boys told me what the teacher had not mentioned.

"I hope you know your lessons well, Induk," Hyun Duk said. "If not, study hard tonight!"

"I do know them," I said confidently.

"Good. Then you are safe," he said.

"Safe?" I asked, becoming uneasy.

"Any student who does not know his lessons is punished," his friend Young Jin explained.

"How?"

"He is whipped across the legs with sticks."

"Everyone watches," Jung Dae, another friend, added.

At home, I studied hard.

The next morning, review day, my heart beat as loudly as it had the first day. I sat cross-legged in my place.

"Induk," called the teacher.

I rose to my feet, a bit wobbly, took a deep breath and began to recite.

The teacher did not look up, but announced, "The prize for the loudest goes to Induk."

Smiling, I sat down. Mother was right. I could learn just like a boy!

Over the next months, I earned the prize for reciting the loudest many times. Never was I whipped, for I always learned what was expected of me. In three months, I was able to read and write one thousand characters of the Chinese language.

Reading was not the only skill I learned because I went to school with boys. My classmates never suspected I was a girl and welcomed me in their games, which girls would never experience.

With their help, I fashioned a kite and ran over the fields of Dukdong to launch it. The chilly spring air brought roses to my cheeks. I loved the feeling of the taut string tugging in my hand as if the kite were saying, "Let me go! Let me free!"

When the wind was too mild for kite flying, we would gather willow branches, now green and supple, to make whistles from them.

One day, my friend Hyun Duk ran up to me as I walked home from school. "Come on," he invited. "We've found a bird's nest. We're going to get the eggs."

What a strange thing to do, I thought, but out loud I asked, "Where?"

He pointed to a gathering of boys a few houses away. One had climbed the side of a house.

Curious, I joined them. The nest was on the thatched roof. Young Jin was higher up in a tree. He called, "I can't quite reach it."

After he had climbed down, he turned to me. "You try it, Induk. Maybe you can reach it."

I doubted it. I wasn't very tall. But here was my chance to try, and I might never get this chance again. I felt my heart racing as I climbed, carefully placing my foot on a branch and testing it for strength before putting my full weight on it. I had seen Young Jin do this, and I copied his way. I did not want the others to know this was the first time I had tried to get a nest. Reaching the roof, I squatted to keep my balance. As I stretched out my arm to the nest, I wobbled but quickly shifted my weight before I could fall.

My concentration was so strong that the shouts of encouragement from my friends seemed far away. In this new position, I could reach the nest. A bit more of a stretch and my fingers caressed the smoothness of an egg.

Suddenly what I was doing seemed silly. Why take the eggs? But glancing down at the expectant faces below told me I had gotten myself too far into this situation. I couldn't back out now, lest someone suspect I was a girl. Slowly I gathered all three eggs, cushioned them in the pocket of my pink jacket, and lowered myself to the ground.

My friends cheered. Hyun Duk shouted, "Hooray for Induk!"

The boys gathered around me as I pulled the eggs out of my pocket. Young Jin thumped me on the back with admiration.

"My mother will cook them for us," Jung Dae said. "Let's go!"

I ran off with them, feeling as free as the wind. I could climb trees! And I was good at it!

When spring gave way to the heat of summer, I climbed trees and swung recklessly from ropes tied to them. Hide-and-seek and other games led me to places I had not yet explored.

One scorching day, my friends and I dropped to the ground, panting, after a game of chase. Sweat trickled down my forehead and Hyun Duk was wiping his neck. Young Jin and Jung Dae fanned themselves.

"I'm so hot," Hyun Duk complained.

"Me too," I added, running my hand over my face.

Jung Dae rolled onto his side and propped himself up on his elbow. "I've got an idea!" he announced.

Young Jin seemed to know what he meant. He sat up.

"And it's a great idea! Come on!"

He jumped up, followed by the others. They began running. I scrambled to my feet, calling after them, "Wait! Wait for me!"

I had no idea where we were going, but I did not want to be left out. Despite the heat, I hurried, hoping to soon catch up with the others.

In the distance, the ground sloped. I watched as Young Jin and Jung Dae disappeared down the embankment. I wondered how steeply the ground dropped as I ran along, now gasping for breath.

I reached the hill some minutes after the others, and what I saw brought me to a halt.

Hyun Duk was pulling off his shoes. Jung Dae had stripped to the waist. And Young Jin? I dared not look! For at the bottom of the hill lay a small pond. They were going to swim!

"Come on, slowpoke!" Hyun Duk called cheerfully to me as he too peeled off his shirt.

Immediately I scurried away, fearful that one of the boys would follow me. My heart was pounding, sweat soaked my back, but I ran. I ran all the way back to my house.

Mother looked up from her weaving, surprised at my hasty entrance.

"What's wrong?" she asked.

"The boys—" I panted. "I was playing with the boys—"

Mother stood up and got me a cup of water.

"Here. Drink this. When you are composed, you may tell me."

I sat down, regained my breath, and gratefully drank the water. Then I began again, "I was playing with Hyun Duk and the others until I realized—they were going swimming!"

For a fleeting moment, I saw a look of amusement cross Mother's face. Then she said calmly, "You did right, of course, to come home."

"But what about when I see them again? They'll want to know why I didn't swim with them. Maybe they'll guess why I didn't!"

My voice was high and frantic. Mother resumed her weaving and the familiar motions calmed me.

"Then you must have a good answer for them. Tell them your mother forbids it because it might be dangerous."

"Dangerous, Mother? Don't the boys swim there all the time?" I asked.

Suddenly I realized I had spoken disrespectfully.

Mother looked up. She was not angry. She understood my fear.

"There is always risk in swimming, especially when children are without adults. And, Induk, for you, it would be especially dangerous—dangerous to your education!"

My friends did question me the next day, and I gave them my mother's words. They pooh-poohed the danger, but understood that a mother's orders must be obeyed.

I asked more questions about what my friends' plans were after that, and if swimming was an option, I declined. Someone would say, mockingly, "Induk's mother treats him like a baby—she won't let him swim!"

They would laugh and I would too. What else could I do?

As I walked home, feeling left out of the fun, I knew my mother was getting a reputation for being overly cautious. Little did they know she was taking a great risk with my life, raising me to go against everything these boys believed in. But this was left unsaid. I was relieved my secret was still safe.

When Imduk could no longer disguise herself as a boy, her mother sent her to a school for girls that had opened seven miles away. Imduk spent her life studying and learning, graduating from high school and college, traveling to the United States, and eventually returning to her country, where she founded two schools, a Technical High School and an Institute of Design. She wanted to give to others the freedom through education that she had always known.

About the Author
Anne E. Neuberger

Anne E. Neuberger first became interested in Korea after she adopted a child who was born there. She read a magazine article about Induk Pahk, a real person who lived in Korea in the early part of the twentieth century, and wanted to tell Induk's story. Ms. Neuberger is a free-lance writer who discovered as a child that she loved to write. She lives in Minnesota with her husband and three children.

About the Illustrator
Cheryl Kirk Noll

Cheryl Kirk Noll always liked to draw. Today she works as an illustrator and specializes in stories about other cultures. Ms. Noll enjoys studying the clothing, landscapes, and homes of people from other times and places. She tries to have her art reflect the "look" of the art of the culture. For "The Disguise," she soaked her paper in tea so that it would have a beige background like the beautiful Korean works of art that she saw at a museum.

Reader Response

Open for Discussion

If you were in the same situation as Imduk, would you want to go to school? Why or why not?

Comprehension Check

1. How does Mother show courage? Give examples.

2. Why does Mother change Imduk's name to Induk? Give details.

3. What skills does Imduk learn from her new friends at school? How do these skills make her feel? Give details.

4. Remember that you include only important details when you **summarize.** Which two of the following statements would you *not* include in a summary of this story? Why? (Summarizing)

   a. Imduk does very well in school.

   b. In most Korean homes, the floors are heated by pipes.

   c. Imduk learns to fly kites.

5. To **summarize** a story, think about the goals. What are the goals of Imduk and her mother, how do they try to reach the goals, and do they succeed? (Summarizing)

Test Prep
Look Back and Write

Look back at pages 450–453. How are Imduk and her mother alike? How are they different? Use evidence from the selection to support your answer.

Back

Test Prep

How to Read a Web Site

1. Preview

- This informational article comes from a Web site. When you visit a Web site, you see links to other information. You decide which links to click on.

- Read the titles on the menu bar at the bottom of the introduction. How would you choose which link to go to first?

2. Read and Decide

- Look over the article. Which link would you click on first? What other links interest you?

- As you read, imagine that you are learning to write using Chinese characters. Decide if you could learn them easily from a Web site.

3. Think and Connect

Think about "The Disguise." Then think about "Chinese Calligraphy."

If Imduk visited your class, what would you ask her about how she learned Korean and Chinese writing? What could you show her that would interest her?

466

Chinese Calligraphy

Introduction

Welcome to the Chinese Calligraphy Web site. This Web site was created by elementary school children to introduce other young people to the art of Chinese calligraphy. We hope you enjoy learning about this ancient art form.

China is the world's oldest ongoing civilization. It is known for many beautiful forms of art—silk painting, pottery, paper cutting, kite making, and calligraphy. It was calligraphy that captured our imaginations because the words evolved from pictures.

This Web site contains information on the tools used by a calligrapher, how to form the characters, and how the characters represent words. We have also included facts about China. We hope that you visit all of the pages, and enjoy Chinese calligraphy as much as we do. Thank you.

HOME   DRAWING   CHINA FACTS   RESOURCES

Chinese Calligraphy
Drawing

Chinese words are made up of characters. These characters have evolved from ancient pictographs.

田 This character means **field.** Can you see the plots of the farmer's field?

山 This one stands for **mountain.** It is easy to see the mountain peaks.

女 The character for **woman** is harder to see. The rectangle represents a baby bundled in a mother's lap.

心 Can you guess this one? This picture represents the **heart.** Each stroke shows the outline of a chamber of the heart.

When you combine two or more characters, you create a new "meaning."

思 If you take the character for **field** and draw it on top of the character for **heart,** you create the new character that means **to think.** Farming was very important in China, and to know what to plant required a lot of thought and planning.

火山 The first symbol means **fire.** The second means **mountain.** Add them together and what do you get? **Volcano!**

安 You recognize the character for **woman.** The woman is under a **roof.** These characters together mean **peace.**

◀ **PREVIOUS**   ▶ **NEXT**

467

Plot

- Stories have **plot,** or a series of events that center on a problem, or conflict.

- A conflict can be a problem between two people or groups, or between a person and nature. Conflicts can also be problems that characters have within themselves.

- The climax is the place where the action of the story builds and the conflict must be faced.

- The resolution is the place where the problem is solved.

Read "One Particular Small, Smart Boy" from *One-Minute Favorite Fairy Tales* **by Shari Lewis.**

Write About It

1. Write a sentence that explains the conflict in this fairy tale.

2. Describe the climax of the story. Explain what kind of voice you would use to read that part of the story aloud.

3. What is the tale's resolution?

One Particular Small, Smart Boy

by Shari Lewis

Once upon a time a little boy was walking home from the village with only an egg and some salt in his pocket. Suddenly a big, mean giant jumped out from behind a tree and said, "Little boy! I'm going to eat you up for lunch!"

The boy, who was small but very smart, quickly said, "Oh great Giant, I know you are strong, but so am I. Let's have a contest to see who's the strongest."

The giant snorted, "Compared to me, you're no bigger than a blade of grass. I'll mow you down right now. On with the contest!"

The boy quickly snuck the egg from his pocket into the palm of his

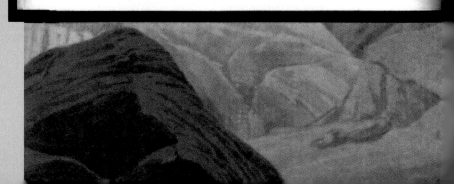

hand where the giant couldn't see it. He picked up a rock in that same hand and said, "I challenge you to squeeze this rock until water comes out, as I will!" Then the boy squeezed the egg and the rock together until the eggshell broke and egg oozed between his fingers. Of course, the giant thought the water actually came from the rock, and he was shocked.

Then the boy secretly took some salt from his pocket, picked up another rock and said, "Now I'm going to squeeze this rock into salt." After a few squeezes, he let the salt pour out. Then he turned to the giant. "And now, give me your *hand* and I'll squeeze it into mud!"

But the giant cried, "Oh no, you won't!" and he ran away, never to bother that particular small, smart boy again.

LOOK AHEAD

Keepers
by Jeri Hanel Watts   illustrated by Felicia Marshall

In *Keepers*, Kenyon loves his grandmother, the Keeper of the family stories. Follow the plot as you read about the problems Kenyon faces in finding her a birthday gift.

Words to Know

considering	definitely	taunted
grounders	reminder	stroke
diamond		

Words that are spelled the same but have different origins and meanings are called **homonyms.** To understand the correct meaning, look for clues in the surrounding words and sentences.

Read the paragraph below. Decide whether *stroke* means "a gentle movement of the hand" or "a sudden attack of illness."

Family Stories

Grandpa's <u>stroke</u> made him lose some memory. He needed a <u>reminder</u> to do simple things. Peter was <u>considering</u> whether he even wanted to tell him what had happened today, but he did. Kids at the playground had <u>taunted</u> Peter about not catching a fly ball. Grandpa told a story about his own days on the ball <u>diamond</u>. He kept missing <u>grounders</u>, balls that bounced on the ground, but practice made him a better catcher than anyone. Peter was determined— and <u>definitely</u> glad he heard Grandpa's story!

Write About It

What special story has someone in your family told you? Write it down, using as many vocabulary words as you can.

Keepers

by Jeri Hanel Watts   illustrated by Tyrone Geter

His grandmother's heavy snoring told Kenyon that she'd finished her storytelling. He liked to listen with his eyes closed, so he hadn't realized she was through until the snore. He loved her stories, as familiar to him as if they had been his own. But he knew she got tired quickly since her stroke, so he rose quietly and eased to the kitchen to glance at the clock.

"Nearly four o'clock," he whispered. He could just make it to the ballfield if he left now. His tired old glove lay in his room, beside the reminder he'd printed in big, bold letters: "ninety in two Saturdays." He didn't want to forget a present for his grandmother's ninetieth birthday. Kenyon pounded his cracked glove with his right hand. He didn't have to worry about that yet. He tiptoed to the front door.

"Where you think you're going, boy?"

Kenyon's quiet, easy glide to freedom was frozen by his grandmother's words. "To play baseball," he mumbled.

"Did you finish your homework?" she demanded.

"Mostly finished, Little Dolly." From the corner of his eye, he saw the white hair snap around. Kenyon let the door fall shut and turned as his grandmother lit into him.

"Mostly? Mostly's not good enough, child. There's some things cain't be done mostly. Cain't mostly be dead. You either dead or you not. Cain't be mostly crazy. You either crazy or you not. And—"

"I'll finish," he interrupted. Man, she did take a lot of words to say no.

Little Dolly's voice kept on muttering with her list of non-mostlys, but Kenyon opened his history book and shut out her talking. Since his mother died six years ago he and his dad had lived with Little Dolly. He still didn't know why she was called Little Dolly. There wasn't much little about her. She was a big-boned woman with great big hands and a great big voice and a great lot of words.

Kenyon tried his best to study his history but he couldn't concentrate on all those long-ago dates and names. His mind was filled up with more important things. Things like Mo Davis's fastball and whether he could hit it today like he did yesterday—clean out of the park.

Mo thought he was some kind of pitcher with his real leather glove, but Kenyon didn't mind on days like yesterday, days when Kenyon felt like a hitting machine that could not be denied. That had been a true wallop-bat day.

By the time Kenyon reached the park diamond, he had to take leftovers on team and position.

"It's about time," Mo taunted. "Did you have to help Granny into the sun?"

Kenyon's knuckles burned as he clenched his fists tightly. He didn't like to hear Little Dolly spoken of poorly. So much for another wallop-bat day, he thought.

That evening, Kenyon sat on the peeling floor of the porch, while Little Dolly rested on the swing.

"Tell me a story, Little Dolly," he begged.

"You tell, instead," she answered. "Tell about the stories you read in your history book."

"Aw, those are boring." Kenyon pushed the swing gently. "The only good stories I can tell are about baseball. And you don't care about that."

"That's true enough, I suppose," Little Dolly agreed. "But a good storyteller can make you care with how she weaves the tale. Course, I ain't needing to tell that. Them words are for the next Keeper."

"Keeper?" Kenyon asked.

"Yes, Keeper. Of stories and legends. My grandma said they had Keepers back in Africa for each tribe, but I cain't say about that. Can say we've had Keepers in our family since always. My great grandma, Daisy, my Grandma Dormeen. And me. The Keeper holds onto the past until she can pass it on to the next." Little Dolly squinched her dark brown eyes. "Don't know who I'll hand my tales to, though." Her large fingers plucked at the sleeve of her blouse.

Kenyon stopped the swing and he knelt beside her. "Little Dolly, I'll be the Keeper. I love your stories."

Her eyes looked deep into his, searching.

"Lord, honey, that's nice, but you a boy. I got to find me a girl Keeper. You cain't be a Keeper if you a boy."

The next day Kenyon picked up an old shoe box and carried it to his bed. He slid the top off and dumped the contents onto the quilt. He'd been saving all of his neighborhood-chores money to buy something for Little Dolly's ninetieth birthday. Even if she did drive him crazy about schoolwork, Kenyon thought she was the best. He headed out to see what he could find.

Kenyon went in the bakery first. "Hey, Mrs. Montgomery." The woman behind the counter reached into the glass display case and pulled an oatmeal cookie from the pile. "Oatmeal is good for you in the morning," she said with a wink as she handed the still-warm cookie to Kenyon. "What can I do for you?"

"I'm trying to figure out what to get Little Dolly for her birthday." Kenyon forced his words around the cookie. "One of the things I was considering was one of your strawberry shortcakes. Little Dolly says no one can come close to touching your cake. Would you make one?"

Mrs. Montgomery smiled gently. "If that's what you want. But they're fifteen dollars."

"Oh, I got that and more," he said. "But I'm just looking today."

Kenyon wandered along Main Street, going in and out of shops, talking of ideas for Little Dolly with all of the shopkeepers, for they all knew his grandmother. The antique store, where she could tell stories about many of the items for sale; the carriage ride place, where Little Dolly always delighted the tourists with her tales; the soldier's cemetery, where she and Kenyon helped the caretaker decorate with flags on holidays.

Kenyon was sliding his fingers along the storefronts when he saw, right under his hand, a leather baseball glove. On sale. Real leather.

He went in. He tried it on. It fit as if it had been made just for him. He punched it with his fist and the rich aroma of new leather filled his head. He thought about Mo Davis, and within five minutes that brand spanking-new leather glove slid into a crisp shopping bag.

Kenyon ran to the field and tried it out. Mo wasn't around, but there were plenty of kids to "ooh" and "aah" over his purchase. He fielded grounders with it, spit into it, and scratched his name on it with a penknife.

And then, when he headed home for lunch, streaked with dust and full of pride, then he remembered Little Dolly.

Kenyon felt as if he couldn't breathe right. His eyes opened wide and he could feel his heart beating against his ribs the way a bat beats a ball when it connects for a homer.

"What'll I do? What'll I do?"

All the way home, folks asked him if he'd decided yet on the gift for Little Dolly. He managed to mumble something. Mrs. Montgomery looked at that ball glove and he knew she'd figured it out.

When he got asked to a pick-up game later, Kenyon said no and went to his room. His dad came in, feeling all over Kenyon's head, making him stick out his tongue.

"I'm not sick," he told his dad.

"You've never said no to a baseball game, son. Never."

Kenyon slumped onto his bed. "I'm not sick. I'm just stupid."

"Why in the world do you say that?"

"Dad, have you ever done something you were sorry for, but you couldn't change it?" Kenyon looked straight into his father's eyes.

His dad let a breath out slow. "Well, sure. Everybody has, I expect."

"So, what did you do?"

"Told myself I'd do better the next time and then, went on. You can't go back. Can only go forward."

Little Dolly wouldn't be ninety again. He couldn't do better. There wouldn't be a next time.

Shoot, he didn't blame Little Dolly for not trusting him with her stories. He couldn't even be trusted with money and—

The stories. That was it. He *could* give her something.

479

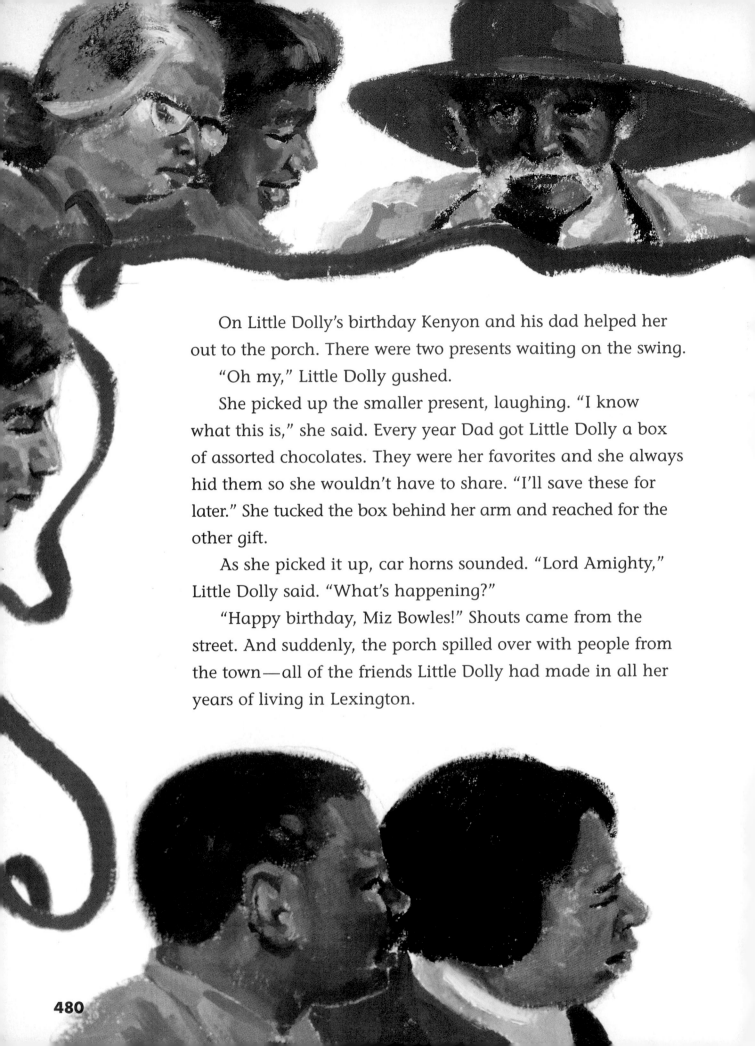

On Little Dolly's birthday Kenyon and his dad helped her out to the porch. There were two presents waiting on the swing.

"Oh my," Little Dolly gushed.

She picked up the smaller present, laughing. "I know what this is," she said. Every year Dad got Little Dolly a box of assorted chocolates. They were her favorites and she always hid them so she wouldn't have to share. "I'll save these for later." She tucked the box behind her arm and reached for the other gift.

As she picked it up, car horns sounded. "Lord Amighty," Little Dolly said. "What's happening?"

"Happy birthday, Miz Bowles!" Shouts came from the street. And suddenly, the porch spilled over with people from the town—all of the friends Little Dolly had made in all her years of living in Lexington.

Mrs. Montgomery strolled up the walk with the biggest strawberry shortcake ever. "Happy Birthday," she said, setting the cake before Little Dolly. "Make a wish and blow out all these candles. It isn't every day you turn ninety, you know." She reached over and hugged Kenyon.

The cake was delicious and everyone had a good time.

"Don't that beat all," Little Dolly said after everyone had left. "Best birthday I've—" Little Dolly stopped as her foot pushed on Kenyon's present.

"Well, looks like it ain't over yet," she said. "Hand that box up to me, Kenyon."

Little Dolly ripped the paper off as Kenyon shifted from foot to foot. He started apologizing. "It's not much, I know. Not like a carriage ride or a strawberry shortcake . . ."

481

He stopped when he saw her eyes sparkling. She carefully lifted the gift from the box and delicately touched the handmade book.

"They showed us how to do that at school," Kenyon explained. "How to bind it and all. And inside I put—"

"My stories," she finished. "A book of my stories."

"Yes, ma'am."

Little Dolly pulled Kenyon next to her. Tears were spilling over and dancing down her cheeks. "It seems that I was wrong, Kenyon," she said. "A Keeper don't have to be a girl. You've done a fine job here, child. Now, I'm going to need to teach you a few things all Keepers got to know. And then, well, you'll need to add some of your own stories. Maybe a few baseball stories, eh?"

Kenyon smiled and slipped his hand into Little Dolly's. It was definitely a wallop-bat day.

About the Author
Jeri Hanel Watts

When Jeri Hanel Watts was in seventh grade, she wrote a story for English class. "The teacher read mine (and another) to the class as examples of good writing," she recalls. "She didn't say names, but I knew it was my piece. She loved the repetition in the story (my first technique!) and told me I should keep writing. It was an exciting moment."

In college, Ms. Watts thought she might like to become a writer. When her first paper was returned with "red marks all over it," she changed her mind and began a teaching career. After her second child was born, she decided to try writing again. She says, "I needed something for myself that was special about me. *Keepers* was published ten years later!"

Ms. Watts says, "Writing isn't easy . . . . I still have to brainstorm, plan, draft, revise—all the things student writers must do. The steps stay the same. But I love to put my ideas on paper and have someone else read them, so it is worth the work."

About the Illustrator
Tyrone Geter

Tyrone Geter grew up in the United States, but he also has traveled to West Africa and lived for seven years in Zaria, Nigeria. His artwork has been exhibited in many countries, including Nigeria, the United States, Senegal, England, Japan, and China. Today Mr. Geter lives with his family in Ohio, where he teaches at the University of Akron School of Art and illustrates children's books.

483

Reader Response

Would you recommend this story to a friend? Why or why not?

Comprehension Check

1. How does Kenyon feel about Little Dolly? Give examples from the story to explain your answer.

2. Reread the conversation between Kenyon and his dad when Kenyon stays home instead of playing baseball. What do the words show about each character? Use examples to explain.

3. What is a Keeper? How does Little Dolly change her mind about Keepers in the end? Use story details to answer.

4. Think about **plot.** Describe the conflict in the story. (Plot)

5. In a **plot,** the action rises to the climax. What is the climax in this story? How is the conflict resolved in the end? (Plot)

Test Prep

Look Back and Write

Look back at pages 478–479. What is the biggest problem Kenyon is facing now that he bought the baseball glove? Give examples from the story to support your answer.

Have-a-Ball! Cake

by Elizabeth Yoder

Ingredients:

2 cups sugar

$\frac{1}{2}$ cup butter

6 heaping tablespoons cocoa

2 eggs

1 cup sour cream

$2\frac{1}{4}$ cups cake flour

1 teaspoon baking soda (heaping)

1 teaspoon salt

1 cup boiling water

can of white frosting

three tubes of frosting: red, yellow, and chocolate

Directions for cake:

1. First, mix sugar and butter well; add eggs, one at a time.
2. Next, add sour cream, cocoa, flour, soda, and salt.
*3. Then, pour boiling water slowly over batter. Stir well.
*4. Last, pour in a greased, 9-inch round pan. Bake in a 325° oven for 40–45 minutes. Let the cake cool for one hour.

*Ask a grown-up to help with this step.

Directions for frosting:

1. Use the white frosting to frost the cake.
2. Decide how you want to decorate the cake.

For baseball decoration: Use red or yellow to make the stitching of a baseball on the cake. With chocolate frosting, write the number of your favorite baseball player in the middle.

For beach ball decoration: Use chocolate frosting to draw two curved lines on the cake as shown. You now have three sections. Use the red and yellow frosting to fill in the outside sections.

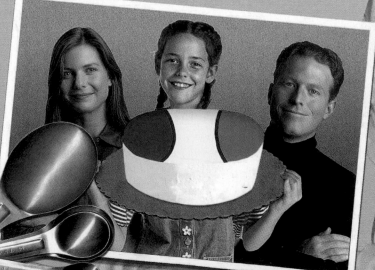

Summer

by Walter Dean Myers

I like hot days, hot days
Sweat is what you got days
Bugs buzzin from cousin to cousin
Juices dripping
Running and ripping
Catch the one you love days

Birds peeping
Old men sleeping
Lazy days, daisies lay
Beaming and dreaming
Of hot days, hot days,
Sweat is what you got days

An Apple a Day

by Lee Blair

"I must eat an apple," said Link,
As he gobbled one down in a wink,
    "For an apple a day
    Keeps the doctor away—
And I just broke his window, I think."

ES VERDAD

by Gary Soto

Es verdad
That Papi saws two boards on Saturday morning,
That he pounds a nail and wipes his brow.

Es verdad
That Moma shakes a rug from the back steps,
That she yells, "*¡Chihuahua!*" when our cat, Slinky,
Tips over the garbage can.

Es verdad
That I pop my fist into my glove
And spit a mouthful of sunflower seeds.
I toss an invisible ball skyward and I think to myself,
I got it! I got it!
And the yapping mouth of my glove eats the ball
In one gulp.

I'm a hero.
That's why Papi saws the boards—a place for trophies.
That's why Moma shakes the rug—a king's path to
    lunch.
That's why I must first pick up the toppled garbage—
A humble beginning
And later, *quién sabe,* center field champ!

Glad to Have a Friend Like You

Song lyrics by Carol Hall

Jill told Bill
That it was lots of fun to cook.
Bill told Jill
That she could bait a real fishhook.

    So they made ooey gooey
    Chocolate cake
    Sticky licky
    Sugar top
    And they gobbled it and giggled.
    And they sat by the river
    And they fished in the water
    And they talked
    As the squirmy wormies wiggled,
    Singin'

    Glad to have a friend like you,
    Fair and fun and skippin' free.
    Glad to have a friend like you,
    And glad to just be me.

Pearl told Earl
That they could do a secret code.
Earl told Pearl
There was free ice cream when it snowed.

So they sent funny letters
Which contained mystery messages
And nobody knew just how they made it.
And they raised up the window
And they scooped all the snow together,
Put milk and sugar in and ate it,
Singin'

Glad to have a friend like you,
Fair and fun and skippin' free.
Glad to have a friend like you,
And glad to just be me.

Peg told Greg
She liked to make things out of chairs.
Greg told Peg
Sometimes he still hugged teddy bears.

So they sneaked in the living room
And piled all the pillows up
And made it a rocket ship
To fly in.
And the bears were their girls and boys
And they were the astronauts
Who lived on the moon
With one pet lion,
Singin'

Glad to have a friend like you,
Fair and fun and skippin' free.
Glad to have a friend like you,
And glad to just be me.

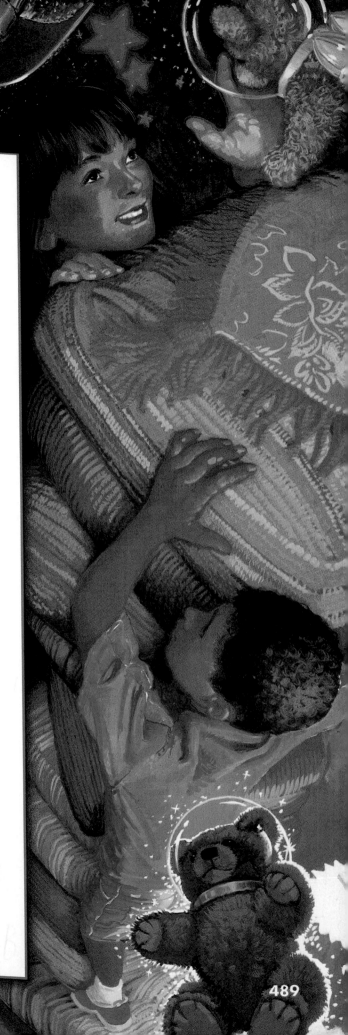

Wrap-Up

How do stories from the past help us live in the present?

To My Future Self

Write a Letter

Stories from the past can be fun to read, and they can also teach us lifelong lessons. What is something you have learned from stories in Unit 4?

1. Choose one or two stories from this unit.

2. Think about what you've learned.

3. Write a letter to your future self. Explain the lesson you learned from the story or stories. Include a reminder about how that lesson can help you in the future.

TV Talk Show

Interview Story Characters

Imagine you and three classmates are on a TV talk show. One of you is the host and the others are guests. The host will interview three characters from this unit.

1. **Choose** three characters. Decide who will play each character and who will play the host.

2. **Write** two questions that ask each character about his or her experiences.

3. Practice the talk show and **perform** it for others.

Be an Illustrator

Illustrate an Event

Photographs, paintings, and drawings help readers imagine stories more clearly. How might you illustrate an event in a story?

1. **Choose** an event from one story in Unit 4 that is not already illustrated.

2. **Illustrate** the event. Your illustration should help someone understand the event better.

3. **Display** your illustration and have classmates guess which event is being shown.

Storytelling Circle

Retell from a Different Viewpoint

Imagine you are Imduk's mother from "The Disguise," or Little Dolly in *Keepers*. You are joining a circle of storytellers. You will tell the story from your viewpoint. How is your story different from the original?

1. **Choose** one character. Look back over the story.

2. **Plan** how you will retell the story from that character's viewpoint. Practice telling it.

3. Join classmates in a storytelling circle and **tell** your story.

Test Talk

Answer the Question

Use Information from the Text

Some test questions tell you to support your answer with details from the text. To answer such questions correctly, you must include information *from the text.* A test about "What Is the Supreme Court?" pages 418–419, might have this question.

Test Question 1

What is the author's purpose for writing this selection? Use details from the text to support your answer.

Understand the question.

Read the question carefully to find the key words. Finish the statement "I need to find out . . ."

Decide where you will look for the answer.

The answer may be *right there* in one place, or you may have to *think and search* for it. The answer may depend on the *author and you.* Make notes about details that answer the question.

Check your notes.

Reread the question and your notes. Ask yourself, "Do I have enough information?" If details are missing, go back to the text.

See how one student uses information from the text to answer the question.

I think the author wants to give me information, but I'll have to search different parts of the article. The first paragraph explains what the Supreme Court is. I'll note that.

Well, I checked my notes. I was right. The author wrote this article to inform people about the Supreme Court. I'll look back at the question to make sure I've got all the details I need.

Try it!

Now use what you've learned to answer these test questions about "What Is the Supreme Court?" pages 418–419.

Test Question 2

How is the Supreme Court like ordinary law courts? How is it different? Support your answer with information from the selection.

Test Question 3

Why are decisions that the Supreme Court made in the past important to Americans now? Use details from the selection to support your answer.

Other Times, Other Places

What can we learn from reading about times and places we've never been?

Summarizing

- A **summary** gives the main ideas of an article, or it tells what happened in a story.

- A summary is short, and it doesn't include unimportant details.

- A summary will help you recall and organize information.

Read "Stagecoaches, Then . . . and Now" by Dorothy Hinshaw Patent from *Spider* magazine.

Talk About It

Which of these is the best summary statement? Explain.

a. Unlike in the movies, real stagecoaches usually provided safe, reliable delivery of passengers and mail.

b. Stagecoaches stopped every twelve miles or so to replace the horses with a fresh team.

c. In the 1850s many settlers and miners traveled by stagecoach. A stagecoach passenger could expect a dusty and boring ride.

Stagecoaches, Then . . . and Now

by Dorothy Hinshaw Patent

If you watch Westerns, you've often seen stagecoaches barreling along rutted roads, pulled by teams of galloping horses. In the movies, the passengers usually include a handsome hero and a beautiful woman, and the stagecoach is almost always ambushed by a gang of masked robbers.

As Westerns show, the companies that ran the stagecoaches, called stages or coaches for short, prided themselves on getting passengers and mail as quickly as possible from town to town. But travel by stage wasn't nearly as exciting as what's shown in the movies. Robbers, called road agents, did sometimes attack, but most trips were uneventful, dusty, and tiring.

By the 1850s the many settlers and miners who had come to California and

Oregon needed a way to travel swiftly between towns. Stagecoaches took on the job of getting mail and people from place to place in the newly settled West.

The name *stagecoach* comes from how the routes were traveled—in stages. Every twelve miles or so, the coach stopped, and the horses, which had been running fast for an hour or more, were replaced by a fresh team. Speed and reliability were important, for the main income for stagecoach operators came from carrying the mail. Passengers brought in extra money.

LOOK AHEAD

Get ready to summarize an adventure about another way to travel as you read "Amazing Alice!"

Words to Know

**blacksmith   telegraph forge
dependable ravines   crank**

Words with similar meanings are called **synonyms.** You can often figure out the meaning of an unknown word by finding a synonym in the words or sentences near it. Read the paragraph below. Notice how *trustworthy* helps you understand the meaning of the word *dependable*.

Postcard from a Cross-Country Trip

I finally got back on the road! After the car broke down, I had it towed to a forge. The blacksmith who owned the metalworking shop pounded the metal crank into place so I could get the car started. I hope the car is dependable now because I need a trustworthy car on this journey. The next part of my trip is through the mountains. I'll look out for those deep ravines next to the roads! When I reach the next town, I'll telegraph you.

Write About It

Picture a place you would like to visit. Write a postcard from the place. Use as many vocabulary words as you can.

Amazing Alice!

from *Coast to Coast with Alice* by Patricia Rusch Hyatt

A Note to the Reader

Hermine Jahns was a real girl who rode across the country with Alice Ramsey in 1909. To create her journal, I drew on long-ago newspaper stories, interviews, books about slang and fads of the early 1900s, and most importantly the memoirs Alice herself wrote in 1961—more than 50 years after her historic trip. The result is this story, which is as true as I could make it. The conversations are imagined, but every event actually happened.

Patricia Rusch Hyatt

Hermine Jahns and Alice Ramsey

June 8, 1909

Hurry Up, Tomorrow—Hackensack, New Jersey

I can't sleep. How could anybody sleep? How much longer 'til morning? I am one of the luckiest girls alive in the United States, the Hemisphere, the World, the Universe, the I-don't-know. My neighborhood friend Alice Ramsey has invited me—yes ME, Hermine Jahns (people call me Minna)—to ride up front with her starting tomorrow morning as she drives a motorcar from New York City all the way to San Francisco, California, on the Pacific Ocean! No woman driver has tried the whole distance yet—Alice is bound to be the first. And I'll be there too.

Only two men have ever driven this distance before. It took each of those fellows more than 60 days. The roads are all wagon ruts west of the Mississippi River, they say, and burro trails through the mountains. Great golliwogs, won't that be an adventure? Will we find buffalo, Indians, and cowboys? Oh, I wish tomorrow would come sooner.

I will be the youngest of the four of us making this trip— I am going on 16—but Alice knows how much I like machines and motoring, and she's already taught me oiling and tire changing. So I will be dependable in the wilderness, like a good first mate on a ship. Unless we . . . oh, dear, there's no sense imagining bad things that could happen. Otherwise, we'd never try.

My family finally agreed to let me ride along after Alice promised we'd have chaperones. So now Alice's two sisters-in-law are coming too. They are Mrs. Nettie Powell and Mrs. Maggie Atwood, and they are maybe 30 or 40—much older than Alice or I.

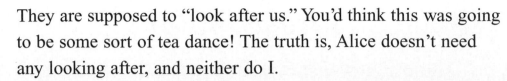

They are supposed to "look after us." You'd think this was going to be some sort of tea dance! The truth is, Alice doesn't need any looking after, and neither do I.

That's exactly what I told my cousin Kermit, the smarty pants, when he laughed at the whole idea of four females making this trip. He thinks we'll give up and head home on a train before we even reach the Mississippi River. "And if you should get so far," he says, "I'll eat my hat!" I hope he likes the taste of straw. Kermit doesn't know Alice and how stubborn she can be. (I mean stubborn in a good way.)

In my secret dreams, I would like to be just like Alice, and maybe I will be in a few years. She is 21 now, but she isn't prissy or bossy at all. I would say she is plucky.

Alice's family lives on our street here in Hackensack. Her father always says Alice was "born mechanical." He taught her about tools in his workshop, and then she took manual training in school instead of homemaking. She learned how to make wooden tables and hatstands rather than how to cook and sew. People think it strange for a girl to take manual training, but I think it is wonderful. I wish I'd thought of it first.

About half a year ago when Alice first learned to drive—after only two lessons!—she started taking me with her on short trips in her family's red Maxwell. Picnics mostly, or sometimes we'd go to a "run," where other drivers in Maxwells or Packards, usually, or Franklins or Cadillacs would show off how well they could back up, handle the wheel on corners, and drive around barrels and hay bales. Alice always scores very high at these meets, and we celebrate afterward with ice cream cones and iced tea—when the weather is warm, that is.

The biggest contest Alice has entered (so far) was the 150-mile Montauk Point Run on Long Island in New York. That day the road to the meet was full of some of the most curious contraptions. I saw a Piano Box Runabout, an electric car that looks like a piano on wheels; a Thomas, which resembles two bicycles locked together; and a new Buick, manufactured by some plumber who also invented the white porcelain bathtub. There were a number of Oldsmobiles whose drivers joked and sang that jolly tune "Come Away with Me, Lucille, in My Merry Oldsmobile." Instead of a steering wheel like the Maxwell, the Olds has a tiller like a sailboat.

There at Montauk, as we fully expected, Alice made another perfect score. A salesman from the Maxwell car company, a Mr. Cadwallader Washburn Kelsey (whew!), watched all her turns and reverses. He came up afterward and declared she was the greatest natural woman driver he'd ever seen and that she had given him a unique idea. How would she like to be the first woman to drive across the United States?

So that's how our adventure started, and tomorrow I'll be sharing the front seat with Alice on the first-time all-women's journey across this great country, courtesy of the Maxwell-Briscoe Company.

Instead of turning a steering wheel, the driver steered this 1903 Oldsmobile with a long stick, or tiller.

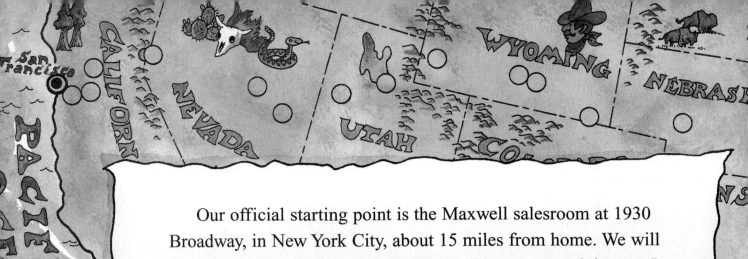

Our official starting point is the Maxwell salesroom at 1930 Broadway, in New York City, about 15 miles from home. We will be driving over rivers and mountains, wildernesses and deserts. I already feel like a pioneer—a modern twentieth-century one. Though I guess it will scare me a bit to be so far from home.

I am going to try to sleep a little now. Good night.

June 15, 1909

Trouble with the Blue Book—Outside Ashtabula, Ohio

How I wish we had a better road map. There are city maps, but no one seems to have drawn one to help motorists get from town to town. Because there are few signposts, we have to rely on a handbook called the Blue Book to figure out where to turn or which fork to follow. It has no drawings or pictures. All the directions are written out. Today, trying to get to Cleveland, Ohio, we checked our Blue Book and read, "At 11.6 miles, yellow house and barn rt. Turn left." We looked and looked for that yellow house, driving back and forth for the longest time. We wondered if Alice had misread the odometer. Nettie spied a woman down the road, and we motored over to her. I asked her which road went to Cleveland. She pointed behind us. Alice told her we saw no yellow house in that direction, only a green one. The woman laughed and said the house owner decided to repaint his house last year because he was "agin' the automobile," and he planned to have some fun confusing motorists. The woman thought the man would be all right when he got an automobile himself!

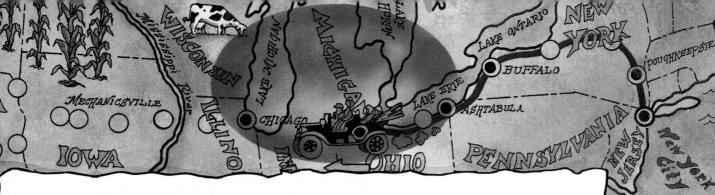

That's when we learned not to trust any directions that mentioned colors. Alice said that Blue Books don't include anything west of the Missouri River, so once we cross over, our book will be useless and we will have to follow our noses.

June 24, 1909

Onward to Iowa—Mechanicsville, Iowa

Just through Dixon to Fulton, Illinois, we spotted the great, long bridge over the Mississippi. The wood planking over the Big River is barely wide enough for two wagons to pass. It is frightening to look down. Nettie and Maggie kept their eyes straight ahead. But Alice and I had to watch for gaps between the planks and for nailheads.

Here, on the other side, we are Out West! Though I must say being here isn't all that inspiring. This Iowa is a bathtub of mud. Late spring rains have left the roads like thick stew. I read somewhere that in the age of dinosaurs, this section between the Mississippi and the Missouri Rivers was underwater. It still is! The mud left behind may be wonderful for corn crops, but it is awful for motoring.

The first new blast of rain hit us in Mechanicsville, Iowa. We headed for the only shelter in sight, a livery stable. With flies buzzing around us and horses snorting and stomping, we waited for two hours for a letup in the storm. Then we ran with our muddy bags to the Page Hotel.

Four proud motorists. Alice is driving, of course, and Maggie is sitting next to her. In back, Nettie is on the left and I, Minna, am on the right.

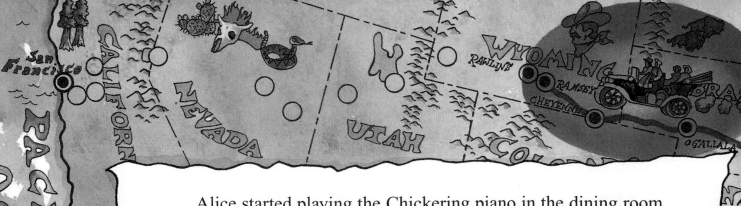

Alice started playing the Chickering piano in the dining room after supper, with rain still beating on the windows outside. If she doesn't stop showing off downstairs for the other guests, I will never get to sleep. Oh, no, here goes "Rock of Ages" again.

July 15, 1909

Careful Timing Between Trains— Near the North Platte River, Wyoming

At Ramsey, Wyoming (no relation to Alice), the road bridge across the North Platte River had been washed away in a flood. The only way across was a railroad track on a trestle bridge 20 feet above the water. The innkeeper back in town told us we'd need an official permit from the stationmaster to cross the bridge, because Alice had to drive between train crossing times. Otherwise, we'd end up wrecked at the bottom of the Platte. And so would the train.

But guess where the station house was? Three-quarters of a mile away, on the OTHER side of the trestle. You had to cross it first to get a permit to cross it. This surely is a backwards world!

I had the idea that Alice should stay in the Maxwell while the three of us walked over the trestle to get the permit. Nettie and Maggie could talk to the stationmaster. I would wait just on the other side of the bridge and wave to Alice when Nettie signaled that he had signed the permit.

Maggie wanted to know what to do if a train came while we were crossing on foot. I told her that we'd dive in for a swim and she should keep her ears open for the whistle.

Maggie and Nettie picked up their skirts and hopped over those railroad ties like jackrabbits. They were already pounding

*Here I am, standing on the running board, scanning the trail ahead.
I don't know if I look like an American pioneer, but I feel like one!*

on the station door before I got even halfway across the trestle.
Then it took a full hour for the stationmaster to telegraph up and
down the line to make sure trains were moving on schedule.

At last he signed the permit. As we had agreed, Maggie next
waved to me. I signaled to Alice, and she began to bump across
the tracks, the left wheels between the two rails, the right wheels
between the rail and the narrow edge of the trestle. First Alice
fed a little gas, then she let out the clutch, then came a bump,
then she hit the brake. One bump at a time, up and down, for
three-quarters of a mile, all the way across the bridge.

By the time Alice got to our side, I could see she was frowning
from some awful pain. "Oh, Minna, I have appendicitis," she
moaned and sat on the roadside, her head down in her lap.

Nettie and Maggie came running, squawking about finding a doctor, about how people could die from appendicitis, about how we would have to cancel the journey, and on and on. But in a few minutes, Alice lifted her head, began to smile, and said she felt quite a bit better: "I think I must have had a sudden bad case of jolt-itis." When she laughed again like the old Alice, we were all relieved.

July 16, 1909

Cliffs and Ravines—Bitter Creek, Wyoming

We've been climbing slowly, slowly toward the Continental Divide—that's the highest point in the Rocky Mountains. Our guides have turned back, nursing a weak axle. They warned us to stop often and cool the motor. Coyotes are yowling nearby. All around us are buttes—those are squatty flat-topped hills—and rocky cliffs. The alkali lakes are not fit to drink because they are full of mineral salts. You can hardly bear to smell them, much less taste. The arroyos—cracks wide enough to swallow us up—are as deep as 60 feet, sometimes with water at the bottom. It would be foolish to travel after dark. Boom we'd go, down to Doom.

As Alice steers the Maxwell up steep inclines, Nettie, Maggie, and I stand beside the car with blocks of wood. Alice presses the gas pedal in low gear and pulls ahead for a few inches. We shove the blocks behind the rear wheels so they won't slide back. Then Alice inches up some more. This way, we climb to the crest of each rising hill. "You're getting a week's worth of exercise all at once," Alice tells us. I'd say it's more like a couple months' worth.

July 24, 1909

Prairie Dogs—Orr's Ranch, Utah

The trail through Utah is full of prairie dog holes. They stretch ahead of us for miles. As we ride over the low hills, thousands of heads pop out of the ground ahead to see us, then pop back down. They must feel the earth shake before we pass by. Alice lay face down on the sand to try to get a picture of one, but the little creatures never failed to pop up in an altogether different hole, then grin and disappear again.

Often there are just two dusty tracks for our wheels. Alice steered carefully all morning. Then at noon we hit our first prairie dog hole. A bolt flew out of the tie-rod connecting the wheels, and the front of the car collapsed. We all tipped forward.

We lose an axle after hitting a prairie dog hole.

Alice got out, slid under the Maxwell's back wheels, and tied everything back together with baling wire and Maggie's extra hairpins until we could reach the blacksmith forge at Orr's Ranch.

July 29, 1909

Another Delay—Callao, Utah

Out West we've learned to watch for dark clouds, because a cloudburst can mean a sudden flood ripping along the ravines and trailways, pulling us underwater. As we were leaving Callao, we had to change plans quickly when our road disappeared into a gaping hole still filled with swirling water from a recent rainstorm. Then, while trying to cross another gullywasher safely, we lost another axle. Because it will take three whole days for a new one to be shipped from San Francisco, Alice will wait in Callao to oversee repairs, and Nettie, Maggie, and I are catching the noon stage to Ely, Nevada. Nettie says Ely is known for its copper mines.

We can't seem to keep the Maxwell in one piece.

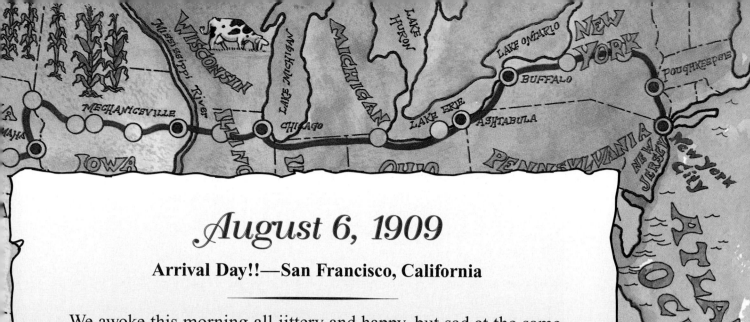

August 6, 1909

Arrival Day!!—San Francisco, California

We awoke this morning all jittery and happy, but sad at the same time. We were 100-percent glad we made it but regretted the trip would soon be over. Maggie says this feeling is called "bittersweet," like the chocolate.

There were only 20 more miles to go until we reached the ferry house at Oakland, where we would board a boat taking us across the wide, blue bay to San Francisco. Time sped by too quickly. We arrived at the Oakland boat dock within an hour after breakfast. Once on the ferry, we set the Maxwell's brakes and raced to the front end of the boat to watch San Francisco bobbing in the water. Great golliwogs! To think that those same Pacific Ocean waves touch the shores of the Chinese Empire!

Our ferry slid out into the bay. Gulls were squawking like New York street vendors. Buoys were clanging. We heard foghorns hoot, though there was no fog. The other passengers seemed very excited to get a look at the Maxwell and us. Who told them I don't know, but everyone knew where we were from and what Alice had done. We did not have a single quiet moment, as every rider wanted to congratulate us.

On the San Francisco wharf, our ferry bumped against the pilings and rocked a little. The captain unhooked the chains across the bow of the ferry. I jumped down and gave the good old Maxwell's crank the last twirl of this trip, hopping aboard as we rolled down the ramp to the dock. "Straighten your cap, Alice," the three of us shouted.

We made it! What a glorious feeling. Here we all are in San Francisco: (left to right) me, Alice, Nettie, and Maggie.

Almost two months since leaving New York City, we at last puttered slowly onto San Francisco's Market Street. All around us were cheers and honks of welcome and so many people you could hardly tell there'd been a big earthquake here only three years ago. What a hubbub! Now I know firsthand what the word *hubbub* means. There was a lineup of other Maxwells, photographers, pressmen, and presswomen too, all wanting to meet Alice and shake her hand. We had come 3,800 miles on 11 tire changes and three axles in only 59 days, faster—for all our delays—than either of the two men driving across country before us. Aren't we proud? Everyone hereabouts is calling Alice "Woman Motorist of the Century."

A reporter took me aside and asked if I would ever take this trip again. Who wouldn't say yes? I want my cousin Kermit to see what great adventure is like. And next time, I'LL drive.

As Alice told the reporters today, it looks like automobiles are here to stay!

September 30, 1909

Back Home—Hackensack, New Jersey

Cousin Kermit took a big bite—not a little nibble—out of his straw boater today, but after a while, I let him spit it out.

About the Author

Patricia Rusch Hyatt

Wherever Patricia Rusch Hyatt goes, her travel diary goes with her. She often writes and sketches in it while traveling. The ideas and information help her when she plans her writing.

When she is not traveling or writing, Ms. Hyatt has a wide variety of other interests. She is a guide for her local Wildscapes Association, an accomplished gardener, and a violinist. She also writes plays for theater groups.

Ms. Hyatt dedicated *Coast to Coast with Alice* to her mother, Winnifred Rusch Hagood, whom she calls "a road-runner herself." Ms. Hyatt was born in Texas and now lives in New Jersey.

Reader Response

Open for Discussion

Suppose you are traveling with Alice. What day would be the most adventurous for you? Tell about it.

Comprehension Check

1. What does "A Note to the Reader" on page 500 tell you about the author's purpose?

2. What makes Alice amazing? Use evidence from the selection to explain your answer.

3. Look back and find details that show how Alice and her companions solve problems.

4. Which of these details would not be included when **summarizing** the events of July 24, 1909? Why? (Summarizing)

   a. Alice tries to get a picture of a prairie dog.

   b. The car hits a prairie dog hole.

5. Which of the following is a better **summary** of this selection? Explain. (Summarizing)

   a. After they leave New York, Alice and her three companions soon learn that the Blue Book is not very useful.

   b. In 1909, an amazing woman named Alice Ramsey, along with three companions, drives across the country in 59 days, faster than either of the two men who made the trip earlier.

Test Prep
Look Back and Write

Look back at pages 501–502. If you didn't know what the word *chaperones* means, what clues would help you figure it out? Use details from these pages to support your answer.

Test Prep

Read a How-to Article

1. Preview

- A how-to article gives step-by-step instructions for making or doing something. Often, it includes a list of necessary materials.

- Skim this how-to article. Look for directions written in a certain order.

2. Read and Locate Information

- Read the article to find out about making a road journal. Before you read, write questions to help you focus on important information. For example,

What is it?
What do I do?
How do I use it?

3. Think and Connect

Think about "Amazing Alice!" Then look back at your questions.

How is Hermine's journal in "Amazing Alice!" alike or different from this road journal? Give details to support your answer.

Keeping a Road Journal

by Joy Beck

Road trips are a lot of fun, especially when you keep track of the interesting things you see and do, the neat new people you meet, and all the new things you learn. Here's how:

516

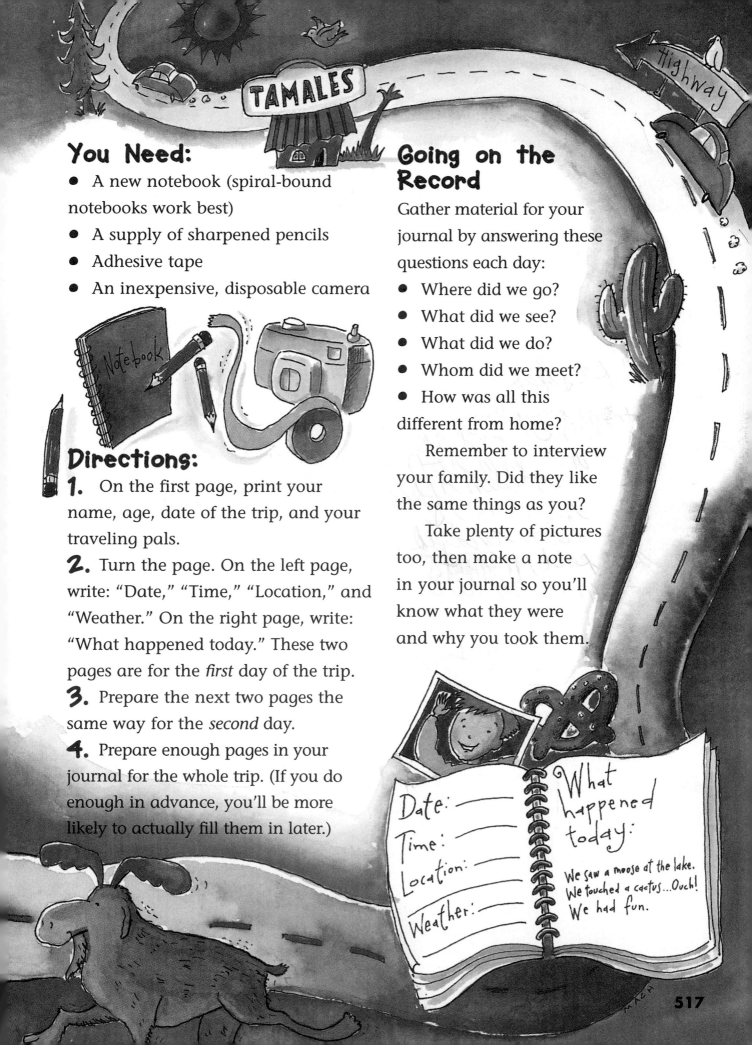

You Need:

- A new notebook (spiral-bound notebooks work best)
- A supply of sharpened pencils
- Adhesive tape
- An inexpensive, disposable camera

Directions:

1. On the first page, print your name, age, date of the trip, and your traveling pals.

2. Turn the page. On the left page, write: "Date," "Time," "Location," and "Weather." On the right page, write: "What happened today." These two pages are for the *first* day of the trip.

3. Prepare the next two pages the same way for the *second* day.

4. Prepare enough pages in your journal for the whole trip. (If you do enough in advance, you'll be more likely to actually fill them in later.)

Going on the Record

Gather material for your journal by answering these questions each day:

- Where did we go?
- What did we see?
- What did we do?
- Whom did we meet?
- How was all this different from home?

Remember to interview your family. Did they like the same things as you?

Take plenty of pictures too, then make a note in your journal so you'll know what they were and why you took them.

Date:
Time:
Location:
Weather:

What happened today:

We saw a moose at the lake.
We touched a cactus...Ouch!
We had fun.

Plot

- Stories have **plot,** or a series of events that center on a problem, or conflict.

- A *conflict* can be a problem between two people or groups, or between a person and nature. Conflicts can also be problems that characters have within themselves.

- The *climax* is where the action of the story builds and the conflict must be faced.

- The *resolution* is where the problem is solved.

Read "Atalanta's Race" from *Greek Myths* retold by Geraldine McCaughrean.

Write About It

1. Write a sentence that explains the conflict in this myth.

2. List the events that happen in the race to move the plot along. Circle the event that is the climax of the story.

3. Explain the resolution of the story.

ATALANTA'S RACE

retold by Geraldine McCaughrean

Beautiful Atalanta has declared that she will only marry a man who can win a race against her. If he loses, he will be killed. Many have died. Handsome Hippomenes falls in love with Atalanta and cannot resist the challenge. The goddess Venus gives him some help in the form of three golden apples.

"Ready, steady, go!" cried the starter.

Away went Hippomenes, as fast as he had ever run. Away went Atalanta, quick as a blink. She soon took the lead.

So Hippomenes threw one golden apple—beyond her, over her head. It caught the light. Atalanta ran to where it lay and picked it up. Hippomenes sped ahead.

But Atalanta caught up with him again and passed him, hair blowing like a flag.

He ran faster than any of the other suitors, but it was not fast enough.

So Hippomenes threw another of the apples. Again Atalanta stopped to pick it up and again Hippomenes took the lead. But Atalanta was so much faster that she could stop, admire, pick up the shiny apple, and *still* catch up with him again.

Hippomenes ran faster than any man has ever run, but it was not fast enough. So he threw the third apple. Would Atalanta be fooled by the trick a third time? She saw—she slowed down— she glanced at the two apples in her hands . . . and she stopped for the third. The crowd cheered as Hippomenes dashed past her, lungs bursting, and threw himself over the winning line. He had won his bride!

And for a champion runner who has just lost a race for the first time Atalanta looked extremely happy.

LOOK AHEAD

A Peddler's Dream

Follow the series of events in *A Peddler's Dream*. Notice the obstacles the peddler must overcome to achieve his dream in his new homeland.

Words to Know

purchased   trudged   bound
peddling   quarters fortune
mission

Words with opposite meanings are called **antonyms.** You can often figure out the meaning of an unknown word by finding a clue in the words around it. Sometimes the clue is an antonym.

Read the paragraph below. How does *run* help you understand its antonym *trudged?*

My Dreams May Come True

With my belongings <u>bound</u> together with a rope, I set off for America to seek my <u>fortune</u>. Because I was too tired to run after the boat trip, I slowly <u>trudged</u> up the pier. First, I needed to find living <u>quarters</u>, so I made my home at the <u>mission</u>. To earn money, I began <u>peddling</u> my paintings, selling them to people in the park. I saved money and <u>purchased</u> my own home. Maybe I'll make my fortune after all!

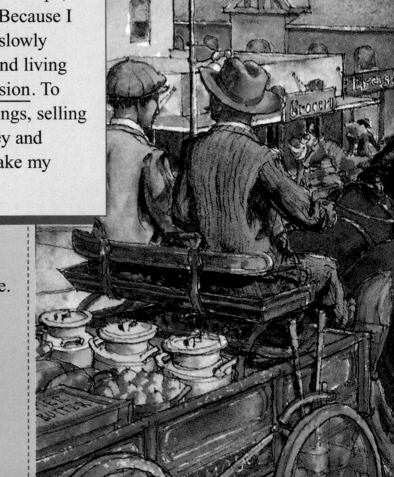

Talk About It

Imagine it's your first day in a new place. Talk about what you would do to get settled. Try to use vocabulary words.

A Peddler's Dream

by Janice Shefelman
illustrated by Tom Shefelman

Solomon Joseph Azar lived in a small village in the mountains of Lebanon, but he had a big dream. He wanted to go to America and seek his fortune.

For a year he studied English at the American mission. Then in the spring he said farewell to his family and friends and Marie, his betrothed.

"When will you return?" asked her father.

"I'll come back for her as soon as I'm settled, *amm*."

"I'll be waiting," Marie said quietly.

For four weeks he sailed across the ocean. The ship was crowded with people who also had dreams. When the weather became rough, many of them had upset stomachs too.

But not Solomon. He stood at the rail and turned his face into the ocean breeze. After all, the blood of seafaring Phoenicians flowed in his veins.

The coast of America looked different from the snowcapped mountains of home. As far as one could see the land was flat.

And Solomon looked different from the people in the streets.

If I am to live in America, I will need American clothes, he thought.

On Market Street he found a store that sold ready-to-wear for men and boys. He bought a new pair of trousers and a cap.

The owner was from the old country too, and Solomon asked if he needed a clerk.

"Sorry," he said, "I can't give you a job, but I'll give you some advice. The best way to get a start here is by peddling. Buy yourself a *quashaat*, a pack, fill it with things a farmer's wife needs, and off you go."

Solomon thanked him for the advice. He bought a pack and filled it with colorful calico, ribbon and thread to match, lace, suspenders, a few spices, and off he went.

He walked from farmhouse to farmhouse showing his wares. Calico sold for eight cents a yard and fancy lace for ten.

At the end of each day, if he was lucky, a farmer's wife would invite him to stay for supper and let him sleep in the barn. Then he would dream of having a real store and going back for Marie.

One cold rainy evening as he trudged through the hill country, two riders approached. They stopped, blocking his way.

"He's too small to be carrying such a big pack," said one. "Why don't we lighten his load?"

"Sure thing," said the other.

And they did.

When he awoke his head ached, his hands and feet were bound, and his pack was gone. So was his purse. Solomon had nothing left but his dream.

It was dark by the time he worked the knots loose. He picked himself up and started walking again. Though his body felt light without the pack, his heart was heavy.

Up ahead he saw the dim light of a farmhouse. Maybe they will let me sleep in the barn, he thought.

"*Wer ist er*, Papa?" asked a small boy in German. "Who is he?"

After Solomon told them who he was and what had happened, Mr. Lindheimer invited him in. His wife gave him some dry clothes and a blanket.

"I could sure use some help around the place, Solomon," said Mr. Lindheimer. "I can't pay much, but at least you will have a roof over your head *und* food in your stomach until you can think what to do."

So Solomon stayed. He painted the barn and chopped enough wood to last for months. Sometimes while he cranked the cream separator, he entertained the little Lindheimers with tales from the old country.

All the while he dreamed of the store he would have one day. It kept getting bigger and bigger until it was four stories tall.

In the evenings after supper, Solomon often wrote letters home:

April 12, 1909

Greetings to the family of my betrothed:

I hope you are all well and the grape harvest was plentiful.

The hills here are not so high as our mountains, but the people are friendly and kind—at least most of them.

I look forward to the day when I can return and marry your beloved daughter. Please extend my greetings to her.

God's blessing on you,
Solomon

One day Mr. Lindheimer said, "I'm going to town tomorrow, Solomon. Why don't you come along? I'll introduce you to a friend of mine who has a dry goods store. It could be that he needs a clerk."

The next morning they hitched up the wagon and set off for Arcadia.

It was noontime when they came to the bustling town beside a river. As the wagon rattled across the bridge Solomon gazed up the broad avenue toward the state house. Streetcars clanged and people rode in horseless carriages.

"Well, what do you think, Solomon?" asked Mr. Lindheimer.

"I think this is the place for my store," he said.

Mr. Lindheimer pulled up in front of Hart's Dry Goods. Solomon tied up the horses and followed him inside. The counters were piled high with boxes, and the store was dark.

"Good day, Mr. Hart. This is my young friend, Solomon Joseph. He peddled his wares across the state until he was beaten and robbed near our place." He told how Solomon had worked hard and learned fast, how he dreamed of having a store of his own someday. "I thought he might be good help to you."

"Well, it happens I do need a clerk," said Mr. Hart. "Someone to live in the apartment upstairs and watch over the place. Would that suit you, my boy?"

It suited Solomon perfectly. For two years he worked in the store, sending money home as he was able. He persuaded Mr. Hart to install new light fixtures and ceiling fans. He cleared the counters so customers could see the rows of colorful ribbons, the fancy umbrellas, straw hats, and comb and brush sets. He always greeted them with a smile even when they wanted to return something. More and more people came to shop in Hart's Dry Goods.

Now that he was settled, the time had come to return for Marie. Happily Mr. Hart agreed, and Solomon sailed back to Lebanon.

On the wedding day his father led the horse carrying Marie through the streets to the church and Solomon. She was more beautiful than he remembered, especially in her headdress.

After days of feasting and dancing, Solomon and Marie returned to Arcadia.

Marie set about making their apartment into a home. She hung curtains in the windows and unrolled a colorful rug that was part of her dowry. The Harts gave the young couple a wing chair and a potted palm.

In the garden at the rear of the store Marie planted a fig seedling brought from the old country.

Before long a daughter was born to them, and they named her Rebecca. Then came another, whom they called Ruth.

While Solomon worked in the store, Marie took care of the little girls. In the afternoons she often invited friends over for sweet Arabic coffee, and the children played in the garden.

One day Mr. Hart said, "Solomon, you've brought new life to this old store. How would you like to be my partner?"

Solomon grinned. "Just what I had in mind."

So the store became Hart & Joseph Dry Goods. Although it was not the store of his dreams, it *was* a beginning.

Because Solomon made sure their store was always stocked with well-made items, business grew. Customers knew that shoes bought from Hart & Joseph would not come apart, that their cloth would not fade nor their underwear shrink.

Solomon's family grew too. When a son, Isaac, was born and another daughter, Nora, he built a house on West Hill, close enough to State House Avenue that he could walk to the store.

Now the store was called simply Joseph's, for Mr. Hart had retired to tend his cattle, sheep, and goats.

Solomon built a mezzanine for his office and remodeled the second floor to sell fine ladies' ready-to-wear from New York and Paris. The clothes were so stylish that the governor's wife came to shop when she needed a new dress for a party in the mansion.

"Only in America!" said Solomon.

Late one night the clanging of fire trucks awakened him. He jumped from bed and looked out the window. A red glow filled the sky over State House Avenue.

"The store! Marie, it's the store!" he cried.

"Oh, Solomon," she gasped. "It can't be."

Hurriedly he pulled on his trousers and ran out the door.

But it was the store. As Solomon stood watching it burn, Marie joined him, clutching Isaac and Nora by the hand. Rebecca and Ruth were right behind, their eyes big.

"Papa," cried Rebecca, with tears running down her cheeks, "it's ruined. Our nice store is all ruined."

Solomon put one arm around her shoulders, the other around Marie. "Yes, Rebecca, ruined but not finished."

Solomon was true to his word. He rented temporary quarters and purchased new merchandise. In two weeks he reopened for business with a fire sale on the sidewalk. Marie made *baklawa*, which they served to customers with coffee.

On New Year's Day Solomon resolved to build the store of his dreams. He bought property on State House Avenue at the corner of Hickory Street and hired an architect, Elijah E. Clayton.

"Make it four stories tall and make it the most beautiful building on the avenue," said Solomon.

So Elijah E. Clayton did.

Each day Elijah came with his roll of drawings to make sure the store was built just as he had designed it. And Solomon came also—to make sure he made sure.

On opening night Solomon and Marie gave a party. The Harts came, the Lindheimers, and the governor too. When the musicians began to play, Solomon took Marie's hand and said, "*Habibati*, my dear, will you dance with an old peddler whose dream has come true?"

She smiled. "A peddler with a dream is *more* than a peddler," she said.

And they danced.

About the Author and the Illustrator
Janice Shefelman and Tom Shefelman

Janice and Tom Shefelman are husband and wife, and they work as a team. *A Peddler's Dream* was created after a neighbor told them about a relative who left Lebanon in search of success in America. Ms. Shefelman wrote the story about Solomon Azar, and Mr. Shefelman drew the pictures, showing a Lebanese mountain village, the hills of central Texas, and an imaginary city much like Austin, Texas, where the Shefelmans live.

Ms. Shefelman writes every day between nine o'clock and five o'clock. She doesn't try to make her writing perfect the first time because she knows that she will be revising her work. For the first draft, she believes it is important only to get ideas down on paper.

In addition to *A Peddler's Dream,* the Shefelmans have created other books together, including three historical novels based on Janice Shefelman's German great-grandparents and their struggles to build a new life in Texas.

Reader Response

Open for Discussion

Choose three illustrations from the story. Pretend you can walk into each picture. Tell what you would see and hear there.

Comprehension Check

1. Why does Solomon leave his home in Lebanon to live in America? Look back and find details to support your answer.

2. What steps does Solomon take to achieve his goals?

3. What part does Marie play in Solomon's dreams and his achievements? Explain your answer with story details.

4. A **plot** begins with a problem or conflict. Is the conflict in this story between Solomon and another person or within Solomon? Use evidence from the story to explain. (Plot)

5. In a **plot,** the climax is just before the conflict is resolved. What is the climax in this story? How is the conflict resolved? Use details from the story to support your answers. (Plot)

 **Test Prep**

Look Back and Write

Look back at pages 524–525. Why didn't Solomon give up and return home after he was attacked by the riders? Use examples about Solomon's personality from pages 530 and 531 to explain your answer.

Welcome to the United States

adapted from *Historical Atlas of the United States* by Lindy Lynk

Over the years immigrants from many countries have come to the United States. Between 1870 and 1920, most immigrants entered through Ellis Island in New York. Read the Ports of Entry graph to see other cities where people entered the United States.

Ports of Entry, 1870–1920

Ports shown if more than 50,000 immigrants arrived between 1870 and 1920.

Key

1 column = 500,000 immigrants

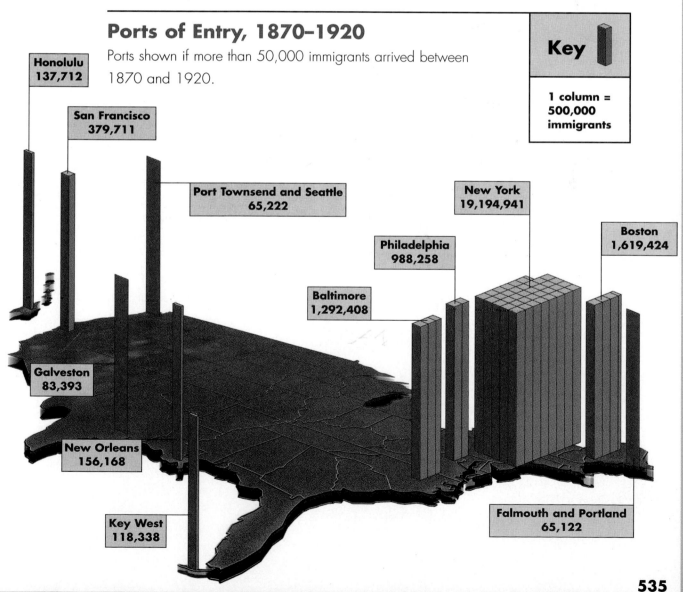

Honolulu
137,712

San Francisco
379,711

Port Townsend and Seattle
65,222

New York
19,194,941

Boston
1,619,424

Philadelphia
988,258

Baltimore
1,292,408

Galveston
83,393

New Orleans
156,168

Key West
118,338

Falmouth and Portland
65,122

Graphic Sources

- Illustrations, charts, graphs, maps, diagrams, tables, lists, time lines, and scale drawings are kinds of **graphic sources.**

- Previewing graphic sources before reading can help you predict what you will learn.

- Graphic sources can help you during reading by showing what the words say or by organizing information in a useful way.

- Maps show places. A physical map shows landforms and bodies of water. A map key explains symbols and the scale of miles.

Read the introduction to *Polar Lands* by Norman Barrett.

Write About It

1. What is the title of the map? What does the map key show?

2. What facts from the article are shown on the map? List them.

3. List questions you have about the North polar region after studying the map.

POLAR LANDS

by Norman Barrett

The polar lands are the regions around the Earth's North and South Poles. They are cold, desolate areas, covered in ice and snow for all or most of the year.

The North Pole is a mostly ice-covered sea, the Arctic Ocean, surrounded by land. The South Pole is a frozen continent, Antarctica, surrounded by seas. Despite the harsh conditions, some plants grow in the polar lands and animals and even people live there.

The lands that surround the Arctic Ocean include Canada, Alaska, Russia, Scandinavia, and a large ice-covered island called Greenland. Many important air routes cross the Arctic, and the defenses of the world's great powers face each other across the ocean.

Antarctica is a huge frozen wilderness larger than Europe. But the seas around it and some coastal areas are rich in animal life.

NORTH POLAR REGION

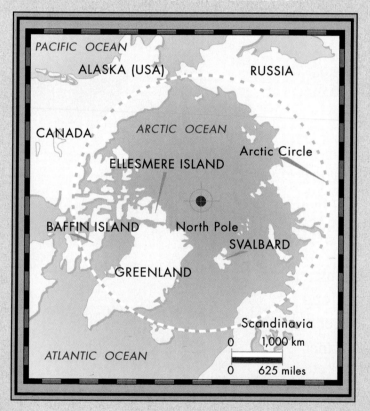

PACIFIC OCEAN

ALASKA (USA)   RUSSIA

CANADA   ARCTIC OCEAN

ELLESMERE ISLAND   Arctic Circle

BAFFIN ISLAND   North Pole   SVALBARD

GREENLAND

Scandinavia

0   1,000 km

ATLANTIC OCEAN

0   625 miles

LOOK AHEAD

Use graphic sources to help you understand the text as you read "The Race for the North Pole," a selection about the first explorers to reach the North Pole.

Words to Know

**adventure navigate region
walruses glaciers**

Many words have more than one
meaning. To decide which meaning
is being used, look for clues in the
surrounding sentences or paragraph.

Read the paragraph below. Decide
whether *navigate* means "manage
an aircraft or ship" or "sail over a
sea or river."

Arctic Mission!

Juan and Tom had the difficult job of making a map
of an unexplored <u>region</u>, a small area of the Arctic.
They had to <u>navigate</u> their plane through the thick
clouds to make a safe landing in a group of <u>glaciers</u>.
The icy surface made for a slippery landing!
Stepping off the plane, the men were greeted by
large <u>walruses</u>. Juan was nervous about their long
tusks, but the walruses left the men alone. After
looking around, Tom knew that he and his partner
were in for quite an <u>adventure</u>.

Write About It

What will the men see on their trip?
Write a journal entry about it. Use as
many vocabulary words as you can.

The Race for the North Pole

by Laurie Rozakis
from *Matthew Henson and Robert Peary:
The Race for the North Pole*

Robert Peary

Matthew Henson

Matthew Henson

On a spring day in Washington, D.C., in 1887, Robert Peary was getting ready to survey Nicaragua, a tropical country in Central America. His job was to find the best place to dig a canal through Nicaragua's jungle that would link the Atlantic and Pacific oceans. That morning, Robert set off to get a hat to protect his head from the blazing tropical sun. He wound up at B. H. Steinmetz and Sons, Hatters.

Inside the store, Robert asked Mr. Steinmetz for a sun helmet. While he was waiting, he mentioned to Steinmetz that he was looking for an assistant. The store owner thought a moment and said, "My clerk, Matthew Henson, might want the job. He is a hard worker, and someone you can depend on." Just then, a young black man came from the back room with Peary's hat. It was Matthew Henson.

Peary (middle row, second from right) with his crew in Nicaragua

Terror in the South

Matthew Alexander Henson was born on August 8, 1866, on his parents' farm in Maryland—only one year after the Civil War ended. Unlike most of their friends, Matthew's parents had never been slaves. But, like many other African Americans living in the South at the time, the Hensons were attacked by the Ku Klux Klan and other groups who did not want to see blacks vote or attend public school. To escape from the racial violence, the Hensons sold their farm and moved to Washington, D.C.

When Matthew was seven years old, his mother died and his father sent him to stay with his uncle, who lived in the area. There, Matthew went to school for the next six years. When he was thirteen years old, Matthew's father died and his uncle could no longer care for him. To support himself, Matthew worked as a waiter in a nearby Washington, D.C., restaurant. The restaurant's owner let him sleep in the kitchen and eat leftover food. Matthew was warm and fed, but he wanted adventure.

An Able-Bodied Seaman

Matthew decided that working on a ship would be more exciting. In the fall of 1879, he walked forty miles to Baltimore's harbor, went up to the silver-haired Captain Childs of the *Katie Hines*, and asked for a job. The captain was so impressed with Matthew that he hired him immediately. For the next five years, Matthew cleaned Captain Childs's room, served his meals, washed his dishes, and helped the cook. The men on the ship liked the hard-working young man. They taught him how to repair engines, navigate by the stars, and build almost anything. The captain liked Matthew so much that he taught him geography, history, mathematics, and lent him books. "These books are the beginning," Captain Childs told Matthew. "Make them your fists."

A sailing ship of the late 1800s

Matthew sailed from China to Japan to the Philippines. He sailed across the Atlantic Ocean to France, Africa, and southern Russia. He even sailed through the Arctic. And all the time, he continued to learn. When Matthew was nineteen, Captain Childs died and was buried at sea. Heartbroken, Matthew returned to Baltimore.

The Meeting of a Lifetime

Matthew tried to find work in Baltimore, but there were not many opportunities for black people in 1885. The young man soon discovered that people didn't care about his skills and learning—only his color. He worked as a driver, a bellhop, a messenger, and a night watchman. Soon, he decided to go to Washington, D.C., where he got a job as a clerk in the Steinmetz and Sons hat shop.

Matthew Henson and Robert Peary looked at each other across the counter on that day they met in 1887. Matthew saw a tall, red-haired man with steely, blue-gray eyes. Robert saw a steady, calm, honest young man. Even though Matthew was only twenty years old, he had already traveled around the world. Robert decided to ask Matthew to be his helper in Nicaragua. "Sir, I'd like that job very much," Matthew answered.

Their first project together was sort of a funny way for these men to begin a partnership. Matthew Henson and Robert Peary, who would later make history by being the first people to reach the North Pole, first had to travel in the opposite direction—to the jungle!

In November 1887, Matthew sailed with forty-five U.S. engineers and one hundred black Jamaican workers to Nicaragua. As Robert's servant, Matthew cooked and cleaned while the engineers measured and the workers chopped through the jungle. Soon, however, Robert recognized Matthew's intelligence and skill and gave him more important and demanding work.

Working in the Nicaraguan jungle

The First Greenland Expedition

After seven months, the Nicaragua survey was done. As the men sailed back to New York, Robert asked Matthew to come with him as he tried to cross Greenland, a snowy country just below the North Pole. Matthew quickly agreed. In June of 1891, the Greenland expedition set off. Their tiny ship, the *Kite,* was packed with many kinds of food, including pemmican—a beef, fat, and raisin mixture that explorers eat for energy. There were also skis and snowshoes, guns and bullets, sledges, woolen clothing, a stove, pots and pans, cameras, and a hundred tons of coal.

Robert planned to become famous by being the first person to cross Greenland. The country's name, however, did not tell the truth about the country: "Greenland" is mostly covered in ice. Robert wanted to cross the southern end, which is the shortest route to travel—but also the most dangerous.

As they set off toward Greenland, the *Kite* sailed past towering white glaciers and struggled through cracks in the stubborn, rugged ice. The little ship finally dropped anchor in McCormick Bay, Greenland. On August 8—Matthew's birthday—he had the first party of his life. Robert's wife (who joined them on the ship) cooked mock turtle soup, stew of auk (a little bird), green peas, eider duck, corn, tomatoes, and apricot pie. The food was so delicious that Matthew remembered this party for the rest of his life.

Soon after they dropped anchor, the explorers set out to meet the local Inuit. They hoped the men would help them hunt polar bears, seals, walruses, reindeer, caribou, and foxes for meat and fur. They also hoped the Inuit women would take the animal hides and sew them into warm clothing.

A ship's crew at a trading post in Greenland

On August 18, four Inuit men walked into camp. They stepped close to Matthew, pointed to his skin, and said, "Inuit! Inuit!" They thought that Matthew was an Inuit who had just returned to his homeland. From that moment on, the Inuit called Matthew "Miy Paluk," which means "dear little Matthew." They taught him how to speak the Inuit language, to eat meat raw and bloody, and to drive a dog sledge with a thirty-foot sealskin whip. Matthew even learned to build a snow igloo with fifty blocks of snow in just an hour. These basic skills would be very important to Matthew in the future. They would help him and his fellow explorers survive in the dangerous and harsh frozen world they were about to explore. But even though Matthew knew the most about surviving in the Arctic, Robert picked another man from the camp to travel with him on this historic journey across Greenland.

On September 24, 1892, the first North Greenland Expedition returned home and Robert was a hero. Matthew, however, was barely noticed.

Reaching the Pole

The never-ending sea ice of the Arctic piles into mountains that reach high into the sky. Under your feet, the ice moves and cracks without warning. One false step and you may plunge into the water, never to come out. The swirling black ocean is cold, dark, and deadly. With all these dangers, no wonder few people have ever reached the North Pole!

The Inuit knew well how dangerous the Arctic Ocean could be. They believed the ocean held a fierce devil, called Tornasuk, the spirit of the frozen sea. The ocean was dangerous because Tornasuk could drag people to their death. But the North Pole had an even more cruel devil they called Kokoyah. They believed that only the bravest person would venture near the North Pole.

Trying for the North Pole

On June 26, 1893, Robert, Matthew, and a crew of ten took off for the frozen north again. This time Matthew was sure that he would be chosen as one of the men to trek with Robert to the North Pole. But once again, Robert picked others to accompany him, and Matthew was left back at camp.

Unlike their first trip, this expedition was a failure. The men could only go 128 miles before the dogs went mad or froze to death in the ice storms. When they returned to camp, all of Robert's men wanted to go home—all except for one: Matthew Henson. Robert was only able to talk one other man, Hugh Lee, into staying. On April 1, 1895, the three men set out for the North Pole again.

Crossing a small open channel through a field of ice

"A Long Race with Death"

It was warm for the north Arctic, only fourteen degrees below zero! It was sunny, too, and the flat fields of ice were so shiny that it hurt to look at them. The three men traveled to where Robert had left a giant pile of supplies, but everything was buried in the snow. "We'll go on anyway," Robert said, "we have enough walrus meat." The others agreed.

Eating the walrus meat, however, would not be easy. When they tried to bite into the meat, it was frozen so hard that it cut the inside of their mouths like glass. They tried to warm it in their tea, but the slippery, raw, red chunks looked too bloody to eat. Lacking enough food, they got weaker and weaker.

Finally, the men found a herd of walrus, and Matthew shot one just as it charged toward Robert. The three starving explorers gobbled the warm, bloody meat and threw chunks to their skinny dogs. With their stomachs filled, the men marched on. They made it as far as Independence Bay, but they could go no further. Towering cliffs that could not be crossed were now in their way. On June 1, bitterly disappointed, they trudged back to camp. Years later Matthew called the trip back to camp "a long race with death."

The men had eaten so little nourishing food that their teeth had started to fall out. Upon returning, only Matthew was brave enough to do what the Inuits told him: He drank bowls and bowls of seals' blood. Sure enough, he recovered first.

On August 3, 1895, the three men returned to Washington, D.C. Robert had to have something to show for his two years in Greenland, so he brought two huge meteorites he had found. Today, visitors can see these meteorites at the Museum of Natural History in New York City.

Tragedy Strikes

On July 4, 1898, Robert and Matthew set off again for the North Pole. This time, however, their ship got trapped in the ice seven hundred miles from their goal. Robert became frantic when he found out that a brave Norwegian explorer named Sverdrup was also heading for the Pole. He knew if their ship was stuck, Sverdrup would beat them to the goal! Robert decided to march through the long Arctic night no matter what the cost. Robert, Matthew, and their expedition finally made it to a stopping point—Fort Conger—and they were ahead of Sverdrup. But their journey had taken a terrible toll. Robert's toes had frozen solid. A fierce storm then trapped the men in their cabin. Matthew cared for Robert until the storm let up. Finally, on February 18, Matthew strapped Robert to a sledge and set off to return to the ship. There, all but two of Robert's toes had to be amputated (cut off). For the rest of his life, he would have difficulty walking.

Peary's Early Attempts to Reach the North Pole

Year	Who Went	What Happened
1893	Matthew, Robert, and crew of ten	Expedition went 128 miles and then failed
1895	Matthew, Robert, and Hugh Lee	The three men got only as far as Independence Bay
1898–1899	Matthew, Robert, and expedition	Expedition ended at Fort Conger where Robert had eight toes amputated
1902	Matthew, Robert, and four Inuit helpers	Expedition got to 84° 16', the farthest north to this time

Peary's team struggling to pull supply sleds over a ridge of ice

On April 6, 1902, Robert, Matthew, and four Inuit helpers once again stepped onto the frozen Arctic ice. Matthew saw once more why the Inuit so feared the region. The ice split apart and jammed with fearsome roars. As it split, floes, or islands of ice, were created. The men tried jumping from ice floe to ice floe, but too often they got stranded on a chunk of ice, and then they had to wait until new ice formed. With Robert still weak from his foot problems, Matthew led the way. He searched in vain for a better way through the treacherous ice but could not avoid the punishment of the Arctic.

On April 21, the men ran out of food and could go no further. They had reached the point 84° 16' north latitude—which was the American record for the farthest north ever traveled—but it was still not the Pole. Disappointed and tired, the expedition returned home. More than three years would pass before Robert and Matthew would feel prepared to face the challenges of the Arctic again.

Accomplishing the Impossible

On July 16, 1905, Matthew and Robert sailed north again with three assistants. As they traveled up the coast of Greenland, they took on thirty-three Inuit families, two hundred dogs, and tons of whale and walrus meat. The ship stank with meat, dogs, and unwashed people.

Humbled by his past attempts, Robert now made a new plan. One group would find the best route and make a trail. Five small groups then would follow and every fifty to seventy-five miles, one of the five groups would go back with the weakest dogs. This would save the food for the strongest.

On March 1, Matthew and his team of Inuits left to try once again to blaze a trail to the Pole. By April 21, they were only 175 miles from the Pole, but they were out of food and were forced to eat their dogs. By the time they arrived back at their ship, only two dogs were left. They had set a new world record, but they still had not reached the Pole.

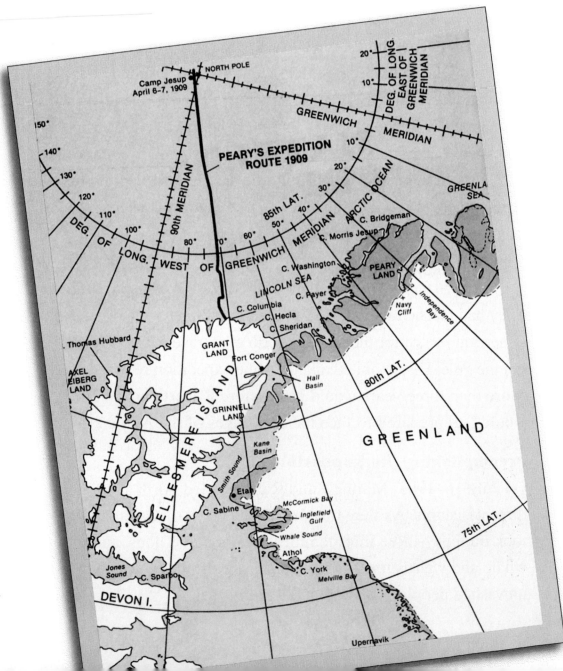

Henson (center) and Inuits celebrating at the North Pole

Victory at Last!

Robert now knew that he would not have too many more chances to reach the Pole. He was nearly fifty years old, and time and money had nearly run out. On July 6, 1908, Robert once again loaded a ship. He picked the six strongest and bravest men he could find, and again all the men marched in teams. But this time, Robert knew enough to ask Matthew to come with him to the Pole.

By April 5, they were only one day's march from their goal. The next day, on April 6, Robert took a reading. At first he couldn't believe what he saw. His reading showed ninety degrees north! They had made it! "We will plant the Stars and Stripes at the North Pole," he shouted. The men gave three cheers and took pictures of themselves with the flag. They also dreamed of what a bright future they would all have.

The future did not turn out to be as bright as Henson and Peary dreamed it would be. During the following summer, Dr. Frederick Cook, another explorer, claimed he had reached the North Pole first. Many people believed Cook's claim, but months later the National Geographic Society ruled that Peary had been the first to reach the Pole. Peary and another member of the team received medals, but it was not until 1944 that Matthew Henson received a medal from Congress for his participation in the North Pole expedition.

About the Author
Laurie Rozakis

Laurie Rozakis doesn't know exactly when the writing bug hit her. "I suppose that I've always been a writer," she says, "scribbling loopy crayon messages as a toddler, writing gossipy notes as a teenager, and typing dense letters in college."

Ms. Rozakis started thinking seriously about writing a book when she took time off from teaching after her son was born. In the extra time between changing diapers and feeding the baby, she started writing. Her first book was for high school students needing to study for an advanced English test.

Since that first book, Ms. Rozakis has written other books to help students study for important tests. She also has written biographies of several other famous people besides Matthew Henson and Robert Peary. If you enjoy watching cartoons, you'll enjoy reading Ms. Rozakis's biography of Bill Hanna and Joe Barbera. These two cartoonists are responsible for creating *The Flintstones, Scooby Doo,* and *The Jetsons.*

When she is writing, Ms. Rozakis follows a set routine. She always has a sharpened pencil behind her right ear, a cup of tea near her on the bookshelf, and the radio tuned to an "oldies" station. She says, "I never use the pencil, know enough to shun the tea, and rarely remember the words to any song, but that's the routine."

Reader Response

Open for Discussion

If you had the chance, would you have volunteered to join Robert Peary on his expedition to the North Pole? Why or why not?

Comprehension Check

1. What dangers did the men who journeyed with Robert Peary face as they traveled across the Arctic? Look back at the selection for examples.

2. What qualities did Peary see in Matthew Henson when they first met? How were those qualities shown during expeditions? Find details in the selection to support your answers.

3. If you had gone on the final journey to the North Pole, what would you have told later about Henson's part in the expedition? Look back and find examples to answer the question.

4. **Graphic sources** are useful in making predictions before you read. What did you predict from the pictures, map, and chart? (Graphic Sources)

5. Charts are one kind of **graphic source.** Use the chart on page 548. List expeditions Robert Peary and Matthew Henson made between 1893 and 1902. Which of these journeys got the farthest north? (Graphic Sources)

Test Prep
Look Back and Write

Look back at pages 546 and 549. Explain how the photographs on these pages help you understand the difficulties these explorers faced. Describe details from these pages to support your answer.

553

The North Pole

by Rupert Matthews

THE DANGEROUS REGIONS of the Arctic were the objects of many 19th-century voyages. Explorers were told to map the regions and to report what they found. These explorers sailed in ships strong enough to handle the pressure of ice and packed with enough supplies to last several years. The teams were equipped with a variety of scientific instruments. The instruments helped them collect rock samples and study wildlife. The long series of expeditions reached a high point with Robert Peary's success in 1909, when he led the first team of men to reach the North Pole.

POLAR PRIZE!
"The Pole at last!" wrote Peary in his diary, "My dream and goal for 20 years." In the afternoon of April 6, 1909, Robert Peary and his team became the first men to reach the North Pole.

ARCTIC TRANSPORT
Polar explorers had to bring supplies and equipment across many miles of snow and ice. Sleds were used for this task.

Sleeping tent for eight men

Load protected by canvas cover

Iron-shod runners

PLEASE DO NOT MOVE!

In 1827 Sir William Parry and a team of men left their ship, the *Hecla,* to set out over land in an attempt to reach the North Pole. The team left this message on board a small boat, which they left behind for future use.

This Boat is left for Captain Parry and his party on their return from attempting to reach the North Pole.

It is particularly requested that she may not be removed; as they will probably be much in want of her.

H.M.Ship Hecla,
May 15th 1827

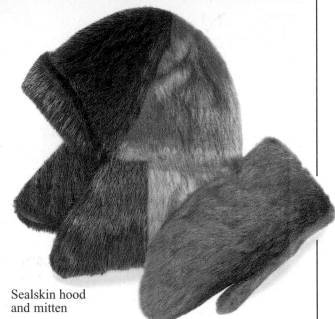

Sealskin hood and mitten

SLED HAULING

Loaded sleds were heavy to pull. Husky dogs and the men shared the job.

SEALSKIN CLOTHING

Arctic explorers learned to wear clothing modeled on local Inuit designs. Sealskin hoods and mittens kept out wind and saved many explorers from frostbite.

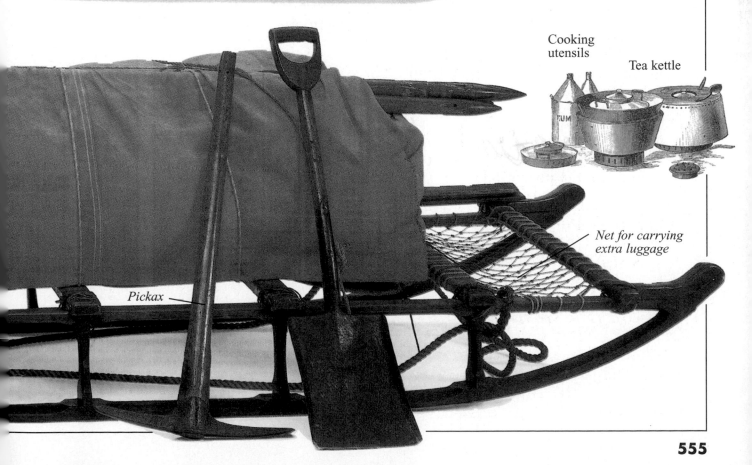

Cooking utensils

Tea kettle

Net for carrying extra luggage

Pickax

Author's Purpose

- An **author's purpose** is the reason for writing something.

- Some purposes for writing are to entertain, to inform, to express, and to persuade.

- Predicting an author's purpose can help you decide whether to read something slowly and carefully or quickly for fun.

Read "Saving Our Wetlands" from *The Aquarium Take-Along Book* by Sheldon L. Gerstenfeld.

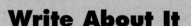

Write About It

1. How does the text structure help you figure out the author's purpose?

2. What purpose or purposes do you think the author had for writing "Saving Our Wetlands"? Explain.

3. What did you learn about wetlands from reading this article? How do you feel about wetlands after reading it?

Saving Our Wetlands

by Sheldon L. Gerstenfeld

- The world's wetlands are being rapidly destroyed for farming, home building, and mining.

- Wetlands are areas that are frequently covered by water. Swamps, marshes, and bogs are all wetlands. For a long time, wetlands were thought to have no value, but now we know that they are among the most important areas on the earth.

The Importance of Wetlands

- Wetlands are feeding, breeding, and nursery areas for fish and shellfish.

Common Loon

- Wetlands are home for a third of the United States' resident bird species and half of the migrating birds.
- Wetlands lock up large amounts of carbon in the form of peat, thus preventing it from entering our atmosphere as carbon dioxide, which would contribute to global warming.
- Wetlands absorb and filter out pollutants that would otherwise make our rivers, lakes, and reservoirs unhealthy.
- Wetlands are the glue that holds the land together. They protect the coast and inland areas from too much water in the wrong place at the wrong time. They hold or sponge up water from storms and floods.

Great Blue Heron

LOOK AHEAD

Into the Sea

Guess the author's purpose for writing *Into the Sea*, a selection about another water environment.

Words to Know

awkward	flippers	ridges
underside	muscles	coral
current	protection	

Many words have more than one meaning. To decide which meaning of a word is being used, look for clues in the surrounding sentences or the paragraph.

Read the paragraph below, paying special attention to its meaning as a whole. Decide whether *current* means "course of events" or "flow of water."

Out of the Nest

The sea turtle left the protection of its nest to make the trip to the sea. It looked awkward—its flippers were for swimming, not walking. In the sea, its strong muscles would help it swim. At first, the turtle floated in the ocean's current. It would have to get used to its new home. The "mountains" ahead were ridges made of coral. They looked like rocks, but coral is actually skeletons of tiny sea creatures. The turtle had to protect its soft underside from the hard coral. There was much to learn.

Talk About It

You are the host of a nature show. Tell about the turtle's journey. Use as many vocabulary words as you can.

Into the Sea

by Brenda Z. Guiberson • illustrated by Alix Berenzy

Tap, tap. Scritch. The tiny sea turtle is the last hatchling to break out of her leathery egg and crawl up the sides of a sandy nest. She is not much bigger than a bottle cap and would make a good meal for a hungry sea bird or a crab. But at this moment, at dawn, the crabs are resting in muddy burrows and the beach is quiet and empty.

The turtle smells the sand and stares at the bright moonlight that glistens across the ocean. She rests a moment and then, like a windup toy, pulls herself quickly across the beach with her flippers. Always she heads straight for the silvery moonlight. *Clack, click-clack.* A crab pops out of its burrow and sees the dark moving shape. Just in time, the turtle reaches the edge of the water. A gentle wave splashes across her back and carries her into the sea.

Instinctively the turtle knows how to paddle with her flippers and dive beneath the surface. She is still swimming hard when the sun moves into the sky. Every few minutes she comes up for a breath of air. Her eyesight is much better in the water. She sees a jellyfish, a starfish, and a barracuda with a big mouth. None of them see the turtle. Her white underside blends in with the shimmering white surface of the ocean.

Splop. The turtle comes up for air in a patch of sargassum weed. A tiny crab and a water strider ride on the floating raft. Below, a sargassum fish uses the plant for camouflage. They all drift with the winds and current while the weeds hide them from the sharp-eyed sea birds above and the hungry fish below. One little turtle floats around in the clump for several months, eating tiny plants and animals called plankton.

As the turtle grows, her shell grows with her and gets a little harder. She likes to dive into long streams of seaweed that grow on the ocean bottom. There, mussels and seahorses sift water for plankton to eat. When a strong current comes up, the seahorses grab on to the seaweed with their tails, while the mussels hold on to rocks with threadlike feet. But the little turtle is not yet strong enough to swim against this current. She drifts away with the moving water.

The turtle spends her first winter in a warm, tropical sea full of brilliant colors and creatures with big mouths. Like all sea turtles, she cannot pull her head and flippers into her shell for protection, but she finds many places to hide in the coral reef. When a butterfly fish swims in her direction, she darts under a ledge. This fish has a dark tail spot that looks just like an eye. The turtle watches closely to see which end is the front and which is the back.

By now the turtle has been in the sea for over a year. She is as big as the sea birds and most of the fish. She has developed strong swimming muscles and swims four times faster than a human.

The turtle has no teeth but bites off pieces of seaweed with the sharp ridges of her jaw. She spends two whole months eating her way through a rich, wavy garden of sea grass.

After several more years, the turtle grows into one of the biggest creatures in the sea. Sharks, however, are still a danger. When one comes near her feeding area, she swims out into a warm current far away from the shallow ocean shelf. She crosses deep, deep water where sunlight cannot reach the bottom and seaweed cannot grow. There is not much to eat in the middle of the ocean, but she continues on her long journey, living on the extra fat in her body.

Even a big turtle can get very tired. Sometimes she stops to sunbathe on the surface of the water. The sunlight discourages the barnacles and marine grasses from growing on her shell. She likes to float for hours in the midday sun. A remora, with a special fin on its head, attaches to her underside for a free ride. Then a tired brown bird flutters down to join them for a rest on the surface of the ocean.

The turtle hears humpback whales singing in the sea. She dives underwater and the bird flies away. She passes a humpback swimming in slow circles and blowing a ring of thick bubbles. Many small fish get caught in the swirling, whirling water of this bubble net. With a strong push of its fluke, the whale comes up through the middle and swallows hundreds of trapped minnows in one huge gulp. The turtle swims swiftly away, but the remora stays behind to catch a ride on the whale.

At three hundred pounds, the turtle is a fully grown adult. Soon eggs begin to form in her body, and she finds a current that seems familiar to her and follows it back across the ocean.

The turtle swims deep under the water for almost two hours, but before she comes up to breathe, she swims below a fishing boat. Suddenly she finds herself trapped in a net. Each time she tries to swim away, her flippers scrape the sides of the net and almost get tangled in the woven ropes.

She bumps into metal bars. *Clunk.* Shrimp and small fish swim through the slots between the bars, but the turtle is much too big. She swims over them and finds an escape door at the bottom. Soon she is at the surface of the ocean, taking in big gulps of fresh air.

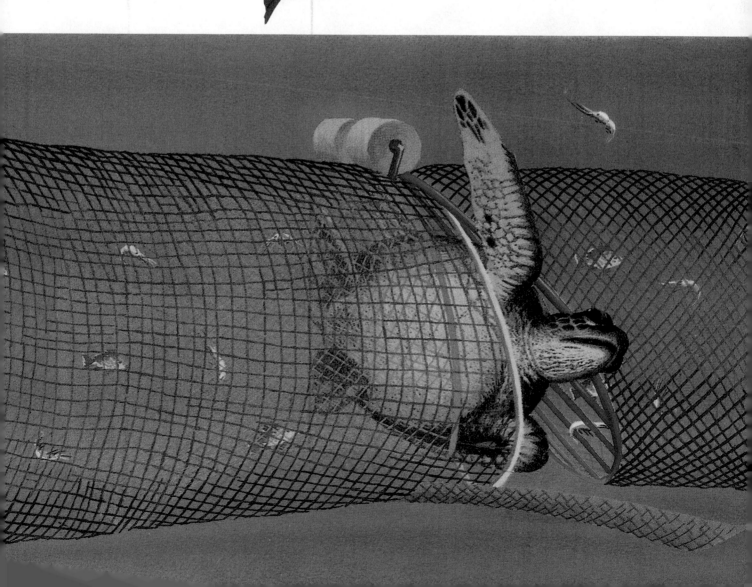

After a rest, the turtle follows the same familiar current through the sea. She swims many hundreds of miles in this flow of water. Finally she crosses over the top of one ocean mountain and along the steep side of another. When she pops her head out of the water, she sees the top of the second mountain. It is a round island, with a warm sandy beach.

After more than twenty years in the sea, the turtle returns to the land. She waits until nighttime, when the tide is high, to come in. She is slow and awkward as she pulls her huge body up onto the sandy beach. She does not see well on land. Tears stream down her cheeks, as they do in the water,

to help her body get rid of extra salt from the sea. She pokes her nose into the sand. The turtle seems to know that she has come back to the same island where she was born.

Slowly she drags herself across the beach. When she gets near a small bush, she stops to rest and then begins to dig a nest in the sand with her flippers. *Thump, scrape, whoosh, wheeze.* It is hard work as she scoops out a hole for her body and a deeper chamber for her eggs. Sand flies everywhere, covering her back and head. She works for three hours, laying over one hundred eggs and then covering them with sand.

Once again the turtle crosses the beach. Waves sweep the sand off her back and lift her into the water. Her huge body feels lighter and she sees clearly again. She leaves the sandy nest behind her. If nothing destroys the eggs, her babies will hatch in two months. Perhaps one or two will get past the crabs and the sea birds, the fish and the fishing nets, and like their mother, will return to lay eggs on the same sandy beach before making their way back into the sea.

Fast in the Sea, Slow on the Sand

It is a difficult and delicate venture for a sea turtle to leave the ocean and lay her eggs on land. In the exposed setting of sand and shallow water, things can go wrong for the turtle, her eggs, or hatchlings.

Centuries ago, settlers, explorers, and pirates landed on New World beaches and discovered the turtle nesting sites. They ate turtle eggs, grabbed the slow, plodding females as they crossed the sand, and caught turtles that came up for air or basked on top of the ocean. Turtles were flipped on their backs and stacked alive on ship decks until fresh meat was needed by the cook. It didn't take long for the population of sea turtles to decline dramatically.

There are other problems for these reptiles. Some turtle eggs are crushed by vehicles on beaches, while others are eaten by dogs, raccoons, jaguars, and snakes. Hatchlings get caught by birds, crabs, and fish, and larger turtles are killed so that fancy items may be made from their shells. And then there are the many turtles that die in fishing nets or after swallowing plastic or other debris in the ocean.

Today sea turtles and their eggs are protected by law, but they still face the loss of their nesting places. Many resorts, homes, and hotels have been built on nesting beaches. Still, turtles return to these beaches and lay eggs if they can find stable, moist sand above the high-tide mark. If the turtles hatch, they can be confused by all the lights around them and may crawl toward the brightness of a resort or highway instead of the sea.

There used to be millions of sea turtles, and now there are only several thousand. However, by working to protect nesting sites, provide safe care for the eggs, and establish new nesting beaches, people hope to dramatically increase the number of turtles in the sea.

Leatherback
74 inches

Green turtle
49 inches

Loggerhead
47 inches

Flatback
39 inches

Hawksbill
35 inches

Kemp's ridley
30 inches

Olive ridley
30 inches

569

About the Author
Brenda Z. Guiberson

Brenda Z. Guiberson likes to write about all kinds of things. "I like to write both fiction and nonfiction," she says. "I like to write about subjects that are interesting and exciting to me." When she decides what she will write about, she knows that she needs to do research first. "A writer can't say that a kangaroo rat stops for a drink of water when research reveals that this creature never drinks," she has said. "And if an alligator is cold-blooded, then how does it behave? It takes a lot of digging into other books to find out." This is part of writing, but Ms. Guiberson doesn't mind. "It's hard work but fun, and surprises pop up all along the way."

About the Illustrator
Alix Berenzy

One thing that makes Ms. Berenzy such a good artist is that she really pays attention to how things look. She stores memories away and uses them for her artwork. "My first interest was in horses—that's what started me drawing," Alix Berenzy says. She would watch for horses on farms that the school bus passed. Sometimes in school, instead of paying attention, Alix drew horses. "I even drew horses on my test papers," she remembers. "Once I got back a test that the teacher had marked in red, 'Great horse, terrible math—D.'"

Reader Response

Open for Discussion

After reading the turtle's life story, what three words would you use to describe her journey?

Comprehension Check

1. Look back at *Into the Sea*. If the beginning, middle, and end were each a chapter in a book, what title would you give each part? Give examples from the selection to explain why.

2. Which stage of the turtle's life do you think is most dangerous? Why? Use details from the selection to explain your answer.

3. The last page of the selection explains dangers that humans present to sea turtles. Which danger might you choose to work against? Use details to explain.

4. The **author's purposes** for writing *Into the Sea* might have been to inform and also to express a feeling for sea turtles. Write a sentence from the story that gives an example of each purpose. (Author's Purpose)

5. What was the **author's purpose** for including "Fast in the Sea, Slow on the Sand" on page 569? Use examples to explain. (Author's Purpose)

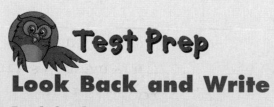

Test Prep
Look Back and Write

Look back at pages 562–563. Explain how the turtle changes. Tell how it grows and becomes stronger. Use specific details and examples from those pages to explain your answer.

Test Prep

How to Read an Informational Article

1. Preview

- "I Work in the Ocean" is a profile. This kind of informational article gives facts and details about someone's skills, personality, and career.

- Read the title and subtitles. Look at the photographs and read the captions. How do you know which caption goes with which photograph?

2. Read and Locate Information

- Read the article to find out about this person's career. As you read use a chart with these headings:

Equipment	Workplace	Goals

3. Think and Connect

Think about "Into the Sea." Then look over your notes on "I Work in the Ocean."

Would Norbert Wu be a good person to take underwater photos for a book about the life cycle of a sea turtle? Give details to support your answer.

"I Work in the Ocean"

A Profile of an Underwater Photographer

by Kristin Ingram

Norbert Wu's coworkers are fish. Instead of putting on a business suit and driving to an office, this underwater photographer puts on scuba gear and dives into the ocean. He travels around the world to photograph all kinds of strange, beautiful, and even dangerous creatures. It's harder than taking pictures on land, but Norbert enjoys the challenge of photographing marine animals in their own environment and showing other people the beauty and mystery of the ocean.

Different Subjects and Locations

Norbert's subjects range from tiny, colorful tropical fish to huge gray whales. He dives in the warm waters of the Red Sea and under icebergs in the near-freezing Greenland Sea. He'll photograph just about anything that lives underwater, but he especially enjoys difficult projects.

On a shoot near Isla del Coco, Costa Rica, he held his breath while kicking furiously to swim beneath a huge school of hammerhead sharks. He had to wait until after he took the photo to exhale, because the cloud of bubbles would have scared the sharks away.

In the Bahamas Norbert had to swim quickly to keep up with a group of wild dolphins. They zipped and dove while playing tag and passing seaweed back and forth. Dolphins like to play with humans, but anyone who's too slow gets left behind.

Norbert doesn't always race around underwater. Sometimes he must keep as still as possible so he won't startle a shy animal. Once in the Caribbean Sea he found a blenny living in a hole in a coral reef. Whenever he tried to photograph it, the fish popped back into its hole. Norbert visited the fish several times over the next

1 Norbert Wu in Monterey Bay, California

2 Large male squarespot fish near Borneo

3 A school of silverside minnows in the Red Sea

4 The blenny that Norbert finally photographed

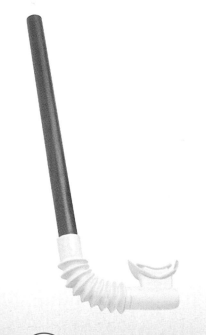

few days. Finally it got used to him and let him get close enough to take the shot.

Thrills and Routines of the Job

Adventure is part of Norbert's job. Would you jump into water swarming with tiger sharks? That's just what Norbert did in the French Frigate Shoals, some tiny islands near Hawaii. A TV wildlife program wanted to show the sharks attacking albatross chicks that landed in the water while learning to fly. Norbert watched the sharks for a long time. They seemed interested only in the birds, ignoring the monk seals swimming nearby. He decided it was safe to go in, but he wore a chain-mail suit just in case. As he'd guessed, the sharks ignored him.

Norbert's work isn't always dangerous and exciting. He spends lots of time in his California office doing paperwork and fixing up equipment. The watertight cases, called housings, that protect his cameras must be free of leaks. Underwater photos need strong lighting, so Norbert attaches strobe lights to bendable arms on the housings. When he tests his equipment in Monterey Bay, it looks as if he's carrying a miniature spaceship. Curious harbor seals and sea lions follow him around. Sometimes they even nuzzle Norbert's camera.

Fun Grows into Work

How did Norbert become an underwater photographer? He has always loved the ocean and its creatures. As a boy his favorite summer activities were swimming and scuba diving. He continued these hobbies through college and added underwater photography to the list. During his years at Scripps Institute of Oceanography in San Diego, Norbert discovered that he had a talent for taking good underwater photos. And he realized that with them he could help people see and understand the ocean the way he did.

Marvelous Sights, Sad Sights

Helping others view the sea in a new way is very important to Norbert. Although he has seen marvelous sights, he has also witnessed many sad things. Pollution has damaged fragile ecosystems such as coral reefs, and overfishing has reduced the populations of some oceans. By taking pictures that show how interesting and beautiful sea animals are, Norbert hopes he'll inspire people to help protect them.

Perhaps one day you, too, will dive into Norbert's underwater world and share his delight at its wonders. Even if you prefer to stay dry, you can always count on him to bring back incredible photographs.

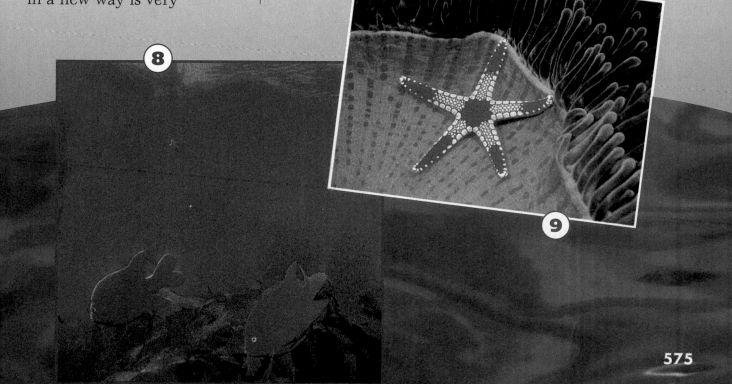

8 Garibaldi fish near California

9 Candy-cane starfish near Borneo

Text Structure

- **Text structure** is the way a piece of writing is organized. There are two main kinds of writing: fiction and nonfiction.

- Fiction tells stories of people and events that an author creates. Fiction is usually organized by the order in which things happen.

- Nonfiction tells of real people and events or tells information about the real world. Some ways to organize nonfiction are cause and effect, problem and solution, and comparison and contrast.

Read "Out-of-This-World Rocks" by John Kontakis from *Contact Kids*.

Talk About It

1. Is "Out-of-This-World Rocks" fiction or nonfiction? How do you know?

2. Much of the text of this article is organized by comparison and contrast. Give examples to show this organization. Explain.

Out-of-This-World Rocks

by John Kontakis

Meteorites may look like plain old rocks. But they're actually tiny pieces of asteroids, comets, planets, and other space objects. These bits of heavenly bodies make it through our atmosphere and land on the Earth's surface.

Space rocks enter the Earth's atmosphere all the time. But most of them are so small, they burn up, or vaporize, before they can reach the ground. Only about five hundred meteorites actually land on the Earth's surface each year.

How can meteorite hunters tell the difference between a space rock and your average Earth rock? Both contain the same types of materials. But meteorites contain more metal than Earth rocks. That makes them heavier. Some meteorites have a glassy crust that's formed when they heat up in the Earth's atmosphere. Also, they're usually darker than the darkest Earth rocks.

Why look for meteorites? They give us information about the types of minerals found in the solar system. And they help us understand what materials were floating about when the solar system was made more than four billion years ago.

LOOK AHEAD

Notice how the author of *Space Probes to the Planets* organizes information as you read more about outer space.

Words to Know

incredible atmosphere probes
craters   spacecraft

When you read, you may come across a word that you do not know. To figure out its meaning, look for clues in the sentences around it.

Notice how *atmosphere* is used in the paragraph below. Read the sentence after *atmosphere*. What do you think *atmosphere* means?

Exploring a Planet

Venus, the brightest planet in the sky, is an incredible sight. Its atmosphere is different from Earth's. It is difficult to see the surface of Venus because the air around it is filled with thick clouds. Most of our knowledge of Venus comes from probes that go through the clouds. The Magellan spacecraft orbited there in 1989 and started sending back pictures that scientists used to make a map of Venus. The map shows volcanoes and craters. Some of these valleys are over one hundred miles across!

Write About It

Make a map of a real or imaginary planet and label its parts. Use as many vocabulary words as you can.

SPACE PROBES
TO THE PLANETS

BY FAY ROBINSON

Mariner 5

Have you ever wanted to visit another planet? Ever since the planets were discovered, people have dreamed of visiting them. But the planets are all very hot or very cold, and very far away. Until scientists learn more, a trip to explore them would be unsafe.

In the meantime we've learned a lot about the planets, partly because of space probes. Space probes are spacecraft with no people on them. With the help of computers and radio signals, they can travel to the planets by themselves.

Earth, the planet we live on, is one of nine planets that circle the sun. The nine planets are Mercury, Venus, Earth, Mars, Jupiter, Saturn, Uranus, Neptune, and Pluto. Most of the planets have moons that travel with them. Rocky objects called meteoroids

and asteroids circle the sun between the planets. The sun and all the planets and objects that circle it are called the solar system.

Space probes have flown close to all the planets except Pluto, and some have landed on Venus and Mars. The planets are all very far away from Earth—so far that it took fifteen months for space probes to get to the closest planet, and twelve years to get to the farthest.

The space probes collected lots of information about each planet's atmosphere, temperatures, moons, and more. But the most exciting information came from pictures the space probes took. When the space probes got up close to the planets, scientists discovered some incredible things.

Pioneer Orbiter

Mercury, the planet closest to the sun, is covered with round holes called craters. Pictures from a space probe showed that Mercury has more craters for its size than any other planet. The craters were formed when millions of big rocks, or meteorites, crashed into Mercury long ago.

Mercury also has long ridges that look a little like wrinkles. Scientists think Mercury shrank after it was formed. The surface wrinkled the same way grapes wrinkle as they dry and shrink to become raisins.

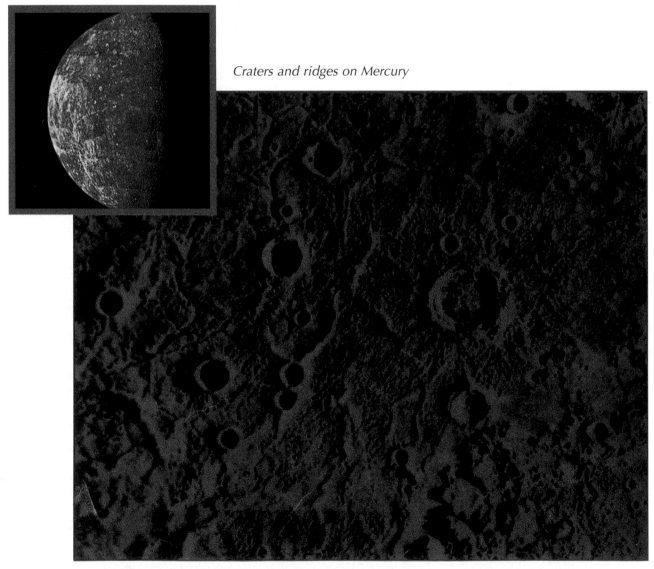

Craters and ridges on Mercury

582

Venus, the second planet from the sun, is wrapped in swirling clouds. Even though Venus is not the closest planet to the sun, it is the hottest. Its clouds are very thick and heavy, so they act like a blanket to trap heat. Powerful lightning bolts may flash through the clouds all the time.

Venus is so hot that when space probes landed on its surface, their parts melted. In order to learn more about Venus without losing any more space probes, scientists developed a way to get pictures through the clouds. These pictures show spots, cracks, and places where melted rock has pushed through the surface to make odd shapes.

Venus with its cloud cover

Venus beneath its cloud cover

Artist's idea of the surface of Venus

Earth is the third planet from the sun and the planet we live on. From far away in space, we can see blue oceans, brown land, and white clouds. Close-up pictures show our forests, mountains, rivers, and seas.

Earth is the only planet with lots of water. Since plants and animals need water to live, Earth is the only planet with plant and animal life. Scientists think it is the only planet in our solar system with *any* kind of life. Earth also has the perfect temperature for people—the other planets would be too hot or cold for us unless we wore special spacesuits.

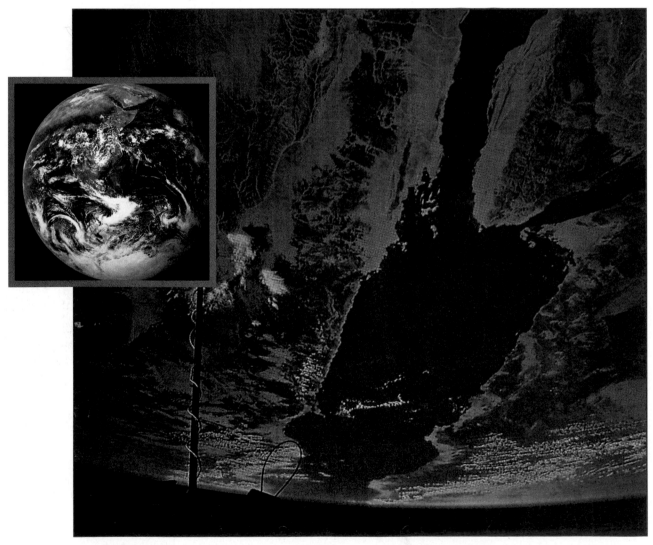

Mercury Venus Earth **Mars** Jupiter Saturn Uranus Neptune Pluto

Mars, the fourth planet from the sun, is nicknamed the Red Planet because of its red-orange color.

In 1997, a space probe landed on Mars. The first photos showed so many rocks that one scientist called it a "rock festival." Scientists named the rocks after cartoon and book characters, such as Pooh Bear, Yogi, Calvin, and Hobbes.

A robot-like car, called a land rover, drove off the space probe to explore. Moving at the speed of a tortoise, the land rover studied Mars's rocks and soil. Scientists learned that Mars's rocks are very much like those on Earth. And, like Earth, Mars was once a planet with warmer weather and lots of water. Although there is no known life on Mars now, maybe, just maybe, there was life on Mars long ago. Scientists are still trying to figure that out.

Jupiter is the fifth planet from the sun and the largest. If you could put eleven Earths side by side, they would not quite equal Jupiter's diameter.

Jupiter has enormous windstorms. One storm, called the Great Red Spot, is a hurricane more than twice the size of Earth.

Scientists knew Jupiter was colorful, but when space probes took these pictures, scientists were amazed. No one knew that the colors made such beautiful designs.

The colors on Jupiter come from different kinds of clouds. The clouds are striped because Jupiter spins very quickly—so quickly that the clouds are stretched into bands. All the planets spin, but Jupiter spins faster than any other.

The Great Red Spot

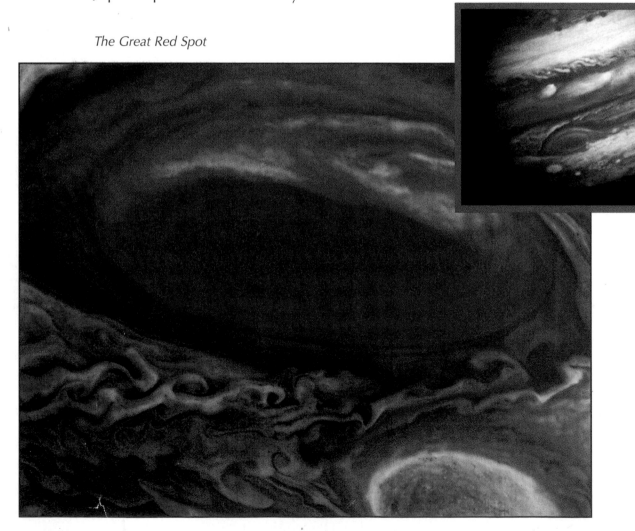

Saturn, the sixth planet from the sun, is surrounded by spectacular rings. Pictures from the space probes showed thousands of thin rings around Saturn, each traveling in its own path. There are three other planets with rings, but no planet has as many as Saturn.

The rings are made of pieces of ice and icy rock. Most pieces are the size of an ice cube, but some are as small as a grain of sand, and some are as large as a house. The space probes also found that Saturn has at least thirty moons—more than any other planet.

	Number of Moons	Number of Rings
Mercury	0	0
Venus	0	0
Earth	1	0
Mars	2	0
Jupiter	27	3
Saturn	at least 30	thousands
Uranus	21	11
Neptune	8	4
Pluto	1	0

Uranus, the seventh planet from the sun, has a hazy glow. When pictures of Uranus started coming in from a space probe, scientists were disappointed that there were no spots, stripes, or designs. One scientist thought Uranus looked like a "fuzzy blue tennis ball."

Uranus has rings that go up and over it instead of around its middle. This is because Uranus is tipped on its side. Some scientists think a planet or other huge object may have bumped into Uranus and knocked it over.

Uranus and its rings

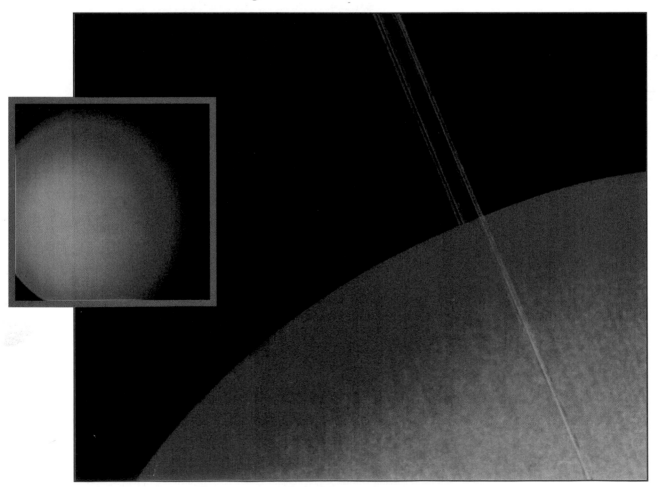

Neptune, the eighth planet from the sun, is deep blue. A space probe took pictures of white clouds that streaked very quickly around the planet. One cloud moved so fast that scientists called it Scooter. Scientists learned that Neptune's strong winds push some clouds to speeds of seven hundred miles per hour—faster than an airplane.

Neptune also has huge storms like those on Jupiter. Scientists named the biggest one the Great Dark Spot. This storm is as large as the planet Earth. Some scientists think there may be pure diamond at Neptune's center, created by a special combination of heat, pressure, and gases.

The Great Dark Spot and Scooter

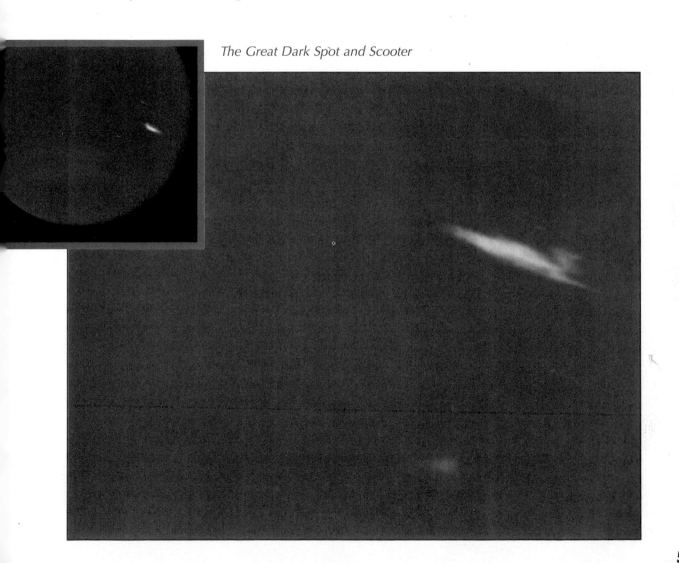

Mercury Venus   Earth   Mars   Jupiter   Saturn   Uranus   Neptune **Pluto**

Pluto is the ninth planet from the sun right now, and most of the time. But because Pluto's path is unusual, it is closer to the sun than Neptune for part of its orbit. Pluto is so far from the sun that it takes 248 Earth-years to go around the sun just once.

Pluto is the only planet that no space probe has explored. Scientists will learn much more when a space probe gets close, but for now they have pictures taken from a telescope in space.

Pluto has a moon that is half its size, so some scientists think of Pluto as a double planet. It is the smallest planet and is so far away from the sun that it is probably frozen solid.

Painting of what Pluto and its moon might look like

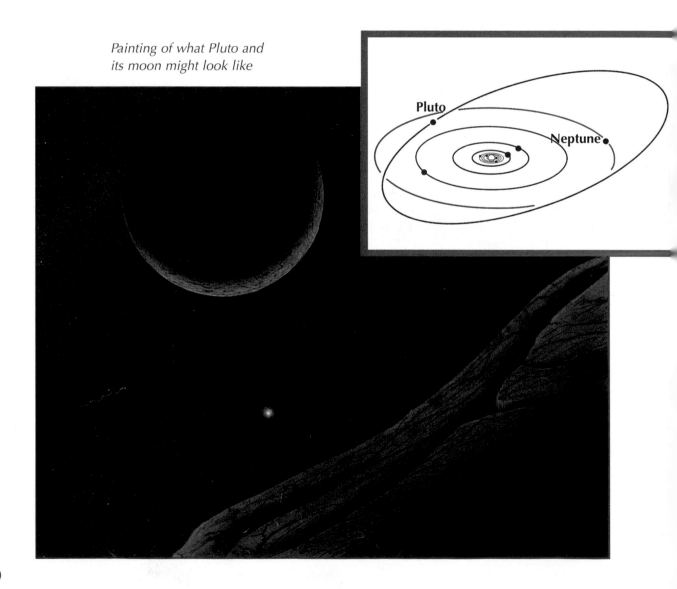

What happened to the space probes that traveled to the planets? They stayed in space. The probes that landed on Mars and Venus are still there. The probes that circled Mars, Venus, and Mercury are still circling. And the probes that flew past the other planets are now flying farther and farther into space.

Someday, they may fly into other solar systems. They will be too far away to send photographs or other information by then. But if there are any living beings who come across those space probes, they may be able to learn about us. Two of the space probes carry a recording that plays sounds from Earth—the voices of people saying hello in many different languages, the sounds of whales, frogs, heartbeats, and rainstorms.

Meanwhile, scientists are studying the information the space probes collected. They are sending other space probes to the planets to learn more. Someday soon, we may be able to visit another planet. We will need all the information the space probes can give us.

Sounds of Earth were recorded on this disk.

More About Space Probes

How do space probes get to the planets?

Space probes are sent into space either by rockets or by space shuttles. These launch vehicles carry the space probes through the Earth's atmosphere, then boost them on their paths to the planets.

How do space probes "know" what to do?

Space probes are run by computers. The computers act like brains to receive instructions from scientists at computers on Earth.

How do scientists get the pictures from the space probes?

The space probes carry special cameras. These cameras don't use film like cameras you may have. Instead, they send pictures down to computers on Earth through electrical signals—similar to the way television pictures are sent through the air to your TV.

Scientists then turn the pictures on the computer screens into photographs.

About the Author

FAY ROBINSON

"I remember my childhood very well compared to a lot of people I know," Fay Robinson says. "I think that is one of the reasons I write for children— I can still remember what I liked to do and what I liked to learn about. When I write a nonfiction book, I pick from my childhood interests."

Ms. Robinson has always been interested in science and sometimes wonders why she didn't become a scientist. Many of her books are about science topics.

Reader Response

Open for Discussion

If you could visit one of the planets, which one would you choose? Which planet would you avoid? Explain your choices.

Comprehension Check

1. What is the purpose of space probes? What happens to space probes? Use evidence from the selection in your answers.

2. If you could send a message about our solar system to another solar system, what would you say? Look back and find details to explain why.

3. Suppose you are on Mars. Use examples from the selection to tell what you would see.

4. How is this nonfiction organized? Think about the order in which the planets are discussed and describe the **text structure**. (Text Structure)

5. Think about the **text structure**. In what two places does the author give information about the space probes themselves? Why does she choose these two places? (Text Structure)

Test Prep
Look Back and Write

Look back at pages 584–585. How were Earth and Mars similar in the past? How are they similar today? How are they different? Find examples from these pages to support your answers.

from The American Museum of Natural History's *Our Place in Space* magazine

Meet the Universe's Main Attraction...

Gravity

If you throw a ball into the air, it will return to the ground. Why? Earth has invisible pulling power called gravity. In fact, our planet isn't the only place with gravity. Every object in the universe—stars, planets, moons, even you—has gravity. Gravity is a force of attraction between all objects. Some things have lots of gravity, some have just a little.

In 1687, a physicist and mathematician named Isaac Newton published a remarkable discovery. He figured out that the same force that causes an apple to fall to the ground also keeps the moon in orbit around Earth.

> How does gravity work? There are two ideas you need to know. These ideas work throughout the universe. The more massive an object is, the more gravity it has. The closer two objects are, the stronger the gravitational pull between them. So, putting these rules together, the more massive and the closer two objects are, the greater the gravitational attraction between them.

ISAAC NEWTON

Try This!

To understand the universe, scientists sometimes do **"thought experiments."** They take a familiar situation and ask, "What would happen if we changed something about it?" Then they apply the laws of the universe and see how the situation would be different. Look at this picture of a carnival. Then ask yourself: **What would happen if the force of gravity were suddenly "turned off" there? What would happen if gravity were "turned off" in the whole universe?**

What Does Gravity Do?

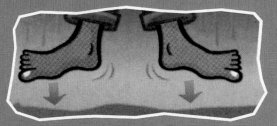

Earth's gravity pulls you back to the ground when you jump in the air. Otherwise, you'd fly out into space.

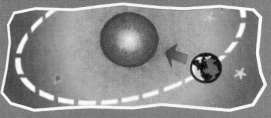

The sun's powerful gravity keeps Earth in orbit around it.

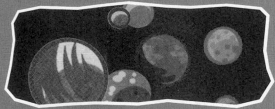

Gravity pulls stars and planets into round shapes called spheres. Did you ever see a **square** planet?

LYLE

by Gwendolyn Brooks

Tree won't pack his bag and go.
Tree won't go away.
In his first and favorite home
Tree shall stay and stay.

Once I liked a little home.
Then I liked another.
I've waved Good-by to seven homes.
And so have Pops and Mother.

But tree may stay, so stout and straight,
And never have to move,
As I, as Pops, as Mother,
From land he learned to love.

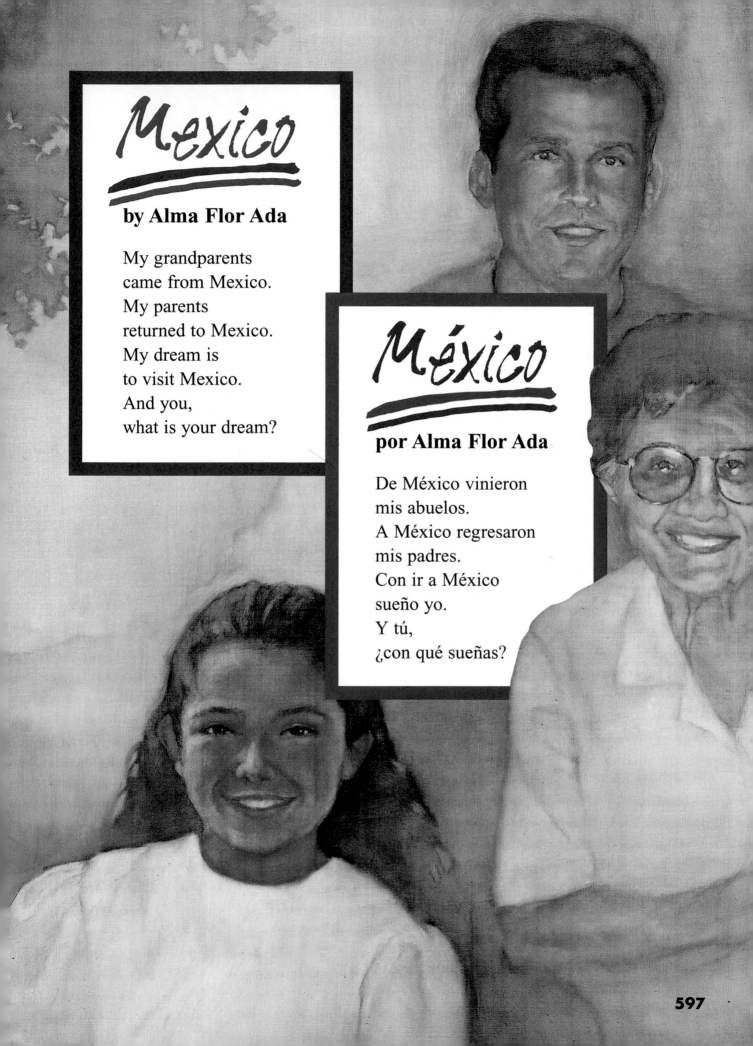

Mexico

by Alma Flor Ada

My grandparents
came from Mexico.
My parents
returned to Mexico.
My dream is
to visit Mexico.
And you,
what is your dream?

México

por Alma Flor Ada

De México vinieron
mis abuelos.
A México regresaron
mis padres.
Con ir a México
sueño yo.
Y tú,
¿con qué sueñas?

597

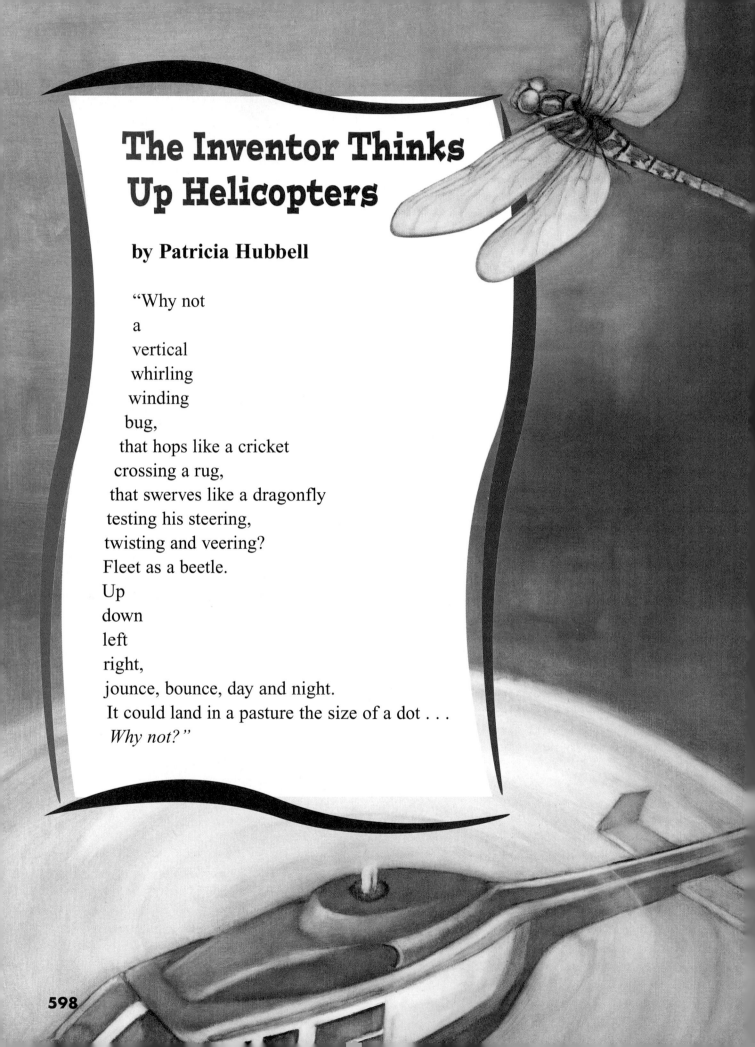

The Inventor Thinks Up Helicopters

by Patricia Hubbell

"Why not
a
vertical
whirling
winding
bug,
that hops like a cricket
crossing a rug,
that swerves like a dragonfly
testing his steering,
twisting and veering?
Fleet as a beetle.
Up
down
left
right,
jounce, bounce, day and night.
It could land in a pasture the size of a dot . . .
Why not?"

from

BLUE

by Claudia Lewis

What is the bluest blue?
To the astronaut ace
Afloat
In space,
Ringing,
Swinging,
Rocket-hurled,
No other blue
So new
So new
So bright
A blue
As the
Great
Blue
Ball
of the
WORLD.

Wrap-Up

What can we learn from reading about times and places we've never been?

Distant Times and Places

Talk with a Partner

Some people and characters in Unit 5 traveled long ago. Some went to places you may never have seen.

1. **Take notes** on each selection. Find details about clothing, speech, and objects that tell about places and time periods that are new to you.

2. Use your notes to **explain** to a partner why it is important to learn about other times and places. Then tell which time seems most interesting to you, and why.

Puppet Show

Retell

With two classmates, choose a selection from Unit 5 that has characters that interest you. Create puppets for some of these characters and use them to retell the story.

1. **Talk** about the selection together. Choose the most important events to retell.

2. **Write** a few sentences about the events in order.

3. **Perform** a puppet show for others.

One Day on Your Journey

Visualize

With a pack on your back, you walk with Solomon Joseph Azar from *A Peddler's Dream*. You join the sea turtle from *Into the Sea,* and swim to a faraway place. You're launched into space, headed for Mars like a space probe from *Space Probes to the Planets*. What is the most exciting part of the journey? What problems do you experience? How do you solve them?

1. **Choose** one of these situations.

2. **Reread** parts that interest you. Imagine being part of what happens.

3. **Write** a diary entry for one day of the journey. Tell about an adventure.

How to Reach a Goal

Think and Write

Each main character in this unit has a dream or a goal. Think about how two characters work toward their goals. Then think about what you have done to reach a goal or a dream of your own.

1. **Brainstorm** and jot down all these ideas.

2. **Choose** your four best ideas.

3. **Write** them in a list to help someone else who is trying to reach a goal.

Test Talk

Answer the Question

Write the Answer

Tests often tell you to write an answer. A test about "I Work in the Ocean," pages 572–575, might have this question.

Test Question 1

Why does Norbert Wu take pictures of ocean creatures? Explain your answer with examples from the selection.

Get ready to answer.

- Read the question to find key words.

- Finish the statement "I need to find out . . ."

- Decide where to look for the answer.

- Make notes and check them.

Write your answer.

- Begin your answer with words from the question. Then include details from your notes.

- Check your answer. Ask yourself:

✓ **Is my answer correct?** Are some details incorrect?

✓ **Is my answer complete?** Do I need to add more details?

✓ **Is my answer focused?** Do all my details come from the selection? Do they all help answer the question?

See how one student writes a correct, complete, and focused response.

I need to start my answer with words from the question. I'll start with "Norbert Wu takes pictures of ocean creatures because" and I'll get the rest of the answer from my notes.

Norbert Wu takes pictures of ocean creatures because he enjoys it and thinks it's challenging. Pollution has damaged ecosystems and hurt animals so Norbert wants people to see how beautiful the animals are. This will make people want to protect the animals. . . .

Try it!

Use what you learned to write answers to these test questions about "I Work in the Ocean," pages 572–575.

Test Question 2

How were Norbert's experiences taking pictures of the hammerhead sharks and the blenny alike and how were they different? Use details from pages 572–575 to explain your answer.

Test Question 3

Why does the author of this article say that it looks like Norbert is "carrying a miniature spaceship"? Use details from the text and from photographs on pages 572–575 to support your answer.

Express Yourself!

How many forms can creativity take?

Visualizing

- **Visualizing** means forming a mental image as you read.

- To help visualize, look for details that tell how things look, smell, sound, taste, and feel.

- Add what you know from your own experience to create an even clearer image in your mind.

- If you cannot visualize, reread or read more slowly to find details.

Read "Seeds" by Linda Montijo from *Cricket* magazine.

Cricket

Talk About It

1. Words can trigger our senses. What words in "Seeds" appeal to your sense of sight? of touch? of taste?

2. Illustrators use the words in stories to get ideas for their drawings. They also use their imaginations. If you were to illustrate the curbside scene in "Seeds," what things would have to be in the picture, and for what things could you use your imagination?

Seeds

by Linda Montijo

The sun licks us like a mother cat, leaving our skin warm and prickly moist. Paco and I sit on the curb, each of us holding a smiling wedge of watermelon. There are certain rules of etiquette for eating watermelon on a curb. Paco is ten and has acquired considerable experience in these matters. I'm only seven and three-quarters, but Paco says I'm OK anyway. I listen good and I learn stuff pretty fast for a girl. I concentrate now and try my best to match his every move: Knees spread body width apart, elbows on tops of knees. Upper arms stationary, lower arms directed toward face. Right and left hand side by side at exact center of wedge. Fingers gripping but not extending beyond the white margin that separates green rind from pink fruit. Commence eating.

"Don't forget to save the seeds." Paco neatly spits three into his hand and slips them into his pocket. I try to do the same. Sugary juice dribbles down my chin, and I am forced to wipe it off on the back of my arm before I can deposit my seeds.

There really won't be any point to the long-distance spitting contest later. Paco will win. He wins at everything. Not just baseball and stuff, but *every*thing. Like when his dad got sick and Paco thought he needed a job. What nine-year-old kid gets a real job that doesn't involve a lawn mower or a dog leash? Well, Paco did. Somehow he talked Mr. Caparelli into letting him work at the deli three or four hours a day after school. He sweeps up and cleans the deli case window and anything else Mr. Caparelli wants.

AHEAD

Koya DeLaney's community is all excited when Koya's famous rock-star cousin visits to perform a concert. Try to visualize each scene as you read "Koya's Cousin Del."

Words to Know

performers	imitation
auditorium	autographs
microphones	impatient
applause	

When you read, you may come across a word that you do not know. To figure out the meaning of the unfamiliar word, look for clues in the sentences around it.

Notice how *microphones* is used in the paragraph. Find an explanation in the sentence. What do you think *microphones* means?

A Night to Remember

I can do an imitation of my favorite performers, but I was really excited when my mom took me to an auditorium to see them in person! I was impatient—it seemed like they would never come out on stage. Suddenly, they appeared and applause broke out. Even with their microphones, it was hard to hear their voices over the roar of the crowd. After the concert, I got all the members of the group to sign their autographs in my program. What a great night!

Write About It

Write a review of the concert. Use as many vocabulary words as you can.

KOYA'S Cousin Del

from
Koya DeLaney
and the
Good Girl Blues

by Eloise Greenfield • illustrated by Tyrone Geter

Everyone in Koya's family is very excited. Koya's cousin, Delbert DeLaney, Jr., a major rock star, is coming to visit. He will stay with her family in their home and give a concert at her school.

At 7:21, Koya and her family were at the airport, watching Gate 6, waiting for Delbert to come through.

Koya and Loritha saw him at the same time, a young man of medium height and build, looking very much like their father. He was dressed in faded blue jeans and matching jacket.

"There he is," Loritha said.

"There's Delbert, Jr.!" Koya said, pointing. Her mother gently pushed her arm down, but it was too late. A man and a woman waiting at the gate had turned to look.

"Isn't that somebody famous?" Koya heard the man ask.

"He does look familiar," the woman answered. She tapped the shoulder of a young man standing next to her.

"Excuse me," she said. "Is that somebody?" She pointed at Delbert.

The young man looked at Delbert and back at the woman as if she were crazy.

"That's Del!" he said. He rushed toward Delbert, grabbed his hand, shook it hard, and kept shaking it. "Del!" he said loudly.

"Your album is bad, man!"

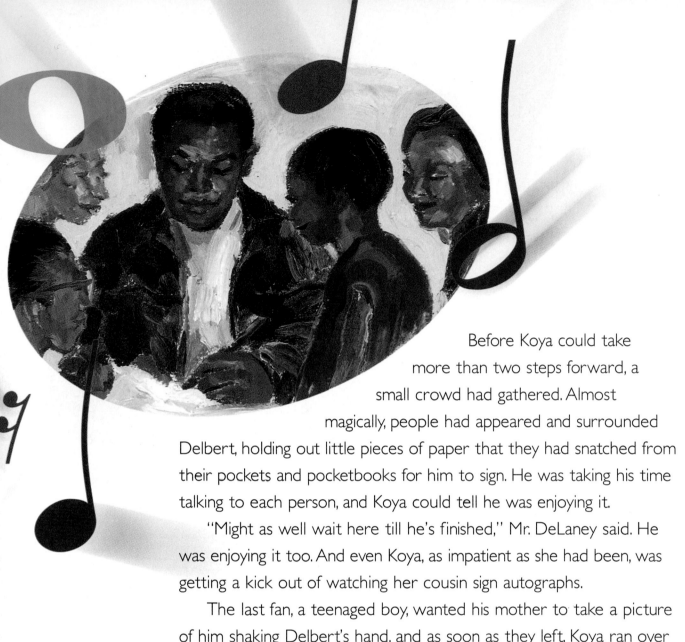

Before Koya could take more than two steps forward, a small crowd had gathered. Almost magically, people had appeared and surrounded Delbert, holding out little pieces of paper that they had snatched from their pockets and pocketbooks for him to sign. He was taking his time talking to each person, and Koya could tell he was enjoying it.

"Might as well wait here till he's finished," Mr. DeLaney said. He was enjoying it too. And even Koya, as impatient as she had been, was getting a kick out of watching her cousin sign autographs.

The last fan, a teenaged boy, wanted his mother to take a picture of him shaking Delbert's hand, and as soon as they left, Koya ran over and hugged Delbert.

"That was *something!*" she said. "I should've had *my* camera."

"We'd better go," Ms. DeLaney said, "before somebody else recognizes you. I'll get my hug later."

Mr. DeLaney picked up the small black overnight bag, and they walked toward the exit. "Is this all the luggage you brought?" he asked.

"It can't be," Koya said. "He couldn't get forty-two trumpets and fifty saxophones in that little bag."

Delbert laughed and put one arm around Koya's shoulder. "I wish I had that many, Cuz," he said. "No, Sherita's driving the van down tomorrow with the band and the rest of the stuff. I came a day early, so I could spend more time with you all."

He had emphasized the word *van* and looked at Loritha, laughing, when he said it, reminding everybody of the time, a few years back, when they were visiting Delbert and his grandparents, and Loritha had hidden in the van, hoping to go traveling with the group.

Loritha pretended that she hadn't gotten the joke. "What are you looking at *me* for?" she asked.

"The Ritha van caper," Koya said. "Right, Delbert, Jr.?" She held out her hand, palm up, and Delbert slapped it twice.

After dinner, the family gathered in the living room to listen to a tape of Delbert's next album. He had brought it to them as a gift.

"It won't be released until summer," he said. He got up and began dancing. "This is the latest thing from us folks up in the big city."

Koya glanced at her mother and was surprised to see that she was smiling. She never let them dance on the carpet. Whenever she caught them doing it, she would point toward the basement, and they knew they had better get down to the rec room, or they'd be sorry.

"Come on," Delbert said to Koya and Loritha, "let me show you how to do it."

Loritha picked up the dance right away, as if she had known it all her life. It took Koya a few minutes to get it, but when she did, she knew she had it because her whole body was working together. It felt right. She reminded herself of the Senegalese dancers she had seen at the theater.

They were all into it, her mother moving her head and neck backward and forward, and her father patting his foot and clapping to the beat, when the doorbell rang. Delbert turned the music down.

"I'll get it," Mr. DeLaney said. He looked through the peephole. "I think it's one of your classmates," he said to Koya as he opened the door.

Loritha looked at Koya.

"I didn't tell *any*body," Koya said. "Honest!" She and Loritha went to the door.

It was Rodney, with another boy, a teenager.

"Is Del here?" Rodney asked.

"You forgot to say good evening," Mr. DeLaney said.

"Oh! Good evening. I'm Rodney, and this is my brother, Kevin." He was rushing his words, not taking a long time the way he usually did. "Is Del here?"

"Well. . . ." Mr. DeLaney started.

Del came out from the living room. "It's okay, Uncle Maurice," he said.

Rodney's eyes widened when he saw Delbert, and Kevin changed the way he was standing to cool.

"How you doing?" Delbert said. He shook their hands.

"I like your music, man," Kevin said, but Rodney, who never stopped talking in school, except when he was drawing, was speechless. Koya thought she must be seeing a mirage.

"Sorry we can't ask you to stay, this time, guys," Mr. DeLaney said, "but this is kind of a special family night."

"How did you know he was here?" Koya asked.

"I deduced it," Rodney said, not taking his eyes off Delbert.

"How'd you deduce it, brother?" Delbert asked.

At the word *brother,* Rodney grinned and took a deep breath, suddenly turning back into his talkative self.

"Well," Rodney said, speaking slowly and deliberately, "first, I told myself that since you were coming to visit our school in the morning, in all probability, you would be arriving in town tonight. And then I said that since you were related to the DeLaneys, there would be at least a bare possibility that you would come here. So. . . ."

Kevin groaned and tapped Rodney on his almost bald head, but Rodney didn't stop talking.

". . . so, I asked myself what was the worst thing that could happen if I just showed up at the door? Well, Mr. and Ms. DeLaney might just throw me out bodily. But I said to myself, 'Rodney, it's well worth the risk.' So here I am."

"Well, I'm glad you made the right decision," Delbert said. "Listen, can you keep a secret?"

"Yeah!" Rodney said.

"You, too, Kevin?"

"Sure!" Kevin said.

"Okay," Delbert said. "I'm going to give you each a photograph, but you can't tell anybody about it until Saturday, after I've left town."

Kevin said, "Wow!" and Rodney lost his voice again.

Delbert went upstairs and got two copies of a glossy photo from his travel bag, a picture of himself and Sherita onstage, singing, microphones in their hands. He signed them, put them in an envelope, and handed them to Rodney.

Kevin had stopped trying to be cool and looked almost as if he might cry. "Thanks, Del, thanks, man," he said. Then he turned to Koya's mother and father. "And thanks for letting us interrupt the family."

Rodney stopped in the doorway as they were leaving. "This is the most stupendous thing that has ever happened to me in my entire life," he said to Delbert. "I promise not to tell one single soul!"

Twenty minutes later, the doorbell rang.

Through the peephole, Koya recognized the girl on the porch as someone she had seen in the neighborhood. She guessed that the woman with her was her mother.

When Koya opened the door, she saw more people standing on the sidewalk, looking as if they wished they could see right through the bricks of her house.

"I hope you don't mind—" the woman started to say.

But the girl was too excited to wait for her mother to finish. "Rodney called me up," she said. "He said Del was here." She was leaning to the side, trying to see around Koya into the living room.

"Did he tell the whole world?" Koya asked, looking at the growing crowd. Older teenagers, kids Koya's age, and little children escorted by adults were streaming, some running, toward her house.

"No," the girl said. "He just told me, and he made me promise not to tell anybody. So I only told Pamela and Jerome. Is he here? Can I see him?"

"He's busy," Koya said. Delbert had been telling them about a dream he had about his father.

"Who is it, Koya?" Ms. DeLaney called. She came to the door.

"They want to see Delbert, Jr.," Koya said.

The woman was starting to look embarrassed. "I didn't mean to barge in," she said. "It's just that my daughter. . . we. . . ." She was too embarrassed to continue. She took her daughter's hand and started to back up.

"I'm so sorry I can't ask you in," Ms. DeLaney said. "We're right in the middle of a discussion."

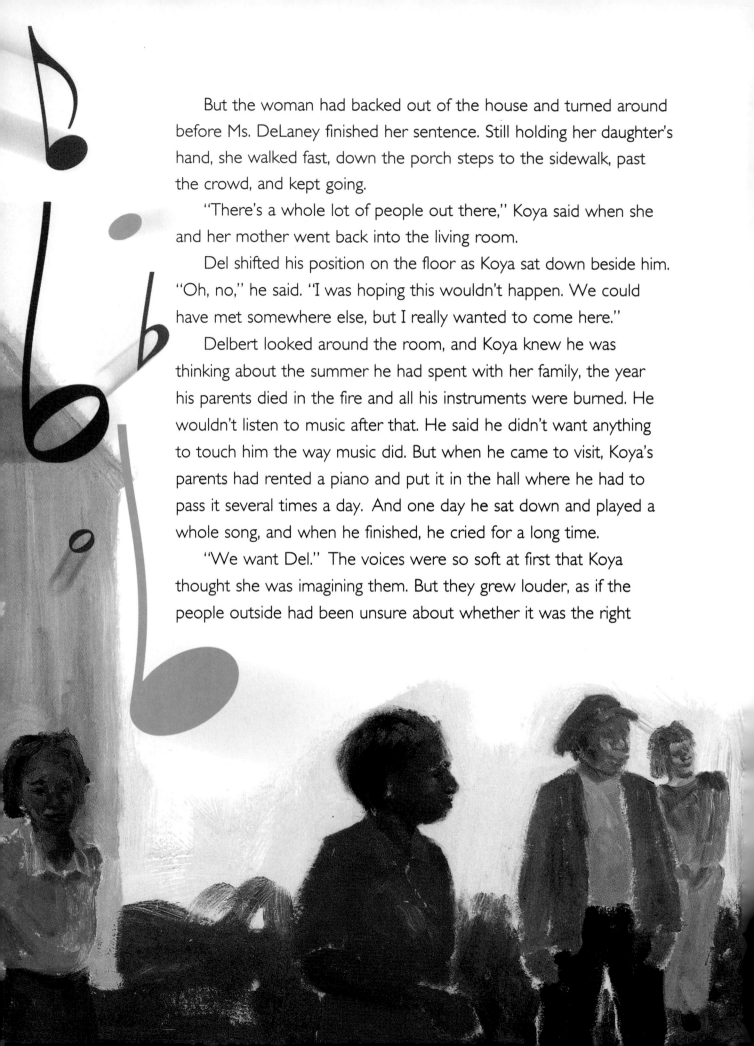

But the woman had backed out of the house and turned around before Ms. DeLaney finished her sentence. Still holding her daughter's hand, she walked fast, down the porch steps to the sidewalk, past the crowd, and kept going.

"There's a whole lot of people out there," Koya said when she and her mother went back into the living room.

Del shifted his position on the floor as Koya sat down beside him. "Oh, no," he said. "I was hoping this wouldn't happen. We could have met somewhere else, but I really wanted to come here."

Delbert looked around the room, and Koya knew he was thinking about the summer he had spent with her family, the year his parents died in the fire and all his instruments were burned. He wouldn't listen to music after that. He said he didn't want anything to touch him the way music did. But when he came to visit, Koya's parents had rented a piano and put it in the hall where he had to pass it several times a day. And one day he sat down and played a whole song, and when he finished, he cried for a long time.

"We want Del." The voices were so soft at first that Koya thought she was imagining them. But they grew louder, as if the people outside had been unsure about whether it was the right thing to do, and then decided it was okay. "We want Del! We want Del!" Now they were shouting.

"I'll just go out for a minute and say hello," Delbert said.

Koya followed him to the door and watched from inside.

"Hey, everybody," Delbert said. He stood on the porch, waving. "It's good to see you."

The crowd began to chant. "Del! Del! Del! Del!"

"Your music is *bump*in', man," a teenaged boy said.

"And you not too bad yourself!" a young woman called out.

A spiral of laughter wound through the crowd. They were beginning to push forward gradually, from the sidewalk onto the lawn. Koya thought they looked like one huge body with a lot of wriggling parts.

"Thanks for coming," Delbert said. "I hope you'll all come out to the show tomorrow night. It's for a good cause." He waved and started into the house. "Good night."

"How about singing a song?" a man yelled.

The crowd surged forward onto the lawn and the neighbor's lawn, trampling two of the neighbor's rosebushes.

"Watch it! Watch the shrubbery!" Delbert said. "Good night, now."

"Hey, you could at least sing one song," the man said. "You wouldn't be making all that money if it wasn't for us."

Delbert came into the house, and as he was closing the door, Koya heard another man say, "Aw, dude, the man worked for it, you didn't give him nothing."

For a few moments, Koya worried that the man who was angry might throw a rock, or something, through the window. But the sounds drifting in were pleasant. Fading sounds of people talking, some older girls singing, harmonizing, and a child's voice asking, "Did you see him? I saw him. Did you see him?"

When there was no more sound, Delbert went next door to apologize and pay for the damage to the bushes. Koya's father went with him. When they came back, they took a small plastic bag outside and picked up the candy wrappers and other little bits of paper that had been left.

Koya felt limp, weary, as if her emotions had been tumbling over one another all day, and her brain had been running, trying to catch up with them. She had been impatient, and happy, and worried, and excited, and now she was tired and very disappointed.

"It's all Rodney's fault," she said. "If he hadn't told—" She stopped when she saw her mother's eyes laughing at her. Then she remembered the other secret, the one *she* hadn't been able to keep, and she laughed with her mother.

Loritha laughed, too, and a loud yawn escaped. "Oh, excuse me!" she said.

She and Koya didn't protest when their mother said it was time for bed.

"Tomorrow night we'll have a chance to really talk," Koya said to Delbert.

"Hope so, Cuz," Delbert answered.

The picture in the newspaper was huge, almost half the size of the page. It was just their faces, turned to the right, hers a little below his. DEL AND SHERITA, MAKIN' A HOME FOR THE HOMELESS. It was the headline on the front page of the Arts Section.

The article, almost two pages long, was all about the young performers whose record, *Makin' a Home,* had surprised the industry with its fast climb up the charts. It told how Del had started performing as a child, at weddings and recitals, and how he and Sherita had met in high school and formed a group of their own.

It also told how heartbroken they had been two years ago when their first album had been snatched off the market after only a few months. The record company didn't think it was selling fast enough.

Delbert had gone to live with his grandparents when he was in high school, the article said. It didn't mention the reason. Koya knew Delbert would never talk to a reporter about that.

Koya read the article before she went to school Thursday morning, and when she got there, everybody was talking about it. Dr. Hanley had posted a copy on the bulletin board outside her office.

By 9:50, the whole school was seated in the auditorium, talking quietly. Koya kept looking back, watching the door. Her mother had kept the car today so that she could bring Delbert to school, and when Koya saw her mother come in and take a seat in the back of the room, she knew Delbert was in the principal's office.

At exactly ten o'clock, there was a burst of applause as Delbert, in a light-blue sweatsuit and white sneakers, walked onto the stage with Dr. Hanley and a little girl from the third grade. Delbert and the girl took seats on the stage.

Dr. Hanley went to the microphone. In her usual way, she said a lot in a few words.

"Welcome, Delbert 'Del' DeLaney. It's an honor to have you with us."

Then, the girl read a short paper about when and where Delbert was born, and how much everybody at Barnett School loved him and his music.

Then it was Delbert's turn.

"I love music too," he said. "I need it the way I need food. Sometimes when I listen to quiet music, I can feel myself breathing it in and becoming a stronger person."

He asked the children how music made them feel.

"Fast music makes me want to do somersaults," a kindergarten boy said.

"Gives you energy, huh?" Delbert said.

"Yeah," the boy said, happy that Delbert understood. "It gives me *en-der-gy.*"

The smiles in the room could almost be heard.

"Music makes me sad, sometimes." It was a girl from fourth grade.

"It makes me happy." A boy.

"It makes me feel like singing." A girl.

"You are all so beautiful," Delbert said, "*you* make *me* feel like singing. And it's a good thing too," he added, laughing a little, "since that's what I had planned to do for you today."

He said he was going to sing three songs. "Last night," he said, "when I was thinking about what I might do, I decided to sing *a cappella.* Who knows what *a cappella* means?"

A boy said it meant just singing, without a piano or horns or anything. Delbert said that was right.

"The song I'm going to sing first," he said, "is very special to me. When I wrote this song, I tried to write the sound of my mother's voice. My mother didn't have a great singing voice, but her speaking voice was like soft music with lots of highs and lows. She would say, 'Delbert, *Junior,* I don't want you to do that any*more.*'"

Koya remembered her aunt saying those words, starting low on "Delbert," a little higher on "Junior," then going up the scale to "more."

The children laughed at Delbert's imitation. He let the laughter end, and then he said, "When I was sixteen years old, my parents died in a fire."

The room got very quiet.

"And after that," Delbert continued, "I didn't want to play music anymore, or even listen to it. But the rest of my family, my grandparents, aunts and uncles and cousins, gave me so much love, that after a while, I became myself again. If they hadn't done that, I wouldn't be here to sing for you today."

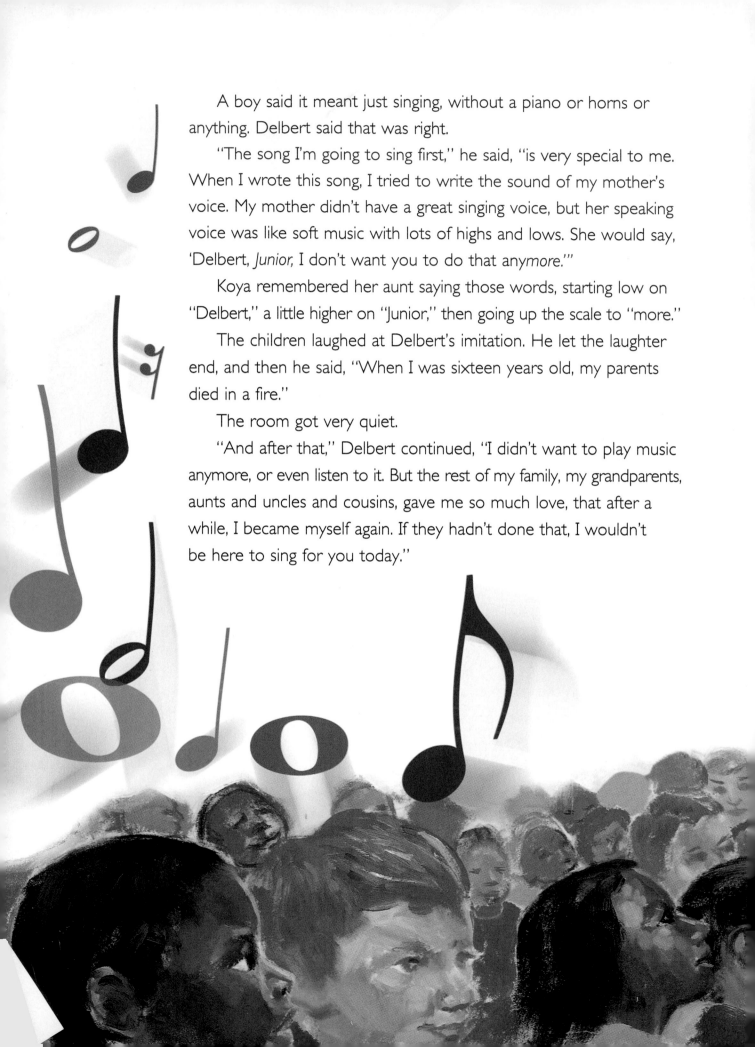

He told the children that the best way to listen to music was to listen all the way through and not to applaud until every bit of the sound had faded away. And then he sang, and Koya thought it was the most beautiful song she had ever heard.

She could hear her aunt's voice in it. It was soft and slow and had notes that Delbert held a long time, notes going from low to high and back again. The very last note, he held and held, and Koya could see his mouth changing shape, making the sound of the note change. Then it got softer and softer until it faded away and there was no more sound.

For a moment, there was absolute silence, as if it, too, were a part of the music. And then the audience broke the silence with applause. Two of the teachers stood up, and then everybody stood up and applauded for a long time.

About the Author
Eloise Greenfield

When Eloise Greenfield was growing up, she never thought about being a writer. All she knew was that she loved reading and she loved words. "I loved their sounds and rhythms," she has said. She even found the oddities of the English language, such as homonyms and silent letters, exciting.

Writing is one of the most important things in Ms. Greenfield's life. She spends a good part of each day writing and rewriting with one goal in mind. Her goal is "trying always to write a book that children will want to live with, live *in,* for as long as it takes them to read it, hoping that some part of the book will stay inside them for the rest of their lives."

Writing does not always come easily to Ms. Greenfield. When asked if writing is fun, she sometimes tells the whole truth—"that writing is fun and serious and interesting and worrisome and exhausting and exciting and challenging and painful and satisfying and magical." Sometimes it is a struggle to find just the right word!

Ms. Greenfield's struggles have brought her recognition, and her books have been selected for numerous awards.

Reader Response

Open for Discussion

If you met Del, what would you ask him? What would he say?

Comprehension Check

1. Why is Koya's family so important to Del? Use story details to explain.

2. How does this story show that being famous is a "wonderful problem"? Use evidence from the story in your answer.

3. Show how music makes the children in the audience feel. Use examples. Compare their answers to your own feelings about music.

4. The author helps you **visualize** the scene in the DeLaney living room after dinner. Describe what you see. What sounds do you hear? (Visualizing)

5. How do you **visualize** the scene in the school auditorium when Del appears on stage? Describe the picture that is created in your mind by the author's words. (Visualizing)

Test Prep
Look Back and Write

Look back at pages 614–615. What does Rodney mean when he uses the word *deduced*? Use context clues to help you write your answer.

On the Beat

by Neil Ardley

Cymbal is free to swing and vibrate

No MUSICIAN is as exciting to watch as the drummer in a rock band is. The drummer sits at a drum set with drums and cymbals. The drummer's hands and feet move the whole time. The set shown here is a basic one, but many drummers have several extra instruments. There may be two bass drums, one for each foot! Other instruments played in rock bands are guitars, bass guitars, saxophones, brass instruments, such as trumpets, and pianos or keyboards.

CRASH CYMBAL
This cymbal, as its name suggests, gives a crash when struck with a stick. It can also be played with a brush. The crash cymbal is suspended from a stand.

Upper cymbal

Lower cymbal

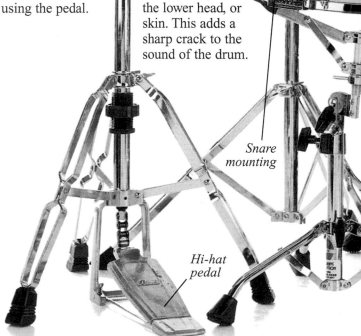

HI-HAT
This is a pair of cymbals mounted on a stand. The drummer can make the upper cymbal ring by striking it with sticks or using the pedal.

SNARE DRUM
Across the base of this drum is a set of tight wires called the snare. Striking the drum causes the snare to vibrate against the lower head, or skin. This adds a sharp crack to the sound of the drum.

Snare mounting

Hi-hat pedal

RICH AND FAMOUS
Hunched over his drum set, the jazz drummer Buddy Rich drives his band forward with energy. Rich began drumming at the age of 18 months.

CAUGHT IN THE ACT
As this picture was taken, the drummer played a fast roll along four tom-toms. A repeating camera flash shows the sticks in action.

RIDE CYMBAL
This cymbal is often played with a stick to create a "riding" rhythm.

TWO TOM-TOMS
Two tom-toms, or "toms," are mounted on top of the bass drum. These small drums give high-pitched, mellow notes.

Stick

Mallet

Brush (wire or plastic bristles)

FLOOR TOM
This large tom-tom gives a deep note. The drummer may use mallets to play the tom-toms or strike them with the palms of the hands.

BEATERS AND BRUSHES
Drummers mainly use sticks, brushes, or mallets to play the drums and cymbals. Sticks and mallets give the loudest sound, and brushes are quiet.

BASS DRUM
The bass drum lies on its side and is played with a pedal connected to a felt-covered beater. It gives a short, deep thud.

Bass drum pedal

Steps in a Process

- Telling the **steps in a process** is telling the order of steps to complete an action.

- Clue words like *first, next,* and *last* or numbers written by the steps can show when each step is done.

- Sometimes illustrations show the steps. At other times you have to picture the steps in your mind and put them in order.

Read "From Drawing to Carousel Critter" by Kathy Kranking from *Ranger Rick* magazine.

Write About It

1. List the steps that artist Milo Mottola followed to make the carousel critters for the Totally Kid Carousel.

2. List the clue words that the author used to help you understand the order of the steps.

From Drawing to Carousel Critter
by Kathy Kranking

Have you ever drawn a picture of your favorite animal? Imagine if someone built an exact copy of your drawing—and made it big enough for you to ride. That's what happened to the drawings of a bunch of lucky kids in New York City. And now the kids can ride their animals any time they want!

The animals are all part of the Totally Kid Carousel in New York's Riverbank State Park. It's the first carousel in the world designed by kids.

So how did it all come about? The wizard behind this magical idea is an artist named Milo Mottola.

So how did each animal go from a drawing to a carousel critter? Here's what happened with this deer, drawn by Edwin

Vargas. (Photo 1) First Milo enlarged the drawing to the size he wanted the animal to be. Then he traced

it onto two big slabs of stiff plastic foam and cut the two shapes out. Next he fit a pole between the cutouts and glued them together to make an animal "sandwich."

Milo's favorite part came next. He carved the foam animal to look just like the drawing, adding eyes, a mouth, and other details. Then he sanded it smooth. (Photo 2)

To make the animal sturdy enough for kids to ride on, Milo and some helpers gave it three coats of fiberglass.

Then Milo brought the animal to life by painting it. (Photo 3) The painted animal was covered with many coats of hard, clear varnish. And a carousel critter was born.

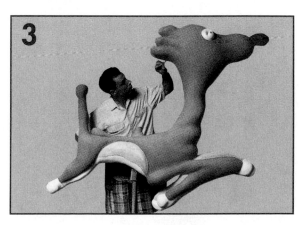

LOOK AHEAD

Children of Clay

As you read "Children of Clay," learn the steps a Pueblo family follows to make another type of sculpture.

Vocabulary

Words to Know

figures	screens	polish
pottery	symbols	

Many words have more than one meaning. To decide which meaning of a word is being used, look for clues in the surrounding sentence.

Read the paragraph. Does *figures* mean "numbers" or "forms or shapes"?

Crafty Clay

Pottery is clay that is shaped and then hardened by baking it in a special oven. You can make dishes and figures using simple materials. If your clay has hard lumps in it, press it through screens to remove stones or twigs. Shape the clay. You can polish your clay dish or figure by dipping it in slip, a kind of liquid clay, and rubbing it to make it shiny. Then you can decorate it before you bake it. You might even paint or stamp special symbols on the piece to make it more meaningful to you.

Write About It

Write an advertisement for a new store that sells arts and crafts supplies. Use as many vocabulary words as you can.

Children of Clay

A Family of Pueblo Potters

by Rina Swentzell / photographs by Bill Steen

*Gia Rose and her large family live in a pueblo in New Mexico.
They are artists who make beautiful objects from clay. When
they need clay to work with, they must dig it from pits in the
mountains far from their desert homes.*

*On the day set aside for digging, the whole family piles into
a truck for the long drive to the clay pits. Their work is done by
noon—so they eat lunch and listen to Gia Rose tell them a story.*

Baby Benito plays by a bucket of clay.

After the story, the family is ready for the long drive back home. The children fall asleep in the car while the grown-ups talk about things going on in the *owingeh*. When they get back to Gia Rose's house, it is late afternoon and everyone is tired. But before they go to their own houses, they help to pick the large sticks and stones out of the clay.

Then Zachary pours water into the buckets and tubs of clay. The clay will be set aside for a few days to slowly soak up the water.

Several days later, Gia Rose and two of her daughters, Judy and Tessie, do more work on the clay. They sit outside Gia Rose's house in the middle of the *owingeh* and push the wet clay through screens to take out small rocks and twigs.

Devonna sits next to her great-grandfather, Michael, Gia Rose's husband. She watches and waits for someone to ask for water or another scraper, or to go answer the telephone.

After the clay is cleaned, fine white sand must be mixed into it. This will keep the clay from cracking during the drying process. Mixing in the sand is a big job. Judy and Tessie take turns working the sand into the clay with their bare feet. Finally, the work is done, and the clay is wrapped in a cloth and set aside to rest for about a week.

When the clay is ready, some of the children and grown-ups of Gia Rose's family get together. They laugh and talk while they coil, pinch, press, and smooth the clay to make bowls and figures of animals and people.

After soaking in water, the hard, dry lumps of clay will be transformed into a soft, smooth material that can be molded and shaped.

Using slabs of clay, Eliza makes a big
figure with sticks on its head.

Eliza rolls out slabs of clay with a rolling pin. She puts the
slabs together to make a big creature with sticks coming out
of its head. Devonna shapes lumps of clay to make a pair of
hands ready to hold something. Micah, another cousin, rolls
ropes of clay to make big and small snakes.

Arin, Micah's sister, works carefully on a small bowl. She
forms the sides of the bowl by coiling ropes of clay around and
around. The adults also play with the clay. Gia Rose makes a
frog, while Eliza and Zachary's mother, Nora, creates figures
of a mother with her two naughty children. Rina, Devonna's
grandmother, makes a small cup.

While they work, Gia Rose tells the children about
Clay-Old-Woman. She says that Clay-Old-Woman lies within
the earth and the clay. If people talk to her with respect, she
will help them to create beautiful things. Gia Rose says

that the pots and figures they make will be alive because Clay-Old-Woman will continue to live and breathe inside of them. In order to know that Clay-Old-Woman is breathing within their pieces, they must be quiet and listen. As they work, the children can feel Clay-Old-Woman in their hands.

Aunt Tessie makes a coiled pot. She winds ropes of clay around and around on a base to form the sides of the pot. The coils are then pinched and scraped together to create a smooth surface.

Great-grandfather Michael watches as Gia Rose, Aunt Rina, and Eliza sand their pots and figures.

When they finish coiling and forming the clay, everyone carefully puts the pieces out of the way to dry. Big pieces like Nora's figures are wrapped in cloth so that they don't dry too fast and crack. The children know not to touch the clay pieces while they are drying because they are very fragile and will break easily.

A week later, it is time to smooth the pieces with sandpaper. Eliza is very careful as she helps to sand the hands that Devonna made. She sits working with her grandmother Rose, her aunt Rina, and her aunt Tessie, while the younger children play close by.

Sanding the pieces is hard work. Children quickly get tired of doing it, but eleven-year-old Eliza works as hard as the adults. Old Great-grandfather Michael loves to sit and watch everyone at work. Ten years ago, before he had a stroke, he helped to sand the pots and put designs on them. He also helped to dig the clay, as Pueblo men usually do.

When the pieces are as smooth as possible, Gia Rose takes out her special polishing stones. Some of the stones are special because her grandmother or aunts gave them to her. Others she found in special places. All the stones are special because they are hard and smooth, and when they are rubbed against the pots, they make the pots shiny.

Before the polishing begins, the pieces are coated with a thin, wet clay called *slip*. Then the children pick up the stones and begin to polish their figures and pots. Their hands move quickly before the wet slip dries. They work quietly because they have to pay close attention to what they are doing.

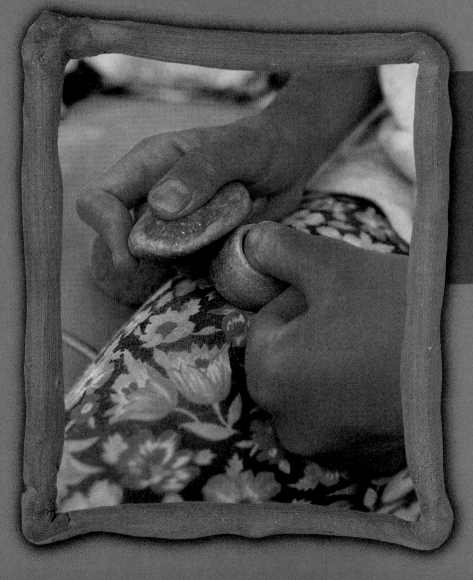

Eliza uses a polishing stone to give a shiny finish to a small pot. The stone was given to Gia Rose by her grandmother.

After each piece is finished, Gia Rose admires it. She talks about how pretty it is and about what design might be put on it. Gia Rose decides to put a lizard on one of her pieces. She will use wet slip to paint the lizard onto the polished surface with a brush. Sometimes she forms a lizard figure out of clay and attaches it to the piece before it is dried. Gia Rose knows many ways to design and decorate pottery.

Eliza decides not to put anything on her piece. Aunt Tessie likes the shiny polish on one of her pots and also decides not to put a design on it. Other pieces are painted with cloud, mountain, bear, lizard, and water-snake symbols. These designs have been used by the Santa Clara *towa* for hundreds of years.

The bear-paw design is used to help make the pot strong and remind people of the healing powers of the bear. The lizard is respected for the way it moves quickly over the ground. Both the clouds and the mountains are symbols of rain, for which the *towa* are always thankful. The water snake reminds people to be respectful of flowing water like the *posongeh*.

Another morning some weeks later, the family gathers again, this time to fire the pots and pieces. At each gathering,

Some traditional Santa Clara pottery designs include the lizard and the water snake.

Devonna places pottery on the rack in the firing pit.

different members of the family are present. Pueblo people work in this way. They help each other make, sand, polish, and fire pots, but the same people seldom do all the work. The group changes, but the pottery-making process remains the same.

Firing makes the clay strong so that the pieces will not melt again or break easily. It can happen almost anywhere that a fire can be built. This time it is being done at the house of Devonna's grandmother Rina. Great-aunt Tessie is one of the oldest women present and is in charge of the firing. Devonna will help her.

The firing process is exciting because if it is not done right, many pieces may break. To get ready, Devonna and Great-aunt Tessie carefully set the pieces on a metal rack in the pit where the fire will be built. Great-aunt Tessie puts a metal cover over the pieces so that the fire will not burn directly on them. Devonna helps to stack wood slabs around the cover.

The fire is started. As the wood burns, everyone watches and listens for popping or cracking sounds. The sounds mean that something has cracked or exploded in the fire. They ask Clay-Old-Woman to help the pots live through the fire.

It seems like a long time before the fire burns out and the pieces can be seen. The grown-ups and children gather to find out what has broken. There are usually some broken pieces, but there are always some good pots and figures too. Devonna is excited about a tiny black water jar with two spouts. A large jar of this kind is used in wedding ceremonies. Members of one family drink water that has been blessed out of one spout, and members of the other family drink from the second spout. Afterwards, the water jar is shattered so that the bond between the bride and groom and their families will never be broken.

Many years ago, the *towa* of Santa Clara and the other *owingehs* made pottery only for their own use—for cooking, eating, or storage. These days the pottery of Santa Clara is highly valued, and many people want to buy it. Some of the pots and figures fired today will be given to friends or family members. Most of the pieces will be sold to visitors or traders who come to the *owingeh*. Others will be sold to art galleries and stores in places nearby or far away.

The people of Santa Clara make figures of animals and people as well as clay jars and pots.

The children of Santa Clara also sell their pots and figures. Devonna and her cousin Arin set up a table outside Gia Rose's house. They put up a sign that reads "Frogs for Sale" and wait for people to come and buy pots, frogs, and other small figures. There are always many tourists visiting Santa Clara Pueblo, so it is not too long before the children sell a frog.

Although many things are changing at Santa Clara Pueblo, pottery-making is still much the same as in the past. It still happens mostly outdoors and is done completely by hand. Making pottery helps children like Eliza, Zachary, Devonna, Arin, and Micah remember the place, the mountains, and the sky as they work and play in clay with their mothers, aunts, grandmothers, and great-grandmothers. It helps them to remember that they are all children of Clay-Old-Woman.

About the Author

Rina Swentzell

Rina Swentzell is from Santa Clara Pueblo in New Mexico, and she herself grew up in a large family of potters. Today she is a writer and educator about the history and culture of Native Americans. Her articles have appeared in magazines such as *Native Peoples* and *Southwest Images and Trends.*

In addition to writing about the Pueblo people, she wrote about the Mimbres people who lived in southern New Mexico about one thousand years ago.

Ms. Swentzell has taught in schools and colleges in New Mexico and Colorado. She is active in many organizations that take an interest in the culture of the Pueblo Indians. She makes her home in Santa Fe, New Mexico.

643

Reader Response

Open for Discussion

What part of making pottery bowls or figures do you think you would enjoy the most? Why?

Comprehension Check

1. Do you think this author's purpose is to inform, entertain, persuade, or express? Explain your answer with examples from the selection.

2. Why is white sand mixed in with the clay? Give examples.

3. Which of the following is a main idea statement for "Children of Clay"?

    a. Firing makes the clay strong so that it won't break easily.

    b. Gia Rose and her family create beautiful works of art.

    c. Some children make frogs and sell them to tourists.

4. Think about the **steps in the process** of making clay pottery. What is the first thing that must be done? What is the last step? (Steps in a Process)

5. How do the photos help us learn the **steps in the process?** Give examples. (Steps in a Process)

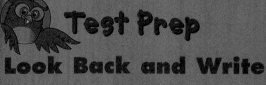

Test Prep
Look Back and Write

Look back at page 641. Why is the firing process important? What can happen to the pottery if the fire is not built correctly? Use details from the selection to support your answer.

Test Prep
How to Read a Myth

1. Preview

- A myth has simple characters and a simple plot. Often, myths try to explain something in nature that people have trouble understanding.

- Read the title and subtitle and look at the illustrations.

2. Read and Locate Information

- As you read, find parts of the myth that offer good advice to someone who makes pots.

- After you read, go back and write the advice you found.

3. Think and Connect

Think about "Children of Clay." Then look over your notes on "Clay Old Woman and Clay Old Man."

Why is it important to Gia Rose to tell the children this story as they work with clay?

Clay Old Woman and Clay Old Man

Cochiti Pueblo myth
told by Joseph Bruchac

Long ago, people did not know how to make pots. So Grandmother Spider made Clay Old Woman and Clay Old Man, and she sent them to the Pueblos.

Clay Old Woman and Clay Old Man walked into the plaza. Clay Old Woman brought clay with her. She brought sand and water and began to mix them together. When she was finished, she rolled the clay into a ball.

As she worked, Clay Old Man danced and sang, "This is how pots will be made."

All the people gathered around them. They watched as Clay Old Woman began to make long coils from the ball of clay. She rolled the clay between the palms of her hands. Then she began to build a pot with those coils. She finished one pot and

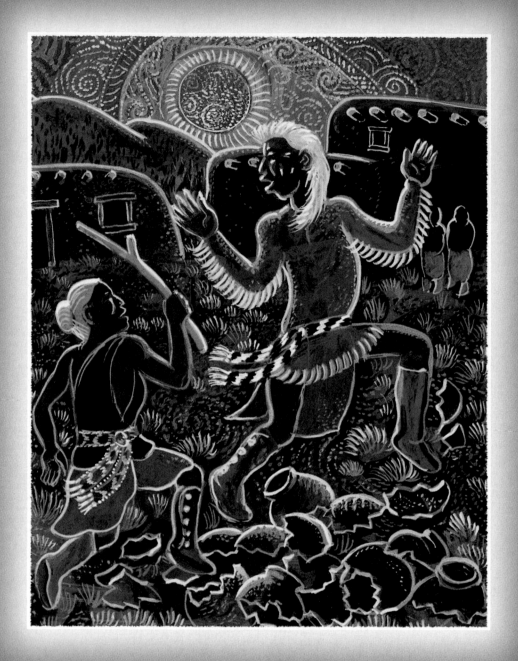

then another. When she had finished
enough pots, she carefully piled wood
around them and made a fire. She piled
wood on top of the pots. People watched
this too. They saw how the pots hardened
in the fire. All this time Clay Old Man
kept singing and dancing.

When the fire had burned out and the
pots were cool, Clay Old Woman took
them out and placed them on the ground.
The people admired what Clay Old
Woman had made.

But although those pots looked good,
they were not strong enough to last. Clay

Old Man knew this. He came dancing up to the pots. Then, to everyone's surprise, he kicked them over. The pots all broke into small pieces. Clay Old Woman chased Clay Old Man around the plaza with a stick, but she did not catch him. As he ran, he still sang his song.

This is how pots will be made.
This is how pots will be made.

Clay Old Woman finally stopped chasing Clay Old Man. She went back to her broken pots and picked up the pieces. She broke them into even smaller pieces and ground them up. Then she mixed those ground-up pieces in with the rest of her clay. Now the pots that would be made would be strong. They would last.

Ever since then, pieces of old broken pots have been used in making new pots. And so it was that people learned that unless something is done the proper way, it will not be good. It might look good, but it would not last.

Then Clay Old Woman divided up the clay. She gave a piece of it to everyone in the village.

"If you need more clay," Clay Old Woman said, "you will find me by the river."

Then Clay Old Woman and Clay Old Man departed from the Pueblos, but they left behind the gift of pottery. Now the people had pots that they could use to carry water and store food. Those pots made their lives much better.

To this day, people who make pots go to the river where Clay Old Woman can be found in the banks of clay. As they gather the clay, they thank her. Often they leave presents for Clay Old Woman. And as the people coil their pots and fire them, they sing songs, just as they were taught to do by Clay Old Woman and Clay Old Man. To this day, that is how the people make pots.

Fact and Opinion

- A **statement of fact** tells something that can be proved true or false.

- A **statement of opinion** tells your ideas or feelings. It cannot be proved true or false, but it can be supported by facts and reasons. Sometimes statements of opinion begin with clues such as *I believe*. Also, words such as *pretty* that express a person's feelings, beliefs, or judgments are clues to statements of opinion.

- Some sentences contain both facts and opinions.

Read the review of *Naomi's Geese* **by student Katie Swegart from** *Stone Soup* **magazine.**

Write About It

1. List five statements of fact that the author of this review tells about the book. How can you check these statements of fact?

2. Copy the statements of opinion in this book review. What words helped you find them?

BOOK REVIEW
BY KATIE SWEGART

Naomi's Geese

by Sanford Evans; Simon & Schuster: New York, 1993

This is a book about a girl who learns to care about other things more than herself. I think that most people who like nature will like this book.

It's about a girl named Naomi and two geese, named Ka and Kee. Naomi's parents buy a summer house in the country, and at first Naomi doesn't like it because it's dirty and ugly. Then she meets two geese. She doesn't like *them,* either, because they hiss at her and chase her away. But, gradually, they come closer to her when she feeds them. Soon they become good friends. Naomi watches them as their chicks hatch and grow. It is time for the geese to migrate, and for the people to go back to the city. At the end, Naomi has to make an important decision

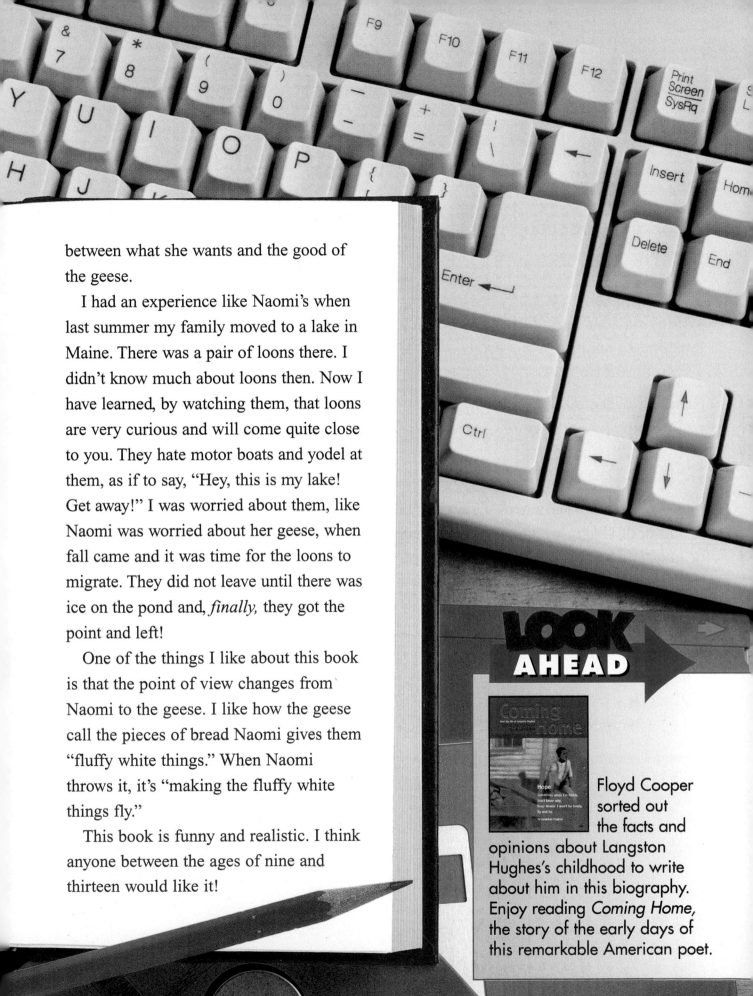

between what she wants and the good of the geese.

I had an experience like Naomi's when last summer my family moved to a lake in Maine. There was a pair of loons there. I didn't know much about loons then. Now I have learned, by watching them, that loons are very curious and will come quite close to you. They hate motor boats and yodel at them, as if to say, "Hey, this is my lake! Get away!" I was worried about them, like Naomi was worried about her geese, when fall came and it was time for the loons to migrate. They did not leave until there was ice on the pond and, *finally,* they got the point and left!

One of the things I like about this book is that the point of view changes from Naomi to the geese. I like how the geese call the pieces of bread Naomi gives them "fluffy white things." When Naomi throws it, it's "making the fluffy white things fly."

This book is funny and realistic. I think anyone between the ages of nine and thirteen would like it!

LOOK AHEAD

Floyd Cooper sorted out the facts and opinions about Langston Hughes's childhood to write about him in this biography. Enjoy reading *Coming Home,* the story of the early days of this remarkable American poet.

Words to Know

librarians   dreamer   rusty
tremble   heroes   drifted

Words with similar meanings are called **synonyms.** You can often figure out the meaning of an unknown word by finding a synonym for it nearby.

Read the paragraph below. How does *shake* help you understand *tremble?*

Books and Bravery

Alex used to be frightened of everything. He would tremble, or shake, when he heard strange noises or met new people. But the librarians at school knew how to help him—with books! When Alex started reading, he became a dreamer. He drifted into a world filled with heroes who battled dragons and saved people in danger. Riding his rusty old bike, Alex imagined he was a knight on a beautiful stallion. Books made Alex feel as if he could conquer anything!

Write About It

What book has really changed the way you feel about something? Write a report about the book. Use as many vocabulary words as you can.

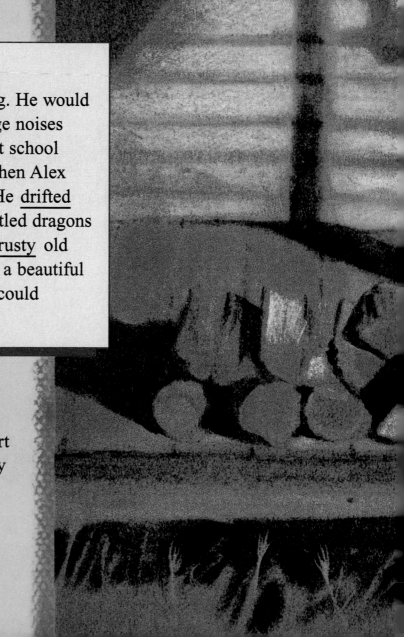

Coming Home

From the Life of Langston Hughes

written and illustrated
by Floyd Cooper

Hope

Sometimes when I'm lonely,

Don't know why,

Keep thinkin' I won't be lonely,

By and by.

by Langston Hughes

James Langston Hughes was a dreamer, there in Lawrence, Kansas, where he lived alone with his Granma Mary Langston. Langston was a dreamer in the fields behind the two-room house he shared with her. Or on the porch.

His grandma didn't much like him playing with the neighborhood kids, so he'd hear kids playing ball or riding bikes, but he'd stay put.

Mostly in his early years, James Langston Hughes was alone.

Unless the distant faint familiar sound of a freight train pressed against his ears. Then Langston would bolt off the porch, hit the ground running, chickens aflutter. Quick! past the woodshed. Swoop! around the pump for drawing water.

He'd hurry across the vacant lot and through the wheat field. He'd run and run until between breaths, he could see the big freighter pulling its load around the curve of tracks, whistle blowing sweet, as it screeched and clanked: clackedy, clackedy, clackedy. The old rusty cars talking, talking.

The old iron snake'd tell him its stories about the places it'd been. Langston would talk back. Dream back. He'd dream of riding the train to Mexico where his pa, James Nathaniel Hughes, went to live after they wouldn't let him be a lawyer in Oklahoma because he was a black man. He'd dream of riding to where his ma, Carrie Hughes, was trying to be an actress on stage. He loved going to the theater with her those times he'd had the chance to be with her.

Mostly, he dreamed of the three of them together, of having a home with his ma and pa. A home he would never have to leave.

But each time the train would trail off, getting quieter and quieter, and quieter still, engine smoke barely clinging to the blue sky before it disappeared; Langston's dreams disappeared too.

Living with Granma wasn't easy. She was poor. Dinner was often dandelion greens and whatever the neighbors passed over the backyard fence.

Sometimes the neighbors passed clothes, too, their used dresses, worn shirts, and old shoes.

Once Langston had to wear a woman's shoes, because his grandma couldn't buy him new ones.

But Granma believed a boy needed heroes, and one day she took Langston all the way to Topeka to hear Booker T. Washington speak. Booker T. Washington in person!

And she would read to young Langston—and storytell. Sometimes she'd read from the Bible. Other times it would be a beautiful tale from the Brothers Grimm.

Almost always, his grandma told stories of heroes. Heroes who were black, just like Langston.

His grandma's first husband, Lewis Sheridan Leary, had ridden with John Brown and was killed in the struggle to free slaves. She still wore his torn, bullet-riddled shawl.

Even on warm summer evenings she'd pull the shawl over Langston and tell him stories of her first husband, and of two uncles who were Buffalo soldiers, named that by the

Indians because of their curly hair, and called the "bravest of
the brave." And about Langston's uncle, John Mercer
Langston, the first black American to hold office. He was a
lawyer and later elected to Congress.

His grandma herself had worked on the Underground
Railroad, helping slaves flee north to freedom, and she told
him those stories.

Langston would hear these stories over and over.
Wrapped in the torn shawl—and wrapped in family stories of
pride and glory—he'd listen and dream.

Sometimes Langston's dreams about having a family
came true. Like the time he, his ma, and grandma really did
go to Mexico to see his father. Maybe, finally, Langston would
have a home of his own.

But on April 14, 1907, the ground in Mexico began to
tremble. Everything shook, including the building they were
in. Langston's pa, carrying Langston, led everyone out into
the street.

Everywhere walls of buildings cracked and split open. Giant tarantula spiders scurried out of the cracks. That was enough for his mama. As soon as the trains were running again, she and his grandma and Langston climbed back on the train and rode back to Kansas. Langston whispered a good-by to Mexico, his father, and to having a home of his own.

Sometimes Langston's ma would send for him. He'd ride the train to the Kansas City Bottoms where she'd meet him and off they'd go. They'd see plays, the opera, and visit the library, where Langston was fascinated by the big, bright, silent reading room, the long smooth tables, and librarians who would so kindly get books for him.

Sometimes, when she was busy, his mother would leave him at his uncle Des's barbershop. He liked it there, right in the center of the black district. He'd go and wander the nearby streets. Speak to folks passing by. A nod here. A hat-tip there.

But mostly Langston would listen.

He'd ride his ears around the city. Through Market Street where everyone sang the song of haggle. Down side streets filled with kids who ran and played forever. Up the block where clubs and dance halls played jazzy old blues music that drifted down the alleys and tickled his soul. Langston felt the rhythms.

Other times Langston's ma would come to Lawrence. Once it wasn't the best of times for her. Money was scarce. She snapped at Langston and it hurt.

Later that evening they went to St. Luke's Church where Langston's ma was giving a performance. She told him that she had a wonderful surprise for him. That he was going to be on the stage with her. That he was going to be a star, just like she was going to be.

Langston didn't like the surprise. That evening he was the one with the surprise. As his ma introduced him, behind her back Langston made faces: He crossed his eyes, stretched his mouth, and imitated her. Everyone burst out laughing.

The more people laughed, the more faces he made. Embarrassed, his mother rushed off stage.

As Langston's grandma got on in years, she grew more and more silent. Then the time came when she hardly spoke at all. The little home where he had lived so long was quiet and lonely, with Granma rocking silent in her rocking chair.

A real home seemed less than ever like something Langston would ever have.

Then he went to live with friends of the family across town, Auntie and Uncle Reed, he called them.

When Langston first saw the dinner table at the Reeds' he had never seen so much food in his life. After the blessing, Uncle Reed smiled and told Langston to eat up. He didn't have to tell Langston twice. Then Auntie, in a voice as sweet as dessert, said there was more out in the kitchen.

Langston soon learned that there would always be "more" from Auntie and Uncle Reed. More food, and more hugs and love.

On Sundays Auntie Reed would take Langston to church. He'd never gone before. Auntie Reed's church was all right,

but in time Langston preferred the Baptist church down the street. The singing and preaching felt so familiar—like the rhythms of the streets in Kansas City. The words seemed to roll out of the preacher's mouth like jazzy old blues.

By now, Langston had grown popular at school, was thought of as "smart," and chosen class poet. He had begun writing poetry and sharing it. One of his first poems was "When Sue Wears Red," about a girl he admired in school. And then he wrote "Just Because I Loves You" and "The Negro Speaks of Rivers."

Now after school, he'd run and play with friends. Sometimes afterward they'd gather around Langston on the Reeds' front porch. There in the dark shadows of a summer night, Langston would tell stories.

Of the time he stood ten feet from Booker T. Washington, of his two uncles who were Buffalo soldiers, the "bravest of the brave." Of John Mercer Langston, the U.S. congressman. About his grandma's first husband, who was killed with John Brown trying to free the slaves, and of Granma herself, who used to work on the Underground Railroad.

Stories of real heroes who were black, just like Langston.

It grew clearer to Langston in those days what home really was. Life with his grandma had never been exactly like home. Life with his ma and pa never had been home, as much as he wanted it to be. Life with his Auntie and Uncle Reed felt like home, it smelled like home and looked like home. And home was all of the things the Reeds' home was.

But home was something more for him.

For him, home was a blues song sung in the pale evening night on a Kansas City street corner. Home was the theater where his ma performed, the library where he sat quiet, reading the books he loved. Home was the church, alive with music, where everybody was "brother" and "sister."

As he grew older, Langston Hughes wrote more and more. About everyday people, common folk. He wrote about

dancers and children, troubled people and people in love; Walt Whitman and the black Pierrot; all kinds of people. And he traveled all over the world, to Russia and France, and to Africa, experiencing the stories and rhythms of yet other people.

He lived in many cities in America, like Cleveland and Los Angeles, but Harlem, New York, where all kinds of black artists gathered—writers, painters, musicians—became the place where he stayed longest and that he knew best.

It seemed Langston Hughes had finally found a home.

But the truth is, Langston never had a home like most people. Home was in him. And it was about his black family that he wrote in words that reached his own people, and all kinds of people of different races and different countries, all over the world.

Floyd Cooper believes that creating
children's books is a very important job.
"I feel children are at the front line in
improving society," he says. "This might sound a little
heavy, but it's true. I feel children's picture books play a
role in counteracting all the violence and other negative
images conveyed in the media."

Mr. Cooper often visits schools to talk to children about
how and why he became an artist. He shows the students
how he draws the illustrations for his books. Sometimes he
creates pictures from scribbles provided by the audience.

Before Mr. Cooper was a book author and illustrator, he
worked in advertising at a greeting card company. He felt
that it was difficult to use his creativity in that type of
work, so he left that job and began a new career writing
and illustrating children's books.

Besides *Coming Home: From the Life of Langston
Hughes,* Mr. Cooper also wrote and illustrated *Mandela*
about the South African leader Nelson Mandela. He has
illustrated several other books as well.

Reader Response

Open for Discussion

Langston Hughes was a dreamer.
How do the illustrations show that he
was a dreamer?

Comprehension Check

1. Compare Langston Hughes's home with his grandma in Lawrence, Kansas, to his home with Auntie and Uncle Reed. Use details.

2. Why do you think the stories Langston Hughes heard as a child were important in his life? Give evidence to support your answer.

3. What happened in Mexico when Langston Hughes went there to visit his father? Use examples from the selection in your answer.

4. A **statement of fact** can be checked, or proved true or false. Which two of the following are statements of fact? (Fact and Opinion)

   a. Langston Hughes lived in Lawrence, Kansas, when he was a boy.

   b. Langston Hughes's two uncles were the "bravest of the brave."

   c. Harlem was the place where Langston Hughes lived the longest.

5. A **statement of opinion** cannot be proved true or false. What is the author's opinion about Langston Hughes's real home? (Fact and Opinion)

Test Prep
Look Back and Write

Look back at pages 652–653. How does the author let you know that Langston isn't happy living with his grandmother? Use examples from the story to support your answer.

The Dream Keeper

by Langston Hughes

Bring me all of your dreams,
You dreamers,
Bring me all of your
Heart melodies
That I may wrap them
In a blue cloud-cloth
Away from the too-rough fingers
Of the world.

Dreamer

by Lee Bennett Hopkins

He let us kiss
the April rain.

He shared his
hope
and
pride
and
pain.

He wrote
of life
with an ebon pen
and the world
was never
the same
again.

He syncopated beats
of Harlem-blues.

O!
The might
of
Langston Hughes

"Bring me all your dreams,"
he said.

And though
he died . . .

He
is
not
dead.

Main Idea and Supporting Details

- The **topic** is what a paragraph or article is about.

- The **main idea** is the most important idea about the topic.

- The main idea is often stated in a single sentence within a paragraph or article. However, sometimes you have to figure out the main idea and put it in your own words.

- **Supporting details** are small pieces of information that tell more about the main idea.

Read "Working on the Railroad" by Gloria A. Harris from *Cobblestone* magazine.

Talk About It

1. What is the topic of "Working on the Railroad"?

2. Which sentence tells the main idea of the article?

3. What details support the main idea of the article?

WORKING ON THE RAILROAD

by Gloria A. Harris

The railroad industry was the biggest employer of black men in the post-Civil War era. The jobs were usually difficult and often dangerous, and many railroad workers created inventions to improve the efficiency and safety of their jobs.

One of the most dangerous jobs on early railroads was that of the brakeman. One of his jobs was to couple, or join, railroad cars together. To do this, he had to walk along the top of the train, then climb down the back of the last car like a spider. Bracing his back against the car, he waited for another train to back up close to his. If he was lucky, he dropped the coupling pin into a lock to connect the cars a split second before they came together. If he was not, he could be crushed between the two cars.

Andrew Beard, an Alabama railroad brakeman, lost his leg in just such an accident. While Beard was not the first to think of a better way to join railroad cars, he was the first to create an automatic coupler, called the Jenny Coupler, in the early 1890s. The genius of Beard's invention was that two railroad cars locked together just by being pushed against each other. A similar device is still used today.

Besides keeping the engine fueled, early railroad firemen were responsible for keeping the engine oiled to prevent overheating. To do this, the engineer had to stop the engine periodically, which usually meant bringing the locomotive to a halt. Oiling the engine was a hot, dirty, and dangerous job.

In 1872, Elijah McCoy invented a self-lubricating cup that dripped oil continuously onto the engine's moving parts even while it was going.

LOOK AHEAD

Find out about Benjamin Franklin and his inventions, ideas, and discoveries in "Out of the Blue." Figure out the main idea of the biography as you read, and notice some details that support it.

Words to Know

circulating	inventions
theory	mysterious
electricity	experiment
calendar	almanac

When you read, you may come across a word you do not know. To figure out the meaning of the unfamiliar word, look for clues in the words or sentences around it.

Read the paragraph below. Notice how the description of *calendar* helps you understand what it means.

Franklin: Man with Many Jobs!

Under the name Richard Saunders, chosen for some mysterious reason, Benjamin Franklin wrote an almanac. It had not only a calendar, a chart showing months and days of the year, but also his own gems of wisdom. It began circulating throughout America. Franklin was a scientist, known for inventions, such as streetlights, and for his "kite experiment." To test his theory about electricity, he tied a key to a kite and flew the kite during a lightning storm.

Write About It

Write some notes to go on a book cover for Franklin's biography. Use as many vocabulary words as you can.

Out of the Blue

from *What's the Big Idea, Ben Franklin?*

by Jean Fritz • Illustrated by Margot Tomes

Benjamin Franklin was born in 1706 into a large family in Boston. Even as a young boy, Benjamin knew he never wanted to be an apprentice, a teenager who worked for no wages to learn a trade. When he was seventeen, Ben left home and his job in his brother James's printing shop and went to Philadelphia.

He was free! He found a job with a printer and began earning his own money. When he had saved enough, he bought a new suit of clothes and a watch with a long gold watch chain. When he had saved some more, he went to Boston to visit his family. He dropped in at the printshop to see James. He didn't come to apologize for running away; he came, in spite of his rules, to show off. He swaggered into the shop, letting James and his apprentices see what a grand thing it was to be your own master in a new suit of clothes. He twirled his watch chain. He jingled the money in his pockets and offered to treat everyone to a drink. (James was so angry that it took years for the brothers to make up.)

Back in Philadelphia Benjamin was better behaved. He had a naturally happy disposition and made friends easily.

Gradually he found other young men who liked to read and argue and try out new ideas. They formed themselves into a club they called the Leather Apron Club and met every Friday night. Each new member had to put his hand on his heart and swear that he loved mankind and the truth.

They talked about all sorts of subjects. Why, they asked, does dew form on the outside of a cold glass in hot weather? If the country has a bad law, should a man obey it? Can a poor man stay honest and still get ahead in the world?

Philadelphia suited young Benjamin perfectly. He lived on High Street, the busiest and noisiest street in town. On one end of the street was the Delaware River to jump into when he felt like a goat leap. On the other end of the street was Debbie Read, whom he courted and married.

Benjamin and Debbie were married in 1730. Benjamin was twenty-four years old now and getting ahead in the world. He had his own printshop, owned his own newspaper, and because he was such a good printer, he did the printing for the government of Pennsylvania. (He always used the blackest ink and the whitest paper he could find.) In addition, Debbie and Benjamin ran a store in the front of their house. They sold books, sealing wax, pencils, maps, pictures of birds and animals, fishnets, chocolate, compasses, codfish, and cloth. And they always had a good supply of Mr. Franklin's soap for sale.

Yet no matter how busy he was, Benjamin found time to try out new ideas. Sometimes he had ideas on why things happen the way they do. He wrote about comets. He formed a theory about hurricanes; they moved, he said, from the southwest to the northeast, contrary to the way winds usually move.

Once he made an experiment with a pot of molasses and an ant. He hung the pot on a string and watched for the ant to crawl down. Soon there was a swarm of ants crawling up the string, so Benjamin concluded that ants have a way of telling each other news.

Sometimes Benjamin's ideas were for the improvement of Philadelphia. He formed the first circulating library in America. He helped organize Philadelphia's fire department. He suggested ways to light the streets, deepen the rivers, dispose of garbage, and keep people from slipping on ice in winter.

Sometimes his ideas turned into inventions. At the head of his bed he hung a cord which was connected to an iron bolt on his door. When he wanted to lock his door at night, he didn't have to get out of bed. He just pulled the cord, rolled over, and shut his eyes.

He invented a stepladder stool with a seat that turned up. And a rocking chair with a fan over it. When he rocked, the fan would turn and keep the flies off his head. He fixed up a pole with movable fingers to use when he wanted to take books down from high shelves. He cut a hole in his kitchen wall and put in a windmill to turn his meat roaster. And he invented an iron stove with a pipe leading outside. The stove produced more heat than an ordinary fireplace, cost less to operate, was less smoky, and became very popular.

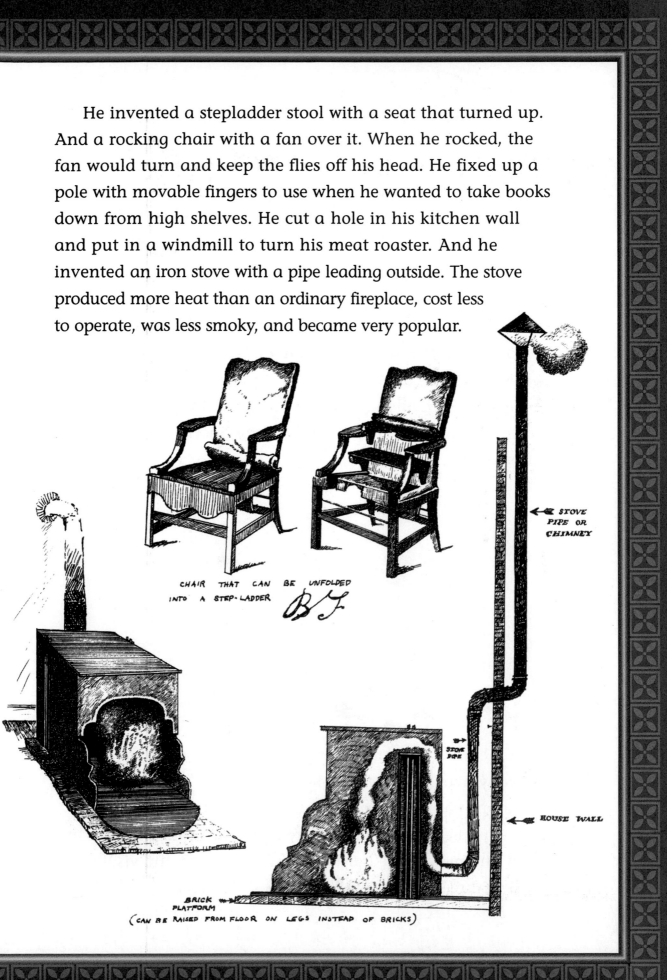

CHAIR THAT CAN BE UNFOLDED
INTO A STEP-LADDER

← STOVE PIPE OR CHIMNEY

→ STOVE PIPE

← HOUSE WALL

BRICK PLATFORM
(CAN BE RAISED FROM FLOOR ON LEGS INSTEAD OF BRICKS)

In 1732, when he was twenty-six years old, Benjamin Franklin had one of his best ideas. He decided to publish an almanac. Every family bought an almanac each year. People read it to find out the holidays, the weather forecasts, the schedule of tides, the time the sun came up and went down, when the moon would be full, when to plant what. It was just the kind of book that Benjamin loved—full of odd pieces of information and bits of advice on this and that. It was, in addition to being a calendar, a grand how-to book and Benjamin figured he knew as many how-to's as anyone else. Besides, he knew a lot of jokes.

He put them all in his almanac, called it *Poor Richard's Almanack,* and published the first edition in 1733. His specialty was short one-line sayings.

Sometimes these one-liners were quick how-to hints for everyday living: "Eat to live, not live to eat"; "A penny saved is a penny earned"; "Half Wits talk much but say little."

Sometimes his one-liners were humorous comments on life: "Men and melons are hard to know"; . . . "Fish and visitors smell in three days."

In a few years Franklin was selling 10,000 copies of his almanac every year. (He kept it up for twenty-five years.)

This was certainly a good idea, but it was not Benjamin Franklin's Big Idea. He was forty years old when he first became interested in the idea that would become the Big one. By this time he had two children—William Temple, who was seventeen, and Sarah, who was two. (A third child, Francis, died in 1736 when he was four years old.)

The idea had to do with electricity, which had become a new fad. For some time it had been known that electricity could be generated by rubbing glass tubes with silk. Now a Dutch scientist had found that this electricity could be stored in specially equipped bottles, then drawn from them by applying wires (or conductors) to the two sides of the bottle.

All over Europe people were meeting in darkened rooms to see these sparks and the tricks that could be performed. Wires twisted into the shape of giant spiders were electrified. Sparks were drawn from a cake of ice and even from the head of a boy suspended from the ceiling by a silk rope. Electrical performers traveled from town to town selling shocks to curious people. Once, before a large audience in Spain, 180 grenadiers were linked together by wire, then given a shock to make them jump into the air at the same time.

Franklin bought electrical equipment and began writing to European scientists. He learned to perform the usual tricks and made up some of his own. Once he gave an electrical picnic. He planned to kill a turkey by an electrical shock, roast it in a container connected to electrical circuits, on a fire lit by an electrical bottle. He was, however, so carried away by his performance in front of his guests that he was careless. He took the whole shock through his own arms and body and was

knocked unconscious. When he came to, he was embarrassed. "What I meant to kill was a turkey," he said. "Instead I almost killed a goose."

His Big Idea was that electricity and lightning were the same. Up to that time most people had thought lightning was (and always would be) as mysterious as heaven itself. And here was Franklin saying it was the same stuff that you saw in parlor tricks—only on a grander scale. What was more, Franklin believed he could prove it. Let a sentry box be built on the top of a high tower, he wrote a scientist in Europe. Put a pointed rod in the tower and let a man stand in the box during a storm. Franklin knew that electricity was attracted to pointed iron rods; if the man in the sentry box could find that lightning was also attracted to a rod, that would prove they were the same. The only reason Franklin didn't make the experiment himself was that Philadelphia didn't have a high enough tower or even a high hill.

In the spring of 1752 three scientists in Europe tried the experiment and all three proved that Franklin's Big Idea was right. (One scientist was killed, but that was because he was careless.) Meanwhile Benjamin thought of a way to prove the Idea himself. One stormy day he raised a kite with a long pointed wire at the tip and felt the electric shock come through a key he had tied to the kite string near his hand. So he already had his own proof when the news reached him about the experiments in Europe. Still, he was surprised to hear how excited people were about his Idea. He was suddenly famous. Indeed, he was becoming the most celebrated man in America.

Franklin is famous for his inventions, but most people feel his greatest contributions were in helping America win independence from England. Among other things, he helped write the Declaration of Independence and the Constitution of the United States. Franklin died in 1790 at the age of eighty-four.

About the Author
Jean Fritz

Because her parents were missionaries, Jean Fritz lived in China for the first thirteen years of her life. Her parents spoke often about the United States, and she became interested in the homeland that she had never seen. Her father would tell her of American heroes, especially his favorite, President Woodrow Wilson. A curiosity about other American heroes led Ms. Fritz into a career of writing biographies.

Ms. Fritz's award-winning biographies are popular because they show historical figures as real people, "warts and all." Besides Ben Franklin, she has written about Paul Revere, John Hancock, Benedict Arnold, and Christopher Columbus.

About the Illustrator
Margot Tomes

Margot Tomes was a fabric designer when her friend, author Barbara Wersba, asked her to illustrate a book she had written. That book led to other illustrating assignments.

Even though she sometimes found illustrating books difficult, Ms. Tomes wanted young people to find pleasure in her art. "I hope at least that some children like and understand my illustrations," she once said.

Reader Response

Open for Discussion

You probably heard of Ben Franklin before reading "Out of the Blue." What surprised you most in this biography?

Comprehension Check

1. What conclusions can you draw about Ben Franklin? Give examples from the selection to support your answer.

2. How do you know that Ben had a sense of humor? Give examples.

3. How did Ben prove his ideas? Give examples from the selection.

4. Reread the first paragraph on page 672. What sentence states the **main idea** of this paragraph? What **supporting details** can you find? (Main Idea and Supporting Details)

5. Now think about the **main idea** of the entire selection. First decide on the topic. Then tell what the selection says about that topic. Finally give a few **supporting details.** (Main Idea and Supporting Details)

 Test Prep
Look Back and Write

Look back at pages 672–673. How do the diagrams and captions on these pages help you understand Benjamin Franklin's inventions? Use details from the selection to support your answer.

from *Kids Discover*
magazine

A Really Bright

IDEA

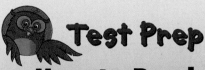

Test Prep

How to Read an Informational Article

1. Preview

- "A Really Bright Idea" is a picture history. It tells about real events that happened in the past.

- Read the title and look at the illustrations. What idea might the title be describing?

2. Read and Locate Information

- Read the article to learn about historical events. Write questions to help you focus on details.

> What was Edison's first
> patented invention?

3. Think and Connect

Think about "Out of the Blue." Then look over your notes on "A Really Bright Idea."

What are some similarities and differences between Franklin's and Edison's inventions? Use details to support your answer.

Thomas Edison, a famous inventor, was nicknamed the "Wizard of Menlo Park." Menlo Park, New Jersey, was not Edison's only laboratory. He and his assistants worked in laboratories in Newark, New Jersey; New York City, New York; West Orange, New Jersey; and Fort Myers, Florida.

Today, electricity lights our homes with the flick of a switch. Radio and television give us instant information. Listening to a CD or watching a video is a favorite pastime for many, and using a computer is commonplace.

What would life be like without these inventions? To find out, you have only to step back in time 100 years.

What Makes a Great Inventor?

Thomas Edison liked to say that genius is "one percent inspiration and ninety-nine percent perspiration." People who have studied successful inventors say that they share certain traits. They are very hard working, willing to put their work ahead of everything else in their lives, including family and fun. And they don't get discouraged by their mistakes and failures. In fact, inventors learn from their mistakes. They know it is important to understand what *doesn't* work in order to arrive at a solution that *does* work.

▲ **EDISON KNEW AMERICANS** would not use electricity unless it was cheaper than gas—and more reliable. His electric light needed a constant flow of electricity to keep burning. Edison proceeded to design the first power station, on Pearl Street in New York City. The station began supplying electricity in 1882.

▲ **EDISON'S FIRST PATENTED** invention was an electrical vote recorder, created in 1869. At the time of his death in 1931, at age 84, Edison had received 1,093 patents, including ones for a motion-picture projector (above), phonograph, telephone transmitter, and a way to make rubber from the goldenrod plant.

THOMAS EDISON EXPERIMENTS ▶ WITH LIGHTS AND LENSES (OPTICS) IN THE 1890s IN HIS WEST ORANGE, NEW JERSEY, LAB.

FILAMENT

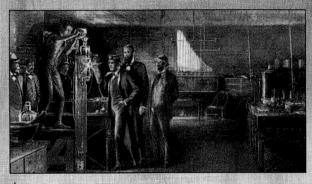

▲ IN 1876 EDISON SET UP WHAT HE CALLED his "invention factory" in Menlo Park, New Jersey. People who worked at his research lab did not work on their own ideas. Their job was to put his ideas into practice. Edison promised the public his lab would turn out a minor invention every ten days and a "big trick" every six months. At times Edison's staff was working on more than 40 ideas at once. He became known as the Wizard of Menlo Park.

◀ FEW INVENTIONS ARE completely new. For example, Edison developed the first practical incandescent lamp (light bulb), but he built on Michael Faraday's experiments in electromagnetic induction. Two other scientists created an electric lamp, but theirs stayed lit for only a few hours because the filament (the thin wire inside the bulb) burned out or caught fire. Edison tried about 6,000 different kinds of filaments before he discovered that one of carbonized cardboard created a long-lasting light.

Hey! Wait a minute... You haven't invented that yet!

▲ AT AGE 12 EDISON GOT A JOB selling magazines and candy on a train that made a daily five-hour round trip ride between Port Huron and Detroit, Michigan. Edison set up a lab for himself in the train's baggage car. During the long wait before the train returned to Port Huron, Edison read science books at the local public library.

Author's Purpose

- An **author's purpose** is the author's reason for writing something.

- Some purposes for writing are to entertain, to inform, to express, and to persuade.

- Predicting an author's purpose can help you decide whether to read something slowly and carefully or quickly for fun.

Read "Breakfast with Brede" from *Not-So-Perfect Rosie* by Patricia Reilly Giff.

Write About It

1. Before you read "Breakfast with Brede," did you decide you should read it slowly or quickly? Why?

2. "Breakfast with Brede" is fiction. What clue does that give you about the author's purpose? Explain.

3. Would you like to read the rest of this story? Explain.

Breakfast with Brede

by Patricia Reilly Giff

We were at the kitchen table, Andrew, and me, and my cousin Brede. We were drinking milk with a teaspoon of tea, and eating scones that Brede had made with her mother in Ireland.

The scones were horrible, just as Grandpa had warned me. "You might just as well be eating horses' hooves," he had said, and winked. "Make sure you eat them, every last rock-hard bite. You don't want to hurt her feelings."

I nibbled around the edges now, trying to bite off a raisin. At the same

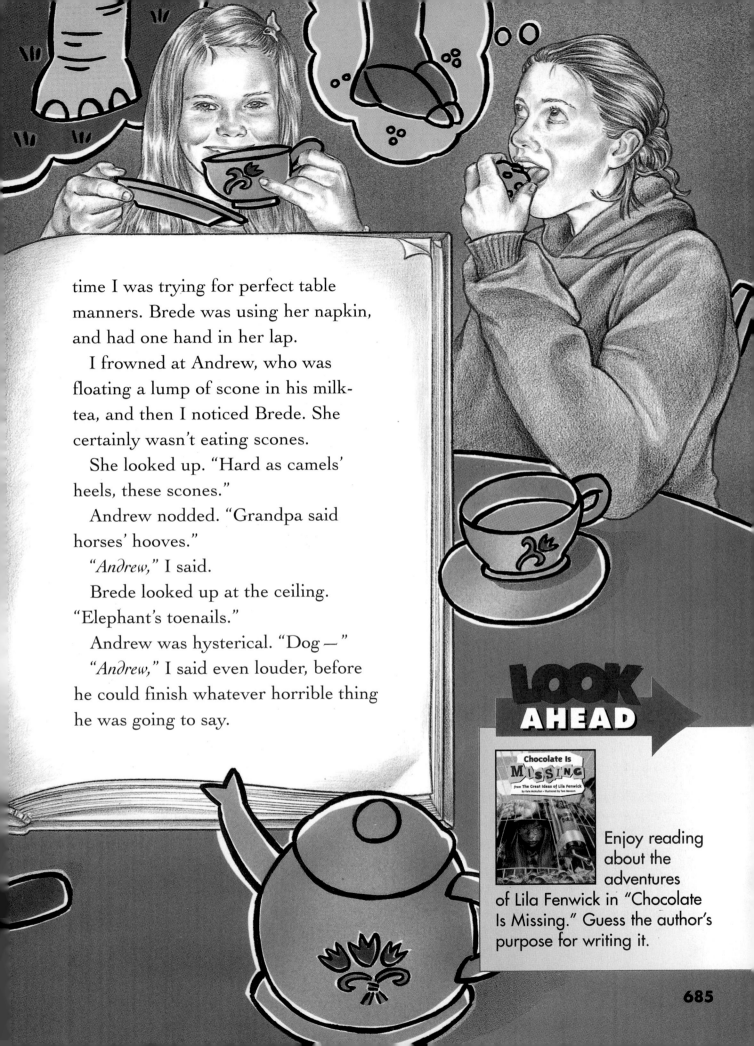

time I was trying for perfect table manners. Brede was using her napkin, and had one hand in her lap.

I frowned at Andrew, who was floating a lump of scone in his milk-tea, and then I noticed Brede. She certainly wasn't eating scones.

She looked up. "Hard as camels' heels, these scones."

Andrew nodded. "Grandpa said horses' hooves."

"*Andrew,*" I said.

Brede looked up at the ceiling. "Elephant's toenails."

Andrew was hysterical. "Dog—"

"*Andrew,*" I said even louder, before he could finish whatever horrible thing he was going to say.

LOOK AHEAD

Chocolate Is
MISSING
from The Great Ideas of Lila Fenwick
by Kate McMullan • Illustrated by Tom Newsom

Enjoy reading about the adventures of Lila Fenwick in "Chocolate Is Missing." Guess the author's purpose for writing it.

Vocabulary

Words to Know

approach   chocolate   angle
presence   poster   brag

Many words have more than one meaning. To decide which meaning of a word is being used, look for clues in the sentences around the word.

Read the paragraph below. Decide if *angle* means "a figure formed by two lines" or "a point of view."

Sniffing Out Clues!

Craig walked in and Anna looked up. Craig had <u>presence</u>. "I don't like to <u>brag</u>, but I know I can solve any mystery," Craig said.

"I solved the case of the missing <u>chocolate</u>," said Anna. "My brother took it. I saw his dark, chocolaty fingerprints on a <u>poster</u> on his wall."

"Those could be dirt!" declared Craig. "Let's look at this from a different <u>angle</u> and try an experiment. I'll leave out some more chocolate."

The two watched Anna's dog Nip <u>approach</u> the chocolate. The thief was caught—red-pawed!

Talk About It

With a partner, discuss situations when you would use each vocabulary word. Take turns using the words in sentences.

Chocolate Is **MISSING**

from **The Great Ideas of Lila Fenwick**

by Kate McMullan • illustrated by Tom Newsom

Chocolate is missing.
He was last seen wearing a dark brown
fur coat and eating a carrot.
If you see him, contact
Lila Fenwick or Gayle Deckert,
in Mr. Sherman's room.
All information strictly confidential.

"**W**hat do you think?" I held the sign up for Gayle's approval.

"I think there's one tiny detail you forgot to mention," she said.

I read my sign over.

"You're right." I added: *Reward: $3.00.*

"You have to say what Chocolate is," Gayle said, "or people won't know what they're looking for."

Gayle had a point. She usually did. She could be as logical as a computer, as practical as notebook dividers. Sometimes I wondered how we ever got to be best friends. We not only thought differently, we looked about as unalike as two fifth graders could. Gayle is big, tall and wide, what you might call queen-sized. Her mother is always harping at her to lose ten pounds, but my mother says Gayle has "presence," which means she is very sure of herself and you notice her when she walks into a room. That's true, but even if Gayle weren't so large, you'd notice her because of her hair—wild, white-blond zig-zaggy hair.

My mother says I would have more presence if I'd trim my hair so that it didn't hang over my glasses and hide my "striking green eyes." But I've been trying to let my bangs grow out for six months, and I'd hate to give up and cut them now. I'm not sure it would help, anyway, because I'm short and bony and I have pretty ordinary brown hair. When I mention this, my mother says it's what's inside that counts.

I added one more line to the poster:

Chocolate answers to the description of a guinea pig.

Gayle sighed. "Too, *too* Nancy Drew."

Gayle had come over to my house after school to help make these posters about Chocolate. Making them had actually been my idea. I don't like to brag, but lots of times I get ideas. Not just good ideas, better than good—*great*. At school, where almost all the kids are known for something, I'm famous for my Great Ideas.

Of course all the kids in Mr. Sherman's room already knew that Chocolate was missing. He'd been our class pet. We'd gotten him on the first day of school, two weeks ago. I had suggested the name Chocolate for him and it had won in the class vote. (The other nominations were Squeaky, Fluffy, and George.) Everyone liked him a lot, and then, this morning, Tuesday morning to be exact, we'd come into the classroom and—no Chocolate. The door to his cage was standing open and he was gone.

Gone! Eddie English, our fifth grade Class President (who is known as T.K.O.—Total Knock-Out in the looks department), called a special meeting to discuss it.

"Does anybody know where Chocolate could be?" he asked, looking very serious.

"There's no way he got out of that cage by himself," volunteered Rita Morgan (also known as Miss Perfect), who had been in charge of changing Chocolate's cedar shavings on Monday. "I closed his cage up, like really tight, just before school let out yesterday." Rita paused dramatically and looked around the room. "I think," she announced, "that someone *stole* Chocolate."

I met Gayle at recess after the meeting. "What are we going to do?" I'd asked.

"About what?"

"Finding Chocolate. We've got to find him."

I had loved holding Chocolate in my lap, stroking his curly brown fur, scratching him behind the ears, and listening to him purr. When I thought that I might never hear that rattly purr again, I felt like crying.

Gayle just shrugged.

I tried to appeal to her interests. "But what if the person who took him doesn't know what to feed him? Doesn't know he likes apples and spinach leaves and peanut butter sandwiches? He could starve!"

"Guinea pigs'll eat anything," said Gayle. Where were her feelings?

What I needed right then was a Great Idea for making Gayle want to help me find Chocolate. With my imagination and Gayle's smarts, we'd be an unbeatable team. I went over to the jungle gym and hung by my knees, hoping that a flow of blood to my brain would stimulate my thinking. I could see Gayle, sitting right side up on the root of a big oak, reading

The Scarlet Band. She loved to read Sherlock Holmes mysteries to see if she could figure out whodunit before Sherlock. Most of the time she could, since she has, as she modestly puts it, a mind like a steel trap. My face was almost scarlet before the Great Idea flowed into my brain.

I was beside Gayle in a nanosecond. Even if she didn't love Chocolate the way I did, I had a plan that would make her wild to find him.

"What we need to do," I'd announced, "is solve the Case of the Missing Chocolate."

Gayle glanced up from her book. "You mean conduct an investigation?"

"Precisely. Find clues, question suspects, the whole detective bit. Fenwick and Deckert, Private Eyes."

"Deckert and Fenwick? I like it." Gayle slammed her book for emphasis. "In three days," she predicted, "the guinea-grabber will be in our hands."

Now Gayle finished drawing one last pathetic picture of Chocolate underneath the notice I had written in black marker. She sat back on her heels and examined our lineup of posters.

"Not bad," she said.

I reached into my book bag and got out the SURPRISE! chocolate bars we'd bought to reward ourselves for doing all this work. I also took out my casebook. In it I'd kept a record of everything about the Case of the Missing Chocolate. That day during a health filmstrip I'd made a list of possible suspects. As we ate our candy bars I showed it to Gayle.

Who took Chocolate?

Possible Suspects/Possible Motives:

1. Rita Morgan

Today I saw Rita's mother's station wagon parked at school and in the back was a shopping bag with three heads of lettuce on top. Guinea pigs eat tons of lettuce.

2. Sandra Guth

Sandra has a snake. I read once that snakes sometimes need to have a live meal. Maybe Sandra took Chocolate to use for snake food.

3. Michael Watson

As everyone knows, Michael is a science genius. As everyone also knows, guinea pigs are often used in science experiments. Michael may have taken Chocolate to use in some awful experiment.

A look of amazement came over Gayle's face as she read my list.

"Sandra's snake," she began, "it's a garter snake. It eats teensy frogs. And Sandra is hardly the type to steal the class pet."

Gayle was right. Sandra was the most popular kid in our class. Besides, Sandra's mom let her have a snake, didn't she? If Sandra wanted a guinea pig, her mom would probably let her get one. She wouldn't have to steal.

"So scratch her off the list."

"As for Rita," Gayle went on, "I overheard her at lunch today saying that her mother has the whole family on another disgusting diet, and for supper they can only eat tossed salads with lemon juice and anchovies."

"Gross." That explained the lettuce. "You'd better hope Rita's mother doesn't tell your mother about this diet."

Gayle ignored my comment. "Plus, what would Rita want with a guinea pig anyway? You do remember her whining about getting stuck with the job of changing the cage yesterday, don't you? She said she'd need a new manicure if she had to touch 'the rodent.'"

It was all coming back to me now. "I guess we can take her off the list too."

"That leaves Michael," said Gayle. "You really think your old buddy Michael would take Chocolate to experiment on?"

"He might," I told her. I'd known Michael practically forever. I could remember baby Michael trying to say Lila, but coming out with YiYa. I think that's why, to this day, he calls me Fenwick. But friend or not, he was still a suspect. "Michael *is* a total science weirdo. He might have stolen Chocolate and not even feel bad about it if he was working on some terribly important project." My imagination clicked into high gear. "Like curing leprosy or . . . or . . . communicating with aliens."

"Leprosy?" Gayle raised her eyebrows. "Aliens? With a guinea pig?"

"Well, curing the common cold, maybe." I wasn't giving up on Michael. "I remember hearing Chocolate sneeze a few times. Maybe Michael just borrowed Chocolate and he's planning to bring him back—if he survives the experiment."

"Borrowed." Gayle looked thoughtful. "It's possible, I guess." She gave me a Sherlockian stare. "Let's interrogate him tomorrow at lunch."

"Hi, Michael," I said as Gayle and I slid our trays next to his at the long, blond cafeteria table where he had been sitting by himself. Michael always ate lunch alone. Today he was reading a book called *Giant Ants of the Third Galaxy* while he ate.

Michael looked up over his book and smiled. "Greetings, earthlings."

Gayle wasn't into beating around the bush. "Say, Michael," she began, "been conducting any experiments lately? You know, any science experiments?"

Michael looked at Gayle strangely.

I tried to help. "Biology experiments maybe?"

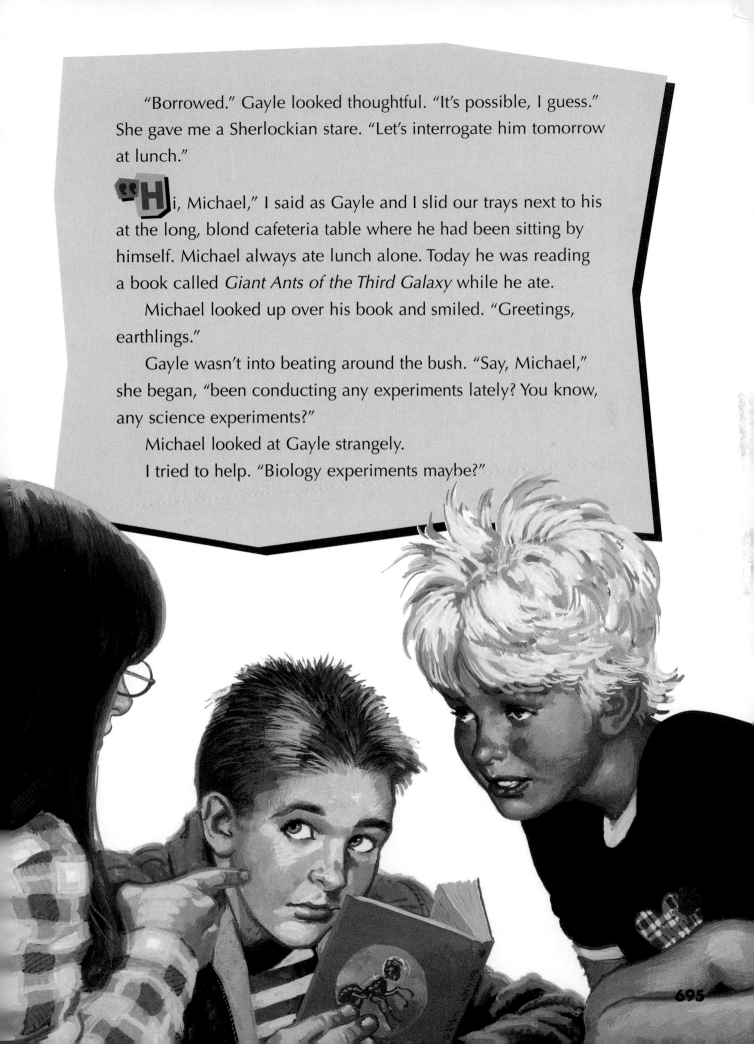

"What's the sudden interest in biology?" Michael asked. He took a large bite of his Sloppy Joe. Michael was one of the few kids who bought a plate lunch every day and actually ate it.

"Uh . . . I'm thinking of taking a Saturday class," I began. "At the Museum of Natural History in . . . uh . . ."

Gayle tried to save me. "In animal experiments."

"That's right," I said.

Michael popped a rubbery orange jello cube into his mouth. Our interrogation was getting nowhere.

"You know," I piped up, "like, maybe, a class in cat dissection."

Michael's eyes widened. "You want to spend your Saturday mornings cutting up dead cats? Boy, Fenwick, you're even weirder than I thought you were."

That's when I remembered Michael's beloved cat, Nelson.

Gayle decided to catch our suspect off guard with the direct approach. "Michael, did you borrow Chocolate to experiment on?"

Michael stared in disbelief first at Gayle and then at me. "You think I've stolen Chocolate and dissected him, is that it?" He looked down at his plate for a few seconds, then he slowly raised his eyes to meet mine. "The truth is, it's even worse than that," he said.

"Worse?" I almost shouted. "What could be worse than being dissected?"

Michael picked up his Sloppy Joe and slowly pried off the top bun. "I'm eating him for lunch!" Michael started laughing like a maniac. "Chocolate on a bun!" He shoved his Sloppy Joe in my face. "Try some!"

"Michael," I said sternly. "This is serious."

But my partner in investigation was cracking up, while I sat there and worried. Now we didn't have one single suspect left on our list.

I always walk home from school alone on Wednesdays because Gayle has her ballet lesson on that day. On this particular

Wednesday I walked slowly. I wanted time to think. I also wanted time to enjoy the SURPRISE! chocolate bar that I'd been saving all day. Maybe it would help me solve the Case of the Missing Chocolate. I peeled the wrapper down. The chocolate coating on the candy bar was just the color of Chocolate's fur. It made me feel sad and hungry at the same time. Who could have stolen Chocolate? Who would be creepy enough to take a class pet? I pulled the candy bar all the way out of the wrapper, reading the label as I walked.
A candy bar that's full of surprises! it said.
A chocolate escape from the ordinary.
A chocolate escape.

And then it hit me like a ten-pound box of bonbons—maybe Chocolate hadn't been stolen at all! He might have escaped! Rita could have thrown us all off the track by claiming to have closed the cage tightly. Snapping that cage door shut wasn't easy. No doubt Rita was afraid if she did it, she'd break a nail. She probably left the cage door wide open but didn't want to get blamed for Chocolate getting out, so she invented the stealing angle. It suddenly seemed so clear to me. Maybe Chocolate was somewhere in the classroom, huddled in a corner, scared, hungry, and miserable!

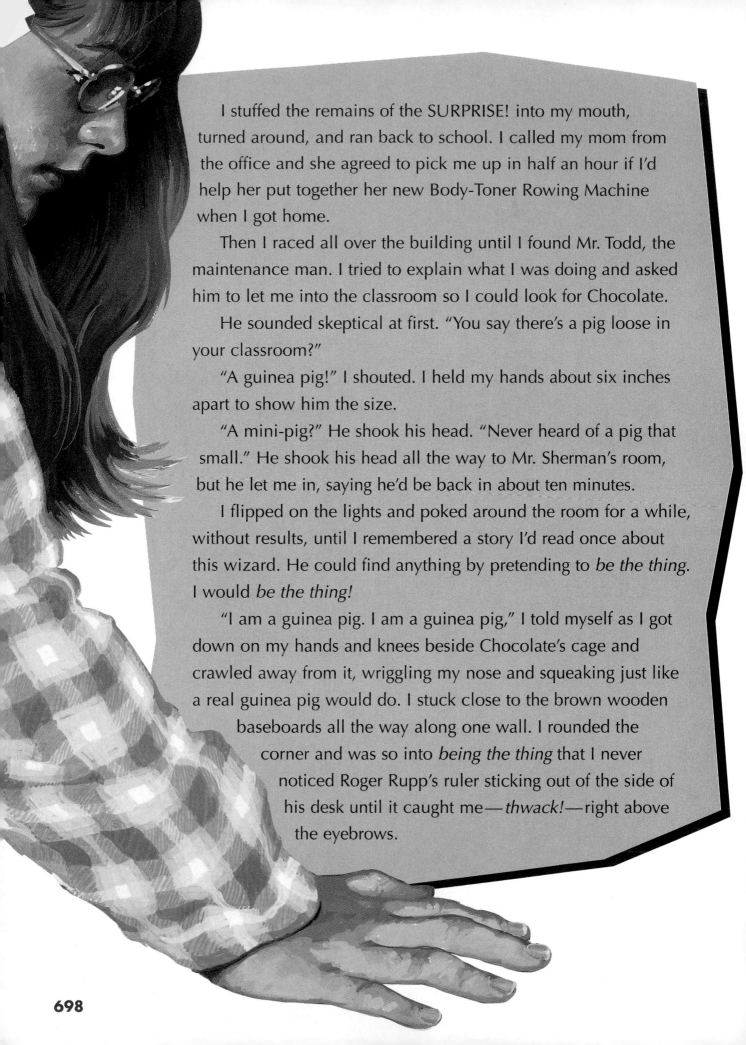

I stuffed the remains of the SURPRISE! into my mouth, turned around, and ran back to school. I called my mom from the office and she agreed to pick me up in half an hour if I'd help her put together her new Body-Toner Rowing Machine when I got home.

Then I raced all over the building until I found Mr. Todd, the maintenance man. I tried to explain what I was doing and asked him to let me into the classroom so I could look for Chocolate.

He sounded skeptical at first. "You say there's a pig loose in your classroom?"

"A guinea pig!" I shouted. I held my hands about six inches apart to show him the size.

"A mini-pig?" He shook his head. "Never heard of a pig that small." He shook his head all the way to Mr. Sherman's room, but he let me in, saying he'd be back in about ten minutes.

I flipped on the lights and poked around the room for a while, without results, until I remembered a story I'd read once about this wizard. He could find anything by pretending to *be the thing*. I would *be the thing!*

"I am a guinea pig. I am a guinea pig," I told myself as I got down on my hands and knees beside Chocolate's cage and crawled away from it, wriggling my nose and squeaking just like a real guinea pig would do. I stuck close to the brown wooden baseboards all the way along one wall. I rounded the corner and was so into *being the thing* that I never noticed Roger Rupp's ruler sticking out of the side of his desk until it caught me—*thwack!*—right above the eyebrows.

I straightened up fast, bashing the back of my head into the plywood board holding Kelly MacConell's salt and flour map of Brazil and sending my glasses flying. Deciding that it was too painful to *be the thing*, I sat down, knocking the metal grate off a heating vent with my knee as I did so. It's a good thing I get Great Ideas, I thought. Otherwise I'd definitely be known as Class Klutz.

I found my specs under Barney Barker's desk, put them on, and then carefully bent down to peer into the dark rectangular hole of the vent. I couldn't see a thing. I was just getting up my nerve to stick my arm into the vent to feel around for Chocolate, when suddenly I sensed that I wasn't alone. Turning my head, I saw a pair of perfectly scuffed sneakers behind me. Slowly I looked up past the sneakers, past the khaki pants, past the plaid shirt, and into the T.K.O. gorgeous face of Eddie English. There he was, wearing his Fifth Grade Safety Patrol Badge, just standing, watching me. From where I was, I noticed, I could see right up his nose.

"Why'd you sneak up on me?" was all I could think to ask.

"Why'd you sneak in here after hours to crawl around?"

"I didn't just sneak in here to crawl around," I explained, wondering whether he had been standing there to see me sniffing, guinea-pig style, along the floor. "On the way home today I happened to think that Chocolate might not have been stolen at all. He might have escaped from his cage and be hiding somewhere in this room, so I came back to have a look."

Eddie sat down by me. "Sounds reasonable," he said. I noticed then that his eyes were dark, dark brown, the color of the bittersweet chocolate my mom uses for making chocolate cakes.

Without my even hinting, Eddie shoved his arm into the furnace vent, all the way up to his shoulder.

"I can't feel anything," he said, "but this goes clear to the furnace. Maybe we should ask Mr. Todd to let us look down there."

"I already thought of that," I said quickly. I mean, Eddie English may be cute, but this was my case, after all. "Lucky thing the furnace hasn't been turned on yet this year."

Just then Mr. Todd poked his head in the door. "Sooey! Sooey!" He laughed. "That's how we used to call the pigs on the farm when I was a boy. Any sign of your pig yet?"

"Guinea pig!" I yelled again. "No, not so far."

Then I showed him the heating vent cover and explained how I'd knocked it off.

Mr. Todd nodded. "It's always falling off. Haven't had time to fix it yet."

That was bad news for Chocolate. Could he have crawled down the vent? As best I could, I shouted to Mr. Todd what I thought might have happened to the poor guinea pig, and he agreed to check the furnace room carefully.

As he let us out of the classroom, Mr. Todd winked. "A pig in the furnace room. I never saw such a thing! Get it? Pig? Never *sausage* a thing?" He chuckled.

I looked at Eddie. He just rolled his chocolate-cake eyes at me. Some joke.

"Well, Lila," my dad said that night as we finished eating supper, "any luck with the Case of the Restless Cavy?"

I shook my head. Was I the only one who didn't think Chocolate's disappearance was something to joke about? When my class got Chocolate at school, I brought home a library book about guinea pigs and my dad and I read it together. Their scientific name really is Restless Cavy. We also found that Chocolate is what's known as a Brazil guinea pig because of his curly hair.

My dad went into the kitchen and came back carrying a tray with three big bowls of what looked like chocolate ice cream drowning in chocolate syrup. We almost always have fresh fruit for dessert, so I could hardly believe my eyes.

My dad gave me a little squeeze. "This is to bring you luck in your search for Chocolate," he said.

"This is *real* chocolate ice cream?" I asked. "Not some phony carob look-alike?"

"It's the genuine article," my mom answered.

"Fifteen extra minutes on the Body-Toner for you tomorrow, Mom," I told her.

"Well worth it," she declared, digging out a huge spoonful of chocolate-smothered ice cream and holding it up as if she were making a toast. My dad and I raised our dripping spoons together to meet hers.

"Here's to you, Chocolate," my mom said. "Wherever you may be."

After helping with the dishes, I went up to my room. I had a funny feeling there was something I was supposed to do. Then I saw my casebook lying on the bed, and I remembered that I'd promised myself to write in it every night until the Chocolate Case was closed. But tonight, I figured, why bother. All I would have written anyway was: *It seems like Lila Fenwick has run out of Great Ideas.*

The next morning our class began as usual with a meeting. This was Mr. Sherman's way of letting us get used to being more grown up and deciding some things for ourselves. So far Sherman Tank, as we had nicknamed him because he was so big, was turning out to be okay. He was fair, he could be both funny and serious, and he treated us as if he just assumed we'd do our best work—even Barney Barker, Class Airhead.

Eddie English and his Oreo eyes were running the meeting, so it was hard not to pay attention, but I was still trying desperately to think of new ways to look for Chocolate. When no one had anything to report about our missing pet, we went on to the next topic on the agenda: the class field trip to the Museum of Natural History. I could feel Michael Watson's eyes on the back of my neck the whole time we were discussing the trip!

When the meeting was over, Mr. Sherman stood up.

"Well," he said, "today is Thursday, September twenty-fifth. I've been looking forward to this date because I am eager to hear your oral reports on South America which are due today."

Desks squeaked open and report folders began appearing in front of everyone. My heart started pounding. Reports! I'd totally forgotten about these reports! Mr. Sherman would think I was the Class Airhead instead of Barney Barker. My report was on the main products of Brazil. Let's see, what had I read that day at the library? There was coffee. I remembered that. And cattle. Sugar. What else?

I saw Gayle waving her hand, hoping Mr. Sherman would let her begin the reports. Oral reports were Gayle's specialty.

She got to show how smart she was and ham it up at the same time. Please, Mr. Sherman, I thought, pick Gayle.

"Why don't we start somewhere in the middle of the alphabet today?" Mr. Sherman said, looking down at his class list. "Let's see. I turn my desk over to Lila Fenwick."

Why me? I thought. What have I done to deserve this? My heart was bonging so loud! It sounded like a stick pounding on a garbage can lid. I didn't even know if I'd be able to walk, but somehow I got to the front of the room, after tripping just a little over Barney Barker's fat foot, which he stuck out on purpose. I stood behind the little podium on Mr. Sherman's desk.

"No notes?" Mr. Sherman asked.

"No, sir," I said. "I guess it's all in my head."

"Excellent." Mr. Sherman smiled. "Go ahead then."

"My report is on the main products of Brazil," I began. "The biggest product of Brazil is coffee, which comes from the coffee bean. Coffee beans grow on low trees. The fact that the trees aren't very tall makes it easy for coffee bean pickers to pick the coffee beans."

I looked around me. I could see that everyone in the whole class was bored already. Rita was writing a note with a pink pen that had a plastic unicorn on top. Even though she was way back in the fifth row, I could smell the strawberry scent of her ink.

"Coffee is a popular drink all over the world, so Brazil exports tons of it each year."

Even Gayle was doodling on her notebook cover. And then, as I talked, I noticed Rita passing her note to Eddie English. Well, there was no way I was going to stand up in front of everyone going on and on about exports and main products while Eddie English read a note from a girl who wrote with phony strawberry ink—a girl who lived on lettuce and little salty fish—a girl who didn't care one little bit that Chocolate was missing! Even if I don't have a lot of information, I thought, I'm going to make Eddie English listen to me. Luckily, at that very moment, I was struck by a Great Idea.

"It might surprise you to learn that something which we all know and love would be missing from our diets if it weren't for the main products of Brazil."

Everyone looked wide awake now.

I kept on. "That's right. First of all, there are lots of cows in Brazil. And as everyone knows, cows give milk. There's also plenty of sugarcane growing there, so sugar is a main product. And then my personal favorite: There are lots of cocoa plants, which produce cocoa beans, which are ground up to make—chocolate. So, if you mix chocolate and sugar and milk together, you get what we all know as a milk chocolate candy bar!"

Everyone in the class, including Eddie English, laughed—even Lynn Williamson, who was incredibly shy and hardly ever even smiled. Then I realized that they were all waiting for me to go on. But my mind was blank. I couldn't remember one more fact about the products of Brazil. I thought about concluding my report by eating a candy bar. I twisted the hair of my bangs. Think, I told myself.

Think! My knees were trembling. I tried to stop them by straightening my legs and tucking the toes of my sneakers under Mr. Sherman's bottom desk drawer, which was open a crack. But as I did this, the toe of one sneaker caught under the drawer, and when I tried to pull it out, the drawer slid open and knocked my other foot out from under me. I lost my balance and fell, hard, right on my behind.

"Chocolate is only one product of a big country like Brazil," I spoke out above the giggles, as I pulled myself back to a standing position on Mr. Sherman's desk. I kept talking, about rubber trees I think, but my mind was on that drawer. I'd seen something dark inside, dark and furry. Careful not to get my foot stuck again, I opened the drawer the rest of the way and there, curled up in a little nest of shredded paper, was the missing Chocolate. Not only that, but nestled beside Chocolate were three little guinea pigs no bigger than after-dinner mints.

"And that concludes my report," I said. One look at Mr. Sherman's face told me that he didn't think it had been such a fantastic report, but I went on quickly. "I have something else to report. Another kind of chocolate from Brazil—our guinea pig Chocolate—has been found. And he, I mean *she*, has three babies!"

So many things happened at once then. The whole class filed quietly by the desk drawer to take a peek at mother Chocolate and her brood. Then everyone got an extra recess while Mr. Sherman and Gayle and I fixed up Chocolate's cage. We put in a big tent-shaped piece of cardboard so that the guinea pigs could have some privacy. We gave them water and lots of food and put the cage in a semi-quiet part of the classroom.

Of course we held another name contest for the babies and ended up with Chocolate Sundae, Chocolate Kiss, and . . . George, which was Barney Barker's idea of a joke.

Later Mr. Sherman called me up to his desk. He said he found my report a bit short on hard facts, but that considering the circumstances which interrupted me, I could turn in a written report later in the week. He also congratulated me on solving the Case of the Missing Chocolate and said that if I'm really a great detective, in a couple of months I'll be able to find good homes for the babies. I've already started working on a list of possible suspects.

About the Author

Kate McMullan

Kate McMullan has written three books about Lila Fenwick. Besides writing her own books, Ms. McMullan has also collaborated with her husband, Jim, to create picture books for young readers. They often base these stories on experiences they have had with their own child. "Our first book emerged because we live in a noisy part of New York City," Ms. McMullan explained, "where garbage trucks crunch trash beneath our window at 3:00 A.M. and fire engine sirens wail all night long. When our daughter was young, these noises frightened her." Together the McMullans made up *The Noisy Giants' Tea Party* to soothe her fears. In this story, a boy named Andrew fits scary city sounds into a dream about a group of giants.

Ms. McMullan has also written several joke books, some of them with Lisa Eisenberg. If you're looking for jokes about pigs, snakes, bugs, fish, chickens, or monsters, check out these books.

Reader Response

Open for Discussion

Pretend you are a detective and give Lila some advice. What would you have done to find the missing guinea pig?

Comprehension Check

1. Are Lila and Gayle well suited to be friends? Use examples to explain.

2. Lila at first concludes that someone stole Chocolate. What is wrong with that conclusion? Give examples.

3. Does Lila solve the disappearance of Chocolate because she has a Great Idea? Explain with story details.

4. Do you think the **author's purpose** is mainly to inform, entertain, persuade, or express? Explain. (Author's Purpose)

5. Figuring out the **author's purpose** helps you adjust the way you read a story. Would you read "Chocolate Is Missing" quickly or slowly? Why? (Author's Purpose)

Test Prep
Look Back and Write

Look back at pages 690–693. What causes Lila and Gayle to think that someone took Chocolate? Use details from the story to support your answer.

by Laura Daily
from *National Geographic World* magazine

The Zoo Crew

"You've got to like animals in this job," says Bethany Patchet, 13. She is one of about 200 kids who sign up every year to work as Junior Zookeepers. The zoo in Dallas, Texas, runs the largest youth volunteer program of any zoo in the United States.

Junior Zookeepers, who call themselves JZs, must be at least 11 years old. They volunteer one day a week for four hours in the Children's Zoo area. Following their training, JZs take care of goats, guinea pigs, snakes, box turtles, lizards, ferrets, chickens, and other small animals. Sometimes they hold an animal so visitors can touch it. "But the best part," says Adam Hunter, 12, "is talking to all the visitors about the animals."

A CORN SNAKE coils in the hands of Bethany Patchet. "Jake, the snake, is harmless," she says, "but I tell people not to touch a snake in the wild because it could be poisonous."

JUNIOR ZOOKEEPERS check a board that lists daily duties and animal feeding schedules. They also clean stalls, aquariums, and cases.

PEANUTS PLEASE a prairie dog fed by Jeniece Martinez. Adam Hunter watches the activity from an observation cage.

The JZs also have behind-the-scenes privileges. They can take tours of the giraffe barn, the rhinoceros and camel habitat, and the reptile house. "The tours are really special," says Jeniece Martinez, 13. "How many kids get to feed a camel or touch a blue-tongued skink?"

During the summer as many as a thousand people visit the Children's Zoo every day. That keeps the volunteers busy.

"Having a job like this is hard work," says Nathan Hartley, 12. "You have to be responsible and show up, even on holidays or when it rains."

The Junior Zookeepers are looking forward to a new, larger Children's Zoo opening later this year. With many more animals, the new area will need even more volunteers. "I can't wait," says Jeniece. "Sign me up!"

NIGERIAN DWARF GOATS don't bite visitors, according to Junior Zookeeper Marthe Turlington, 12.

Dreams

by Langston Hughes

Hold fast to dreams
For if dreams die
Life is a broken-winged bird
That cannot fly.

Hold fast to dreams
For when dreams go
Life is a barren field
Frozen with snow.

Dream Dust

by Langston Hughes

Gather out of star-dust
　　　Earth-dust,
　　　Cloud-dust,
　　　Storm-dust,
And splinters of hail,
One handful of dream-dust
　　　Not for sale.

When I Grow Up

by Janet S. Wong

I want to be an artist, Grandpa—
write and paint, dance and sing.

Be accountant.
Be lawyer.
Make good living,
buy good food.
Back in China,
in the old days,
everybody
so, so poor.
Eat one chicken,
work all year.

Grandpa, things are different
here.

Purple Snake

by Pat Mora

"It's in there, sleeping,"
Don Luis says and winks.
He knows I want to feel
the animal asleep in a piece of wood,
like he does
turning it this way and that,
listening.

Slowly he strokes the wood,
rough and wrinkled. Like his hands.
He begins to carve his way.
"*Mira*. Its head, its scales, its tail."
Don Luis rubs and strokes
the animal before he paints
its eyes open.
When the paint dries,
I place the purple snake
by the green bull and red frog
that Don Luis found asleep
in a piece of wood.

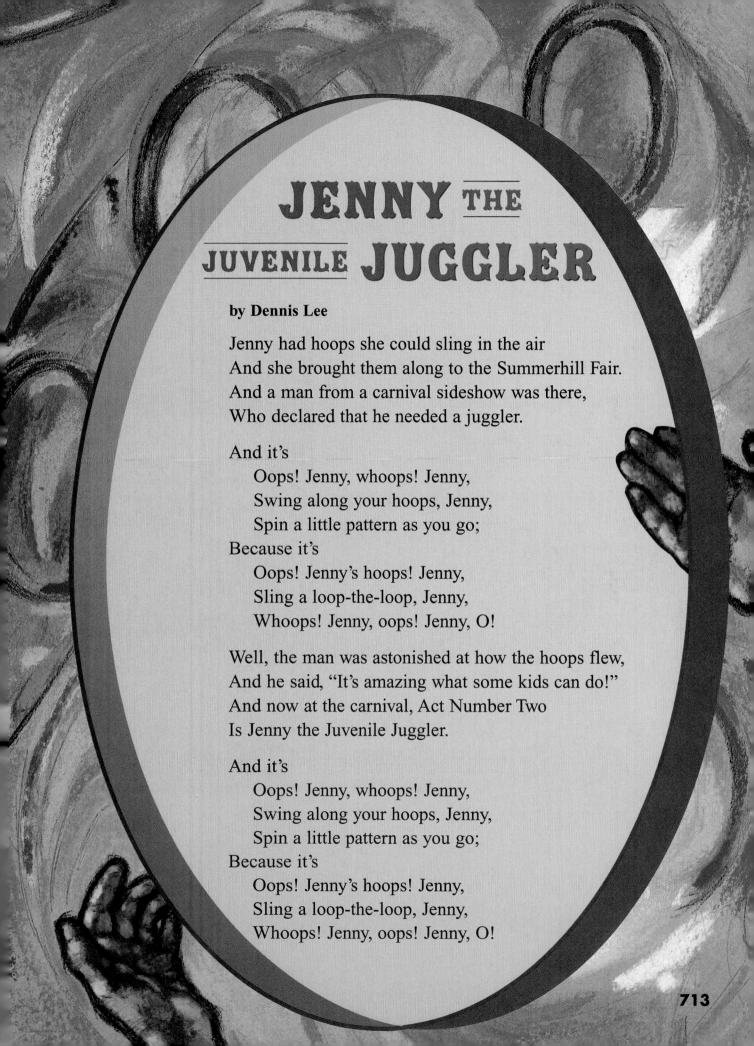

JENNY THE
JUVENILE JUGGLER

by Dennis Lee

Jenny had hoops she could sling in the air
And she brought them along to the Summerhill Fair.
And a man from a carnival sideshow was there,
Who declared that he needed a juggler.

And it's
    Oops! Jenny, whoops! Jenny,
    Swing along your hoops, Jenny,
    Spin a little pattern as you go;
Because it's
    Oops! Jenny's hoops! Jenny,
    Sling a loop-the-loop, Jenny,
    Whoops! Jenny, oops! Jenny, O!

Well, the man was astonished at how the hoops flew,
And he said, "It's amazing what some kids can do!"
And now at the carnival, Act Number Two
Is Jenny the Juvenile Juggler.

And it's
    Oops! Jenny, whoops! Jenny,
    Swing along your hoops, Jenny,
    Spin a little pattern as you go;
Because it's
    Oops! Jenny's hoops! Jenny,
    Sling a loop-the-loop, Jenny,
    Whoops! Jenny, oops! Jenny, O!

Unit 6 Wrap-Up

How many forms can creativity take?

Talent Festival

Create a Model

The characters and people in Unit 6 all have unique talents that take different forms. Imagine what it might be like if several of the characters and people displayed their talents and abilities in booths at a festival.

1. **Imagine** how characters from this unit would present their talents.

2. **Choose** a character whose talents are like yours or are interesting to you.

3. **Create** a model or diorama of that character's booth at your talent festival.

Problem-Solvers

Write a Slogan

Benjamin Franklin, from "Out of the Blue," and Lila, the narrator of "Chocolate Is Missing," solve problems. What makes them good problem-solvers?

1. **Make a list** of problems and solutions for each character. Record information from each selection.

2. **Discuss** the information on your lists with a partner.

3. Together, **write** a slogan about problem-solving.

Songwriter's Workshop

Write a Song or a Rap

Del, from "Koya's Cousin Del," is teaching a songwriter's workshop. Some characters from this unit are in the workshop. They are writing music about their lives.

1. Choose one character and **brainstorm** with a partner the most important events of the character's life.

2. Together, **write** a song or a rap that describes those events.

3. **Practice** your song once. Then share it with others. You may even record it to play later.

Ad Agency

Create an Advertisement

Pretend that you work for an advertising agency. Your boss asks you to work with a client—a character from Unit 6.

1. **Select** the character or person. Then choose one talent he or she has, or one product he or she invented or created.

2. **List** details about the talent or product. Explain why it is valuable.

3. **Advertise** the talent or product. Create a magazine, radio, or TV ad that gets people interested in the talent or product.

Test Talk

Answer the Question

Score High!

A scoring checklist shows you what makes up a good answer to a test question. You can learn how to write answers that score high by using a scoring checklist.

Read the scoring checklist at the right.

A test about "Chocolate Is Missing," pages 690–692, might have this question.

Test Question 1

What is Lila's Great Idea for making Gayle want to help with her search for Chocolate? Use details from this section to support your answer.

Look at the First Try answer on page 717. Then see how the student used the scoring checklist to improve the answer.

Scoring Checklist

✓ **The answer is correct.** It has only correct details from the text.

✓ **The answer is complete.** It has all the necessary details from the text.

✓ **The answer is focused.** It has only details from the text that answer the question.

First Try

It's not complete. It needs more details about how Gayle gets interested.

It's not correct. Gayle likes reading mysteries, not Lila.

Lila's Great Idea for making Gayle want to help with her search for Chocolate is to tell Gayle that she's worried about Chocolate starving. Lila likes reading Sherlock Holmes mysteries. Lila says that they must solve the Case of the Missing Chocolate.

It's not focused. The detail about Chocolate starving doesn't belong.

Improved Answer

Tell why this is a better answer. Look back at the scoring checklist for help.

Lila's Great Idea for making Gayle want to help with her search for Chocolate is to turn the search into a mystery case. Gayle likes to read Sherlock Holmes mysteries. Lila says they must solve the Case of the Missing Chocolate.

Try it!

Now look at the First Try answer below. Then rewrite the answer and improve it. Look back at the scoring checklist for help.

Test Question 2

What is Lila's Great Idea for getting her classmates' attention during her oral report on Brazil? Use details from the selection to support your answer.

First Try

Lila's Great Idea for getting her classmates' attention during her oral report on Brazil is to talk about coffee. She also tells the class about how there are a lot of cows in Brazil. Lila mentions other products, such as milk, sugar, and cocoa.

How to Use This Glossary

This glossary can help you understand and pronounce some of the words in this book. The entries in this glossary are in alphabetical order. There are guide words at the top of each page to show you the first and last words on the page. A pronunciation key is at the bottom of every other page. Remember, if you can't find the word you are looking for, ask for help or check a dictionary.

The entry word is in dark type. It shows how the word is spelled and how the word is divided into syllables.

The pronunciation is in parentheses. It also shows which syllables are stressed.

Part-of-speech labels show the function or functions of an entry word and any listed form of that word.

a•dopt (ə dopt′), VERB. to take a child of other parents and bring up as your own: *My parents plan to adopt another child.* ❏ VERB **a•dopts, a•dopt•ed, a•dopt•ing.** —**a•dop•tion** (ə dop′shən), NOUN.

Sometimes, irregular and other special forms will be shown to help you use the word correctly.

The definition and example sentence show you what the word means and how it is used.

Aa

ac•ci•dent (ak′sə dənt), NOUN. something harmful or unlucky that happens unexpectedly: *She was hurt in a car accident.*

a•chieve•ment (ə chēv′mənt), NOUN. something achieved; some plan or action carried out with courage or with unusual ability: *The new painting was her greatest achievement.*

ad•he•sive (ad hē′siv), ADJECTIVE. holding tight; sticky: *an adhesive label.*

a•dopt (ə dopt′), VERB. to take a child of other parents and bring up as your own: *My parents plan to adopt another child.* ❏ VERB **a•dopts, a•dopt•ed, a•dopt•ing.** —**a•dop•tion** (ə dop′shən), NOUN.

ad•ven•ture (ad ven′chər), NOUN. an unusual or exciting experience: *The trip to Alaska was quite an adventure for her.*

ad•vi•sor•y (ad vī′zər ē), NOUN. bulletin or report to advise of developments: *An advisory by the Weather Bureau warned of a storm.* ❏ PLURAL **ad•vi•sor•ies.**

a•gent (ā′jənt), NOUN. person or company having the authority to act for another: *She is a real-estate agent and can help you sell your house.*

al•ma•nac (ȯl′mə nak), NOUN. a reference book published yearly, with tables of facts and information on many subjects: *My almanac is out-of-date.*

an•ces•tor (an′ses′tər), NOUN. someone from whom you are directly descended. Your grandfathers and your grandmothers are ancestors.

an•gle (ang′gəl), NOUN.
1 the figure formed by two lines or surfaces that meet.
2 a point of view: *We are treating the problem from a new angle.*

a·pol·o·get·i·cal·ly (ə pol′ə jet′ik lē), ADVERB. in a way or manner that makes an excuse or expresses regret: *"I got mud on the carpet, but I'll clean it up," she said apologetically.* **—a·pol·o·get·ic**, ADJECTIVE.

a·pol·o·gize (ə pol′ə jīz), VERB. to make an apology; say you are sorry; offer an excuse: *I heard my sister apologizing for her mistake.* ❑ VERB **a·pol·o·giz·es, a·pol·o·gized, a·pol·o·giz·ing.**

ap·pall·ing (ə po′ling), ADJECTIVE. causing horror; dismaying; terrifying: *The mystery movie on television was appalling.* **—ap·pall′ing·ly**, ADVERB.

ap·plause (ə plôz′), NOUN. approval shown by clapping the hands or shouting: *Applause for the singer rang out from the audience.*

ap·pren·tice (ə pren′tis), NOUN. person learning a trade or art. In return for instruction, apprentices agree to work for their employers a certain length of time with little or no pay. ❑ VERB **ap·pren·tic·es, ap·pren·ticed, ap·pren·tic·ing.**

ap·proach (ə prōch′), NOUN. a method of starting work on a task or problem: *Drawing an outline is a good approach to writing an essay.*

arc·tic (ärk′tik *or* är′tik), NOUN. **the Arctic,** the north polar region: *We explored the Arctic with our team of dogs.*

ar·mor (är′mər), NOUN. a covering, usually of metal or leather, worn to protect the body in fighting.

as·sist·ant (ə sis′tənt), NOUN. person who assists another; aid; helper: *He was my assistant in the library for a time.*

as·ter·oid (as′tə roid′), NOUN. any of thousands of rocky objects smaller than 620 miles (1000 kilometers) across, orbiting the sun mainly between the orbits of Mars and Jupiter; planetoid: *We looked at models of asteroids traveling around the sun.*

at·las (at′ləs), NOUN. a book of maps. A big atlas has maps of every country. ❑ PLURAL **at·las·es.**

at·mo·sphere (at′mə sfir), NOUN. the mass of gases that surrounds a planet, star, or other object in outer space: *The atmosphere of Venus is cloudy.*

at·trac·tion (ə trak′shən), NOUN. the act or power of attracting; the drawing or gathering together of something: *The pins were drawn to the magnet by attraction.*

au·di·tion (ò dish′ən), NOUN. a hearing to test the ability, quality, or performance of a singer, actor, or other performer: *He had a trumpet audition with the band director.*

au·di·to·ri·um (ò′də tôr′ē əm), NOUN. a large room for an audience in a theater, school, or the like; large hall.

au·to·graph (ò′tə graf), NOUN. someone's signature: *Many people collect the autographs of celebrities.*

awk·ward (òk′wərd), ADJECTIVE. clumsy; not graceful or skillful in movement: *Seals are very awkward on land but graceful in the water.*

B b

badg·er (baj′ər), NOUN. any of eight kinds of hairy gray mammals that feed at night and dig holes in the ground to live in. The badger is related to the weasel but is larger and more heavily built. It usually has some white and black fur on its head and face.

bel·low (bel′ō), NOUN. a loud, deep noise; roar: *The lions let out frightening bellows.*

be·trothed (bi trōŦHd′ *or* bi trôŦHt′), NOUN. person engaged to be married: *My sister introduced me to her betrothed.*

a	hat	ė	term	ô	order	ch	child	⎧a in about
ā	age	i	it	oi	oil	ng	long	e in taken
ä	far	ī	ice	ou	out	sh	she	ə⎨i in pencil
â	care	o	hot	u	cup	th	thin	o in lemon
e	let	ō	open	ù	put	ŦH	then	⎩u in circus
ē	equal	ò	saw	ü	rule	zh	measure	

bil·low (bil′ō), NOUN. any great wave or mass of smoke, flame, sound, or the like: *Billows of steam rose from the pot.*

bis·cuit (bis′kit), NOUN. a small piece of baked bread dough that is made without yeast. Biscuits can be made with baking powder or baking soda.

black·smith (blak′smith′), NOUN. someone who makes things out of iron by heating it in a forge and hammering it into shape on an anvil. Blacksmiths mend tools and shoe horses.

blis·ter (blis′tər), NOUN. a swelling in the skin filled with watery liquid. Blisters are caused by burns or rubbing.

boar (bôr), NOUN. a male pig, hog, or guinea pig: *The boars were kept in a different pen from the rest of the pigs.* ❑ PLURAL **boars** or **boar.**

bo·de·ga (bō dā′gə), NOUN. a grocery store in a Spanish-speaking neighborhood: *Maria and her mother bought bananas and flour at the bodega.* ❑ PLURAL **bo·de·gas.**

bond (bond), NOUN. anything that ties, binds, or unites: *a bond of affection.* ➡**bond′a·ble,** ADJECTIVE. ➡**bond·er,** NOUN.

book·keep·er (bùk′kē′pər), NOUN. a person who keeps a record of business accounts: *The bookkeeper calculated the amount of money the company had earned that year.*

bor·der (bôr′dər), NOUN. the side, edge, or boundary of anything, or the part near it: *We camped near the Mexican border.*

boul·der (bōl′dər), NOUN. a large rock, rounded or worn down by the action of water and weather.

bound (bound), VERB. the past tense of **bind;** tied together; fastened: *She bound the package with string.*

brag (brag), VERB. to speak too highly of yourself, what you have, or what you do; boast: *You're a good athlete, but don't brag about it!*

brand (brand), VERB. to mark by burning the skin with a hot iron: *brand the cows.*

bri·dle (brī′dl), NOUN. the part of a harness that fits around a horse's head, including the bit and reins: *My father bought two new bridles for our horses.*

bris·tle (bris′əl), VERB. to stand up straight: *The dog growled, and its hair bristled.* ❑ VERB **bris·tles, bris·tled, bris·tling.**

bristled

Cc

cal·en·dar (kal′ən dər), NOUN. a chart showing the months, weeks, and days of the year. A calendar shows the day of the week on which each day of the month falls.

calf (kaf), NOUN. a young cow or bull: *The calves were only two hours old.* ❑ PLURAL **calves.**

cal·i·co (kal′ə kō), NOUN. a cotton cloth that usually has colored patterns printed on one side: *Her dress was made of pink calico.* ❑ PLURAL **cal·i·coes** or **cal·i·cos.**

cal·lig·ra·phy (kə lig′rə fē), NOUN. the art or practice of beautiful handwriting. You need a special kind of pen or brush to do calligraphy.

can·yon (kan′yən), NOUN. a narrow valley with high, steep sides, usually with a stream at the bottom: *The canyon was so deep that I couldn't see the bottom.*

car·riage (kar′ij), NOUN. a light, four-wheeled vehicle, often having a top that can be folded down. Some carriages are pulled by horses and are used to carry people.

cat·a·log (kat′l og), NOUN. a list. A library usually has a catalog of its books, arranged in alphabetical order. Many companies print catalogs showing pictures and prices of the things that they have to sell.

cau·tious (ko′shəs), ADJECTIVE. very careful to avoid danger: *Cautious drivers obey the speed limits.*

ca·vy (kā′vē), NOUN. any of a family of South American rodents. The best known cavy is the guinea pig. ❑ PLURAL **ca·vies.**

cel·e·brate (sel′ə brāt), VERB. to do something special in honor of a special person or day: *Americans celebrate many different holidays.* ❑ VERB **cel·e·brates, cel·e·brat·ed, cel·e·brat·ing.**

chain mail (chān māl), (long ago) a kind of flexible armor, made of metal rings linked together. **–chain-mail,** ADJECTIVE.

chant (chant), VERB. to sing a song in which several words or syllables are sung in one tone: *The priest was chanting a prayer.* ❑ VERB **chants, chant·ed, chant·ing.**

chap·e·ron or **chap·e·rone** (shap′ə rōn′), NOUN. a person, especially a married or an older woman, who accompanies a young unmarried woman in public for the sake of her safety and reputation: *When my great-grandmother was a teenager, she was not allowed to go shopping without her two aunts, who were her chaperones.* ❑ VERB **chap·e·rones, chap·e·roned, chap·e·ron·ing.**

char (chär), VERB. to burn enough to blacken; scorch: *After the fire a carpenter replaced the badly charred floor.* ❑ VERB **chars, charred, char·ring.**

char·ac·ter (kar′ik tər), NOUN.
1 personality; moral strength: *He had to judge the character of the witness.*
2 a person or animal in a play, poem, story, book, or movie.
3 a letter, number, mark, or sign: *This Korean character means* child.

char·ac·ter·is·tic (kar′ik tə ris′tik), NOUN. a typical quality or feature; whatever distinguishes one person or thing from others: *A deer's antlers are its most noticeable characteristic.*

char·mer (chärm′ər), NOUN. one who guides or controls as if by magic: *Snake charmers sat on the floor and made the snakes move.*

chirp (chėrp), VERB. to make a short, sharp sound, as do some small birds and insects: *A sparrow started to chirp outside my window.*

chit (chit), NOUN. a signed note or ticket for a purchase, a meal, etc., that is to be paid for later: *The worker submitted a chit so that he would be paid for his work.*

choc·o·late (chok′lit or chok′ə lit), NOUN. a candy made from roasted and ground cacao beans and sugar.

cinch (sinch), NOUN. a strong strap for fastening a saddle or pack on a horse: *She tightened the cinches on her horse's saddle before she went riding.* ❑ PLURAL **cinch·es.**

cin·ders (sin′dərz), NOUN PLURAL. wood or coal partly burned but no longer flaming. Cinders are made up of larger and coarser pieces than ashes are.

cir·cuit (sėr′kit), NOUN. the complete path over which an electric current flows. *He needed to add two batteries to complete the circuits.*

a	hat	ė	term	ô	order	ch	child	⎧ a in about
ā	age	i	it	oi	oil	ng	long	e in taken
ä	far	ī	ice	ou	out	sh	she	ə⎨ i in pencil
â	care	o	hot	u	cup	th	thin	o in lemon
e	let	ō	open	ů	put	ŦH	then	⎩ u in circus
ē	equal	ò	saw	ü	rule	zh	measure	

cir·cu·late (sėr′kyə lāt), VERB. to go around or to send around: *Open windows allowed air to circulate through the building. A memo from the principal is circulating throughout our school.* ❏ VERB **cir·cu·lates, cir·cu·lat·ed, cir·cu·lat·ing.**

circulating library (sėr′kyə lāt ing li′brer′ē), library whose books can be rented or borrowed.

cit·i·zen·ship (sit′ə zən ship *or* sit′ə sən ship), NOUN. the quality of an individual's responsibility or contribution to his community; social conduct: *Mark showed good citizenship by picking up trash in the park.*

civ·il (siv′əl), ADJECTIVE. of the government, state, or nation: *Police departments are civil institutions that protect citizens.*

coax (kōks), VERB. to persuade a person or animal to do something by using gentle words and kindness: *She coaxed me into letting her use my bike.* ❏ VERB **coax·es, coaxed, coax·ing.**

co·bra (kō′brə), NOUN. any of several very poisonous snakes of Asia and Africa. When excited, a cobra flattens its neck so that its head seems to have a hood. ❏ PLURAL **co·bras.**

coil (koil), VERB. to wind around and around, forming a pile, a tube, or a curl: *The wire spring was tightly coiled.* ❏ VERB **coils, coiled, coil·ing.**

cold-blood·ed (kōld′blud′id), ADJECTIVE. having blood that is about the same temperature as the air or water around the animal. The blood of such animals is colder in winter than in summer. Turtles, snakes, and many other animals are cold-blooded; birds and mammals are warm-blooded. **–cold′-blood′ed·ly,** ADVERB. **–cold′-blood′ed·ness,** NOUN.

colt (kōlt), NOUN. a young, male horse, donkey, or zebra. A male horse is a colt until it is four or five years old.

comb (kōm), NOUN. the thick, red, fleshy piece on the top of the head of chickens and some other fowl: *I recognized the chicken by the comb on its head.*

com·mer·cial (kə mėr′shəl), ADJECTIVE. of or about trade or business: *My uncle owns a store and several other commercial establishments.*

com·mis·sion (kə mish′ən), NOUN. group of people appointed or elected with authority to do certain things: *A commission was appointed to investigate the disappearance of the statue of the town's founder.*

com·mu·ni·cate (kə myü′nə kāt), VERB. to give or exchange information or news: *When my brother is away at school, I communicate with him by e-mail.* ❏ VERB **com·mu·ni·cates, com·mu·ni·cat·ed, com·mu·ni·cat·ing.**

con·duc·tor (kən duk′tər), NOUN. director of an orchestra, chorus, etc.: *The conductor pointed his baton at the violin section.*

con·fi·den·tial (kon′fə den′shəl), ADJECTIVE. told or written as a secret: a confidential report. **–con′fi·den′ti·al′i·ty,** NOUN. **–con·fi·den·tially,** ADVERB.

con·sec·u·tive (kən sek′yə tiv), ADJECTIVE. following one right after another; successive: *Monday, Tuesday, and Wednesday are consecutive days of the week.* **–con·sec·u·tive·ly,** ADVERB. **–con·sec·u·tive·ness,** NOUN.

con·ser·va·tion·ist (kon′sər vā′shə nist), NOUN. someone who wants to preserve and protect the forests, rivers, and other natural resources of a country: *The conservationist raised money to help protect the rainforest.*

con·sid·er (kən sid′ər), VERB. to think about something in order to decide: *I was considering the problem.* ❏ VERB **con·sid·ers, con·sid·ered, con·sid·er·ing.**

con·ti·nent (kon′tə nənt), NOUN. one of the seven great masses of land on the Earth. The continents are North America, South America, Europe, Africa, Asia, Australia, and Antarctica: *We flew to the continent of Asia last summer.*

con·trap·tion (kən trap′shən), NOUN. odd, complicated device or gadget; contrivance: *She built several contraptions to scare rabbits out of her garden.*

con·ver·sa·tion (kon′vər sā′shən), NOUN. friendly talk; exchange of thoughts by talking informally together: *Dena and I had a conversation about what we planned to do over the weekend.*

con·vince (kən vins′), VERB. to make someone believe something: *The mistakes she made convinced me that she had not studied her lesson.* ❑ VERB **con·vinc·es, con·vinced, con·vinc·ing.**

co·ral (kôr′əl), NOUN. a hard substance formed from the skeletons of tiny sea animals. These animals live in large colonies.

cord (kôrd), NOUN.
1 a thick string; very thin rope: *He tied the package with a cord.*
2 a unit for measuring cut wood. A pile of wood 4 feet wide, 4 feet high, and 8 feet long is a cord.

cor·ner·stone (kôr′nər stōn′), NOUN. a stone built into the corner of a building as its formal beginning. Cornerstones are often marked with important information, such as the name of the builder and the date of completion.

corn·meal (kôrn′mēl′), NOUN. coarsely ground dried corn: *We made bread with cornmeal.*

cor·ral (kə ral′), NOUN. a fenced-in place for keeping horses, cattle, and other animals.

corral

coun·ter·clock·wise (koun′tər klok′wīz′), ADVERB OR ADJECTIVE. in the direction opposite to that in which the hands of a clock go.

cou·ple (kup′əl), NOUN. a man and woman who are married, engaged, or dance partners.

cou·ra·geous (kə rā′jəs), ADJECTIVE. brave; fearless. **—cou·ra′geous·ly,** ADVERB.

court·room (kôrt′rüm′), NOUN. a room for holding trials.

crank (krangk), NOUN. a part or handle connected to a machine, that you turn in a circle to set the machine in motion: *I turned the crank of the pencil sharpener.*

cra·ter (krā′tər), NOUN. a hole in the ground shaped like a bowl: *These craters were made by meteorites.*

cross-leg·ged (kròs′leg′id *or* kròs′legd), ADJECTIVE. with one leg over the other and the knees crossed: *The class sat cross-legged on the floor.*

crouch (krouch), VERB. to stoop over with the legs bent: *The cat crouched in the corner, waiting for the mouse to come out of its hole.* ❑ VERB **crouch·es, crouched, crouch·ing.**

a	hat	ė	term	ô	order	ch	child	ə	a in about
ā	age	i	it	oi	oil	ng	long		e in taken
ä	far	ī	ice	ou	out	sh	she		i in pencil
â	care	o	hot	u	cup	th	thin		o in lemon
e	let	ō	open	ù	put	ŦH	then		u in circus
ē	equal	ò	saw	ü	rule	zh	measure		

cur·rent (kėr′ənt),

1 NOUN. a flow or stream of water, electricity, air, or any fluid: *The current swept the stick down the river. The current went off when the storm hit.*
2 ADJECTIVE. of or about the present time.

Dd

dan·ger·ous (dān′jər əs), ADJECTIVE. not safe; likely to harm you: *Shooting off firecrackers is dangerous.* **–dan′ger·ous·ly,** ADVERB.

decimal point (des′ə məl point), a period placed before a decimal fraction, as in 2.03 or .623.

de·duce (di düs′), VERB. to reach a conclusion by reasoning; infer: *I deduced from your lack of appetite what had happened to the cookies.* ❑ VERB **de·duc·es, de·duced, de·duc·ing. –de·duc′i·ble,** ADJECTIVE.

de·fend·ant (di fen′dənt), NOUN. person accused or sued in a court of law: *The defendant is charged with theft.*

defense mechanism (di fens′ mek′ə niz′əm), any physical feature that protects a plant or animal from predators or other dangers. A turtle's shell is a defense mechanism.

def·i·nite·ly (def′ə nit lē), ADVERB. certainly: *I am definitely not going.*

de·lib·er·ate·ly (di lib′ər it lē), ADVERB. in a way or manner that is carefully thought out beforehand, made or done on purpose, or intended: *He deliberately lied when he made that excuse.* ❑ VERB **de·lib·er·ates, de·lib·er·at·ed, de·lib·er·at·ing. –de·lib·er·ate,** ADJECTIVE. **–de·lib′er·ate·ness,** NOUN.

de·pend·a·ble (di pen′də bəl), ADJECTIVE. reliable; trustworthy: *My friend works hard and is dependable.* **–de·pend·a·bil′i·ty,** NOUN.

de·pot (dē′pō), NOUN. a railroad or bus station.

de·scend·ant or **de·scend·ent** (di sen′dənt), NOUN. someone born of a certain family or group: *a descendant of the Pilgrims.*

dia·mond (dī′mənd), NOUN. (in baseball) the area inside the square formed by home plate and the three bases; infield.

dig·it (dij′it), NOUN. any of the figures 0, 1, 2, 3, 4, 5, 6, 7, 8, 9. Sometimes 0 is not called a digit: *What are the last four digits of your telephone number?*

dis·crim·i·na·tion (dis krim′ə nā′shən), NOUN. the act of showing an unfair difference in your treatment of people or groups: *Racial discrimination in hiring is against the law.*

dis·guise (dis gīz′),

1 VERB. to hide what something really is; make something seem like something else: *I will disguise myself as a gorilla for the costume party.*
2 NOUN. the clothes or actions used to hide or deceive.

❑ VERB **dis·guis·es, dis·guised, dis·guis·ing.**

dis·pos·a·ble (dis pō′zə bəl), ADJECTIVE. made or meant to be thrown away after use: *disposable diapers, disposable cups.*

dis·pute (dis pyüt′), NOUN. an angry argument or quarrel: *There is a dispute over where to build the new school.*

dis·tinc·tive (dis tingk′tiv), ADJECTIVE. clearly showing a difference from others; special: *Police officers wear a distinctive uniform.*

di·ur·nal (dī ėr′nl), ADJECTIVE. active in the daytime: *Butterflies are diurnal.* **–di·ur′nal·ly,** ADVERB.

do·mes·tic (də mas′tik), ADJECTIVE. living with or cared for by human beings; not wild; tame. Horses, dogs, cats, cows, and pigs are **domestic animals.**

dough (dō), NOUN. a soft, thick mixture of flour, liquid, and other things from which bread, biscuits, cake, and pie crust are made.

dow•ry (dou′rē), NOUN. money or property that a woman brings to the man she marries: *Caroline gave her husband a chest of drawers as her dowry.* ❏ PLURAL **dow•ries.**

dream•er (drē′mər), NOUN. someone who lives in a world of imagination and daydreams.

drift (drift), VERB. to go along without knowing or caring where you are going: *Some had a purpose in life, but she just drifted.* ❏ VERB **drifts, drift•ed, drift•ing. –drift′er,** NOUN.

dug•out (dug′out′), NOUN. a rough shelter or dwelling formed by digging into the side of a hill or trench.

dy•na•mite (dī′nə mīt), NOUN. a powerful explosive made of nitroglycerin mixed with an absorbent material and pressed into round sticks. It is used in blasting rock, tree stumps, etc.: *The workers used dynamite to blast through the mountain.* ❏ VERB **dy•na•mites, dy•na•mit•ed, dy•na•mit•ing. –dy′na•mit′er,** NOUN.

Ee

eaves•drop (ēvz′drop′), VERB. to listen to talk you are not supposed to hear; listen secretly to a private conversation: *I caught her eavesdropping on our conversation.* ❏ VERB **eaves•drops, eaves•dropped, eaves•drop•ping. –eaves′drop′per,** NOUN.

e•co•sys•tem (ē′kō sis′təm *or* ek′ō sis′təm), NOUN. a physical environment with its community of living things, and their relationship with each other. Ecosystems may be lakes, deserts, and so on.

e•lec•tric•i•ty (i lek′tris′ə tē), NOUN. a form of energy that can produce light, heat, or motion. Electricity is produced by machines called generators, by batteries, and by solar cells.

em•bar•rass•ment (em bar′əs mənt), NOUN. shame; an uneasy feeling: *He blushed in embarrassment at such a silly mistake.*

em•bed (em bed′), VERB. to stick something firmly into something else: *Precious stones are often found embedded in rock.* ❏ VERB **em•beds, em•bed•ded, em•bed•ding.**

em•pha•size (em′fə sīz), VERB. to give extra force to in speaking: *He emphasized her name as he read the list of winners.* ❏ VERB **em•pha•siz•es, em•pha•sized, em•pha•siz•ing.**

en•cour•age (en kėr′ij), VERB. to give someone courage or confidence; urge on: *We enjoy encouraging our team with loud cheers.* ❏ VERB **en•cour•ag•es, en•cour•aged, en•cour•ag•ing.**

en•er•get•ic (en′ər jet′ik), ADJECTIVE. full of energy; active; vigorous: *I feel energetic in the morning.* **–en′er•get′i•cal•ly,** ADVERB.

en•gi•neer (en′jə nir′), NOUN. an expert in building or managing engines, machines, roads, bridges, buildings, electrical systems, and so on.

en•gulf (en gulf′), VERB. to swallow up; overwhelm: *We saw the wave engulf the small island.* **–en•gulf′ment,** NOUN.

es•cort (e skôrt′), VERB. to go with as a person or group of persons to give protection to or to show honor, etc.: *Three police cars escorted the governor's limousine in the parade.*

a	hat	ė	term	ô	order	ch	child		a in about
ā	age	i	it	oi	oil	ng	long		e in taken
ä	far	ī	ice	ou	out	sh	she	ə {	i in pencil
â	care	o	hot	u	cup	th	thin		o in lemon
e	let	ō	open	ù	put	₮H	then		u in circus
ē	equal	ò	saw	ü	rule	zh	measure		

ev·i·dence (ev′ə dəns), NOUN. anything that shows what has happened; facts; proof: *The evidence showed that he had caused the accident.*

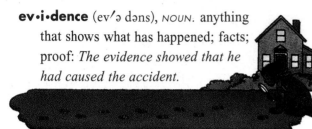

evidence

ex·pe·di·tion (ek′spə dish′ ən), NOUN. journey for some special purpose, such as exploration, scientific study, or for military puposes: *The scientists went on an expedition to study mountain lions.*

ex·per·i·ment (ek sper′ə mənt), NOUN. a carefully planned trial or test to find out something: *We made an experiment to learn the weight of the air in a basketball.*

ex·per·i·men·tal (ek sper′ə men′tl), ADJECTIVE. still being tested or tried: *He saw an experimental car at the auto show.*

Ff

fare·well (fâr′wel′), NOUN. good wishes when saying good-by: *We said our farewells at the station.*

fierce (firs), ADJECTIVE. wild and frightening; dangerous: *The hunter was attacked by a fierce lion.* ❏ ADJECTIVE **fierc·er, fierc·est.**

fig·ure (fig′yər), NOUN.
1 a symbol for a number. 1, 2, 3, 4, and so on, are figures.
2 a form or shape: *In the darkness she saw dim figures moving.*

fil·a·ment (fil′ə mənt) NOUN. a very fine thread; very slender, threadlike part. The wire that gives off light in a light bulb is a filament.

fire·break (fir′brāk′), NOUN. a strip of cleared or plowed land created to prevent the spreading of a forest fire or a prairie fire: *After Pa built our sod house, he dug a firebreak around it.*

flap·jack (flap′jak′), NOUN. a flat, round kind of bread made of liquid batter and fried in a pan; pancake: *I made flapjacks for breakfast.*

flash·back (flash′bak′), NOUN. a break in the continuous series of events of a novel, motion picture, etc., to introduce some earlier event or scene: *The grandfather character had several flashbacks of when he was a young boy.*

flip·per (flip′ər), NOUN. one of the broad, flat body parts used for swimming by animals such as seals and walruses: *The dolphin splashed the water with its flippers.*

floe (flō), NOUN. field or sheet of floating ice: *Two polar bears were sleeping when the floe broke, and each floated away.*

flung (flung), VERB. the past tense of **fling;** threw with force: *I flung my coat on the chair.*

fond (fond), ADJECTIVE. loving or liking: *She gave her daughter a fond look.* **–fond′ly,** ADVERB.

forge (fôrj), NOUN. a blacksmith's shop.

for·tune (fôr′chən), NOUN. a great deal of money or property; riches; wealth: *The family made a fortune in oil.*

frag·ile (fraj′əl), ADJECTIVE. easily broken, damaged, or destroyed; delicate; frail: *Be careful; that thin glass is fragile.* **–frag′ile·ly,** ADVERB. **–fra·gil′i·ty,** NOUN.

fright·ful (frit′fəl), ADJECTIVE. causing fear or terror: *Being lost in the forest was a frightful experience.* **–fright′ful·ly,** ADVERB. **–fright′ful·ness,** NOUN.

fur·i·ous·ly (fyur′ē əs lē), ADVERB. done with great energy, speed, or intensity; wildly: *The dog ran furiously, but couldn't catch the rabbit.*

fu·ture (fyü′chər), NOUN. all time to come; what is to come; what will be: *You cannot change the past, but you can do better in the future.*

Gg

gal·ler·y (gal′ər ē), NOUN. room or building used to show collections of pictures and statues: *We walked through the galleries and saw many famous paintings.* ❑ PLURAL **gal·ler·ies.**

gal·lop (gal′əp), NOUN. the fastest gait of a horse or of many other four-footed animals. In a gallop, all four feet are off the ground at the same time in each leap. *The horse moved in a gallop across the field.*

gau·cho (gou′chō), NOUN. cowboy in the southern plains of South America, usually of mixed Spanish and American Indian descent: *The gauchos rounded up the cattle and put them back in the corral.* ❑ PLURAL **gau·chos.**

gen·e·rate (jen′ə rāt′), VERB. to cause to be; bring into being; produce: *The team generated several good ideas.* ❑ VERB **gen·e·rat·es, gen·e·rat·ed, gen·e·rat·ing.**

ge·nus (jē′nəs), NOUN. a group of related living things. Wolves, coyotes, and dogs belong to the same genus. ❑ PLURAL **ge·nus·es** or **gen·er·a** (jen′ər ə).

gla·cier (glā′shər), NOUN. a great mass of ice moving very slowly down a mountain or along a valley, or spreading very slowly over a land area. Glaciers are formed from snow on high ground wherever winter snowfall exceeds summer melting for many years.

glimpse (glimps), NOUN. a very quick look: *I caught a glimpse of the falls as our train went by.*

gnaw (no′), VERB. to bite at and wear away: *A mouse was gnawing right through the cover of this box.* ❑ VERB **gnaws, gnawed, gnaw·ing.**

gourd (gôrd), NOUN. any of various fleshy fruits that grow on vines and are related to squash. A gourd has a hard rind and is often dried and hollowed out for use as a cup, bowl, or other utensil. **−gourd′like′,** ADJECTIVE.

grad·u·al·ly (graj′ü ə lē), ADVERB. happening slowly; by small steps or degrees: *She gradually learned how to ride a bike.*

graph (graf), NOUN. a line or drawing that shows information, especially how one quantity is related to another quantity.

grav·i·ty (grav′ə tē), NOUN. the natural force that causes objects to move or tend to move toward the center of the Earth. Gravity causes objects to have weight. *Gravity caused the book to fall to the floor.*

griz·zly (griz′lē), NOUN. a very large, fierce, brownish gray bear of western North America; **grizzly bear.** ❑ PLURAL **griz·zlies.**

ground·er (groun′dər), NOUN. (in baseball) a batted ball that bounces or rolls along the ground; ground ball: *He hit four grounders during the game.*

guilt·y (gil′tē), ADJECTIVE. having done something wrong; deserving to be blamed and punished: *The jury found her guilty.*

guinea pig, any of about 20 kinds of small, fat, harmless rodents with short ears and either short tails or no tail. Guinea pigs make good pets and are often used for laboratory experiments.

Hh

hab·i·tat (hab′ə tat), NOUN. the particular kind of place where a living thing is naturally found: *The jungle is the habitat of monkeys.*

hag·gle (hag′əl), VERB. to dispute, especially about a price or the terms of a bargain: *I watched my brother haggle with the hat salesman.* ❑ VERB **hag·gles, hag·gled, hag·gling. −hag′gler,** NOUN.

a	hat	ė	term	ô	order	ch	child	(a in about
ā	age	i	it	oi	oil	ng	long	e in taken
ä	far	ī	ice	ou	out	sh	she	ə ⟨ i in pencil
â	care	o	hot	u	cup	th	thin	o in lemon
e	let	ō	open	ů	put	ŦH	then	(u in circus
ē	equal	ò	saw	ü	rule	zh	measure	

hand·ker·chief (hang′kər chif), NOUN. a soft, usually square piece of cloth used for wiping your nose, face, or hands.

hand·made (hand′mād′), ADJECTIVE. made by hand, not by machine: *handmade pottery.*

harsh (härsh), ADJECTIVE. rough to the touch, taste, eye, or ear: *His voice is the harshest I've ever heard.* ❏ ADJECTIVE **harsh·er, harsh·est.**

hatch·ling (hach′ling), NOUN. recently hatched animal: *The hatchling was so young that it couldn't open its eyes yet.*

ha·zy (hā′zē), ADJECTIVE. full of haze; misty; smoky: *a hazy sky.* ❏ ADJECTIVE **ha·zi·er, ha·zi·est. −ha′zi·ly,** ADVERB. **−ha′zi·ness,** NOUN.

herd (hėrd), NOUN. group of animals of one kind, especially large animals: *a herd of cows.*

her·o (hir′ō), NOUN. someone admired for his or her bravery, great deeds, or noble qualities. ❏ PLURAL **her·oes.**

hol·ler (hol′ər), VERB. to cry or shout loudly: *"Come quick," she hollered from the yard.* ❏ VERB **hol·lers, hol·lered, hol·ler·ing.**

home·stead·er (hōm′sted′ər), NOUN. a settler granted public land to farm by the United States government. *Homesteaders were common in the mid-1800s.*

ho·ri·zon (hə rī′zn), NOUN. the line where earth and sky seem to meet. You cannot see beyond the horizon.

hus·ky or **Hus·ky** (hus′kē), NOUN. a strong, medium-sized dog used to pull sleds in arctic regions. A husky usually has a thick coat and a bushy tail. ❏ PLURAL **hus·kies** or **Hus·kies.**

hy·brid (hī′brid), ADJECTIVE. bred from two different kinds or species: *A mule is a hybrid animal produced from a horse and a donkey.*

Ii

il·lu·mi·nate (i lü′mə nāt), VERB. to light up; make bright: *The room was illuminated by four large lamps.* (VERB **il·lu·mi·nates, il·lu·mi·nat·ed, il·lu·mi·nat·ing, -il·lu′mi·na′tive,** ADJECTIVE. **−il·lu′mi·nat′tor,** NOUN.

im·i·ta·tion (im′ə tā′shən), NOUN. something that looks, acts, sounds, smells, or tastes like something else: *He does a good imitation of a rooster crowing.*

im·mi·grant (im′ə grənt), NOUN. someone who comes into a country or region to live there: *Canada has many immigrants from Europe.*

im·pa·tient (im pā′shənt), ADJECTIVE. not patient; not willing to put up with delay, annoyance, pain, or bother: *He is impatient with his little brother's whining.* **−im·pa′tient·ly,** ADVERB.

im·press (im pres′), VERB. to have a strong effect on someone's mind or feelings: *The policewoman's bravery impressed us all.* ❏ VERB **im·press·es, im·pressed, im·press·ing.**

im·print (im′print), NOUN. a mark made by something pressed on a soft surface: *Your foot made an imprint in the sand.*

in·can·des·cent (in′kən des′nt), ADJECTIVE. glowing with heat; red-hot or white-hot: *The incandescent light bulb lit up the room.*

in·cred·i·ble (in kred′ə bəl), ADJECTIVE. impossible to believe; unbelievable: *The hurricane's power was incredible.* **−in·cred′i·bly,** ADVERB.

in·flu·ence (in′flü əns), VERB. to have some power or influence on: *What we read influenced our thinking.* ❏ VERB **in·flu·enc·es, in·flu·enced, in·flu·enc·ing.**

i·ni·tial (i nish′əl), NOUN. the first letter of a word or name: *The initials U.S. stand for United States.*

in·spire (in spīr′), VERB. to cause someone to do something good; have a positive influence on: *His poor grade inspired him to study harder for the next test.* ❑ VERB **in·spires, in·spired, in·spir·ing.**

in·stinc·tive·ly (in stingk′tiv lē), ADVERB. in a way or manner that is born in an animal or person, not learned: *Spiders instinctively spin webs.*

in·stru·ment (in′strə mənt), NOUN. a device for producing musical sounds: *wind instruments, stringed instruments. A violin, cello, and piano were the instruments in the trio.*

In·u·it (in′ü it *or* in′yü it), ADJECTIVE. of or about the people or the language of the people living mainly in the arctic regions of Canada and Greenland: *an Inuit word.*

in·ven·tion (in ven′shən), NOUN. something new that someone makes or thinks of: *Computers are twentieth-century inventions.*

in·ves·ti·ga·tion (in ves′tə gā′shən), NOUN. a careful search; detailed or careful examination: *An investigation of the accident by the police put the blame on the drivers of both cars.*

in·volve (in volv′), VERB. to take up the attention of; absorb: *She was involved in working out a puzzle.* ❑ VERB **in·volves, in·volved, in·volv·ing. −in·volve′ment,** NOUN.

Jj

jeal·ous (jel′əs), ADJECTIVE. unhappy because someone has something that you want to have: *He is jealous of his brother's good grades.*

joint·ed (join′tid), ADJECTIVE. having places at which two things or parts are joined together: *Crabs have jointed legs.*

Ll

lame (lām), ADJECTIVE. not able to walk properly; having a hurt leg or foot: *The dog limps because he has been lame since birth.* ★ **Lame** is often considered offensive when used about people.

lat·i·tude (lat′ə tüd), NOUN. distance north or south of the equator, measured in degrees. A degree of latitude is about 69 miles (111 kilometers).

laun·dry (lȯn′drē), NOUN. clothes, towels, and so on, that have been washed or need to be washed.

laundry

li·brar·i·an (lī brer′ē ən), NOUN. someone who directs or helps to manage a library: *Three librarians work in our school library.*

liv·er·wurst (liv′ər wèrst′), NOUN. sausage, mostly liver: *We ate liverwurst for lunch.*

liz·ard (liz′ərd), NOUN. a reptile that usually has scaly skin, four legs, and a narrow body. Iguanas, chameleons, and horned toads are lizards.

lo·co·mo·tive (lō′kə mō′tiv), NOUN. engine that moves from place to place under its own power, used to pull railroad trains: *The locomotive pulled the train through the tunnel and around the mountain.*

log·ging (lȯ′ging), NOUN. work of cutting down trees, sawing them into logs, and moving the logs out of the forest: *My uncle's logging company worked in forests in northern Michigan.* ❑ VERB **logs, logged, log·ging.**

lum·ber·jack (lum′bər jak′), NOUN. person whose work is cutting down trees and sending the logs to the sawmill; woodsman; logger: *The lumberjacks worked all day to clear the forest.*

a	hat	ė	term	ô	order	ch	child		a in about
ā	age	i	it	oi	oil	ng	long		e in taken
ä	far	ī	ice	ou	out	sh	she	ə {	i in pencil
â	care	o	hot	u	cup	th	thin		o in lemon
e	let	ō	open	ù	put	ŦH	then		u in circus
ē	equal	ȯ	saw	ü	rule	zh	measure		

Mm

mal·let (mal′it), NOUN. a hammer with a large head. One kind of mallet is used to play musical instruments.

mam·mal (mam′əl), NOUN. one of a large group of warm-blooded animals with backbones, usually having hair. Human beings, cattle, dogs, cats, and whales are all mammals.

mane (mān), NOUN. the long, heavy hair on the back of the neck of a horse, or around the face and neck of a male lion: *The lions′ manes are beautiful.*

marsh (märsh), NOUN. low, soft land covered at times by water, where grasses and reeds but not trees grow. ❑ PLURAL **marsh·es.**

mas·sive (mas′iv), ADJECTIVE. big and heavy; bulky: *A massive boulder blocked the road.*

meas·ure (mezh′ər), NOUN.
1 a size or amount: *The man at the clothing store asked for the measure of my waistline.*
2 a unit of rhythm in music, containing one or more notes or a rest. Measures are also called **bars.**

mel·o·dy (mel′ə dē), NOUN. a pleasing or easily remembered series of musical notes; tune. Music has melody, harmony, and rhythm.

mem·o·ry (mem′ər ē), NOUN. a person, thing, or event that you can remember: *I have many pleasant memories from my childhood.*
❑ PLURAL **mem·or·ies.**

mer·chan·dise (mėr′chən dīz *or* mėr′chən dīs), NOUN. goods for sale; articles bought and sold: *Most drugstores sell games, books, pencils, and other sorts of merchandise besides medicines.*
❑ VERB **mer·chan·dis·es, mer·chan·dised, mer·chan·dis·ing. —mer′chan·dis′er,** NOUN.

me·te·or·ite (mē′tē ə rīt′), NOUN. mass of stone or metal that has fallen from outer space to a planet or moon; a fallen meteor: *Scientists believe the craters were caused by meteorites.*

me·te·or·oid (mē′tē ə roid′), NOUN. mass of stone or metal that travels through space and will become a meteor if it enters a planet′s atmosphere: *The meteoroids hurtled toward Jupiter.*

me·thod·i·cal·ly (mə thod′ə kə lē), ADVERB. in a way or manner that is done according to a method; in an orderly or systematic way: *She methodically examined the fossils.*
—me·thod′i·cal, ADJECTIVE.
—me·thod′i·cal·ness, NOUN.

mi·cro·phone (mī′krə fōn), NOUN. an electrical device that makes your voice sound louder. Television and radio stations use microphones for broadcasting.

mis·er·y (miz′ər ē), NOUN. great unhappiness or suffering caused by being poor, worried, or in pain: *Think of the misery of having no home or friends.* ❑ PLURAL **mis·er·ies.**

mis·sion (mish′ən), NOUN. a center or headquarters for religious or social work: *The church set up a mission with a soup kitchen to help local homeless people.*

mon·goose (mong′güs), NOUN. any of several slender, flesh-eating mammals of Asia and Africa that resemble ferrets. Some types of mongooses are noted for their ability to kill cobras and other poisonous snakes.
❑ PLURAL **mon·goos·es.**

mon·i·tor (mon′ə tər), NOUN. any of several large, flesh-eating lizards of Africa, southern Asia, Australia, and the East Indies. The Komodo dragon is a type of monitor. A monitor has a long head and neck and is most often brown or black with yellow markings.

mus·cle (mus′əl), NOUN. a special bundle of tissue in the body of a person or animal which is made of fibers and moves some particular bone or part: *Feel the muscles in my arm!* ■ Another word that sounds like this is **mussel.**

mus•sel (mus′əl), NOUN. any of numerous shellfish that resemble clams. Sea mussels can be eaten: *When we took the boat out of the water, there was a mussel attached to the bottom of it.*
■ Another word that sounds like this is **muscle.**

mys•ter•i•ous (mi stir′ē əs), ADJECTIVE. hard to explain or understand; full of mystery: *The mysterious call echoed across the lake.*

Nn

naugh•ty (no′tē), ADJECTIVE. bad; not behaving well: *The naughty child refused to pick up her toys.*

nav•i•gate (nav′ə gāt), VERB.
1 to sail, manage, or steer a ship, aircraft, or rocket: *It's difficult to navigate an airplane in stormy conditions.*
2 to sail on or over a sea or river: *Many steamboats used to navigate the Mississippi River.* ❏ VERB **nav•i•gates, nav•i•gat•ed, nav•i•gat•ing.**

no-hit•ter (nō′hit′ər), NOUN. a baseball game in which a pitcher gives up no base hits to the opposing team.

non•tox•ic (non′tok′sik), ADJECTIVE. not poisonous: *The label said that the crayons were nontoxic.*

nuz•zle (nuz′əl), VERB. to rub your nose against someone in a gentle, loving way: *The mother nuzzled her baby.* ❏ VERB **nuz•zles, nuz•zled, nuz•zling.**

Oo

oc•ca•sion (ə kā′zhən), NOUN. a special event: *The coronation was an impressive occasion.*

o•dom•e•ter (ō dom′ə tər), NOUN. device for measuring the distance a vehicle has gone, by recording the number of turns of a wheel. Every car has an odometer showing its total distance traveled.

or•ches•tra (ôr′kə strə), NOUN. a group of musicians playing stringed, brass, woodwind, and percussion instruments. An orchestra is usually led by a conductor. ❏ PLURAL **or•ches•tras.**

or•phan (ôr′fən), NOUN. child whose parents are dead; child whose father or mother is dead: *The orphans went to live with their aunt and uncle.*

Pp

pad•lock (pad′lok′), NOUN. a lock that can be put on and removed. It hangs by a curved bar, hinged at one end and snapped shut at the other.

par•a•pet (par′ə pet), NOUN. low wall or mound of stone, earth, etc., to protect soldiers: *The soldiers were hidden from view behind parapets.*

pat•ent (pat′nt), VERB. to get a patent for: *She patented her new invention.* ❏ VERB **pat•ents, pat•ent•ed, pat•ent•ing.**

ped•dle (ped′l), VERB. to carry things from place to place and sell them: *The salesman was peddling brushes from house to house.* ❏ VERB **ped•dles, ped•dled, ped•dling.**

pe•nin•su•la (pə nin′sə lə), NOUN. an area of land with water lying almost all the way around it. Florida is a peninsula. ❏ PLURAL **pe•nin•su•las.**

perch (pėrch), NOUN. a bar, branch, rod, and so on, that a bird can land on. ❏ PLURAL **perch•es.**

percussion instrument, a musical instrument that produces sound when a part of it is struck. The drums and the piano are percussion instruments.

per•form•er (pər fôr′mər), NOUN. someone who acts, plays, sings, or does tricks to entertain other people. Singers, dancers, and magicians are performers.

a	hat	ė	term	ô	order	ch	child	
ā	age	i	it	oi	oil	ng	long	a in about
ä	far	ī	ice	ou	out	sh	she	e in taken
â	care	o	hot	u	cup	th	thin	ə i in pencil
e	let	ō	open	ů	put	ŦH	then	o in lemon
ē	equal	ȯ	saw	ü	rule	zh	measure	u in circus

pic·to·graph (pik′tə graf), NOUN. a picture used as a sign or symbol: *That Chinese character developed from a pictograph.*

pier (pir), NOUN. structure supported on columns extending into the water, used as a walk or landing place for ships: *We walked out on the pier to get a closer look at the cruise ship that was arriving.*

placing-out, a system of caring for dependent children by placing them in private families rather than in orphanages.

plank·ton (plangk′tən), NOUN. the small living things that float or drift in water, especially at or near the surface: *I watched the plankton float around our rowboat.*

pla·teau (pla tō′), NOUN. a large, flat area in the mountains or high above sea level: *We climbed on top of the plateau so we could see farther.* ❏ PLURAL **pla·teaus** or **pla·teaux** (pla tōz′).

plat·form (plat′fôrm), NOUN. a raised level surface for people to stand or sit on: *There is a platform beside the track at the railroad station.*

plen·ti·ful (plen′ti fəl), ADJECTIVE. more than enough: *We had a plentiful supply of food.*

plunge (plunj), VERB. to throw yourself into something suddenly: *She plunged into the lake to save the drowning swimmer.* ❏ VERB **plung·es, plunged, plung·ing.**

plunged

poi·son (poi′zn), NOUN. anything that is very dangerous to your life or health if you swallow it or breathe it in. Arsenic and lead are poisons.

pol·ish (pol′ish), VERB. to make something smooth and shiny: *to polish wood, to polish silverware.*

pol·lu·tion (pə lü′shən), NOUN. the act or process of dirtying any part of the environment, especially with waste material: *Exhaust from cars causes air pollution.*

port of entry (pôrt uv *or* ov en′trē), a place where people and merchandise may enter legally into a country. ❏ PLURAL **ports of entry.**

post·er (pō′stər), NOUN. a large printed picture or message put up on a wall.

pot·ter·y (pot′ər ē), NOUN. pots, dishes, or vases made from clay and baked until they are hard.

prai·rie (prâr′ē), NOUN. a large area of level or rolling land with grass but few or no trees.

prea·ching (prēch′ing), NOUN. the act of speaking on a religious subject or delivering a sermon: *We heard preaching on the radio.* ❏ VERB **preaches, prea′cher, prea′ching. —prea′cher,** NOUN.

pred·a·tor (pred′ə tər), NOUN. an animal that lives by killing and eating other animals. Tigers, bears, hawks, and wolves are predators.

pres·ence (prez′ns), NOUN. the impression that a person makes on others; manner. Presence involves the way a person stands, walks, talks, and behaves: *The queen is a person of noble presence.*

prey (prā), NOUN. an animal that is hunted or seized for food by another animal: *Mice and birds are the prey of cats.* ❏ PLURAL **prey.**

prin·ci·pal (prin′sə pəl), NOUN. someone who is the head of a school.

print·shop (print′shop), NOUN. an establishment where books, magazines, newspapers, etc., are printed: *We had pamphlets printed at a printshop.*

priv·i·lege (priv′ə lij), NOUN. a special right, advantage, or favor that someone has: *My sister has the privilege of driving the family car.*

probe (prōb), NOUN. a spacecraft carrying scientific devices to record or report back information about planets or other objects in outer space: *lunar probes.*

pro·tec·tion (prə tek′shən), NOUN. the act of keeping someone or something safe from harm; defense: *We have a large dog for our protection.*

pro·to·type (prō′tə tīp), NOUN. the first or original type or model of anything that is designed or constructed: *We had to finish the prototype before the car could be built.*

pun·ish (pun′ish), VERB. to cause pain or unhappiness to someone who did something wrong: *Parents may punish children who don't behave.*

pur·chase (pėr′chəs), VERB. to buy something: *We purchased a new car.* ❏ VERB **pur·chas·es, pur·chased, pur·chas·ing.**

Qq

quar·ters (kwôr′tərz), NOUN PLURAL. a place to live or stay in: *My summer camp offers very comfortable quarters.*

Rr

ra·cial (rā′shəl), ADJECTIVE. of or about a race of people: *racial traits.*

rail·road (rāl′rōd′), NOUN. a road or track with two parallel steel rails on which the wheels of trains run.

rain (rān), NOUN. the fall of water in drops from the clouds: *The summer rains helped our crops.* ■ Another word that sounds like this is **rein.**

rai·sin (rā′zn), NOUN. a small, sweet, dried grape: *We ate raisins for a snack.*

ra·vine (rə vēn′), NOUN. a long, deep, narrow valley: *The rivers had worn ravines between the hills.*

re·cite (ri sīt′), VERB. to say something from memory, especially in front of an audience: *We recite poems in class each month.* ❏ VERB **re·cites, re·cit·ed, re·cit·ing.**

re·gion (rē′jən), NOUN. any place, space, or area: *Bighorn sheep are found in a mountainous region.*

re·hears·al (ri hėr′səl), NOUN. the act of rehearsing; process of preparing for a performance: *The rehearsal for the show was a disaster, but the actual performance was great.*

rein (rān), NOUN. Often, **reins,** PLURAL. a long, narrow strap fastened to a bridle or bit, used to guide and control an animal. ■ Another word that sounds like this is **rain.**

re·li·a·ble (ri lī′ə bəl), ADJECTIVE. able to be depended on: *Send her to the bank for the money; she is reliable and honest.*

re·mind·er (ri mīn′dər), NOUN. something to help you remember: *The note taped to my mirror is a reminder of things I need to do.*

rep·tile (rep′til), NOUN. one of a group of cold-blooded animals that have backbones and lungs and are usually covered with scales. Snakes, lizards, turtles, and dinosaurs are reptiles.

rep·u·ta·tion (rep′yə tā′shən), NOUN. what people think and say the character of someone or something is; character in the opinion of others; *My brother has an excellent reputation for being a fine policeman.*

res·cue (res′kyü), VERB. to save someone from danger, capture, or harm; free; deliver: *She rescued the man from drowning.* ❏ VERB **res·cues, res·cued, res·cu·ing.** —**res′cu·er,** NOUN.

re·source (ri sôrs′ or rē′sôrs), NOUN. a material that is useful or necessary for life. Land, water, minerals, and forests are **natural resources.**

a	hat	ė	term	ô	order	ch	child		a in about
ā	age	i	it	oi	oil	ng	long		e in taken
ä	far	ī	ice	ou	out	sh	she	ə {	i in pencil
â	care	o	hot	u	cup	th	thin		o in lemon
e	let	ō	open	ú	put	ᴛʜ	then		u in circus
ē	equal	ò	saw	ü	rule	zh	measure		

re·spon·si·ble (ri spon′sə bəl), ADJECTIVE. expected to take care of someone or something: *You are responsible for keeping your room cleaned up.*

rhythm (riŦH′əm), NOUN. any movement with a regular repetition of a beat, accent, rise and fall, or the like: *the rhythm of dancing, the rhythm of the tides.*

ridge (rij), NOUN. any raised narrow strip: *the ridges in plowed ground, the ridges on corduroy cloth.*

roam (rōm), VERB. to walk around with no special plan or aim; wander: *to roam through the fields.*

ro·dent (rōd′nt), NOUN. any of many mammals with large front teeth that are used for gnawing. Rats, mice, squirrels, and beavers are rodents.

ro·tate (rō′tāt), VERB. to move around a center or axis; turn in a circle; revolve. *The Earth rotates on its axis.* ❑ VERB **ro·tates, ro·tat·ed, ro·tat·ing.**

rum·ple (rum′pəl), VERB. to make something wrinkled, crumpled, or messy: *I accidentally rumpled my new shirt.* ❑ VERB **rum·ples, rum·pled, rum·pling.**

rush (rush), NOUN. a grasslike plant with a hollow stem that grows in wet soil or marshy places. The seats of chairs are sometimes made from the stems of rushes. ❑ PLURAL **rush·es.**

rust·y (rus′tē), ADJECTIVE. covered with rust; rusted: *Don't cut the apple with that rusty knife.*

S s

sac (sak), NOUN. a part like a bag inside an animal or plant, often one that holds liquids: *Some snakes have poison sacs.*

sad·dle·bag (sad′l bag′), NOUN. one of a pair of bags laid over an animal's back behind the saddle, or over the rear fender of a bicycle or motorcycle: *Emma and Brian filled the saddlebags with snacks and supplies before they set out for a trail ride.*

sand·pa·per (sand′pā′pər), NOUN. a strong paper with a layer of sand or similar substance glued on it, used for smoothing, cleaning, or polishing: *Adrian sanded the board with sandpaper in order to make it smooth.*

scene (sēn), NOUN. something to look at; view: *The white sailboats in the blue water made a pretty scene.*

scorn·ful·ly (skôrn′fəl lē), ADVERB. in a way or manner that shows contempt or mocking: *He looked scornfully at the girl who had broken his science project.* **–scorn′ful,** ADJECTIVE. **–scorn′ful·ness,** NOUN.

screen (skrēn), NOUN. wire woven together with small openings in between: *We have screens in our windows.*

script (skript), NOUN. writen letters, figures, characters, etc.; handwriting: *German script.*

scrounge (skrounj), VERB. to search about for what you can find that is useful: *I saw my brother scrounging material in the garage to build a model car.* ❑ VERB **scroung·es, scrounged, scroung·ing. –scroung′er,** NOUN.

scu·ba (skü′bə), NOUN. portable equipment used to breathe underwater, including tanks of compressed air, a mouthpiece with valves to regulate the flow of air, a face mask, fins, and so on.

scuba

scythe (sīⱦH), NOUN. a long, slightly curved blade on a long handle, for cutting grass, grain, etc.: *The farmer used a scythe to cut wheat.*

seed·ling (sēd′ling), NOUN. a young plant grown from a seed: *Our garden club planted seedlings in the city park on Saturday.*

Sem·i·nole (sem′ə nōl), NOUN. a member of a tribe of American Indians that settled in Florida in the 1700s. The Seminole now live in the Florida Everglades and in Oklahoma. ❑ PLURAL **Sem·i·nole** or **Sem·i·noles.**

shal·low (shal′ō), ADJECTIVE. not deep: *shallow water, a shallow dish, a shallow mind.*

sheep·ish·ly (shē′pish lē), ADVERB. in a way or manner which is awkwardly bashful or embarrassed: *He smiled sheepishly at his new teacher.* **—sheep′ish,** ADJECTIVE. **—sheep′ish·ness,** NOUN.

shiv·er (shiv′ər), VERB. to shake with cold, fear, or excitement: *I shivered in the cold wind.* ❑ VERB **shiv·ers, shiv·ered, shiv·er·ing.**

short·en·ing (shôrt′n ing), NOUN. butter, lard, vegetable oil, or other fat, used to make pastry, cake, etc., crisp or crumbly: *Maia added shortening to the pie-crust dough.*

singe (sinj), VERB. to burn a little; scorch: *A spark from the fireplace singed the rug.* ❑ VERB **sing·es, singed, singe·ing. —sing′er,** NOUN.

skep·ti·cal (skep′tə kəl), ADJECTIVE. of or like a skeptic; inclined to doubt; not believing easily: *He was skeptical when his sister told him she could walk on her hands.* **—skep′ti·cal·ly,** ADVERB.

skil·let (skil′it), NOUN. a shallow pan with a long handle, used for frying; frying pan: *Dad made pancakes in a skillet.*

skink (skingk), NOUN. any of a family of small, smooth-scaled lizards, often with short, weak legs. A skink may eat both plant and animal matter.

sledge (slej), NOUN. a heavy sled or sleigh, usually pulled by horses: *We rode a sledge through the deep snow.*

sledge·ham·mer (slej′ham′ər), NOUN. a large, heavy hammer, usually swung with both hands: *The construction worker used a sledgehammer to break down the old wall.*

smart (smärt), VERB. to feel or cause sharp pain: *The cut on her finger smarted when she got salt in it.* ❑ VERB **smarts, smart·ed, smart·ing.**

snare (snâr), NOUN. one of the strings of wire or gut stretched across the bottom of a snare drum: *The snare rattled as she struck the drum.*

snow·shoe (snō′shü′), NOUN. a light wooden frame with strips of leather stretched across it. Snowshoes are worn on your feet to keep you from sinking into deep, soft snow.

solar system, the sun and all the planets, satellites, comets, etc., that revolve around it.

soothe (süⱦH), VERB. to quiet or comfort someone or something: *After soothing the excited dog, I answered the front door.* ❑ VERB **soothes, soothed, sooth·ing.**

south·ern·most (suⱦH′ərn mōst), ADJECTIVE. farthest south: *We swam to the southernmost part of the lake.*

sou·ve·nir (sü′və nir′), NOUN. something given or kept as a reminder; keepsake: *She bought a pair of moccasins and a hat as souvenirs of her trip out West.*

sow[1] (sō), VERB. to scatter seed on the ground; plant seed in: *She sowed grass seed in the yard.* ❑ VERB **sows, sowed, sown** or **sowed, sow·ing. —sow′er,** NOUN.

a	hat	ė	term	ô	order	ch	child	⎧ a in about
ā	age	i	it	oi	oil	ng	long	⎪ e in taken
ä	far	ī	ice	ou	out	sh	she	ə⎨ i in pencil
â	care	o	hot	u	cup	th	thin	⎪ o in lemon
e	let	ō	open	ù	put	ⱦH	then	⎩ u in circus
ē	equal	ȯ	saw	ü	rule	zh	measure	

sow² (sou), *NOUN.* a fully grown female pig or guinea pig.

space·craft (spās′kraft′), *NOUN.* a vehicle used for flight in outer space; spaceship. ❏ *PLURAL* **space·craft.**

spe·cial·ist (spesh′ə list), *NOUN.* person who pursues one particular branch of study, business, etc. Heart specialists are doctors who treat diseases of the heart.

spe·cies (spē′shēz), *NOUN.* a group of related living things that have the same basic characteristics. ❏ *PLURAL* **spe·cies.**

sphere (sfir), *NOUN.* a round solid object; globe. Every point on the surface of a sphere is the same distance from the center. The sun, moon, Earth, and stars are spheres.

squat (skwät), *VERB.* to crouch on your heels: *He squatted on the grass watching a caterpillar.* ❏ *VERB* **squats, squat·ted, squat·ting.**

squinch (skwinch), *VERB.* to squeeze together; squint: *I squinched my eyes and tried to read the distant sign.*

stats (stats), *NOUN.* a short form of **statistics;** facts in the form of numbers.

sto·ry·tell·ing (stôr′ē tel′ing), *NOUN.* act or art of telling stories: *My uncle is famous for his storytelling.*

stringed in·stru·ment, a musical instrument having strings, played either with a bow or by plucking. The harp, violin, cello, and guitar are stringed instruments.

stroke¹ (strōk), *NOUN.*
   1 a sudden attack of illness, especially paralysis caused by injury to the brain when a blood vessel breaks or becomes blocked.
   2 a movement or mark made by a pen, pencil, or brush: *She writes with a heavy stroke.*

stroke² (strōk), *NOUN.* a gentle movement of the hand: *to brush away the crumbs with one stroke.*

sub·way (sub′wā′), *NOUN.* an underground electric railroad that runs beneath the surface of the streets in a city.

sug·gest (səg jest′ *or* sə jest′), *VERB.* to bring up an idea; propose: *She suggested a swim, and we all agreed.* ❏ *VERB* **sug·gests, sug·gest·ed, sug·gest·ing.**

sus·pect (sə spekt′), *VERB.* to believe that someone is guilty, false, or bad without proof: *The police suspected them of being thieves.* ❏ *VERB* **sus·pects, sus·pect·ed, sus·pect·ing.**

sus·pend (sə spend′), *VERB.* to hang something by fastening it to something above: *The lamp was suspended from the ceiling.* ❏ *VERB* **sus·pends, sus·pend·ed, sus·pend·ing.**

swamp (swämp), *NOUN.* wet, soft land: *The swamp near the woods has many wild animals living in it.*

sym·bol (sim′bəl), *NOUN.* an object, diagram, icon, and so on, that stands for or represents something else: *The olive branch is a symbol of peace. The marks +, −, ×, and ÷ are symbols for add, subtract, multiply, and divide.*

sym·pa·thet·i·cal·ly (sim′pə thet′ə klē), *ADVERB.* in a way or manner which shows kind feelings toward others; sympathizing: *I sympathetically hugged my upset friend.* **—sym′pa·thet′ic,** *ADJECTIVE.*

Tt

ta·ble·land (tā′bəl land′), *NOUN.* a high plain; plateau; table: *We climbed up to the tableland and looked out over the valley.*

ta·ma·le (tə mä′lē), *NOUN.* a Mexican food made of cornmeal and minced meat, seasoned with red peppers, wrapped in cornhusks, and roasted or steamed: *We made tamales for dinner.*

tan·gle (tang′gəl), VERB. to twist and twine together in a confused mass: *The kitten had tangled the ball of twine.* ❏ VERB **tan·gles, tan·gled, tan·gling.**

taunt (tȯnt), VERB. to make fun of someone by saying unkind things to him or her: *My classmates taunted me for being teacher's pet.* ❏ VERB **taunts, taunt·ed, taunt·ing.**

tease (tēz), VERB. to pester, annoy, or upset someone by jokes, questions, noises, and so on: *Stop teasing the dog!* ❏ VERB **teas·es, teased, teas·ing.**

tech·nique (tek nēk′), NOUN. a special method or system used to do something: *Please show me the technique you use to change a tire.* ❏ PLURAL **tech·niques.**

tel·e·graph (tel′ə graf), VERB. to send a coded message over wires by means of electricity: *Mother wants to telegraph congratulations to the bride and groom.*

tempt (tempt), VERB. to appeal strongly to; attract: *I was tempted by the candy.* **—tempt′a·ble,** ADJECTIVE. **—tempt′er,** NOUN.

ten·don (ten′dən), NOUN. a tough, strong band of tissue that joins a muscle to a bone: *I pulled a tendon when I was running.*

the·a·ter or **the·a·tre** (thē′ə tər), NOUN. place where plays are acted or movies are shown: *We saw an exciting movie at the theater last night.*

the·or·y (thē′ər ē), NOUN. an explanation of something, based on observation and reasoning: *Sir Isaac Newton developed a theory about gravity.* ❏ PLURAL **the·or·ies.**

ther·a·pist (ther′ə pist), NOUN. person who specializes in some form of treatment of disease, injury, or disorder: *Two physical therapists helped me recover from surgery.*

threat·en (thret′n), VERB. to give warning of coming trouble. *Black clouds threatened rain.* ❏ VERB **threat·ens, threat·ened, threat·en·ing.**

thun·der·clap (thun′dər klap′), NOUN. a loud crash of thunder: *The thunderclap woke him from sound sleep.*

till·er (til′ər), NOUN. bar or handle used to turn the rudder in steering: *At the exhibit of old-fashioned cars, there was a demonstration on how the tiller was used to steer.*

tor·na·do (tôr nā′dō), NOUN. a very violent and destructive windstorm with winds as high as 300 miles per hour; twister. A tornado extends down from a mass of dark clouds as a twisting funnel and moves across the land in a narrow path. ❏ PLURAL **tor·na·does** or **tor·na·dos.**

traf·fic (traf′ik), NOUN. people, motor vehicles, ships, and so on, coming and going along a way of travel: *Police control the traffic in large cities.*

trait (trāt), NOUN. a quality of body, mind, or character; characteristic: *Red hair is a lovely trait.*

tram·ple (tram′pəl), VERB. to walk or step heavily on something; crush: *Don't trample the flowers.* ❏ VERB **tram·ples, tram·pled, tram·pling.**

trans·form (tran sfôrm′), VERB. to change in condition, nature, or character: *Watch the tadpole gradually transform into a frog.* ❏ VERB **trans·forms, trans·formed, trans·form·ing.**

trans·por·ta·tion (tran′spər tā′shən), NOUN. a vehicle used to transport people or things: *When the bus broke down, we had no other transportation to school.*

a	hat	ė	term	ô	order	ch	child		a in about
ā	age	i	it	oi	oil	ng	long		e in taken
ä	far	ī	ice	ou	out	sh	she	ə {	i in pencil
â	care	o	hot	u	cup	th	thin		o in lemon
e	let	ō	open	ů	put	ᴛʜ	then		u in circus
ē	equal	ȯ	saw	ü	rule	zh	measure		

trem•ble (trem′bəl), VERB. to shake because you are feeling fear, excitement, weakness, cold, and so on: *I trembled during the scary scenes of the movie.* ❑ VERB **trem•bles, trem•bled, trem•bling.**

tres•tle (tres′əl), NOUN. a braced framework of timber, steel, etc., used as a bridge to support a road or railroad tracks: *The trestle shook as a train rushed over it.*

tri•an•gle (trī′ang′gəl), NOUN. a musical instrument made of a steel bar bent into a three-sided shape. To play a triangle, you strike the side of it with a steel rod.

tri•umph (trī′umf), NOUN. victory or success after great effort: *The exploration of outer space is a great triumph of modern science.*

trudge (truj), VERB. to walk wearily or with effort: *She trudged slowly through the deep snow.* ❑ VERB **trudg•es, trudged, trudg•ing.**

tuft (tuft), NOUN. a bunch of feathers, hair, grass, and so on, held together at one end: *Lions have tufts of black hair at the ends of their tails.*

tun•nel (tun′l), NOUN. an underground road or path: *The railroad passes through a tunnel.*

U u

Underground Railroad, system by which people secretly helped fugitives from slavery escape to the free states or Canada before the Civil War.

un•der•side (un′dər sīd′), NOUN. the bottom side of something: *They painted the underside of the table.*

u•ni•form (yü′nə fôrm), NOUN. the clothes worn by the members of a group that is on duty. Soldiers, police officers, and nurses wear uniforms so that they may be easily recognized.

u•nique (yü nēk′), ADJECTIVE. very uncommon or unusual; rare; remarkable: *Making a vest out of your father's old ties is a rather unique idea.* **—u•nique′ly,** ADVERB. **—u•nique′ness,** NOUN.

up•held (up held′), VERB. the past tense of **uphold;** gave support to something: *The judge's decision was upheld by the jury.*

V v

vac•ci•nate (vak′sə nāt), VERB. to give someone a vaccine by a shot or other means to protect against a disease: *Doctors vaccinate their patients to protect them from measles for several years.* ❑ VERB **vac•ci•nates, vac•ci•nat•ed, vac•ci•nat•ing.**

vain (vān), ADJECTIVE. having too much pride in your looks, ability, or achievements: *Some good-looking people are vain.* **—vain′ly,** ADVERB.

val•iant (val′yənt), ADJECTIVE. brave; courageous: *A neighbor's valiant efforts saved the children from the burning building.* **—val′iant•ly,** ADVERB. **—val′iant•ness,** NOUN.

vane (vān), NOUN. a flat piece of metal, wood, etc., turning on a rod to indicate the direction of the wind; weather vane; weathercock: *The vane on our barn showed us that the wind was coming from the southeast.*

va•ri•e•ty (və rī′ə tē), NOUN. a kind or sort: *Which varieties of fruit are on sale?* ❑ PLURAL **va•ri•e•ties.**

vast (vast), ADJECTIVE. very, very large; immense: *Texas and Alaska cover vast territories.*

ven•ture (ven′chər), VERB. to go somewhere that is dangerous: *As they were venturing out on the thin ice, it cracked.* ❑ VERB **ven•tures, ven•tured, ven•tur•ing.**

ver•dict (vėr′dikt), NOUN. the decision of a jury: *The jury returned a verdict of "Not guilty."*

vi·brate (vī′brāt), VERB. to move rapidly back and forth: *Piano strings vibrate and make sounds when keys are struck.* ❏ VERB **vi·brates, vi·brat·ed, vi·brat·ing.**

vice·reine (vīs′rān), NOUN. the wife of a viceroy: *The viceroy and vicereine lived in a large house near the palace.*

vice·roy (vīs′roi), NOUN. a person who rules a country or province, acting as the king's or queen's representative: *The viceroy reported directly to the king.*

vic·tor·y (vik′tər ē), NOUN. defeat of an enemy or opponent; success in a contest: *The game ended in a victory for our school.* ❏ PLURAL **vic·tor·ies.**

vol·un·teer (vol′ən tir′), NOUN. someone who works without pay. A fire department is often made up of volunteers.

Ww

wail (wāl), NOUN. a sound similar to a long, loud cry of grief or pain: *We heard the wail of a coyote as we sat around the campfire.*

wal·rus (wȯl′rəs), NOUN. a large sea animal of the arctic regions, closely related to the seal. Walruses are hunted for their hides, tusks, and blubber. ❏ PLURAL **wal·rus** or **wal·rus·es.**

walrus

wares (wârz), NOUN PLURAL. manufactured things or articles for sale: *Household wares are on the third floor at this store.*

wa·ter·spout (wȯ′tər spout′), NOUN. a rapidly spinning column or cone of mist, spray, and water, produced by the action of a whirlwind over the ocean or a lake.

weath·er·cock (weᴛʜ′ər kok′), NOUN. vane to show which way the wind is blowing, especially one in the shape of a rooster: *It was so windy that the weathercocks were spinning in circles.*

whole number (hōl num′bər), a number such as 1, 2, 3, 4, 5, and so on, that is not a fraction or a mixed number. 15 and 106 are whole numbers; $\frac{1}{2}$ and $\frac{7}{8}$ are fractions; $1\frac{3}{8}$ and $23\frac{2}{3}$ are mixed numbers.

wit·ness (wit′nis), NOUN. person who gives evidence or testifies under oath in a court of law: *The witness claimed she had seen the defendant climb a fence and run away.*

wolf·like (wůlf′līk), ADJECTIVE. similar to a flesh-eating mammal related to dogs: *He has long, pointed, wolflike teeth.* ❏ NOUN **wolf,** PLURAL **wolves.**

wood·wind (wůd′wind′), NOUN. any of a group of wind instruments which were originally made of wood, but are now often made of metal or plastic. Clarinets, flutes, oboes, and bassoons are woodwinds.

wrin·kled (ring′kəld), ADJECTIVE. having folds or creases on the surface of something that is usually flat or smooth: *He decided to iron his wrinkled shirt.*

a	hat	ė	term	ô	order	ch	child	(a in about
ā	age	i	it	oi	oil	ng	long	e in taken
ä	far	ī	ice	ou	out	sh	she	ə{ i in pencil
â	care	o	hot	u	cup	th	thin	o in lemon
e	let	ō	open	ů	put	ᴛʜ	then	u in circus
ē	equal	ȯ	saw	ü	rule	zh	measure	

How to Use This Handbook

The following reading skills and definitions are found throughout this book. Understanding these skills can help you as you read. In this section, the skills are arranged in alphabetical order. Use these pages to help you review the terms and definitions. When reading, look back at these pages as often as you need.

Author's Purpose

- An **author's purpose** is the author's reason for writing.

- Some purposes for writing are to entertain, to inform, to express, and to persuade.

- Authors don't usually tell you their purposes. You have to figure them out.

- Predicting an author's purpose can help you decide whether to read something slowly and carefully or quickly for fun.

Cause and Effect

- A **cause** is why something happens. An **effect** is what happens.

- Sometimes there are clue words, such as *because, so, if, then,* or *since,* to help you figure out what happened and why.

Character

- **Characters** are the people or animals in a story or nonfiction article.

- You can learn about characters by what they think, do, and say.

- You can also learn about characters by paying attention to how other characters in the story treat them and what these other characters say about them.

Compare and Contrast

- To **compare** is to tell how two or more things are alike. To **contrast** is to tell how two or more things are different.

- Clue words such as *like* or *as* show comparisons. Clue words such as *but, instead,* and *unlike* show contrasts. Other clue words are words of comparison, such as *smaller.*

Context Clues

- **Context clues** are words around an unfamiliar word that can be used to figure out meaning.

- The context may give a definition or an explanation of an unfamiliar word. Often the definition or explanation comes just before or just after the word.

- Sometimes a synonym, a word with nearly the same meaning as another word, is used as a context clue.

Drawing Conclusions

- A conclusion is a decision you reach after you think about the details or facts that you have read.

- When you make decisions about the characters or events, you are **drawing conclusions.**

- **Drawing conclusions** is sometimes called *making inferences.*

Fact and Opinion

- A **fact** tells something that can be proved true or false.

- An **opinion** tells your ideas or feelings. It cannot be proved true or false, but it can be supported by facts and reasons.

- Statements of opinion may begin with clues such as *I believe.* Also, words such as *pretty* that express a person's feelings, beliefs, or judgments are clues to statements of opinion.

- Some sentences or passages contain both facts and opinions.

Generalizing

- A **generalization** is a broad statement or rule that applies to many examples.

- Often clue words, such as *all, most, many, some, sometimes, usually, seldom, few,* or *generally,* signal generalizations.

- When you read, you may be given ideas about several things or people. You can generalize, or make a statement, about all or most of them together.

- A valid generalization is supported by facts and your own knowledge. A faulty generalization is not.

Graphic Sources

- Illustrations, charts, graphs, maps, diagrams, tables, lists, time lines, and scale drawings are kinds of **graphic sources.**

- Previewing graphic sources before reading can help you predict what you will learn.

- Graphic sources can help you during reading by showing what the words say or by organizing information in a useful way.

Handbook of Reading Skills

Main Idea and Supporting Details

- The **topic** is what a paragraph or article is about.

- The **main idea** is the most important idea about the topic.

- The main idea is often stated in a single sentence within a paragraph or article. However, sometimes you have to figure out the main idea and put it into your own words.

- **Supporting details** are small pieces of information that tell more about the main idea.

Making Judgments

- **Making judgments** means thinking about and deciding how to react toward people, situations, and ideas in stories and articles that you read.

- When making judgments, use what you know from the story or article and your own experience. Ask yourself if the author is trying to influence you. Does the author support the ideas he or she presents?

Paraphrasing

- **Paraphrasing** is explaining something in your own words but keeping the writer's meaning.

- A paraphrase should include all of the author's ideas, but it should be easier to read than the original.

Plot

- Stories have a **plot,** or a series of events that center on a problem or conflict.

- A *conflict* can be a problem between two people or groups or between a person and nature. Conflicts can also be problems that characters have within themselves.

- The *climax* is the point where the action of the story builds and the conflict must be faced.

- The *resolution* is where the problem is solved.

Predicting

- To **predict** means to tell what you think might happen next in a story or article based on what has already happened. Your prediction is what you say might happen next.

- When you make predictions, use your personal knowledge about a topic to help you.

- Predicting is a process of checking and changing your predictions as you read, based on new information.

Sequence

- **Sequence** means the order in which things happen. Sequence can also mean the steps followed to do something.

- Clue words, such as *first, then, next,* and *finally,* can help you figure out the sequence of events. Dates and times of day also show sequence.

- Some events in a story may take place at the same time. Authors may use words like *meanwhile, while,* or *during* to show this.

- Sometimes events are told out of order. Verb tenses or clue words can show this.

Setting

- The **setting** is the time and place in which a story occurs.

- Sometimes the setting is important to the plot of a story. At other times, setting is only a background.

- Pictures sometimes show the setting of a story. At other times you have to imagine the setting. Details the author has written can help you see, hear, feel, and smell what it is like to be there.

Steps in a Process

- Telling the **steps in a process** is telling the order of steps to complete an action.

- Clue words, such as *first, next,* and *last,* or numbers written by the steps can show when each step is done.

- Sometimes illustrations show the steps. At other times you have to picture the steps in your mind and put them in order.

Summarizing

- A **summary** is a short statement, no more than a few sentences, that tells the main idea of a selection.

- A story summary tells the goals of the characters, how they try to reach them, and whether they reach them.

- A summary of an article should tell the main idea, leaving out unnecessary details.

Text Structure

- **Text structure** is the way a piece of writing is organized.

- Fiction is usually organized by the order in which things happen.

- Nonfiction can be organized in many different ways: sequence of events, main ideas and details, cause and effect, comparison and contrast, fact and opinion, or problem and solution.

- Biographies and autobiographies are often organized in chronological, or time, order.

- Figuring out the organization of a text can help you make sense of it as you read.

Theme

- The **theme** of a story is its underlying meaning or big idea.

- A theme can stand alone outside the story. It does not mention characters or plot events that are specific to the story.

- Sometimes an author states the theme directly. Sometimes readers have to figure out the theme on their own, using evidence from the text to support their big idea.

- A story can have more than one theme.

Visualizing

- **Visualizing** means forming a mental image in your mind as you read.

- To help visualize, look for details that tell how things look, smell, sound, taste, and feel.

- Add what you know from your own experience to create an even clearer image in your mind.

- If you cannot visualize, reread or read more slowly to find details that will help you "see" the picture more clearly.

Unit 1

A Visit with Grandpa

huge	excuse	confuse	few	nephew
curfew	usual	pupil	fuel	menu
cool	mood	shoot	school	shampoo
fruit	suit	juice	bruise	cruise

Train to Somewhere

them	went	fence	credit	engine
contest	speak	reason	beat	least
steal	treat	season	money	valley
honey	monkey	hockey	alley	donkey

Yingtao's New Friend

band	cash	January	blanket	backpack
river	finger	build	guilt	window
pond	block	forgot	closet	chop
trouble	young	cousin	couple	tough

Family Pictures

station	danger	April	vacation	cable
bacon	wild	behind	pint	lion
hide	decide	invite	arrive	whole
broke	drove	smoke	remote	stole

Addie in Charge

throat	through	screen	scratch	scream
strange	street	strike	square	squeeze
threat	thrown	thrill	scrub	skyscraper
strawberry	strength	squeal	squirm	squirt

Unit 2

---

from The Cricket in Times Square

stood	took	wood	football	brook
bush	July	cushion	butcher	pudding
power	however	shower	crowd	loud
house	outside	mountain	cloud	proud

A Big-City Dream

often	might	known	they	remember
surprised	caught	island	finally	really
several	everyone	everybody	interesting	swimming
camera	December	evening	beginning	February

I Love Guinea Pigs

baseball	basketball	upstairs	myself	highway
classroom	anyway	newspaper	something	earrings
driveway	chalkboard	nighttime	motorcycle	downstairs
softball	weekend	classmate	doorbell	sometimes

The Swimming Hole

wood	would	too	to	two
there	their	they're	your	you're
beat	beet	break	brake	clothes
close	piece	peace	thrown	throne

Komodo Dragons

storm	morning	forest	Florida	form
pour	fourteen	court	fourth	course
serve	herself	certain	nerve	perfect
dirty	first	girlfriend	thirsty	skirt

Unit 3

John Henry

smaller	larger	happier	hotter	sadder
deeper	closer	scarier	funnier	fatter
smallest	largest	happiest	hottest	saddest
deepest	closest	scariest	funniest	fattest

Marven of the Great North Woods

monkeys	holidays	delays	flowers	friends
tigers	supplies	enemies	hobbies	memories
mysteries	eyelashes	ashes	beaches	bunches
circuses	glasses	classes	taxes	suffixes

On the Pampas

happened	opened	danced	studied	stopped
chased	worried	dried	robbed	slipped
happening	opening	dancing	studying	stopping
chasing	worrying	drying	robbing	slipping

The Storm

change	village	edge	except	excited
explain	expect	Texas	quick	equal
charge	bridge	fudge	excellent	relax
extra	queen	quart	liquid	quilt

Rikki-Tikki-Tavi

other	number	October	another	color
doctor	motor	people	simple	angle
title	model	barrel	angel	broken
sudden	oven	common	gallon	button

Unit 4

Half-Chicken

shown	short	punish	shelter	flashlight
trash	March	chapter	chocolate	church
watch	kitchen	pitcher	catcher	whatever
anywhere	whenever	wheat	awhile	somewhere

Blame It on the Wolf

we'll	I'm	I'd	you'd	I'll
we've	it's	that's	what's	doesn't
he'll	she'll	they'll	they'd	he'd
would've	could've	wouldn't	shouldn't	let's

Lou Gehrig: The Luckiest Man

set	sit	off	of	when
win	our	are	than	then
lose	loose	were	we're	where
quiet	quite	quit	whose	who's

The Disguise

powerful	peaceful	beautiful	cheerful	painful
thoughtful	slowly	safely	daily	suddenly
carefully	weekly	lately	truthfully	hopefully
action	location	invention	correction	pollution

Keepers

tomorrow	borrow	different	supper	matter
written	bottle	ridden	odd	bubble
offer	suffer	slipper	grasshopper	worry
current	lettuce	paddle	shudder	hobby

Unit 5

Amazing Alice!

dislike	disappear	distrust	dishonest	disagree
incomplete	recall	incorrect	invisible	inactive
misplace	misspell	misled	mistreat	misbehave
rebuild	reuse	react	replace	independent

A Peddler's Dream

knot	unknown	know	knit	knob
kneel	sign	design	assign	writing
wrist	wreck	wreath	wrench	wren
climb	thumb	limb	comb	lamb

The Race for the North Pole

Dad's	friend's	girl's	girls'	teacher's
teachers'	baby's	babies'	family's	families'
grandma's	grandpa's	brother's	brothers'	boy's
boys'	aunt's	aunts'	lady's	ladies'

Into the Sea

machine	especially	usually	probably	giant
buffalo	Canada	canoe	relatives	stomach
moment	cement	yesterday	animals	iron
favorite	welcome	support	suppose	August

Space Probes to the Planets

coming	always	almost	didn't	upon
wasn't	until	during	want	father
hamster	a lot	ugly	washed	hotel
missed	eleven	crazy	lazy	feelings

Unit 6

Koya's Cousin Del

piece	friend	field	believe	weird
said	again	asked	only	brought
height	weight	neighbor	heard	heart
tongue	rattle	pickle	toes	hospital

Children of Clay

May	Memorial Day	Kwanzaa	Christmas	September
Hanukkah	June	Chinese New Year	November	Valentine's Day
Sun.	Dec.	Dr.	Mrs.	Rd.
Feb.	Wed.	Ms.	Mr.	Ave.

Coming Home

care	because	cover	record	brake
Kansas	track	pocket	snack	attack
stiff	muffin	giraffe	enough	laughed
rough	photo	alphabet	dolphin	elephant

Out of the Blue

helpless	careless	breathless	spotless	hopeless
worthless	useless	payment	statement	movement
pavement	treatment	punishment	goodness	softness
brightness	business	greatness	fairness	darkness

Chocolate Is Missing

able	ability	sign	signal	mean
meant	deal	dealt	soft	soften
relate	relative	heal	health	meter
metric	compose	composition	crumb	crumble

Acknowledgments

Text

Dorling Kindersley (DK) is an international publishing company specializing in the creation of high quality reference content for books, CD-ROMs, online, and video. The hallmark of DK content is its unique combination of educational value and strong visual style—this combination allows DK to deliver appealing, accessible, and engaging educational content that delights children, parents, and teachers around the world. Scott Foresman is delighted to have been able to use selected extracts of DK content within the Scott Foresman Reading program.
68–69: "The American Railroad" from *Train* by John Coiley. Copyright © 2000 by Dorling Kindersley Limited; **230–231:** "Badger Toes and Rabbit Feet" from *Mammal* by Steve Parker. Copyright © 1989 by Dorling Kindersley Limited; **364–365:** "The Deadly Cobra" from *Amazing Snakes* by Alexandra Parsons. Copyright © 1990 by Dorling Kindersley Limited; **392–393:** "Chicken Farming" from *Farm* by Ned Halley. Copyright © 2000 by Dorling Kindersley Limited; **554–555:** "The North Pole" from *Explorer* by Rupert Matthews. Copyright © 1991 by Dorling Kindersley Limited; **628–629:** "On the Beat" from *Music* by Neil Ardley. Copyright © 2000 by Dorling Kindersley Limited.

16, 90: © 1998 Lensey Namioka; **20:** From "The Red Fox" by Donna Stringfellow from *Spider,* March 1995, Volume 2, Number 3, pg. 8. Text copyright © 1995 by Donna Stringfellow. Reprinted by permission of the author; **22:** Chapter 6, "Riding Fence," and Chapter 7, "About Black Cowboys," from *Justin and the Best Biscuits in the World* by Mildred Pitts Walter, pp. 49–68. Text copyright © 1986 by Mildred Pitts Walter. Used by permission of HarperCollins Publishers; **41:** "Understanding Horses" from *Your First Horse Book* by Peter R. Winkelaar. Copyright © 1996 by Sterling Publishing Co., Inc. Used by permission of Balloon Books, a division of Sterling Publishing Co., Inc.; **44:** From *Sarah, Plain and Tall* by Patricia MacLachlan, pp. 54–55. Copyright © 1985 by Patricia MacLachlan. Reprinted by permission of HarperCollins Publishers, Inc.; **46:** *Train to Somewhere* by Eve Bunting. Illustrated by Ronald Himler, pp. 4–32. Text copyright © 1996 by Eve Bunting. Illustrations copyright © 1996 by Ronald Himler. All rights reserved. Reprinted by permission of Clarion Books/Houghton Mifflin Company; **70:** From *From Anna* by Jean Little, pp. 89–90. Text copyright © 1972 by Jean Little. Reprinted by permission of HarperCollins Publishers, Inc.; **72:** From *Yang the Youngest and His Terrible Ear* by Lensey Namioka, pp. 23–39. Text copyright © 1992 by Lensey Namioka. Used by permission of Lensey Namioka. All rights are reserved by the Author; **94:** From *Hear! Hear! The Science of Sound* by Barbara Taylor, copyright © 1990 by Grisewood & Dempsey Ltd. Used by permission of Random House Children's Books, a division of Random House, Inc.; **96:** From "Painting Mist and Fog" by Molly Bang from *Spider*, October 1994, Volume 1, Number 10, pg. 16. Copyright © 1994 by Molly Bang. Reprinted by permission of the author; **98:** Adapted from *Family Pictures* by Carmen Lomas Garza, pp. 1, 3, 6–7, 10–11, 14–17, 22–23, & 30–31. Copyright © 1990 by Carmen Lomas Garza. Reprinted by permission of GRM Associates, Inc., Agents for Children's Book Press; **114:** "Family Photo" and "New Baby" from *Relatively Speaking: Poems About Family* by Ralph Fletcher. Published by Orchard Books, an imprint of Scholastic Inc. Copyright © 1999 by Ralph Fletcher. Reproduced by permission of Scholastic Inc.; **116:** From *Black-Eyed Susan* by Jennifer M. Armstrong, pp. 14, 16, & 17. Text copyright © 1995 by Jennifer M. Armstrong. Used by permission of Crown Children's Books, a division of Random House, Inc.; **118:** From Chapter 9, "Fraidycat," and Chapter 10, "Trapped!" from *Addie Across the Prairie* by Laurie Lawlor, pp. 110–126**.** Text copyright © 1986 by Laurie Lawlor. Excerpted by permission of Albert Whitman & Company; **133:** *Thehistorynet* Web page, *www.thehistorynet.com/HistoricTraveler/articles/0696_text.htm,* article, "Merle Builds a Sod House" by Anne Hattes, *March '96 Historic Traveler Feature*. Reprinted by permission of the author; **136:** "Changing" from *The Llama Who Had No Pajama: 100 Favorite Poems* by Mary Ann Hoberman. Copyright © 1981 by Mary Ann Hoberman. Reprinted by permission of Harcourt, Inc.; **137:** "Enchantment" by Joanne Ryder. Copyright © 1990 by Joanne Ryder. Reprinted by permission of the author; **138:** "My Grandma's Songs" from *Laughing Tomatoes and Other Spring Poems* by Francisco X. Alarcón, pg. 9. Poems copyright © 1997 by Francisco X. Alarcón. Reprinted by permission of the publisher, Children's Book Press, San Francisco, CA; **139:** "August Cowboy" from *Gingerbread Days,* poems by Joyce Carol Thomas. Text copyright © 1995 by Joyce Carol Thomas. Reprinted by permission of HarperCollins Publishers, Inc.; **146:** From *The Attic Mice* by Ethel Pochocki, pp. 44–46. Text copyright © 1990 by Ethel Pochocki. Reprinted by permission of the author; **148:** Chapter Three, "Chester," and Chapter Four, "Harry Cat," from *The Cricket in Times Square* by George Selden. Illustrated by Garth Williams, pp. 18–34. Copyright © 1960 by George Selden Thompson and Garth Williams. Copyright renewed © 1988 by George Selden Thompson. Reprinted by permission of Farrar, Straus & Giroux, LLC; **165:** "The Country Mouse and the City Mouse" from *Aesop's Fables,* retold by Anne Terry White, pp. 10–13. Copyright © 1964 by Anne Terry White. Reprinted by permission of Random House, Inc.; **168:** From "Super Cooper Scoopers!" from *Kid City,* April 1998, pg. 6. Reprinted by permission from Kid City. Copyright 1998 Sesame Workshop. All rights reserved; **170:** "A Big-City Dream" from *The Big Idea* by Ellen Schecter; illustrated by Bob Dorsey. Text copyright © 1996 by Ellen Schecter. Illustrations © 1996 by Bob Dorsey. Reprinted by permission of Hyperion Paperbacks for Children; **190:** "River of Grass" from *Kids Discover,* Vol. 7, Issue 10, December 1997. Copyright © 1997 Kids Discover. Reprinted by permission; **194:** From "Your Best Friend" from *Me and My Pet Dog* by Christine Morley and Carole Orbell, pp. 4–5. Copyright © 1996 by Two-Can Publishing Ltd. Reprinted by permission of the publisher; **196:** *I Love Guinea Pigs* by Dick King-Smith, illustrated by Anita Jeram. Text copyright © 1994 by Foxbusters Ltd. Illustrations copyright © 1994 by Anita Jeram. Published by Candlewick Press, Cambridge, MA. Reprinted by permission of Walker Books Limited, London; **210:** "What You Always Wanted to Know About Pets" from *101 Questions and Answers About Pets and People* by Dr. Ann Squire. Copyright © 1988 by Ann Squire. Reprinted by permission; **212:** "Ant and Dove" from *Fables from Aesop,* retold by James Reeves. Copyright © 1961 by James Reeves and Blackie and Son Limited. Reprinted by permission of the James Reeves Estate; **214:** Cover of book from *On the Banks of Plum Creek* by Laura Ingalls Wilder, illustrated by Garth Williams. Illustrations copyright 1953, renewed © 1981 by Garth Williams. Reprinted by permission of HarperCollins Publishers, Inc.; **216:** "Rushes and Flags," "Deep Water," and "Strange Animal" from *On the Banks of Plum Creek* by Laura Ingalls Wilder, illustrated by Garth Williams, pp. 18–36. Text copyright 1937 by Laura Ingalls Wilder, renewed © 1965, 1993 by Roger Lea MacBride. Illustrations copyright 1953, renewed © 1981 by Garth Williams. Reprinted by permission of HarperCollins Publishers, Inc.; **232:** From *Roaring Reptiles* by D. M. Souza, pp. 6–8. Copyright © 1992 by Carolrhoda Books, Inc., a division of Lerner Publishing Group. Used by permission of the publisher. All rights reserved; **234:** *Komodo Dragons* by Thane Maynard, pp. 7–8, 11–12, 14, 17–18, 21–22, 25, 27–28, & 31. Copyright © 1997 by The Child's World®, Inc. Reprinted by permission of The Child's World®, Inc.; **248:** "Horned Lizard" from *Microsoft® Encarta® 96 Encyclopedia*. Copyright © 1993–1995 by Microsoft Corporation. Copyright © by Funk & Wagnalls Corporation. All rights reserved; **249:** "Glass Lizard" from *Microsoft® Encarta® 96 Encyclopedia*. Copyright © 1993–1995 by Microsoft Corporation. Copyright © by Funk & Wagnalls Corporation. All rights reserved; **250:** "The Circle of Thanks" from *The Circle of Thanks* retold by Joseph Bruchac. Text copyright © 1996 by Joseph Bruchac. Reprinted by permission of BridgeWater Books, an imprint of Troll Communications L.L.C.; **251:** "Food/Comida" by Victor M. Valle from *Fiesta in Aztlan*. Reprinted by permission of Capra Press; **252:** "House Crickets" from *Joyful Noise* by Paul Fleischman, pp. 36–38. Text copyright © 1988 by Paul Fleischman. Reprinted by permission of HarperCollins Publishers, Inc.; **260:** From *McBroom's Ear* by Sid Fleischman, pp. 3–4. Text copyright © 1969 by Sid Fleischman. Reprinted by permission of the author; **262:** *John Henry* by Julius Lester, pictures by Jerry Pinkney. Text copyright © 1994 by Julius Lester. Pictures copyright © 1994 by Jerry Pinkney. Reprinted by permission of Dial Books for Young Readers, a division of Penguin Putnam, Inc.; **280:** "John Henry" from *Doc Watson Sings Songs for Little Pickers*. Reprinted by permission; **282:** From "Winter of the Snowshoe Hare" by Gillian Richardson from *Cricket,* February 1995, Volume 22, Number 6, pp. 5–6. Copyright © 1995 by Gillian Richardson. Reprinted by permission of the author; **284:** *Marven of the Great North Woods* by Kathryn Lasky, illustrated by Kevin Hawkes. Text copyright © 1997 by Kathryn Lasky Knight. Illustrations copyright © 1997 by Kevin Hawkes. Reprinted by permission of Harcourt, Inc.; **302:** Chapter 3, Lesson 12, "Counting Money" from *Scott Foresman – Addison Wesley Math* Grade 4 by Randall I. Charles et al., pp. 126–127. Copyright © 1998 by Addison Wesley Longman, Inc.; **304:** Excerpts from *Salmon Summer* by Bruce McMillan. Copyright © 1998 by Bruce McMillan. All rights reserved. Reprinted by permission of Houghton Mifflin Company; **306:** *On the Pampas* by María Cristina Brusca. Copyright © 1991 by María Cristina Brusca. Reprinted by permission of Henry Holt and Company, Inc.; **322:** Excerpts from *Argentina: A Book* by Michael Burgan. Copyright © 1999 Children's Press® a Division of Grolier Publishing Co., Inc. Reprinted by permission; **323:** Excerpts from *The Statesman's Year-Book: 1998–1999.* Copyright © Macmillan Reference Ltd., 1998. Reprinted by permission. **324:** Excerpt from *Seal Surfer* by Michael Foreman. Copyright © 1996 by Michael Foreman. Reprinted by permission of Harcourt, Inc.; **326:** *The Storm* by Marc Harshman, illustrated by Mark Mohr. Text Copyright © Marc Harshman, 1995. Illustrations Copyright © Mark Mohr, 1995. Published by arrangement with Dutton Children's Books, a division of Penguin Putnum Inc.; **341:** "Tornado Tales" from *Weather Explained* by Derek Elsom, pp. 30–31. Copyright © 1997 by Marshall Editions Developments Ltd. Reprinted by permission of Henry Holt and Company, Inc.; **344:** From Chapter 5, "Another Bloody Murder," from *The Original Adventures of Hank the Cowdog* by John R. Erickson, pp. 45–46. Copyright © 1983 by John R. Erickson. Reprinted by permission of Viking Penguin, a division of Penguin Putnam, Inc.; **346:** *Rikki-Tikki-Tavi* by Rudyard Kipling, adapted and illustrated by Jerry Pinkney. Copyright © 1997 by Jerry Pinkney. Used by permission of Harper Collins Publishers; **366:** "74th Street" from *The Malibu and Other Poems* by Myra Cohn Livingston. Copyright © 1972 by Myra Cohn Livingston. Reprinted by permission of Marian Reiner for the author; **367:** "Crystal Rowe (Track Star)" from *Class Dismissed II* by Mel Glenn. Text copyright © 1986 by Mel Glenn. Reprinted by permission of the author; **368:** "My Teacher in the Market" from *Canto Familiar* by Gary Soto, pp. 58 & 60–61. Copyright © 1995 by Gary Soto. Reprinted by permission of Harcourt, Inc.; **376:** From "Blue Jay and Swallow Take the Heat" from *When Birds Could Talk & Bats Could Sing* told by Virginia Hamilton. Text copyright © 1996 by Virginia Hamilton. Published by The Blue Sky Press, an imprint of Scholastic Inc. Reprinted by permission of Scholastic Inc.; **378:** *Mediopollito/Half-Chicken* by Alma Flor Ada, illustrated by Kim Howard, translated by Rosalma Zubizarreta. Text copyright © 1995 by Alma Flor Ada. Illustrations copyright © 1995 by Kim Howard. All rights reserved. Used by permission of Dell Publishing, a division of Random House, Inc.; **394:** From *Wolves* by Gail Gibbons. Text copyright © 1994 by Gail Gibbons. All rights reserved. Reprinted by permission of Holiday House; **396:** Adaptation of "Blame It on the Wolf" Copyright © 1993 by Douglas Love from *Blame It on the Wolf* published by HarperCollins. Reprinted by permission of McIntosh and Otis, Inc.; **418:** "What Is the Supreme Court?" from *The Supreme Court* by Barbara Aria. Copyright © 1994 by Barbara Aria. Reprinted by permission; **420:** From "When I Was a Kid: Cal Ripken, Jr." by Elizabeth Schleichert from *National Geographic World,* Number 261, May 1997, pg. 35. Copyright © 1997 by National Geographic Society. Reprinted by permission of National Geographic Society; **422:** *Lou Gehrig: The Luckiest Man* by David A. Adler, illustrated by Terry Widener. Text copyright © 1997 by David A. Adler. Illustrations copyright © 1997 by Terry Widener. Reprinted by permission of Harcourt, Inc.; **439:** From Chapter One, "Take Me Out to the Ball Game: The Birth of Baseball" and from Chapter Two, "Buy Me Some Peanuts and Cracker Jacks: The Game Grows" from *The Baseball Hall of Fame* by Terry Janson Dunnahoo & Herma Silverstein, pp. 5, 11, & 13. Copyright © 1994 by Crestwood House. Reprinted by permission of Macmillan Library Reference USA, a Simon & Schuster Macmillan Company; **442:** From Chapter 12, "Korean Food Is Highly Seasoned," from *North & South Korea* by Gene and Clare Gurney, pp. 42 & 44. Copyright © 1973 by Franklin Watts, Inc. Reprinted by permission of Grolier Publishing Company; **444:** From Chapter One, "The Gift That Changed My Life," and Chapter Two, "The Girl-Son," from *The Girl-Son* by Anne E. Neuberger, pp. 18–34. Copyright © 1995 by Anne E. Neuberger. All rights reserved. Reprinted by permission of the publisher; **466:** Excerpts from *Chinese Calligraphy* Web site. Reprinted by permission; **468:** From "One Particular Small, Smart Boy" from *One-Minute Favorite Fairy Tales* by Shari Lewis, pp. 16–17. Text copyright © 1985 by Shari Lewis Enterprises, Inc. Used by permission. All rights reserved; **470:** *Keepers* by Jeri Hanel Watts. Text copyright © 1997 by Jeri Hanel Watts. Reprinted by permission of Lee & Low Books, Inc., 95 Madison Avenue, New York, NY 10016; **486:** "Summer" from *Brown Angels* by Walter Dean Myers. Copyright © 1993 by Walter Dean Myers. Reprinted by permission of HarperCollins Publishers, Inc.; **487:** "Es verdad" from *Canto Familiar* by Gary Soto, pg. 75. Copyright © 1995 by Gary Soto. Reprinted by permission of Harcourt, Inc.; **488:** Lyrics and music from "Glad to Have a Friend Like You" by Carol Hall from *Free to Be . . . You and Me and Free to Be . . . A Family,* created by Marlo Thomas, developed and edited by Christopher Cerf et al., designed by Samuel N. Antupit and Barbara Cohen, pp. 63 & 226–229. Copyright © 1997, 1987, 1974 by the Free to Be Foundation, Inc. Reprinted by permission of Running Press Book Publishers; **496:** From "Stagecoaches, Then . . . and Now" by Dorothy Hinshaw Patent from *Spider,* October 1995, pp. 20–21. Copyright © 1995 by Dorothy Hinshaw Patent. Reprinted by permission of the author; **498:** From *Coast to Coast with Alice* by Patricia Rusch Hyatt, pp. 5, 7–11, 22, 31, 44–48, 51–52, 60, & 62–63. Copyright © 1995 by Carolrhoda Books, Inc. All rights reserved. Reprinted by permission of the publisher; **516:** "Keeping a Road Journal" by Joy Beck from *U. S. Kids* magazine, copyright © 1996 by Children's Better Health Institute, Benjamin Franklin Literary & Medical Society, Inc., Indianapolis, Indiana. Used by permission; **518:** From "Atalanta's Race" from *Greek Myths,* retold by Geraldine McCaughrean, pp. 76–77. Text copyright © 1992 by Geraldine McCaughrean. Reprinted with the permission of Margaret K. McElderry Books, an imprint of Simon & Schuster Children's Publishing Division. First published in the UK by Orchard Books in 1992, a division of The Watts Publishing Group Limited, 96 Leonard Street, London ECK2A 4XD; **520:** *A Peddler's Dream* by Janice Shefelman, illustrated by Tom Shefelman, pp. 3–32. Text copyright © 1992 by Janice Shefelman. Illustrations copyright © 1992 by Tom Shefelman. Reprinted by permission of RLR Associates, Ltd.; **535:** "Ports of Entry, 1870–1920" Graph adapted from *Historical Atlas of the United States,* p. 54. Copyright © 1988 by National Geographic Society. Reprinted by permission of National Geographic Society; **536:** From Introduction and Map, "North Polar Region," from*: Polar Lands* by Norman Barrett, pp. 6–8. Copyright © 1989 by Franklin Watts, Inc. First published in the UK by Franklin Watts, a division of the Watts Publishing Group Ltd., 96 Leonard Street, London EC2A 4XD.; **538:** From Chapter 3, "Matthew Henson," and Chapter 4, "Reaching the Pole," from *Matthew Henson and Robert Peary: The Race for the North Pole* by Laurie Rozakis, pp. 19–29, 31, & 33–36. Copyright © 1994 by Blackbirch Press, Inc. Reprinted by permission of Blackbirch Press, Inc.; **556:** "Saving Our Wetlands" and "The Importance of Wetlands" from *The Aquarium Take-Along Book* by Sheldon L. Gerstenfeld V.M.D., pg. 98. Text copyright © 1994 by Sheldon L. Gerstenfeld. Reprinted by permission of Harold Ober Associates Incorporated; **558:** *Into the Sea* by Brenda Z. Guiberson, illustrated by Alix Berenzy. Text copyright © 1996 by Brenda Z. Guiberson. Illustrations copyright © 1996 by Alix Berenzy. Reprinted by permission of Henry Holt and Company, Inc.; **572:** "I Work in the Ocean" by Kristin Ingram from *Spider,* January 1998, Volume 5, Number 1, pp. 26–31. Copyright © 1998 by Kristin Ingram. Reprinted by permission of *Spider Magazine,* a division of Carus Publishing Company; **576:** "Out-of-This-World Rocks" from "Camp Meteorite" by John Kontakis from *Contact Kids,* June 1998, pp. 13–14. Reprinted with permission from Kid City. Copyright © 1998 by Sesame Workshop. All rights reserved; **578:** *Space Probes to the Planets* by Fay Robinson. Text copyright © 1993 by Fay Robinson. Illustrations copyright © 1993 by Albert Whitman & Company. Reprinted by permission of Albert Whitman & Company; **594:** "Meet the Universe's Main Attraction . . . Gravity" from *Our Place in Space, A Kid's Guide to the Universe* by American Museum of Natural History. Copyright © 2000. Reprinted by permission; **596:** "Lyle" from *Bronzeville Boys and Girls* by Gwendolyn Brooks, pg. 25. Copyright © 1956 by Gwendolyn Brooks Blakely. Reprinted by permission of HarperCollins Publishers, Inc.; **597:** "México/Mexico" from *Gathering the Sun* by Alma Flor Ada, English translation by Rosa Zubizarreta. Text copyright © 1997 by Alma Flor Ada. Used by permission of HarperCollins Pubishers; **598:** "The Inventor Thinks Up Helicopters" from *The Tigers Brought Pink Lemonade* by Patricia Hubbell. Copyright © 1998 by Patricia Hubbell. Reprinted by permission of Marian Reiner for the author; **599:** From "Blue" from *Poems of Earth and Space* by Claudia Lewis. Copyright © 1967 by Claudia Lewis. Reprinted by permission of Dutton Children's Books, a division of Penguin Putnam, Inc.; **606:** From "Seeds" by Linda Montijo from *Cricket,* April 1995, Volume 22, Number 8, pp. 16–17. Copyright © 1995 by Linda Montijo; **608:** From Chapters Fourteen, Fifteen, and Sixteen from *Koya DeLaney and the Good Girl Blues* by Eloise Greenfield, pp. 88–104. Copyright © 1992 by Eloise Greenfield. Reprinted by permission of Scott Treimel New York; **630:** From "Carousel Designed by Kids" by Kathy Kranking from *Ranger Rick,* June 1998, Vol. 32, No. 6, pp. 4 & 6. Copyright © 1998 by the National Wildlife Federation. Reprinted by permission of the National Wildlife Federation; **632:** From *Children of Clay: A Family of Pueblo Potters* by Rina Swentzell, pp. 22–37. Copyright © 1992 by Lerner Publications, a Division of the Lerner Pubishing Group. All rights reserved. Used by permission of the publisher; **645:** "Clay Old Woman and Clay Old Man," Cochiti Pueblo myth from *Four Ancestors* told by Joseph Bruchac, pictures by S. S. Burrus, Jeffrey Chapman, Murv Jacob, & Duke Sine, pp. 45–47. Text copyright © 1996 by Joseph Bruchac. Illustrations copyright © 1996 by Murv Jacob. Reprinted by permission of BridgeWater Books, an imprint of Troll Communications L.L.C.; **648:** From Book Review by Katie Swegart, age 11, of *Naomi's Geese* by Sanford Evans, from *Stone Soup,* the magazine by young writers and artists, © 1994 by the Children's Art Foundation; **650:** From *Coming Home: From the Life of Langston Hughes* by Floyd Cooper. Copyright © 1994 by Floyd Cooper. Published by arrangement with Philomel Books, an imprint of Penguin Putnam Books for Young Readers, a division of Penguin Putnam, Inc.; **651:** "Hope" from *Collected Poems* by Langston Hughes. Copyright © 1994 by the Estate of Langston Hughes. Reprinted by permission of Alfred A. Knopf, Inc.; **664:** "The Dream Keeper" from *The Collected Poems of Langston Hughes* by Langston Hughes, copyright © 1994 by the Estate of Langston Hughes. Used by permission of Alfred A. Knopf, a division of Random House, Inc.; **665:** "Dreamer" by Lee Bennett Hopkins from *Lives: Poems About Famous Americans,* selected by Lee Bennett Hopkins. Copyright © 1999 by Lee Bennett Hopkins. Reprinted by permission; **666:** From "Working on the Railroad" by Gloria A. Harris. Excerpted from *Cobblestone's* February, 1992 issue: *African American Inventors.* © 1992, Cobblestone Publishing Company, 30 Grove Street, Suite C, Peterborough, NH 03458. All rights reserved. Reproduced by permission of the publisher; **668:** From *What's the Big Idea, Ben Franklin?* by Jean Fritz, illustrated by Margot Tomes, pp. 20–36. Text copyright © 1976 by Jean Fritz. Illustrations copyright © 1976 by Margot Tomes. Reprinted by permission of Coward-McCann, Inc., a division of Penguin Putnam, Inc.; **681:** "A Really Bright Idea" from *Kids Discover,* Vol. 8, Issue 8, August 1998. Copyright © 1998 Kids Discover. Reprinted by permission; **684:** From Chapter 2 from *Not-So-Perfect Rosie* by Patricia Reilly Giff, pp. 9–10. Text copyright © 1997 by Patricia Reilly Giff. Reprinted by permission of Viking Penguin, a division of Penguin Putnam, Inc.; **686:** "Chocolate Is Missing" from *The Great Ideas of Lila Fenwick* by Kate McMullan, pp. 3–8 & 10–23. Text copyright © 1986 by Kate McMullan. Published by Dial Books for Young Readers. All rights reserved. Used with permission. **708:** "The Zoo Crew" by Laura Daily. Copyright © 2000 National Geographic Society. Used by permission of NGS Images; **710:** "Dreams" from *Collected Poems* by Langston Hughes. Copyright © 1994 by the Estate of Langston Hughes. Reprinted by permission of Alfred A. Knopf, Inc.; **710:** "Dream Dust" from *Collected Poems* by Langston Hughes. Copyright © 1994 by the Estate of Langston Hughes. Reprinted by permission of Alfred A. Knopf, Inc.; **711:** "When I Grow Up" from *A Suitcase of Seaweed and Other Poems* by Janet S. Wong, pg. 19. Copyright © 1996 by Janet S. Wong. Reprinted with the permission of Margaret K. McElderry Books, an imprint of Simon & Schuster Children's Publishing Division; **712:** "Purple Snake" from *Confetti,* poems by Pat Mora. Text copyright © 1996 by Pat Mora. Reprinted by permission of Lee & Low Books, Inc., 95 Madison Avenue, New York, NY 10016; **713:** "Jenny the Juvenile Juggler" from *The Ice Cream Store* (HarperCollins Publishers Ltd., 1991). Copyright © 1991 by Dennis Lee. With permission of the author. Selected text and images in this book are copyrighted © 2002

Artists

Cover: Dan Craig; **4–5, 22–38:** Catherine Stock; **6–7, 196–209:** Anita Jeram; **8–9, 262–279, 346–361:** Jerry Pinkney; **10–11, 396–417:** Franklin Hammond; **12–13, 558–571:** Alix Berenzy; **14–15, 486–489, 686–707:** Tom Newsom; **20–21, 282–283:** Joel Spector; **44–45:** Pat Maire; **46–67:** Ronald Himler; **72–90:** Kees de Kiefte; **96–97, 118, 120, 122, 124, 126, 128, 130, 132–135 (Web art), 142–143, 190 (map), 256–257, 322 (map), 372–373, 466–467 (Web art), 492–493, 528, 535–537, 576–577, 594, 600–603, 716–717:** Tony Klassen; **98–113:** Carmen Lomas Garza; **114–115, 490–491:** Stacey Schuett; **116–117:** Kathy Lengyel; **118–132:** Bill Farnsworth; **136–139:** Roseanne Kaloustian; **140–141:** Wendy Wax; **148–164 (collage), 254–255:** Stephanie Garcia; **148–164 (drawings), 214–227:** Garth Williams; **165–167:** John Sandford; **170–189:** Lori Lohstoeter; **194–195:** Diane Blasius; **210–211:** Mark Zahnd; **212–213, 214, 228, 537:** Sharon Hoogstraten; Melinda Levine; **232–233, 578–593:** Patrick Gnan; **250–253:** Lee Lee Brazeal; **260–261:** JoAnn Adinolfi; **280–281, 370–371:** Stephanie Carter; **284–301:** Kevin Hawkes; **284–289, 291, 296, 300, 301:** Kelly Hume; **306–321:** María Cristina Brusca; **324–325:** Joseph Daniel Fiedler; **326–340:** Mark Mohr; **344–345, 556–557:** Gregory Berger; **376–377:** Antonio Cangemi; **378–391:** Kim Howard; **422–437:** Terry Widener; **444–465:** Cheryl Kirk Noll; **468–469:** Marty Blake; **470–484, 608–625:** Tyrone Geter; **472, 474, 476, 482–484:** Tracy L. Taylor; **485:** Lou Beach; **494–495:** Wendy Ackison; **496–497:** Andy Newsom; **498–515:** Arvis Stewart; **516–517:** Steven Mach; **518–519:** Mike Reed; **520–534:** Tom Shefelman; **520, 522, 534:** Margaret Cusack; **538–553, 596–599, 681–683:** Todd Leonardo; **604–605:** Paul Selwyn; **606–607:** Harry Roolaart; **632–644 (borders):** Karen Blessen; **645–647:** Murv Jacob; **650–663:** Floyd Cooper; **664–665:** Teresa Flavin; **666–667:** Jack Graham; **668–679:** Margot Tomes; **684–685:** Lisa Adams; **710–713:** Jeff Meyer; **714–715:** Cameron Eagle

Photographs

Every effort has been made to secure permission and provide appropriate credit for photographic material. The publisher deeply regrets any omission and pledges to correct, in subsequent editions, errors called to its attention.

Unless otherwise acknowledged, all photographs are the property of Scott Foresman, a division of Pearson Education. Page abbreviations are as follows: **(t) top, (b) bottom, (c) center, (l) left, (r) right, (ins) inset, (s) spot, (bk) background.**
17, 39(bk), 70–71, 91–93, 146–147, 216–229, 236, 238, 240, 246–247, 278–279, 366–369, 440–441(bk), 442–443, 648–649: Sharon Hoogstraten; **18–19:** Steven

Glossary

The contents of the glossary have been adapted from *Thorndike Barnhart Intermediate Dictionary* Copyright © 1999 Addison Wesley Educational Publishers, Inc., Glenview, Illinois and *Thorndike Barnhart Children's Dictionary* © 2001, 1999 Scott Foresman, a division of Addison-Wesley Educational Publishers, Inc.